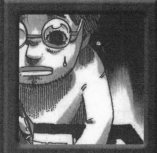

Sometimes at night I have to stop work when I get that chill up my spine, and I start wondering what's behind me... Too bad, because nighttime is one of my most productive times. I tend to not go to the bathroom either.

– Yoshiyuki Nishi

Yoshiyuki Nishi was born in Tokyo. Two of his favorite manga series are *Dragon Ball* and the robot-cat comedy *Doraemon*. His latest series, *Muhyo & Roji's Bureau of Supernatural Investigation*, debuted in Japan's *Akamaru Jump* magazine in 2004 and went on to be serialized in *Weekly Shonen Jump*.

MUHYO & ROJI'S
BUREAU OF SUPERNATURAL INVESTIGATION

VOL. 11
The SHONEN JUMP Manga Edition

STORY AND ART BY
YOSHIYUKI NISHI

Translation & Adaptation/Alexander O. Smith
Touch-up Art & Lettering/Brian Bilter
Design/Yukiko Whitley
Editor/Amy Yu

Editor in Chief, Books/Alvin Lu
Editor in Chief, Magazines/Marc Weidenbaum
VP, Publishing Licensing/Rika Inouye
VP, Sales & Product Marketing/Gonzalo Ferreyra
VP, Creative/Linda Espinosa
Publisher/Hyoe Narita

Printed in Canada

Published by VIZ Media, LLC
P.O. Box 77010
San Francisco, CA 94107

SHONEN JUMP Manga Edition
10 9 8 7 6 5 4 3 2 1
First printing, June 2009

www.viz.com   www.shonenjump.com

THE WORLD'S
MOST POPULAR MANGA

SHONEN JUMP MANGA EDITION

Muhyo & Roji's

Bureau of Supernatural Investigation

BSI

Vol. 11   **Rescue Mission**

Story & Art by **Yoshiyuki Nishi**

Dramatis Personae

Jiro Kusano (Roji)

Assistant at Muhyo's office, recently promoted from the lowest rank of "Second Clerk" to that of (provisional) "First Clerk." Roji has a gentle heart and has been known to freak out in the presence of spirits. Lately, he has been devoting himself to the study of magic law so that he can pull his own weight someday.

Toru Muhyo (Muhyo)

Young, genius magic law practitioner with the highest rank of "Executor." Always calm and collected (though sometimes considered cold), Muhyo possesses a strong sense of justice and even has a kind side. Sleeps a lot to recover from the exhaustion caused by his practice.

Yu Abiko (Biko)

Muhyo's classmate and an Artificer. Makes seals, pens, magic law books, and other accoutrements of magic law.

Yoichi Himukai (Yoichi)

Judge and Muhyo's former classmate. Expert practitioner of all magic law except execution.

Rio Kurotori (Rio)

Charismatic Artificer who turned traitor when the Magic Law Association stood by and let her mother die.

Soratsugu Madoka (Enchu)

Muhyo's former classmate and Executor-hopeful until one event turned him onto the traitor's path.

The Demon Lord

Page wagered his own life to summon this envoy in the fight against Isabi.

Isabi

Forbidden magic law practitioner who made himself an envoy to obtain eternal life. Sole possessor of means to kill Teeki.

Page Klaus

Chief Investigator for the Magic Law Association, Yoichi's boss, and Muhyo and Enchu's former instructor.

Seven-Faced Dog

An envoy with the ability to change shape. Specialist at uncovering spectral crimes.

Umekichi Sasanoha

First clerk and Busujima's assistant. In his true envoy form he is called *Unryuso*. "Umekichi" is his human-form alias.

Harumi Busujima

Executor and one of the only practitioners in the world capable of "remote magic law."

The Story

Magic law is a newly established practice for judging and punishing the increasing crimes committed by spirits; those who use it are called "practitioners."

On the way to the Wailing Vale, base of the forbidden magic law practitioners, our heroes run afoul of Ark, and in the ensuing fray, Judge Imai is kidnapped! What's more, Muhyo's book of magic law is ruined. The team joins up with Executor Busujima, hoping to use her remote magic law for a rescue mission into the Vale. Meanwhile, Page and Yoichi battle Isabi, the only entity that knows how to defeat Teeki. The battle turns sour and Page is forced to invoke the Bells of Troy, enabling him to wager not only his tempering but his flesh and blood as well to bind an envoy to him. The rules of magic law have been changed...

Reiko Imai

Brave Judge who joined Muhyo and gang during the fight against Face-Ripper Sophie.

Mick

Member of the forbidden magic law group known as Ark. A heartless man who would as soon abandon a friend as kill a foe.

Teeki

Dangerous entity marked as a traitor to the Magic Law Association for 800 years.

Muhyo & Roji's
Bureau of Supernatural Investigation
BSI

CONTENTS

11

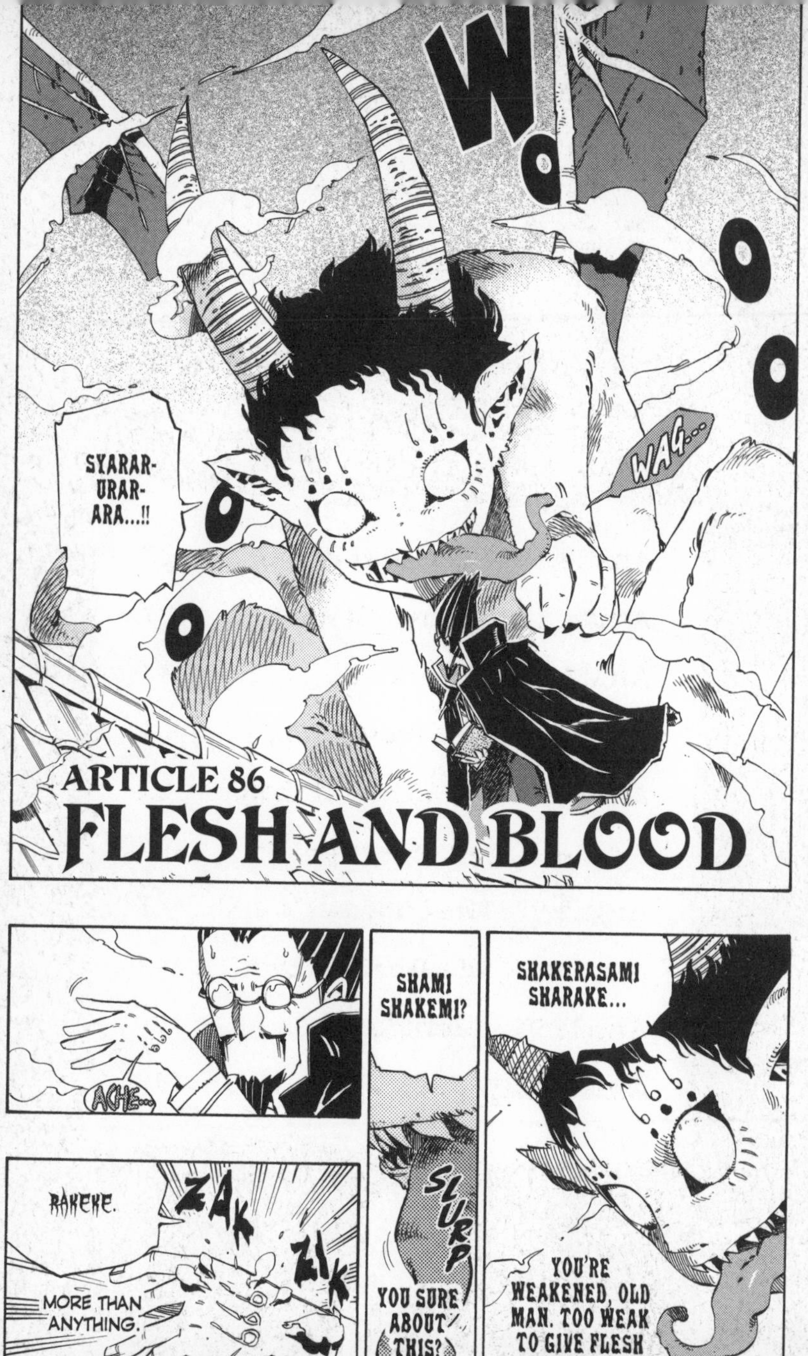
WOOOO
WAG...
SYARAR-URAR-ARA...!!
ARTICLE 86
FLESH AND BLOOD
SHAKERASAMI SHARAKE...
YOU'RE WEAKENED, OLD MAN. TOO WEAK TO GIVE FLESH AND BLOOD.
SHAMI SHAKEMI?
SLURP
YOU SURE ABOUT THIS?
ACHE...
RAKEKE.
ZAK
ZIK
MORE THAN ANYTHING.

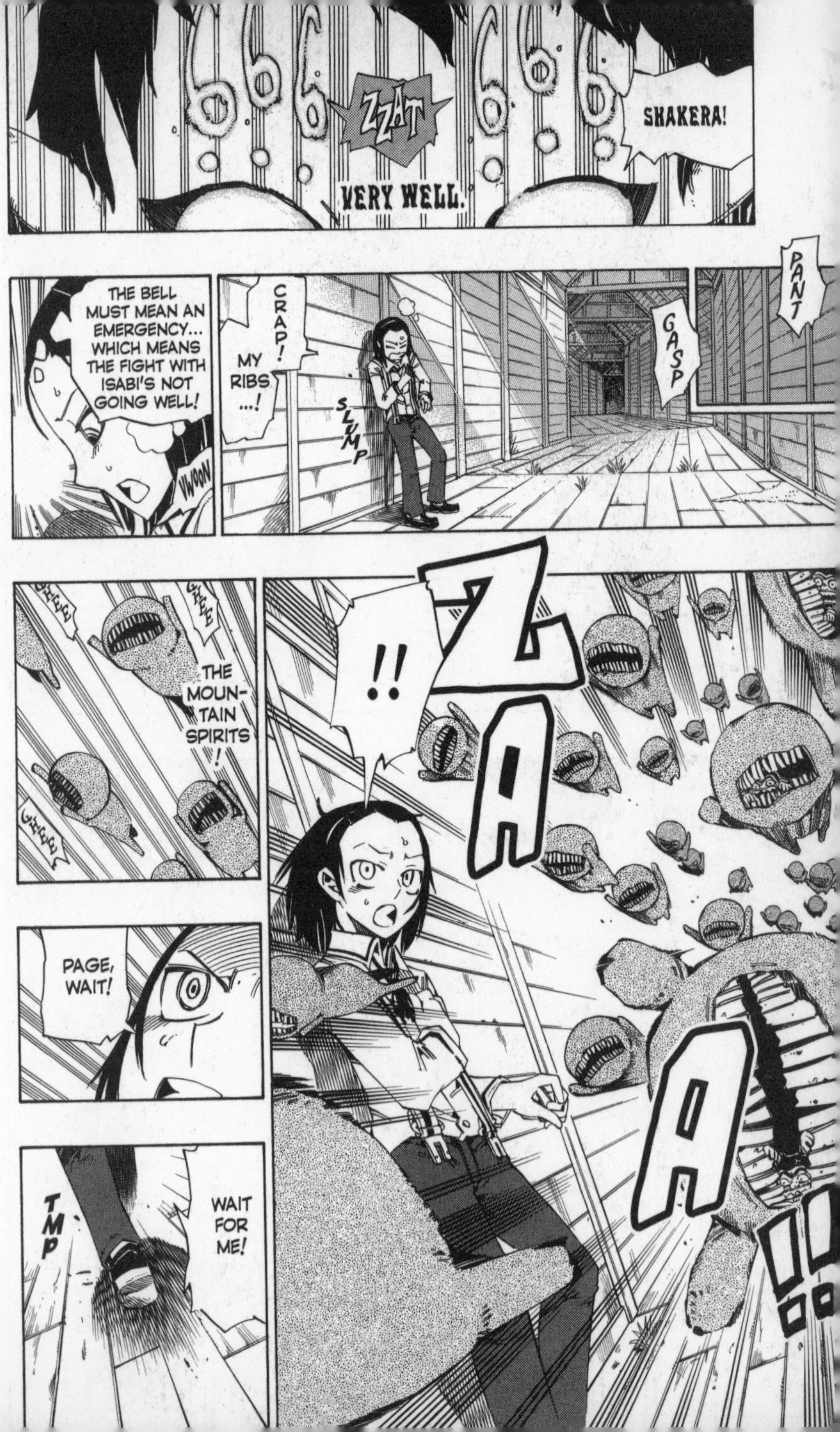
SHAKERA!
ZZAT
VERY WELL.
PANT
GASP
CRAP! MY RIBS ...!
SLUMP
THE BELL MUST MEAN AN EMERGENCY... WHICH MEANS THE FIGHT WITH ISABI'S NOT GOING WELL!
VWOON
!!
ZAAA!!
GHEE
THE MOUN-TAIN SPIRITS!
PAGE, WAIT!
WAIT FOR ME!
TMP

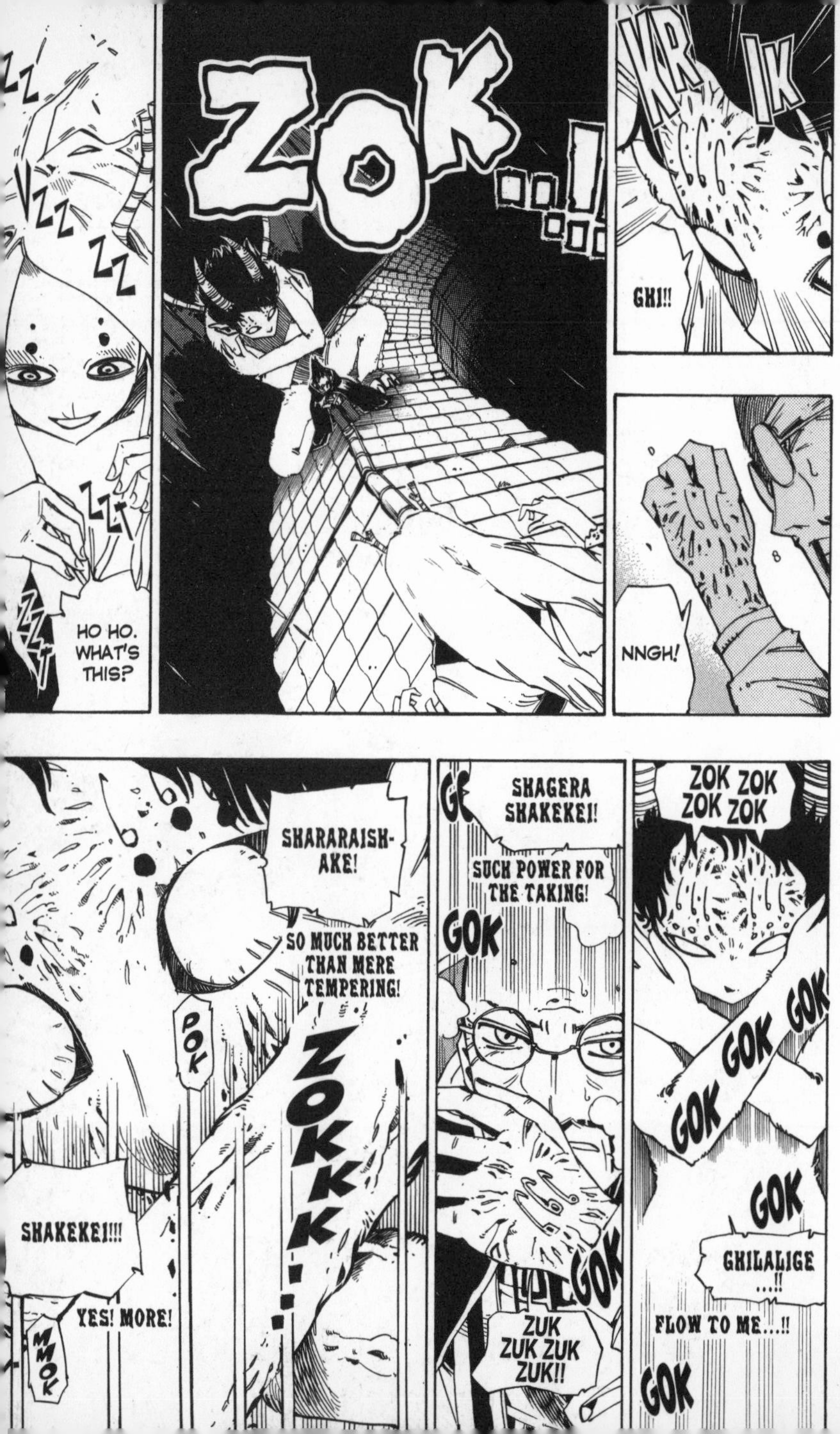

KRIK
GHI!!
NNGH!
ZOK...!!
ZZZ
HO HO. WHAT'S THIS?
ZOK ZOK ZOK ZOK
GOK GOK GOK GOK
GOK
GHILALIGE ...!!
FLOW TO ME...!!
GOK
GE
SHAGERA SHAKEKEI!
SUCH POWER FOR THE TAKING!
GOK
GOK
ZUK ZUK ZUK ZUK!!
SHARARAISH-AKE!
SO MUCH BETTER THAN MERE TEMPERING!
ZOKKK...!!
DOK
SHAKEKEI!!!
YES! MORE!
MMOK

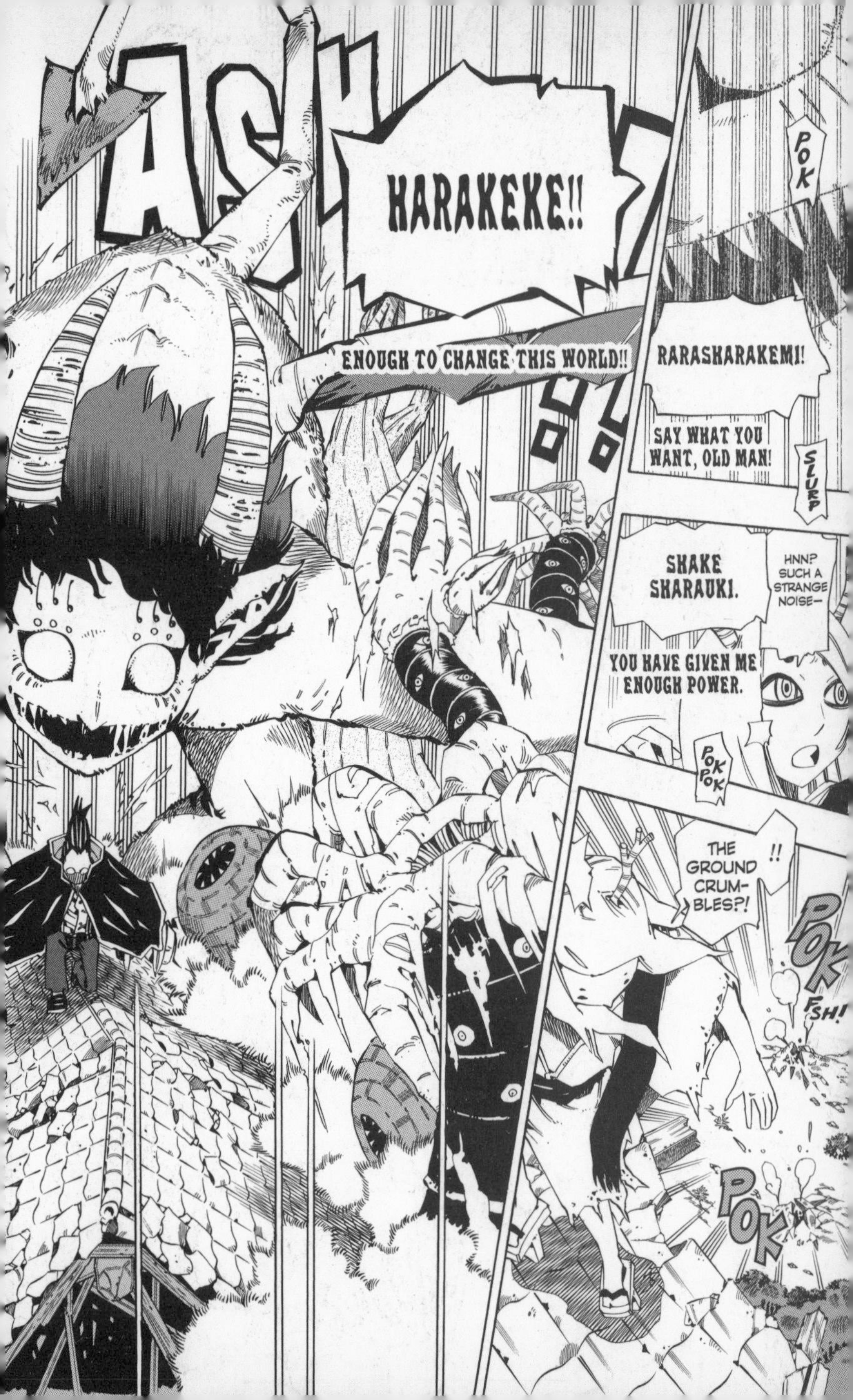
POK
RARASHARAKEMI!
SAY WHAT YOU WANT, OLD MAN!
SLURP
HNN? SUCH A STRANGE NOISE—
SHAKE SHARAUKI.
YOU HAVE GIVEN ME ENOUGH POWER.
POK POK
!!
THE GROUND CRUMBLES?!
POK
FSH!
POK
HARAKEKE!!
ENOUGH TO CHANGE THIS WORLD!!

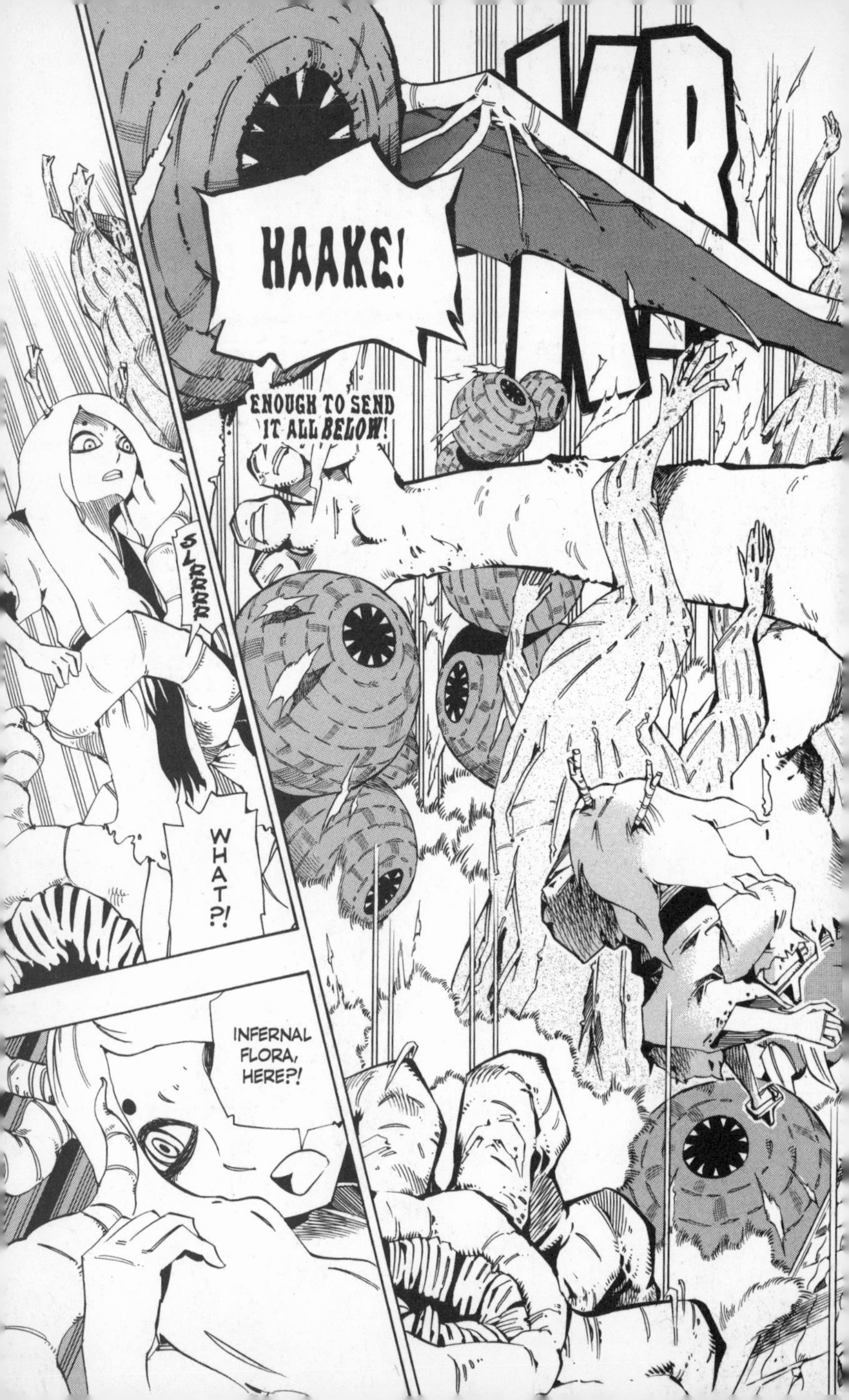
HAAKE!
ENOUGH TO SEND IT ALL BELOW!
SLRRRR
WHAT?!
INFERNAL FLORA, HERE?!

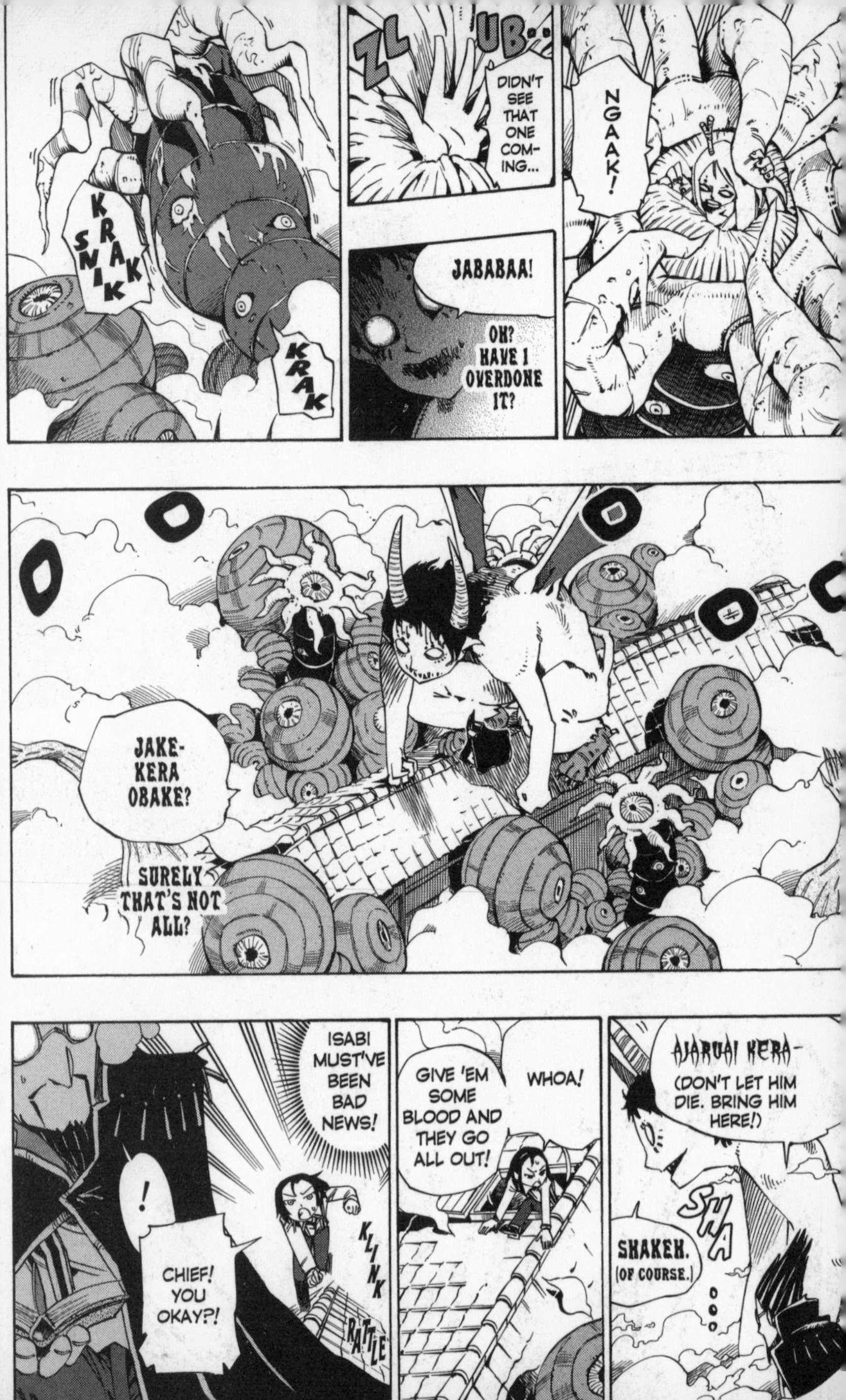
NGAAK!
ZL UB..
DIDN'T SEE THAT ONE COMING...
JABABAA!
OH? HAVE I OVERDONE IT?
KRAK SNIK
KRAK
JAKE-KERA OBAKE?
SURELY THAT'S NOT ALL?
AJARUAI KERA-
(DON'T LET HIM DIE. BRING HIM HERE!)
SHA
SHAKEH. (OF COURSE.)
WHOA!
GIVE 'EM SOME BLOOD AND THEY GO ALL OUT!
ISABI MUST'VE BEEN BAD NEWS!
KLINK
RATTLE
!
CHIEF! YOU OKAY?!

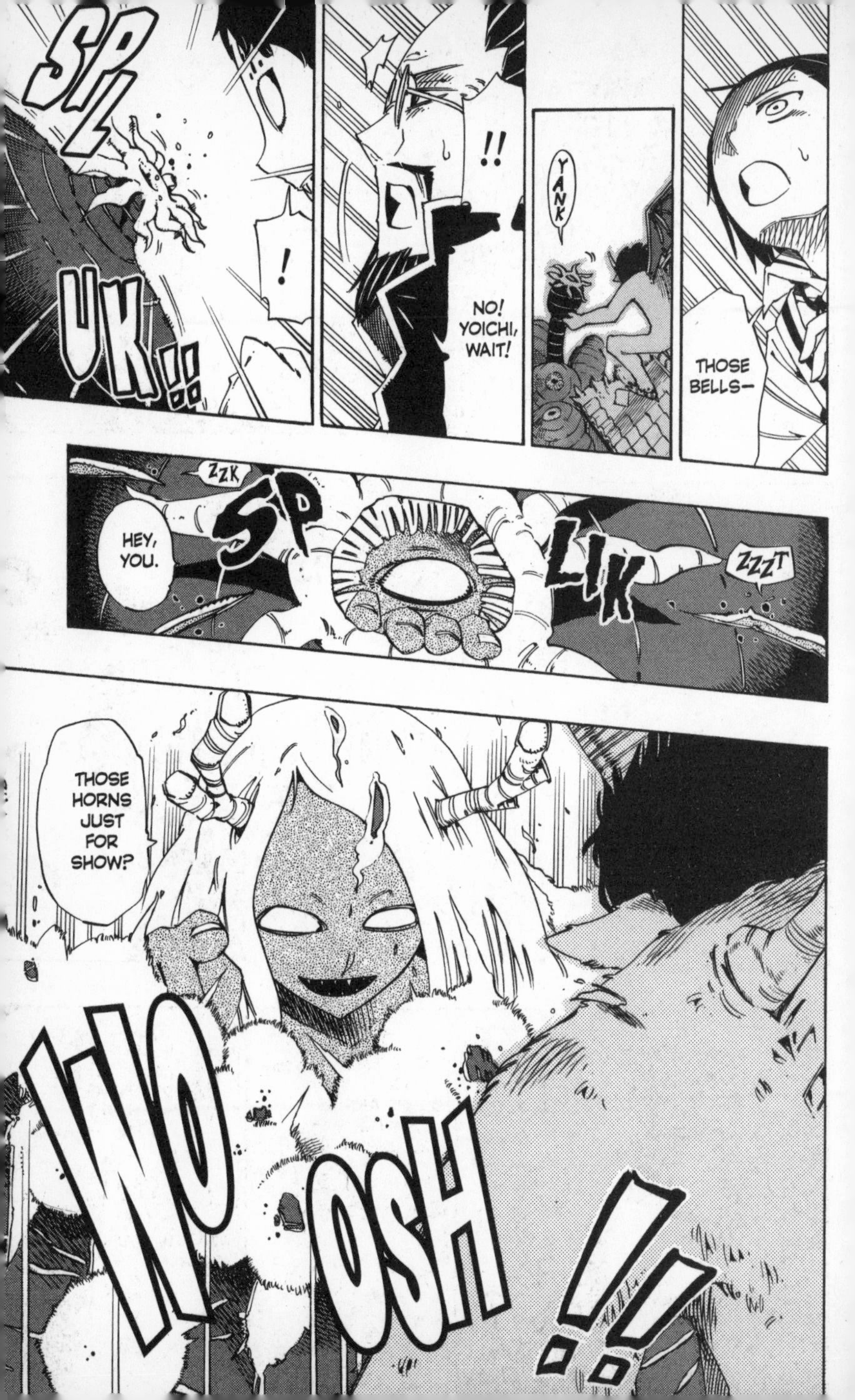
THOSE BELLS—
YANK
!!
NO! YOICHI, WAIT!
SPLUK!!
!
ZZZT
SPLIK
ZZK
HEY, YOU.
THOSE HORNS JUST FOR SHOW?
WHOOSH!!

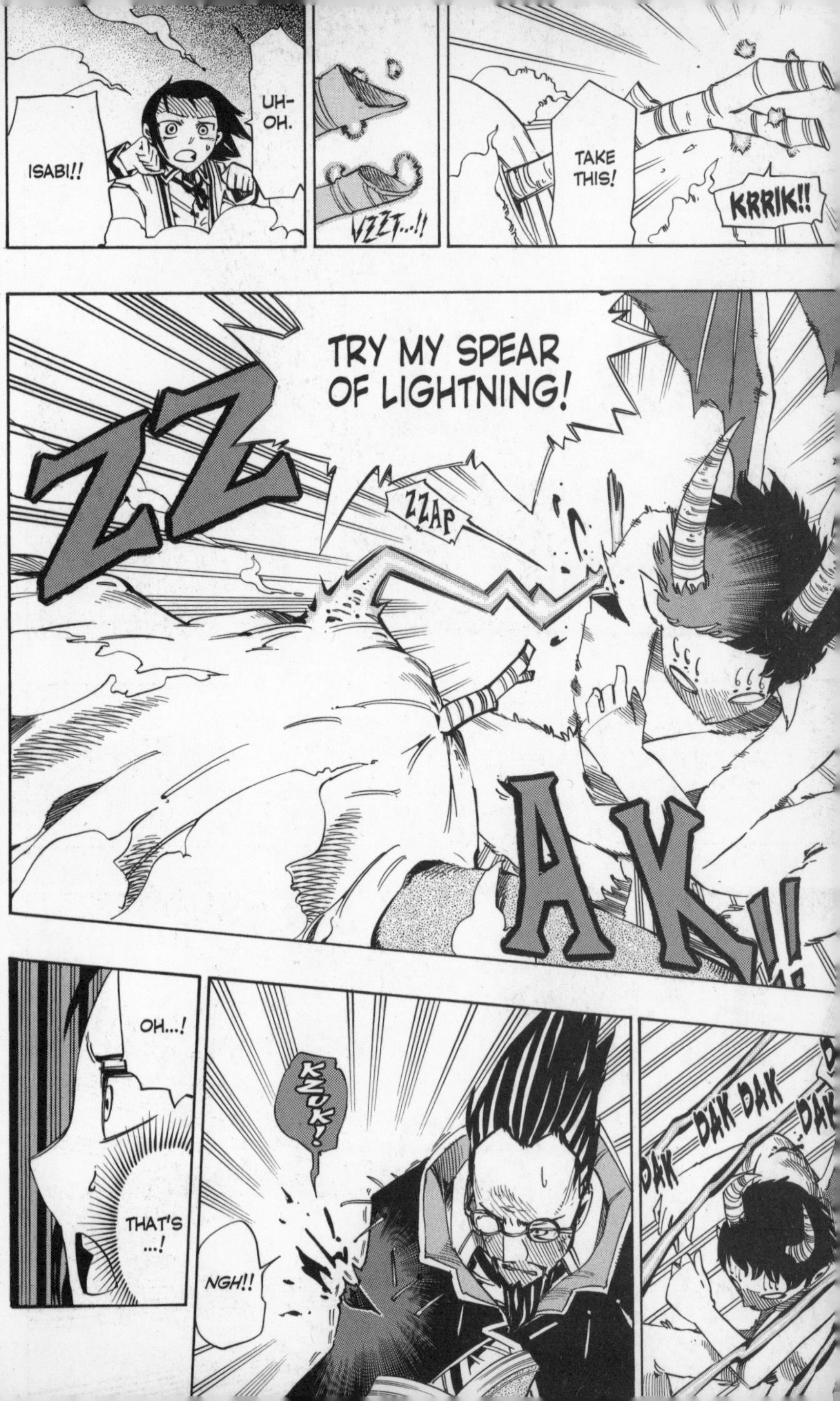
TAKE THIS!
KRRIK!!
VZZT...!!
UH-OH.
ISABI!!
TRY MY SPEAR OF LIGHTNING!
ZZAP
ZZ
AK!!
DAK DAK DAK DAK DAK
KZUK!
NGH!!
OH...!
THAT'S ...!

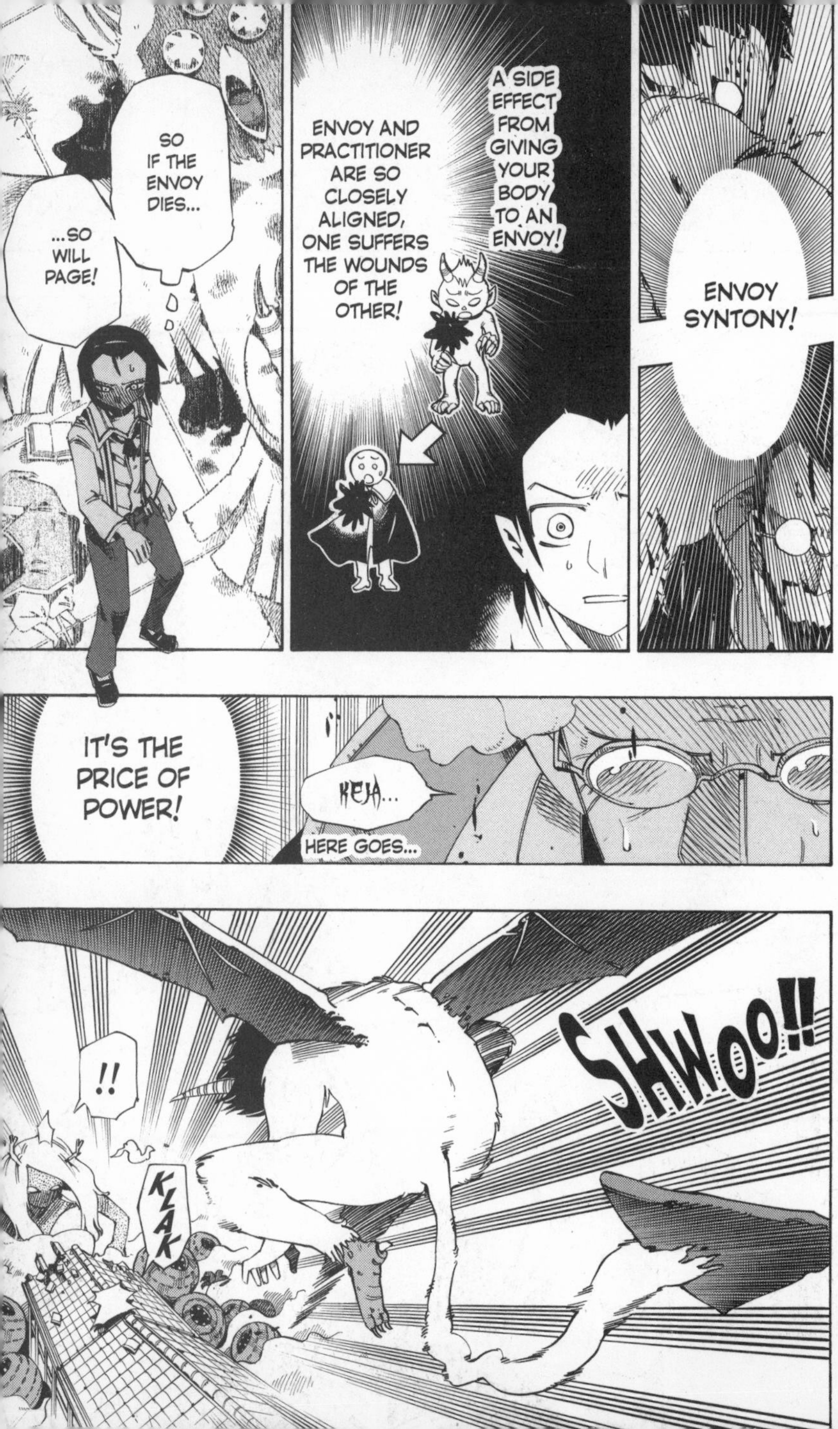
ENVOY SYNTONY!
A SIDE EFFECT FROM GIVING YOUR BODY TO AN ENVOY!
ENVOY AND PRACTITIONER ARE SO CLOSELY ALIGNED, ONE SUFFERS THE WOUNDS OF THE OTHER!
SO IF THE ENVOY DIES...
...SO WILL PAGE!
KEJA...
HERE GOES...
IT'S THE PRICE OF POWER!
SHWOO!!
!!
KLAK

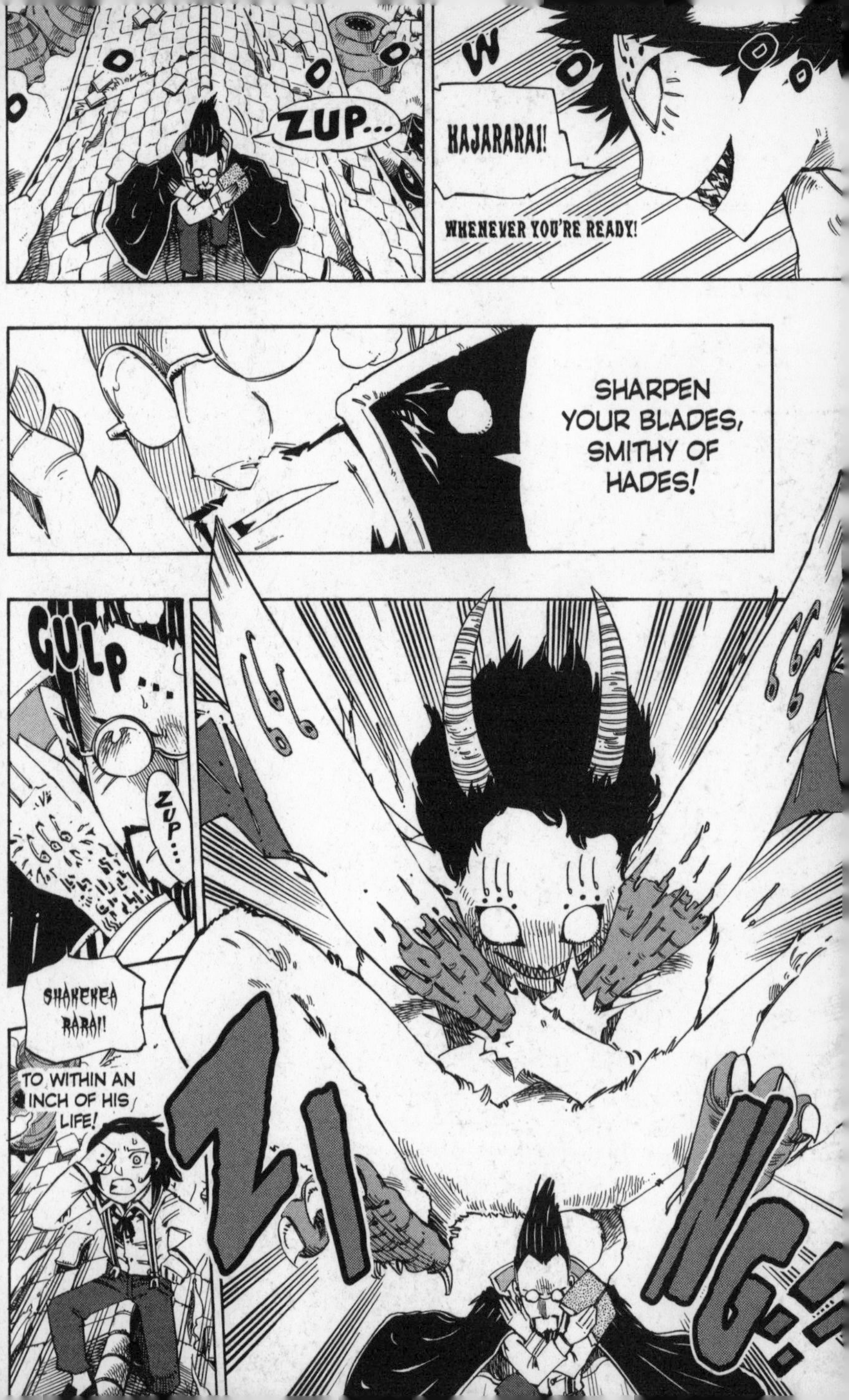
WOOOO
HAJARARAI!
WHENEVER YOU'RE READY!
WOOOO
ZUP...
SHARPEN YOUR BLADES, SMITHY OF HADES!
ZIIG...
GULP...
ZUP...
SHAKEKEA RARAI!
TO WITHIN AN INCH OF HIS LIFE!

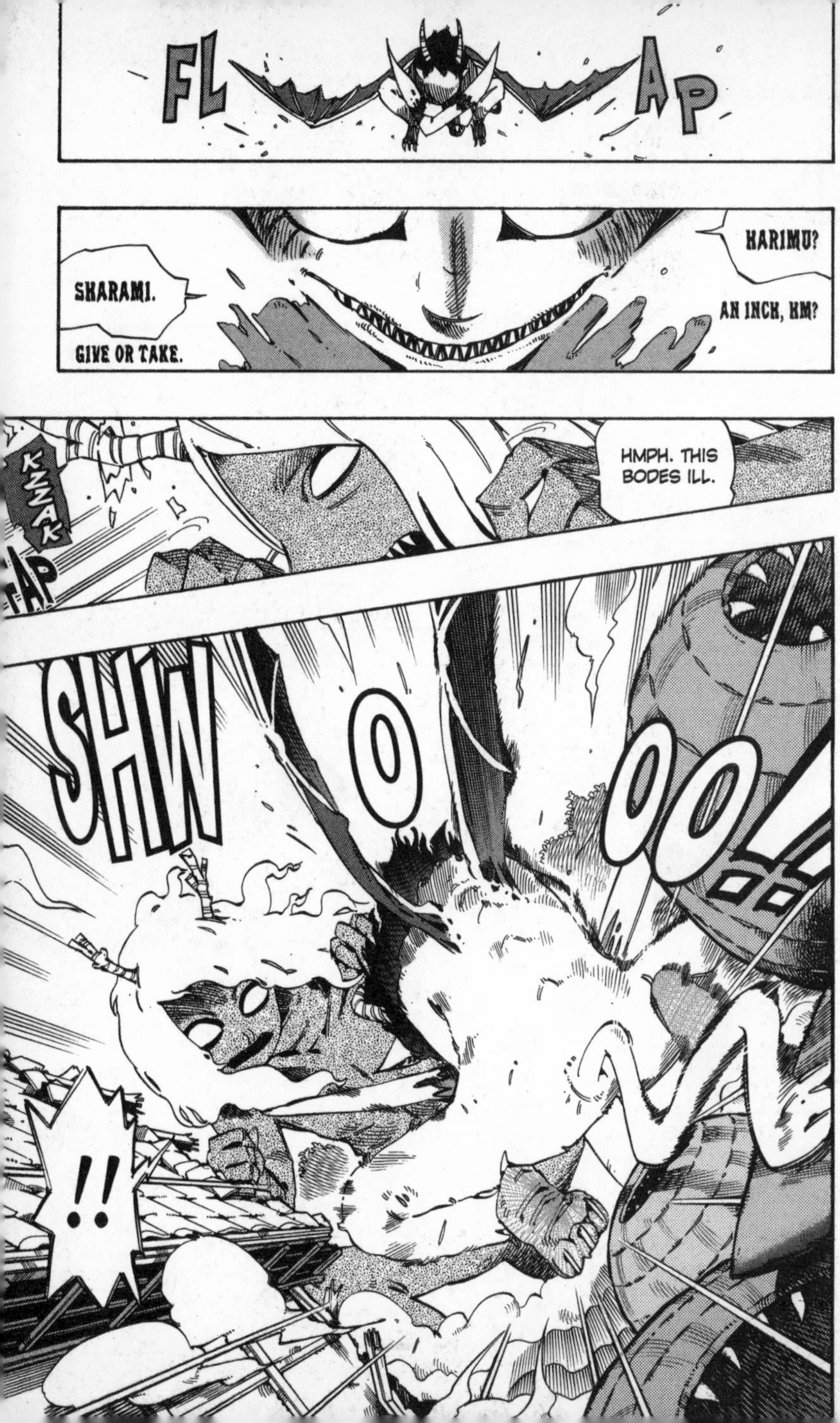
FLAP
KARIMU?
AN INCH, HM?
SHARAMI.
GIVE OR TAKE.
HMPH. THIS BODES ILL.
KZZAK
FAP
SHWOOO
!!

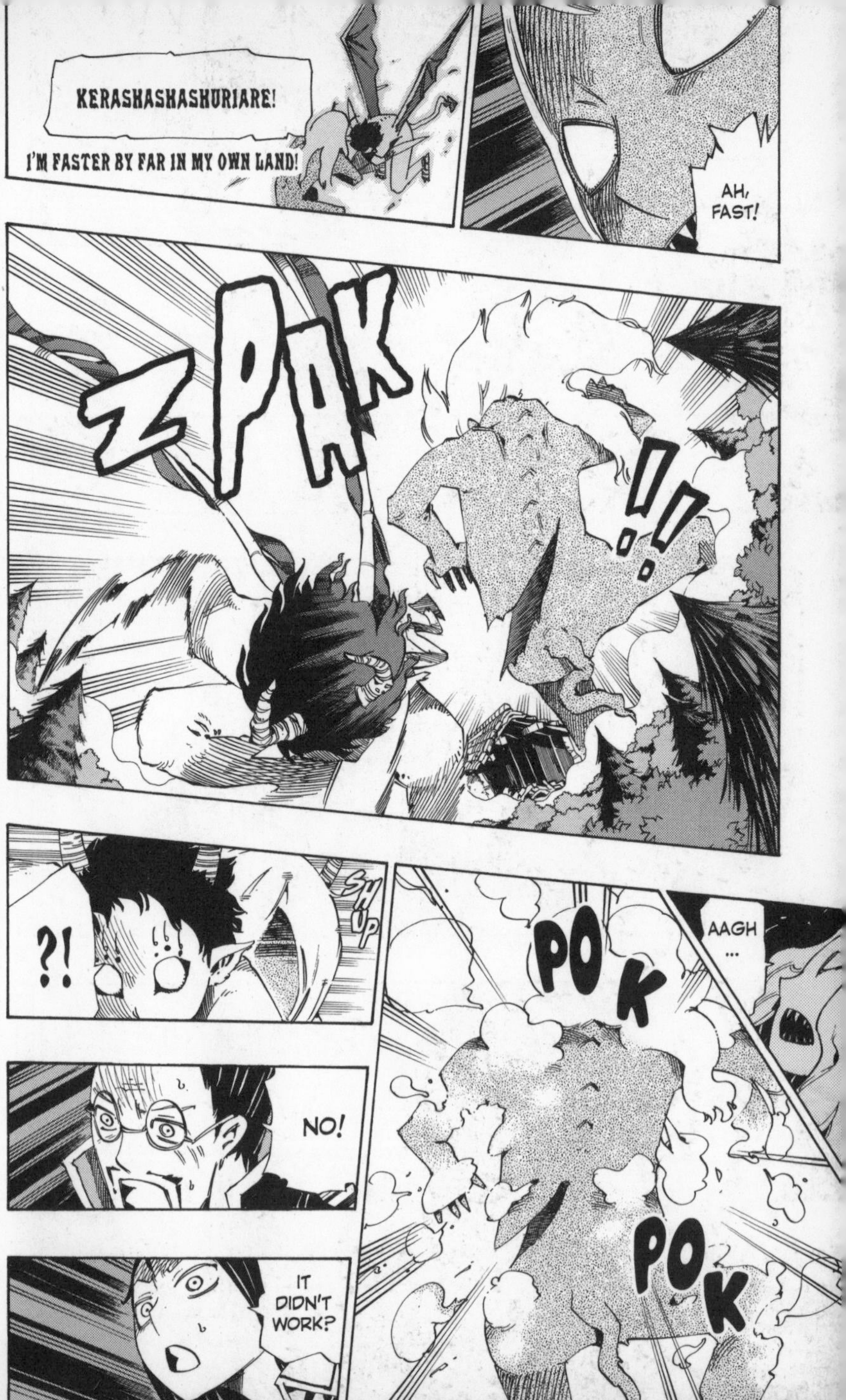
AH, FAST!
KERASHASHASHURIARE!
I'M FASTER BY FAR IN MY OWN LAND!
ZPAK
!!
AAGH...
POK
POK
SHUP
?!
NO!
IT DIDN'T WORK?

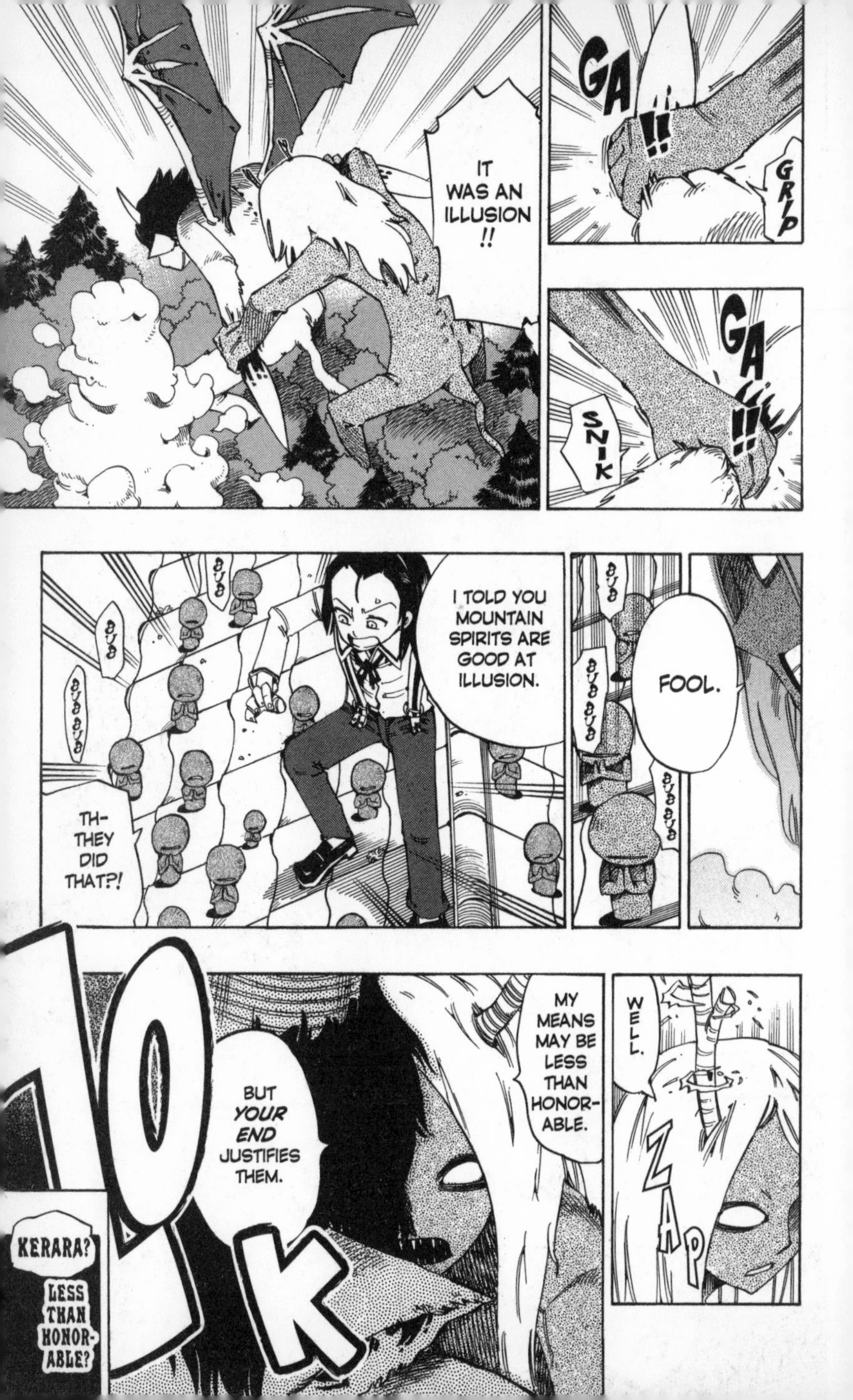

GA!!
GRIP
GA!!!
SNIK
IT WAS AN ILLUSION!!
FOOL.
BUB
BUB BUB BUB
BUB BUB BUB
I TOLD YOU MOUNTAIN SPIRITS ARE GOOD AT ILLUSION.
BUB
BUB
BUB BUB BUB
TH- THEY DID THAT?!
WELL.
ZAP
MY MEANS MAY BE LESS THAN HONOR-ABLE.
BUT *YOUR END* JUSTIFIES THEM.
KERARA?
LESS THAN HONOR-ABLE?

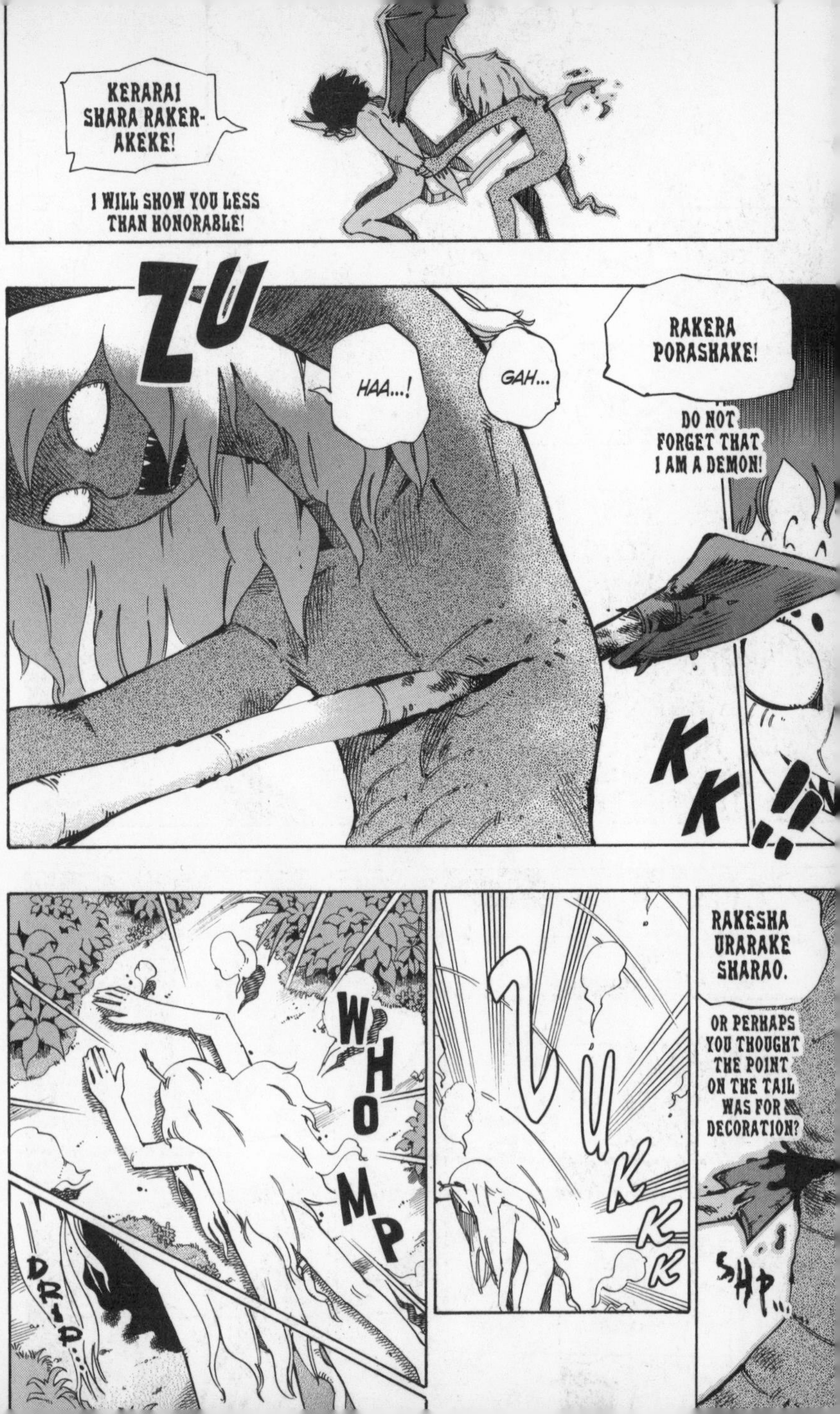
KERARAI SHARA RAKER-AKEKE!
I WILL SHOW YOU LESS THAN HONORABLE!
RAKERA PORASHAKE!
DO NOT FORGET THAT I AM A DEMON!
GAH...
HAA...!
ZU
KK!!
RAKESHA URARAKE SHARAO.
OR PERHAPS YOU THOUGHT THE POINT ON THE TAIL WAS FOR DECORATION?
SHP...
ZUKKKK
WHOMP
DRIP...

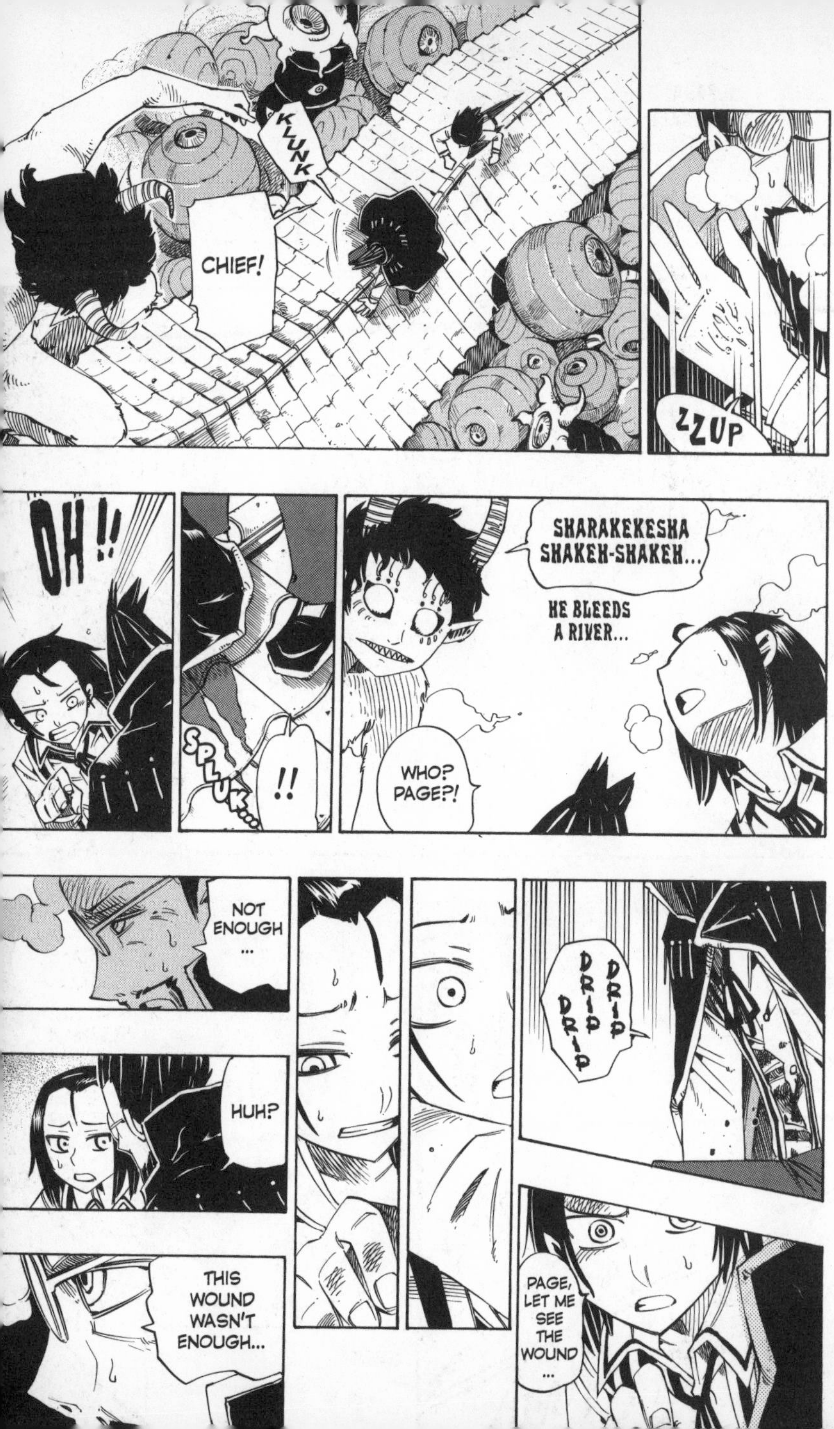
ZZUP
KLUNK
CHIEF!
SHARAKEKESHA SHAKEH-SHAKEH...
HE BLEEDS A RIVER...
WHO? PAGE?!
!!
SPLUK...
OH!!
DRIP DRIP DRIP
PAGE, LET ME SEE THE WOUND...
NOT ENOUGH...
HUH?
THIS WOUND WASN'T ENOUGH...

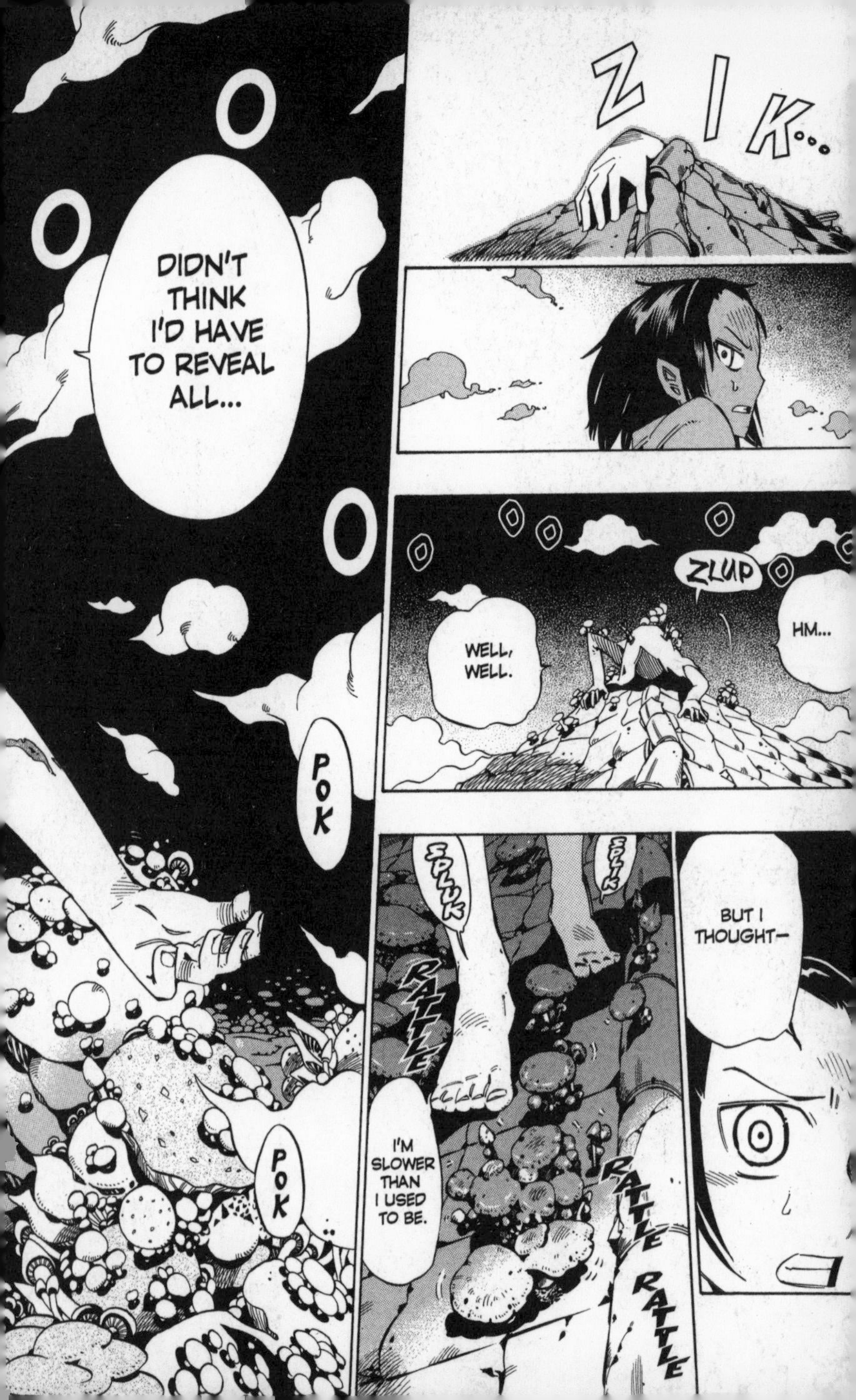

ZIK...
ZLUP
HM...
WELL, WELL.
BUT I THOUGHT—
SPLIK
SPLUK
RATTLE
I'M SLOWER THAN I USED TO BE.
RATTLE RATTLE
DIDN'T THINK I'D HAVE TO REVEAL ALL...
POK
POK

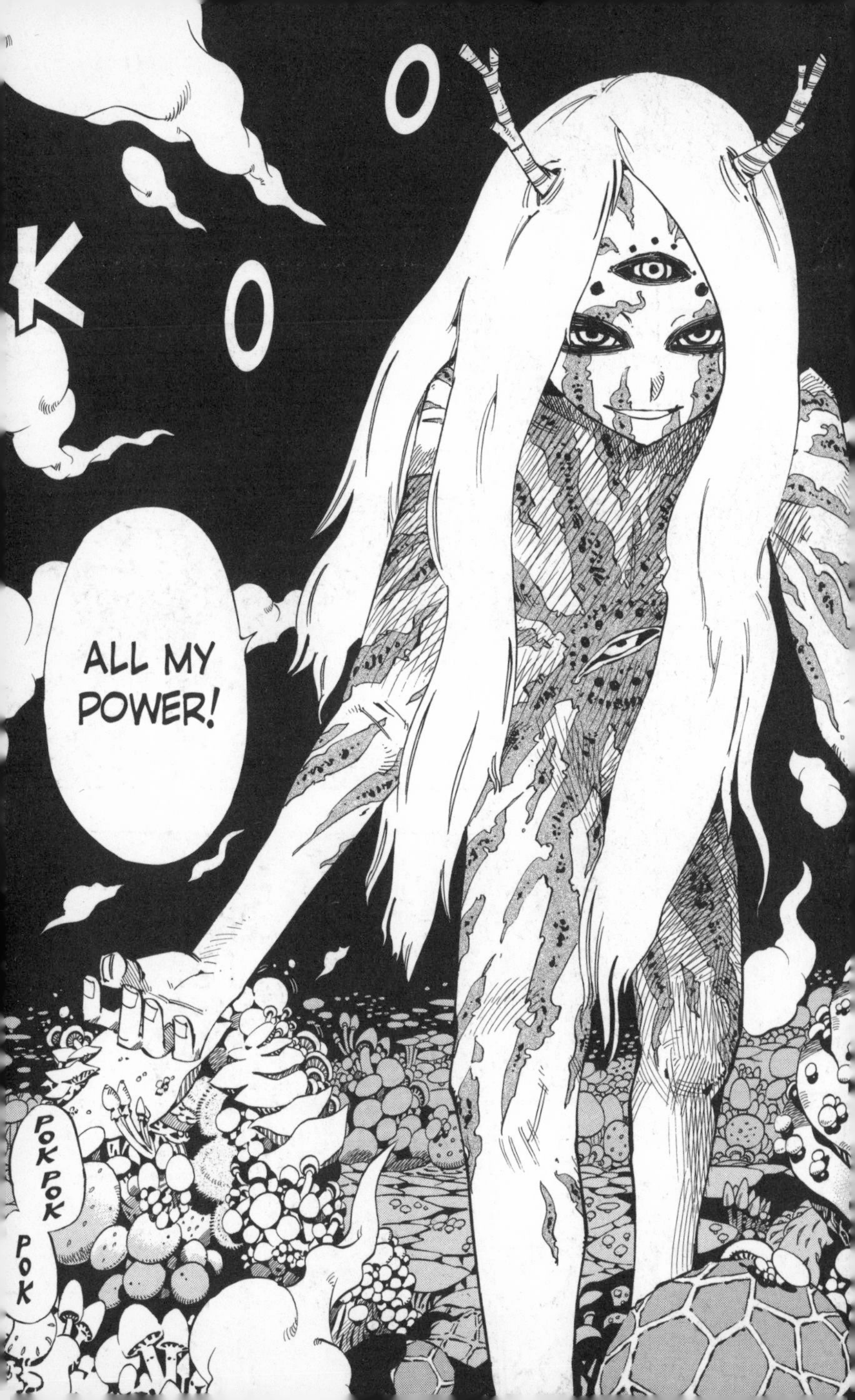
KOO
ALL MY POWER!
POKPOK POK

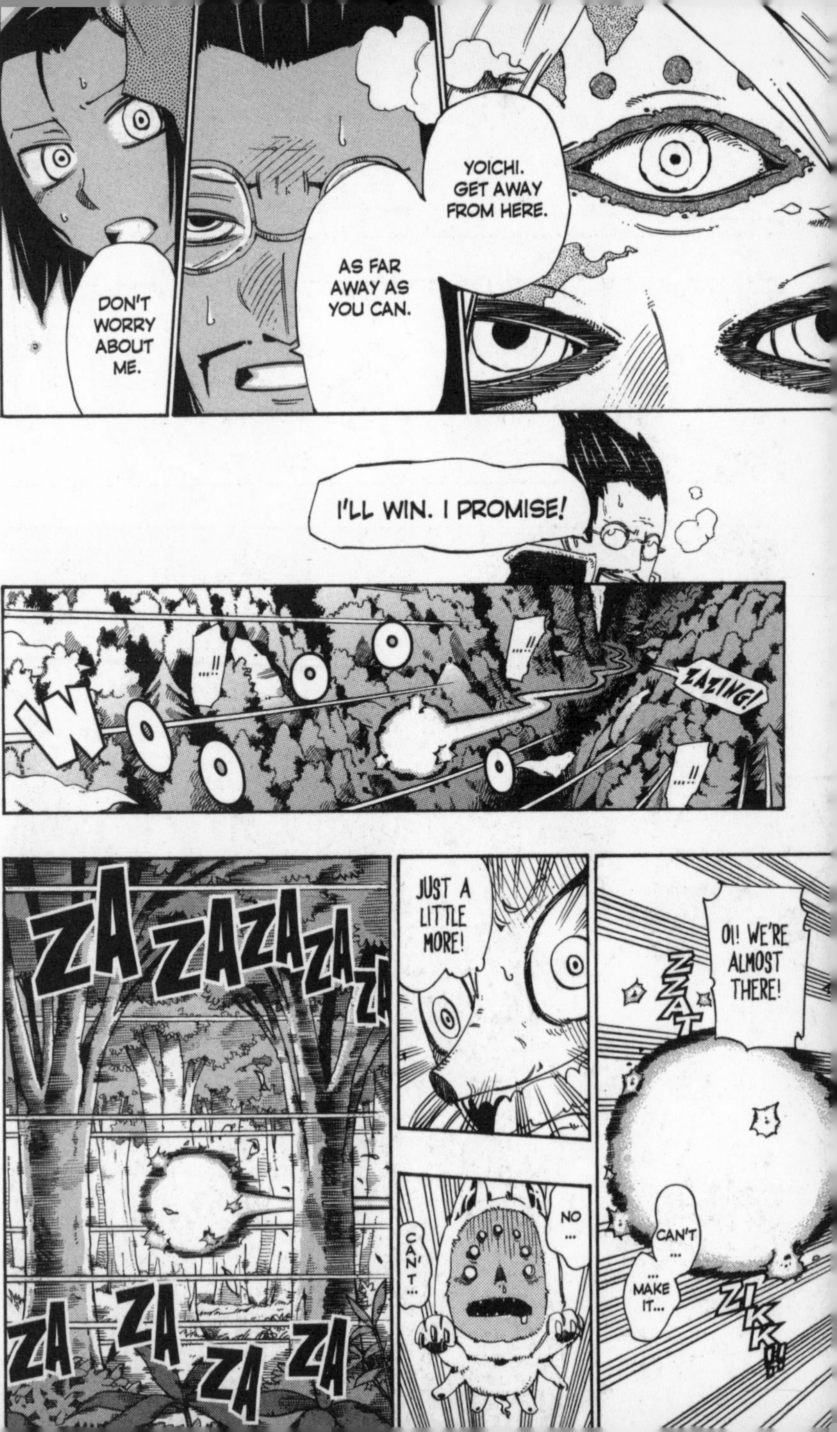
YOICHI. GET AWAY FROM HERE.
AS FAR AWAY AS YOU CAN.
DON'T WORRY ABOUT ME.
I'LL WIN. I PROMISE!
...!!
ZAZING!
...!!
WOOOOO
...!!
OI! WE'RE ALMOST THERE!
ZZAT
CAN'T ... MAKE IT...
ZIKK!!
JUST A LITTLE MORE!
NO ...
CAN'T...
ZA ZA ZA ZA ZA ZA ZA
ZA ZA ZA ZA ZA

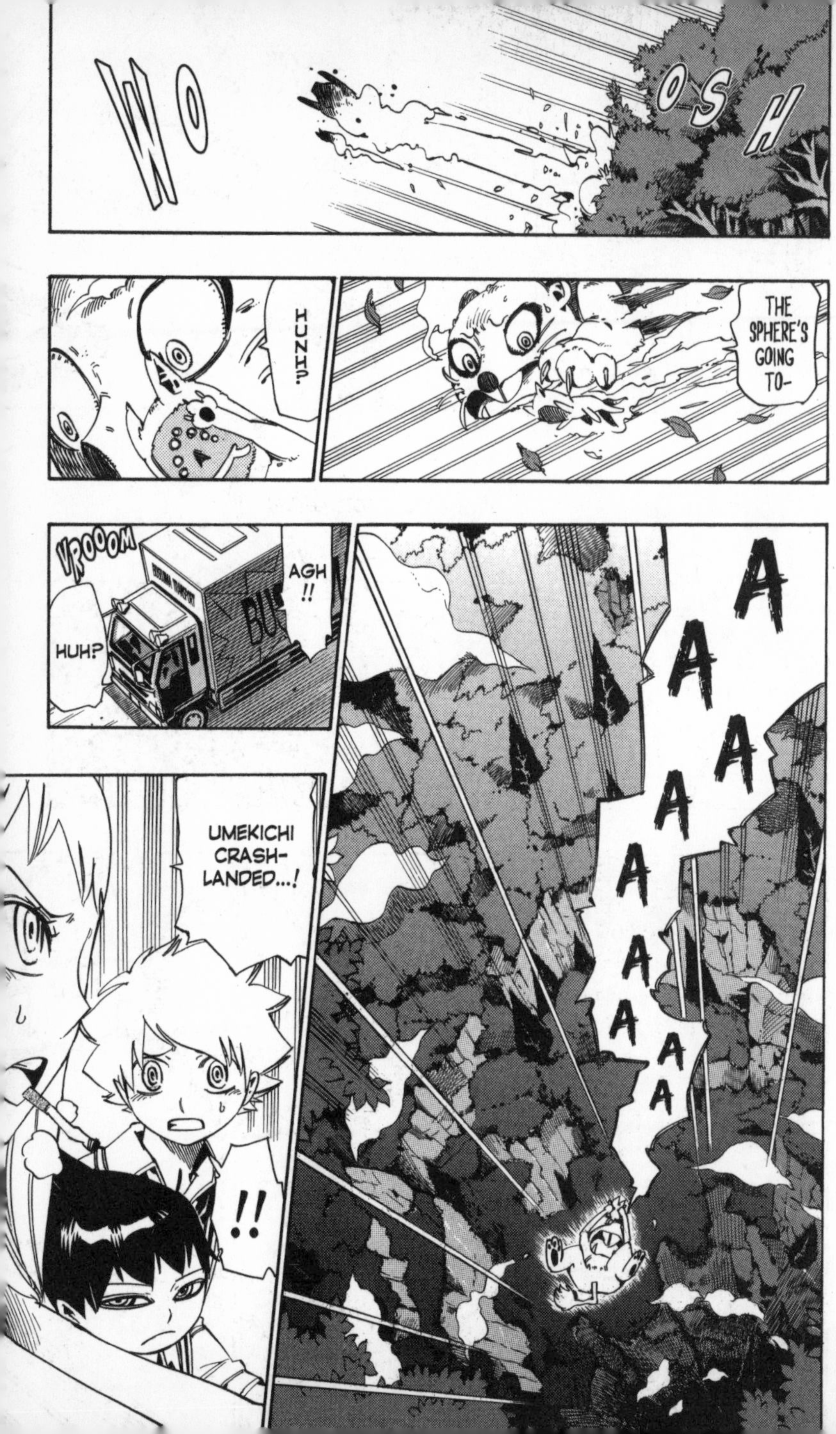
WO
OSH
THE SPHERE'S GOING TO-
HUNH?
AAAAAAAAAAA
AGH!!
VROOOM
HUH?
UMEKICHI CRASH-LANDED...!
!!

HEY EVERYONE, THANKS FOR BUYING VOLUME 11! LET'S GET BACK TO THE QUESTIONS, SHALL WE?

Q: IN VOLUME 9, SEVEN-FACED DOG SAID HE MESSED UP THE LAUGH TWICE, BUT I COUNTED THREE TIMES. WHAT GIVES?

-S.S, GIFU PREFECTURE

A: GAK! FACT-CHECKING THIS EARLY? VOLUME 9, WAS IT? YEAH. I GUESS IT WAS THREE TIMES... UM, HEY! SEVEN-FACED DOG! WHAT GIVES?

MUN CH

YOU MADE ME DO IT!!!

YOU'RE THE AUTHOR!

AH HA HA. TRUE. TOO TRUE. *SIGH*...

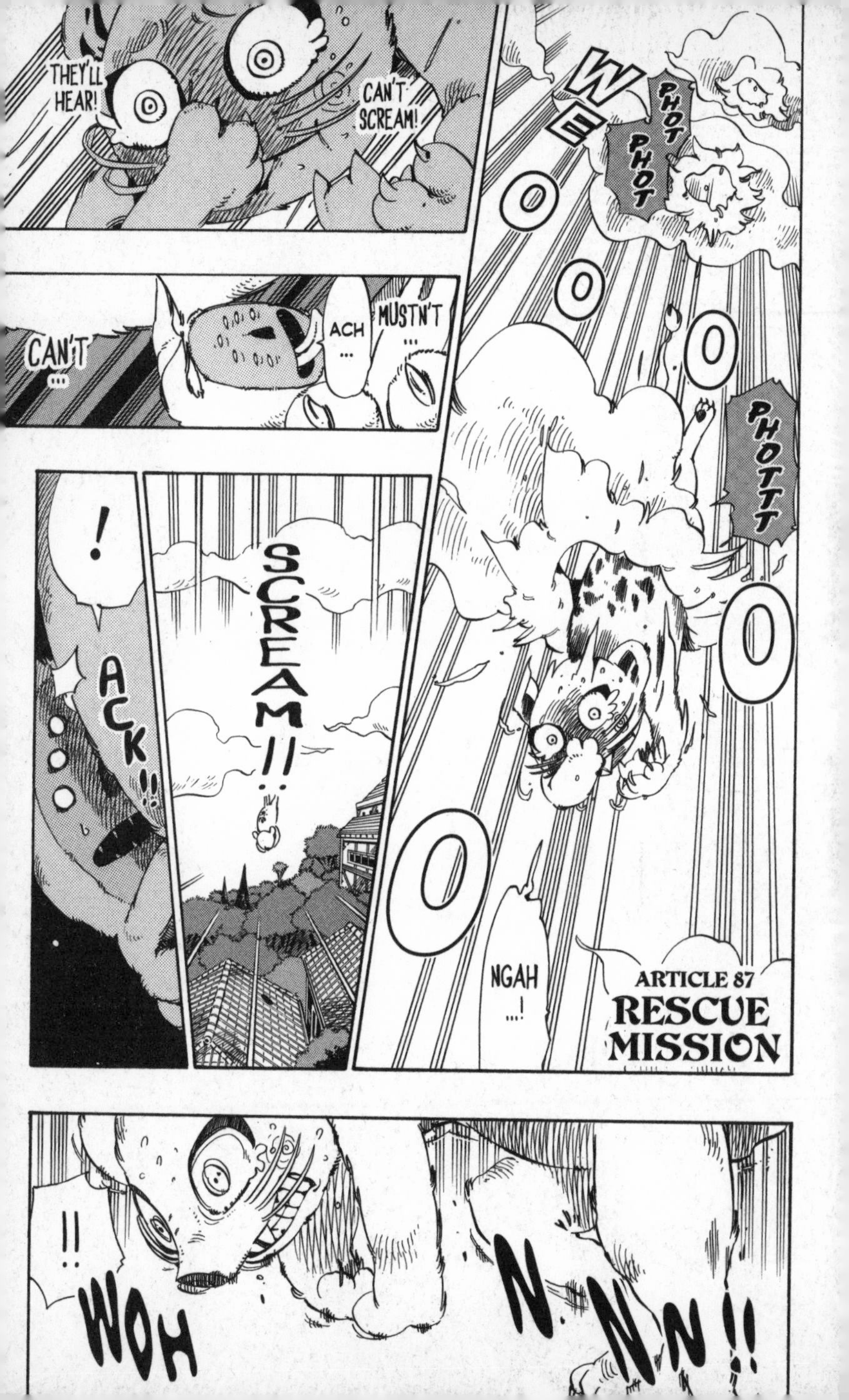
WEOOOOO
PHOT PHOT PHOT
PHOTTT
NGAH ...!
ARTICLE 87
RESCUE MISSION
CAN'T SCREAM!
THEY'LL HEAR!
MUSTN'T ...
ACH ...
CAN'T ...
SCREAM!!
!
ACK!!
...
!!
HOWNNN!!

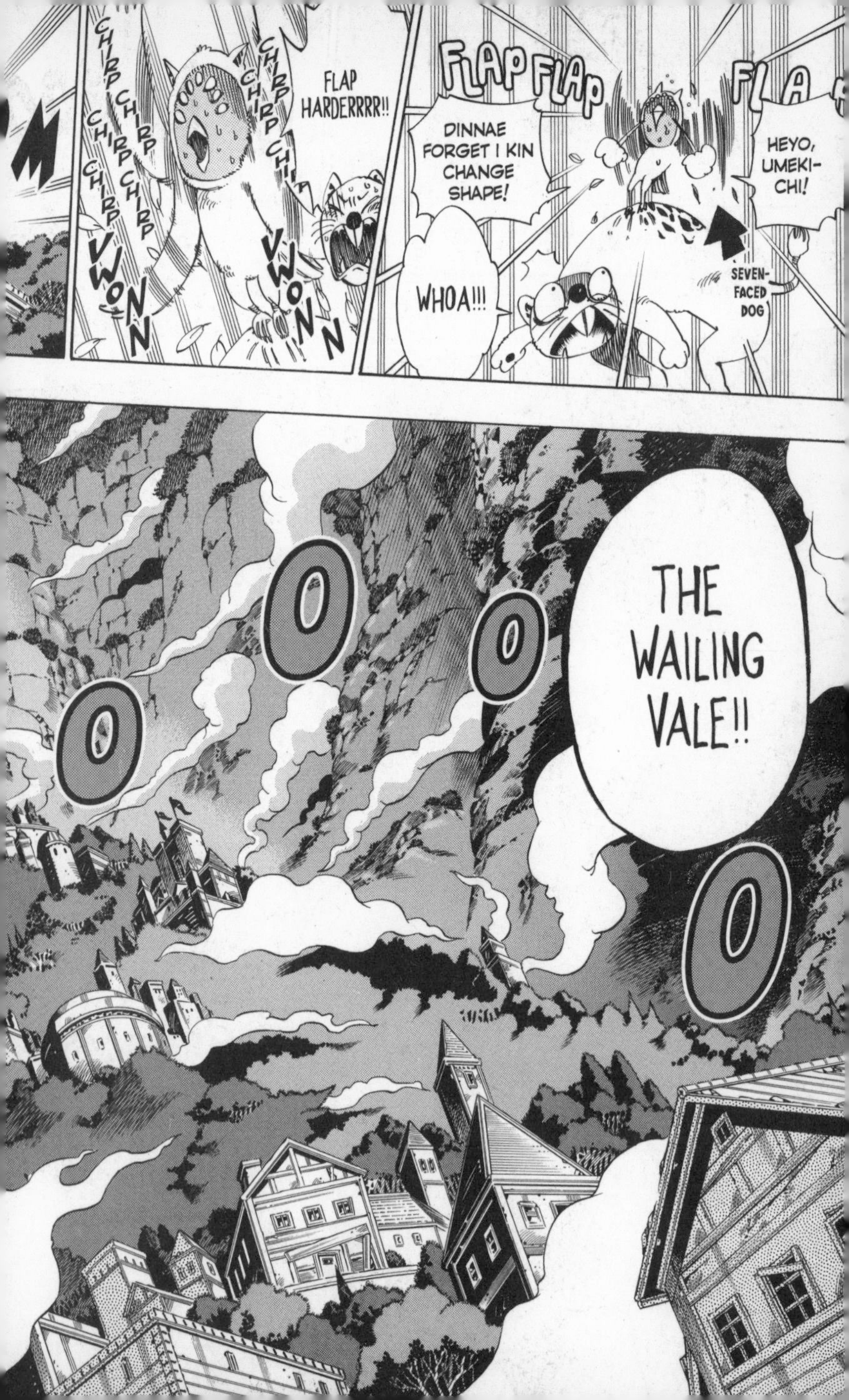
FLA
HEYO, UMEKI-CHI!
FLAP FLAP
DINNAE FORGET I KIN CHANGE SHAPE!
SEVEN-FACED DOG
WHOA!!!
FLAP HARDERRRR!!
CHIRP CHIRP CHIRP
CHIRP CHIRP CHIRP CHIRP
VWONN
VWONN
THE WAILING VALE!!
O
O
O
O
O

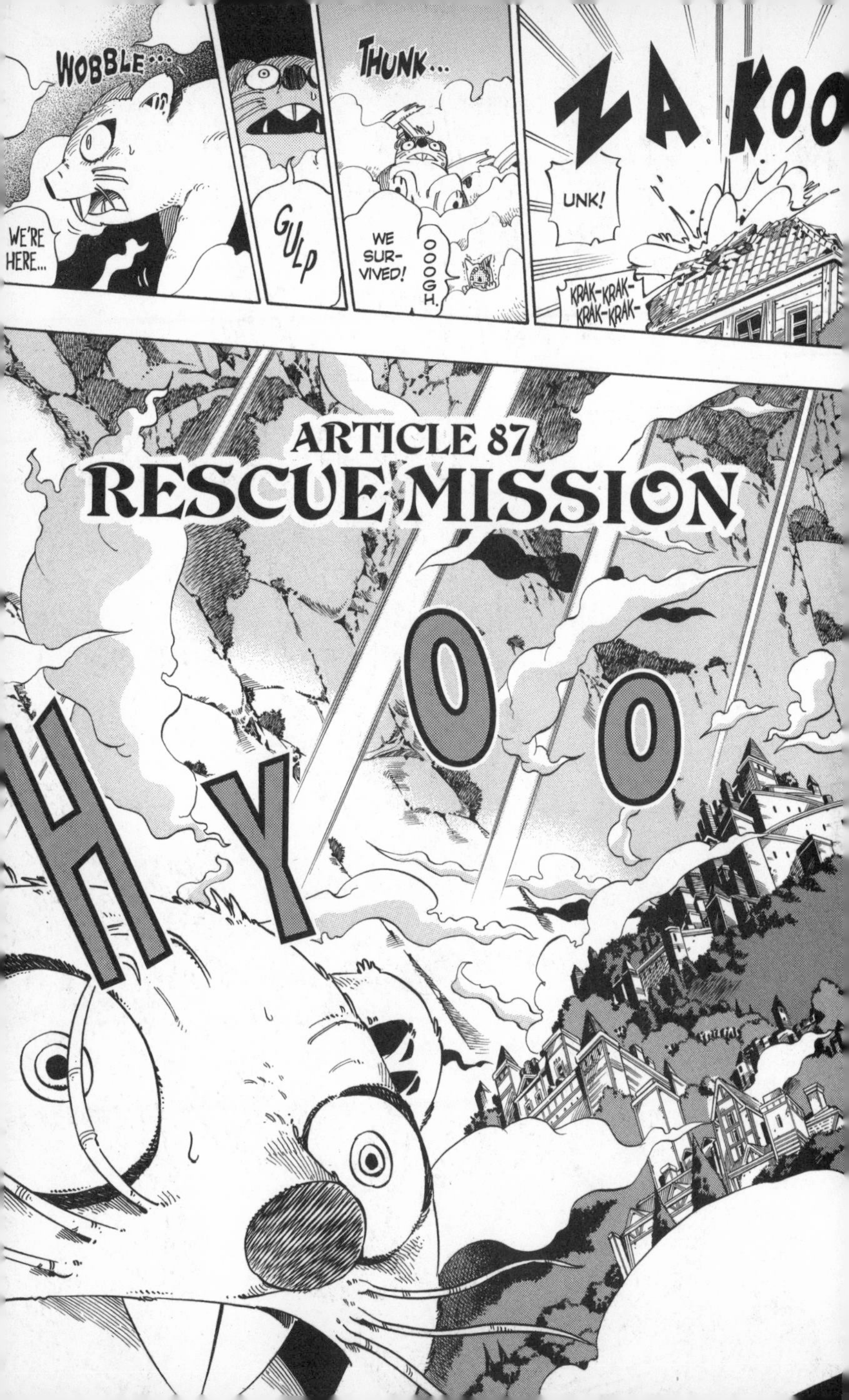
ZA KOO
UNK!
KRAK-KRAK-KRAK-KRAK-
THUNK...
WE SUR-VIVED!
OOOGH.
GULP
WOBBLE...
WE'RE HERE...
ARTICLE 87
RESCUE MISSION
HYOO

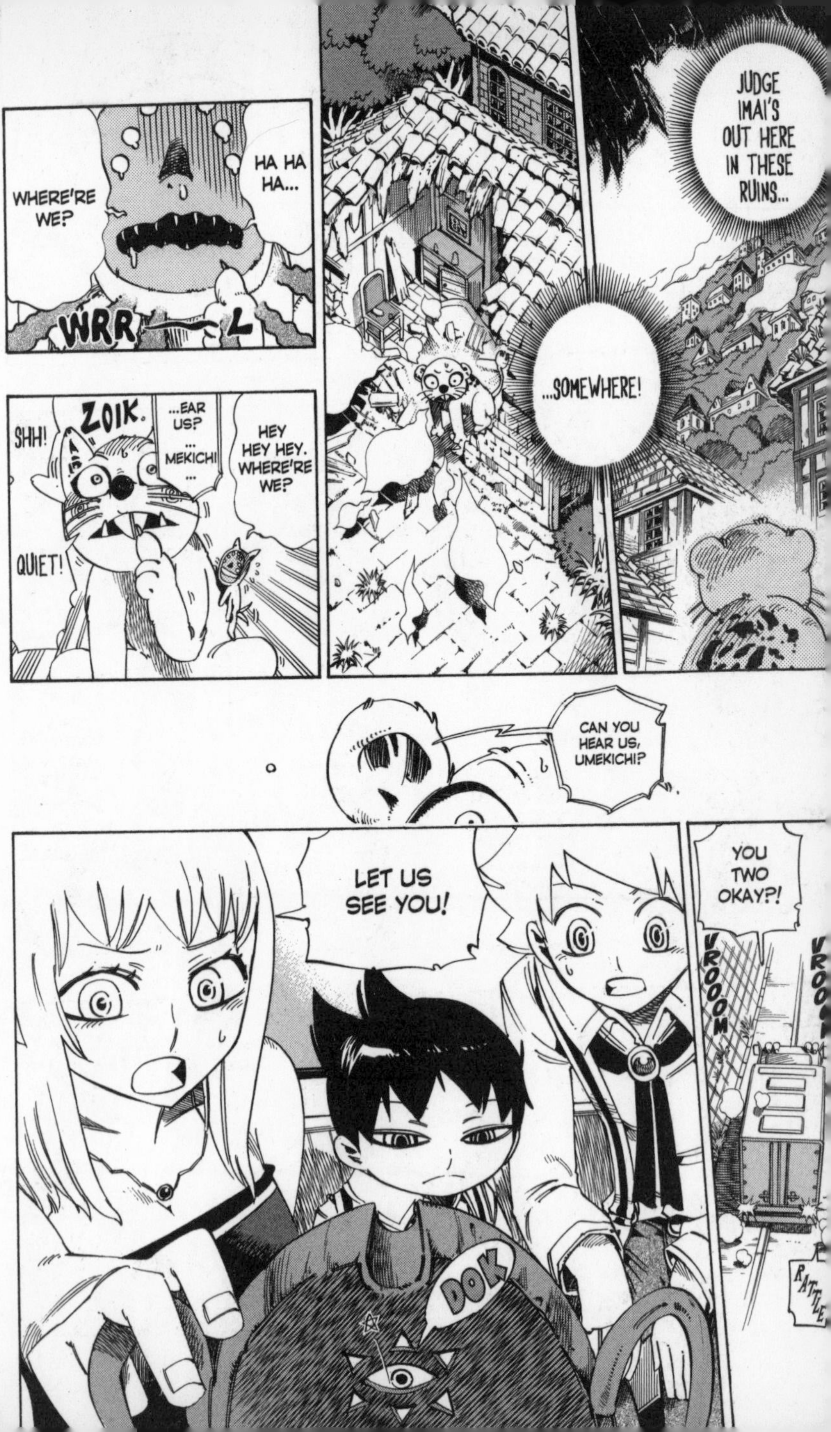
JUDGE IMAI'S OUT HERE IN THESE RUINS...
...SOMEWHERE!
HA HA HA...
WHERE'RE WE?
WRR—L
HEY HEY HEY. WHERE'RE WE?
...EAR US? ... MEKICHI ...
ZOIK.
SHH!
QUIET!
CAN YOU HEAR US, UMEKICHI?
YOU TWO OKAY?!
VROOOM
VROOO
RATTLE
LET US SEE YOU!
DOK

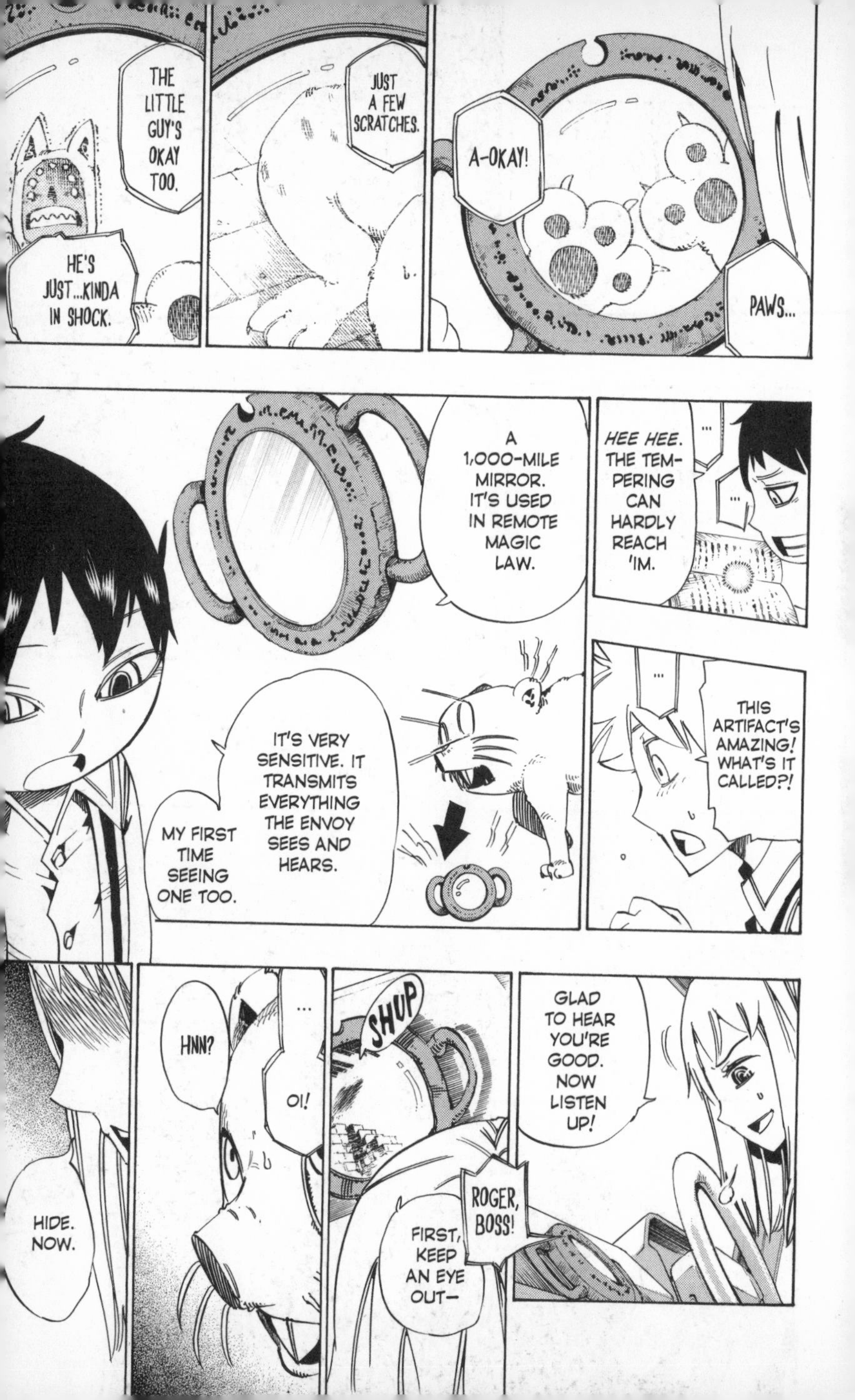
PAWS...
A-OKAY!
JUST A FEW SCRATCHES.
THE LITTLE GUY'S OKAY TOO.
HE'S JUST...KINDA IN SHOCK.
...
...
HEE HEE. THE TEMPERING CAN HARDLY REACH 'IM.
...
THIS ARTIFACT'S AMAZING! WHAT'S IT CALLED?!
A 1,000-MILE MIRROR. IT'S USED IN REMOTE MAGIC LAW.
IT'S VERY SENSITIVE. IT TRANSMITS EVERYTHING THE ENVOY SEES AND HEARS.
MY FIRST TIME SEEING ONE TOO.
GLAD TO HEAR YOU'RE GOOD. NOW LISTEN UP!
ROGER, BOSS!
FIRST, KEEP AN EYE OUT—
SHUP
...
HNN?
OI!
HIDE. NOW.

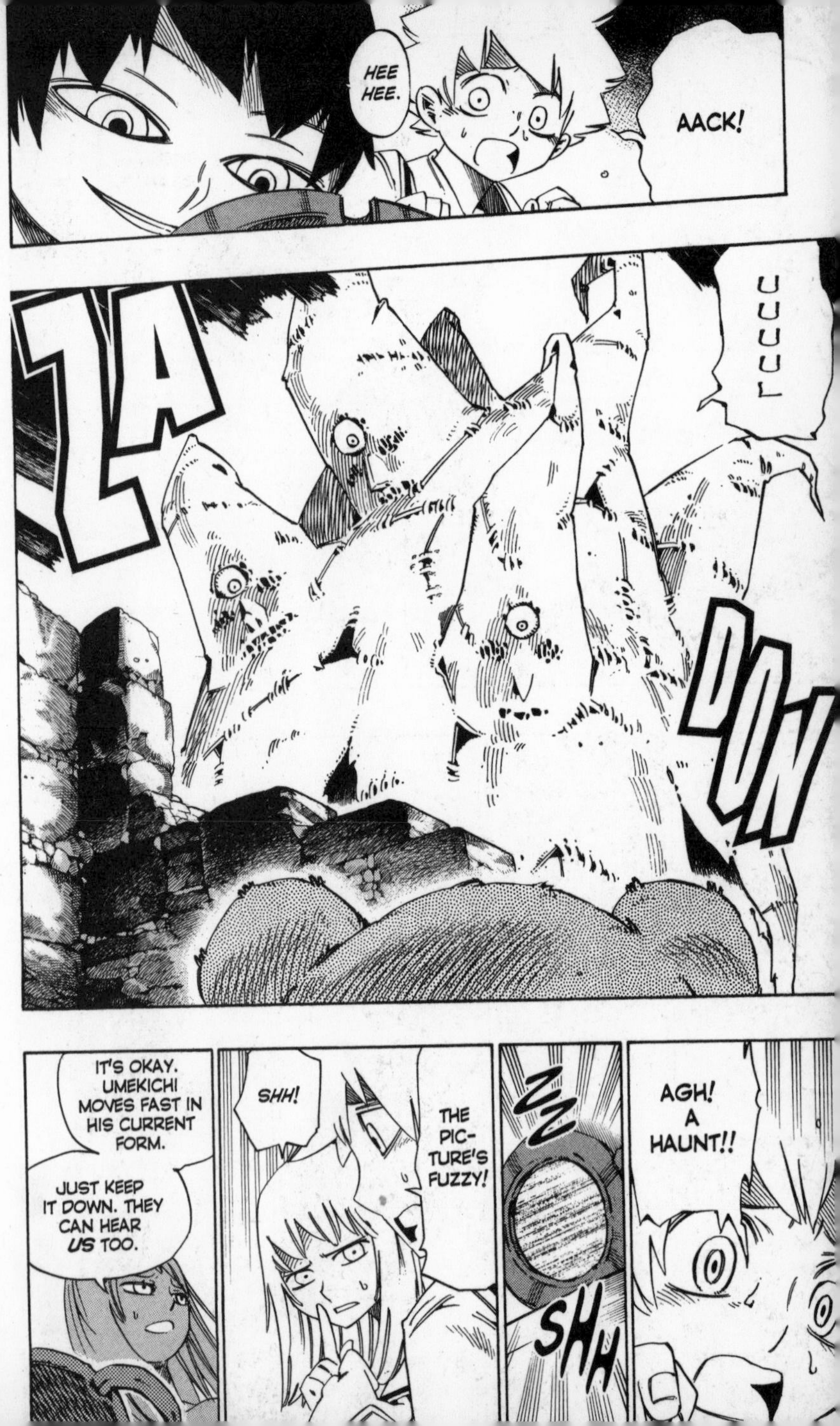
AACK!
HEE HEE.
UUUUL
DON
ZA
AGH! A HAUNT!!
SHH
THE PIC-TURE'S FUZZY!
SHH!
IT'S OKAY. UMEKICHI MOVES FAST IN HIS CURRENT FORM.
JUST KEEP IT DOWN. THEY CAN HEAR *US* TOO.

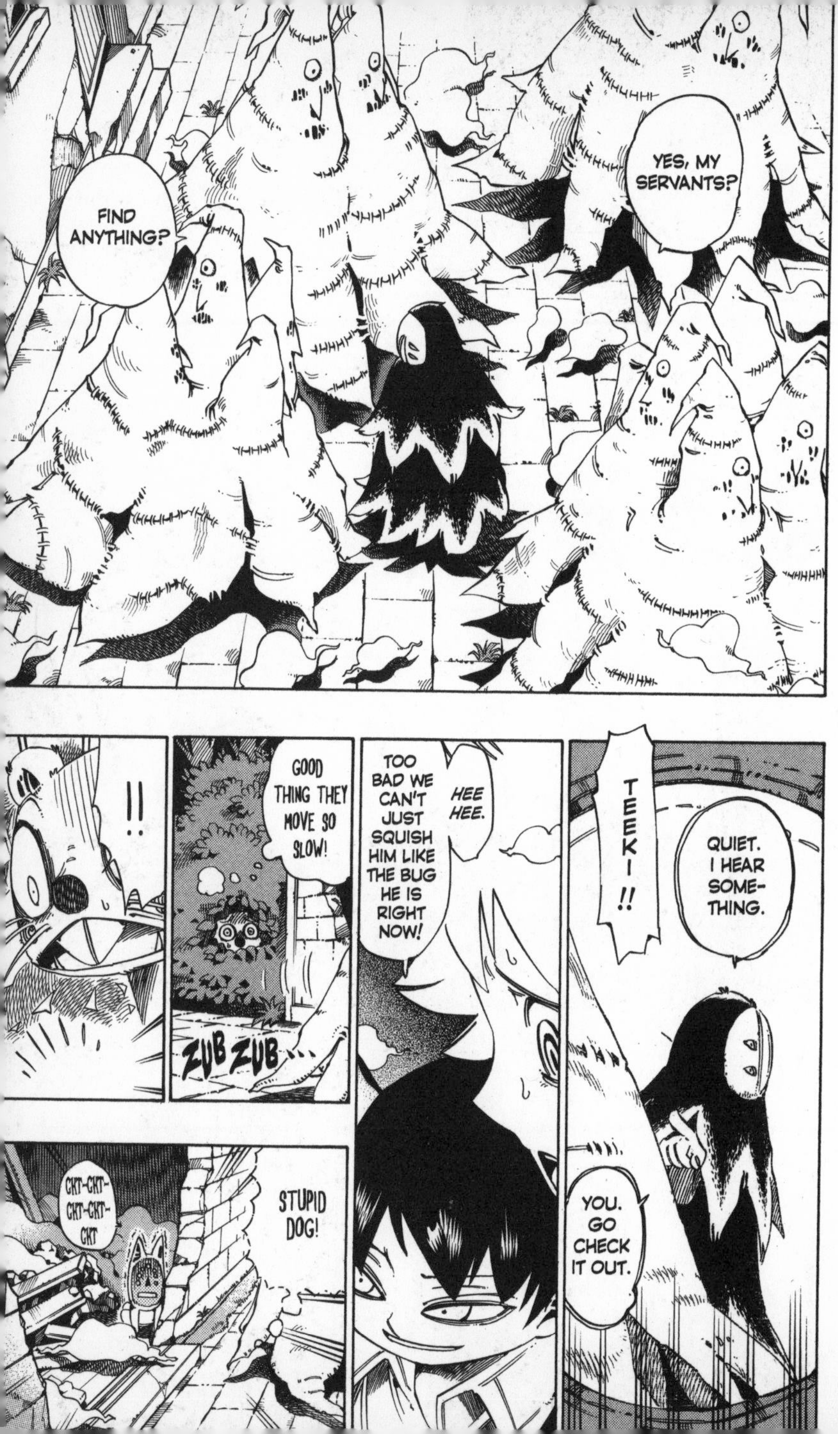
YES, MY SERVANTS?
FIND ANYTHING?
TEEKI!!
QUIET. I HEAR SOME-THING.
YOU. GO CHECK IT OUT.
HEE HEE.
TOO BAD WE CAN'T JUST SQUISH HIM LIKE THE BUG HE IS RIGHT NOW!
GOOD THING THEY MOVE SO SLOW!
ZUB ZUB...
!!
STUPID DOG!
CKT-CKT-CKT-CKT-CKT

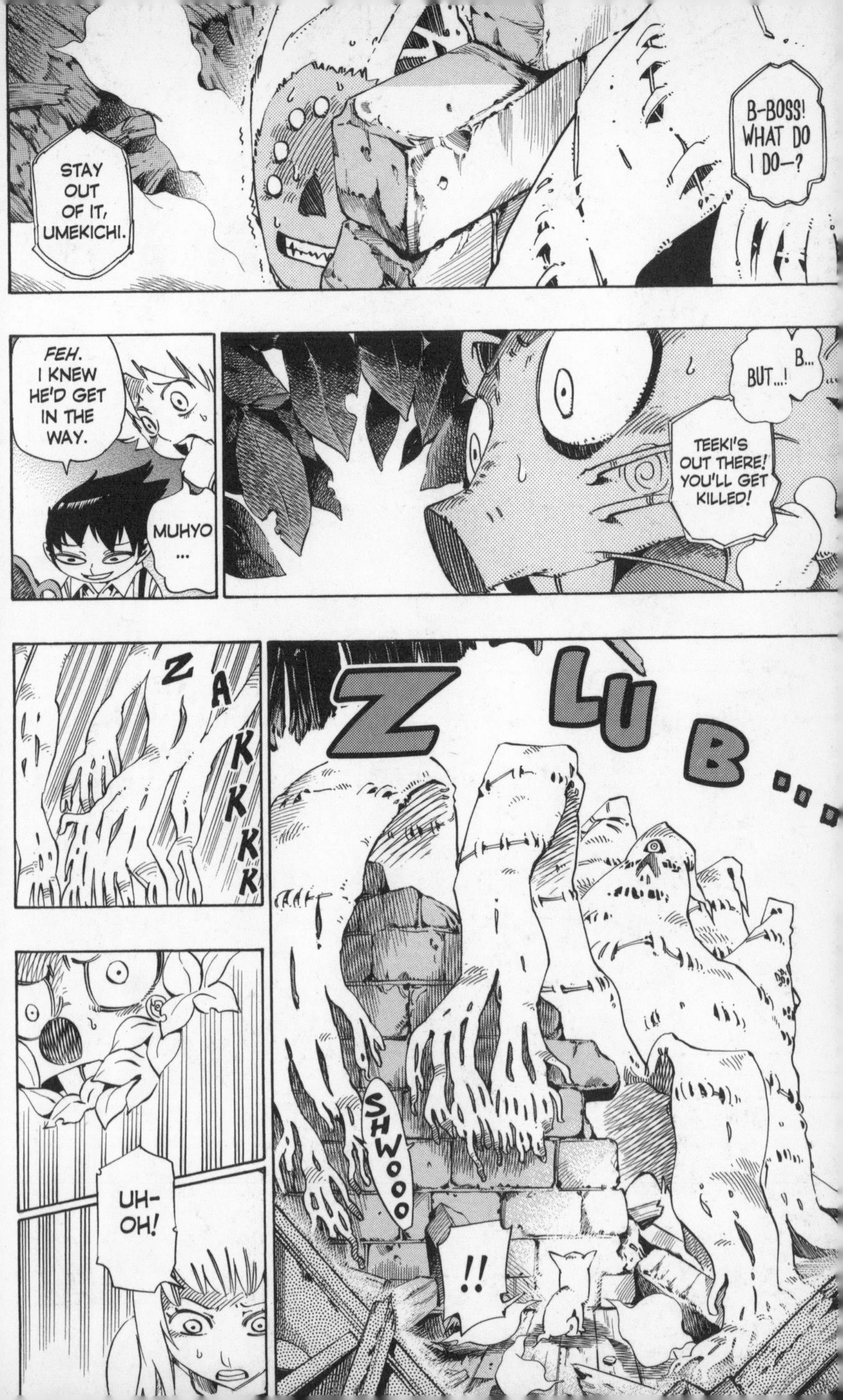
B-BOSS! WHAT DO I DO—?
STAY OUT OF IT, UMEKICHI.
B...
BUT...!
TEEKI'S OUT THERE! YOU'LL GET KILLED!
FEH. I KNEW HE'D GET IN THE WAY.
MUHYO ...
ZLUB...
SHWOOO
!!
ZAKKKK
UH-OH!

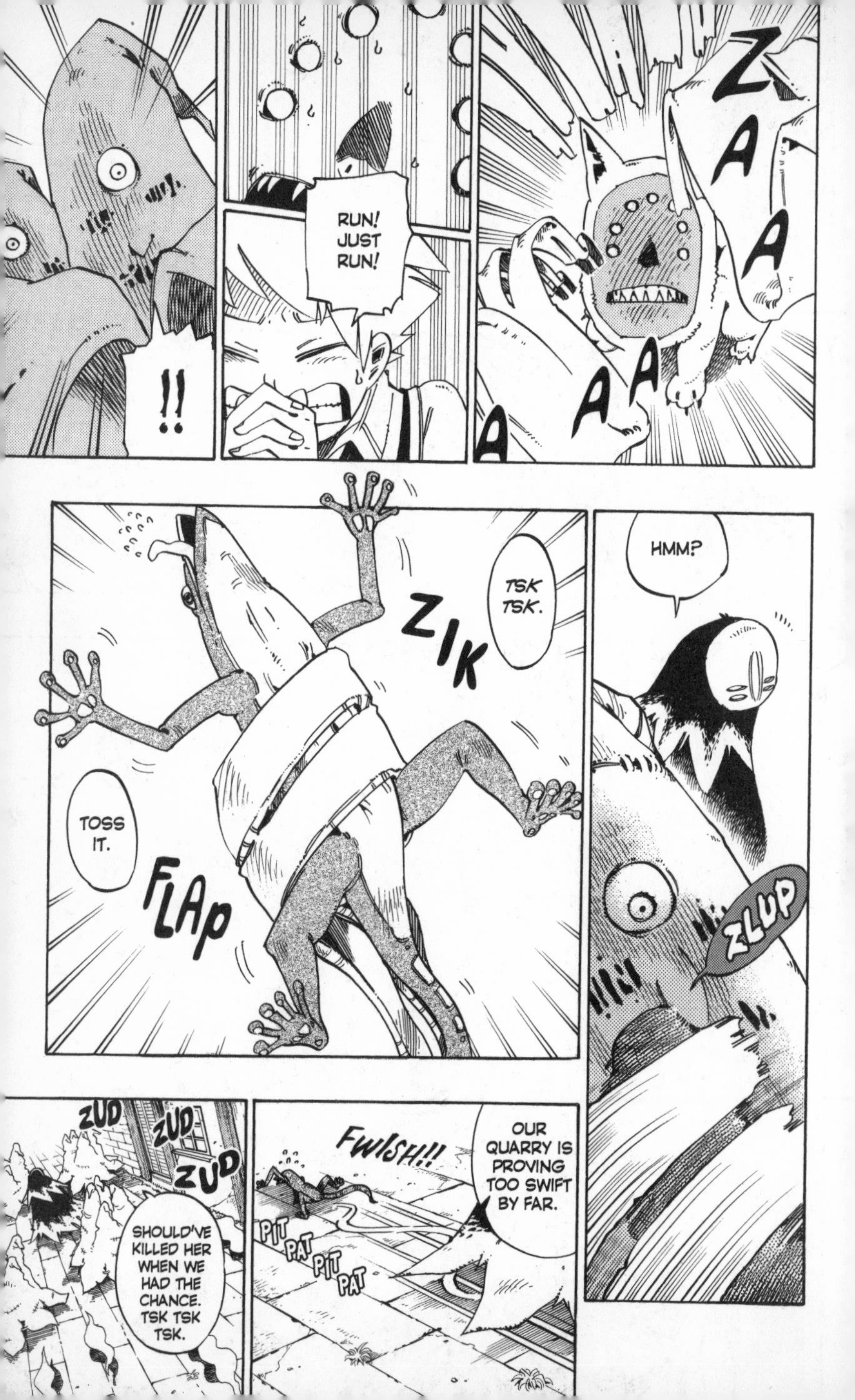
ZAAAAAA
RUN! JUST RUN!
!!
HMM?
ZLUP
TSK TSK.
ZIK
TOSS IT.
FLAP
FWISH!!
OUR QUARRY IS PROVING TOO SWIFT BY FAR.
PIT PAT PIT PAT
ZUD ZUD ZUD
SHOULD'VE KILLED HER WHEN WE HAD THE CHANCE. TSK TSK TSK.

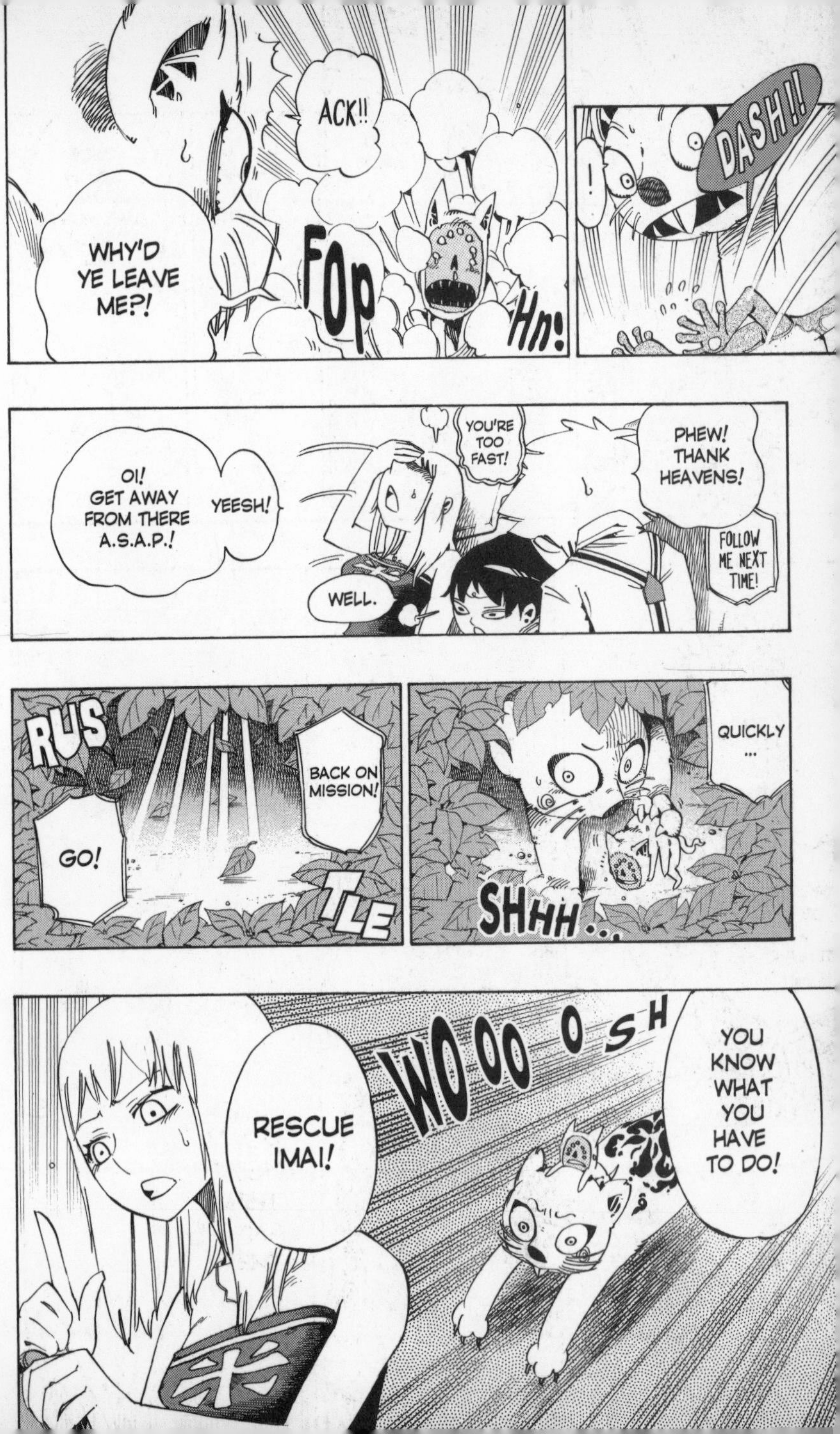
!
DASH!!
ACK!!
Hn!
FOp
WHY'D YE LEAVE ME?!
PHEW! THANK HEAVENS!
FOLLOW ME NEXT TIME!
YOU'RE TOO FAST!
YEESH!
OI! GET AWAY FROM THERE A.S.A.P.!
WELL.
QUICKLY ...
SHHH...
BACK ON MISSION!
RUS
TLE
GO!
YOU KNOW WHAT YOU HAVE TO DO!
WOOOOSH
RESCUE IMAI!

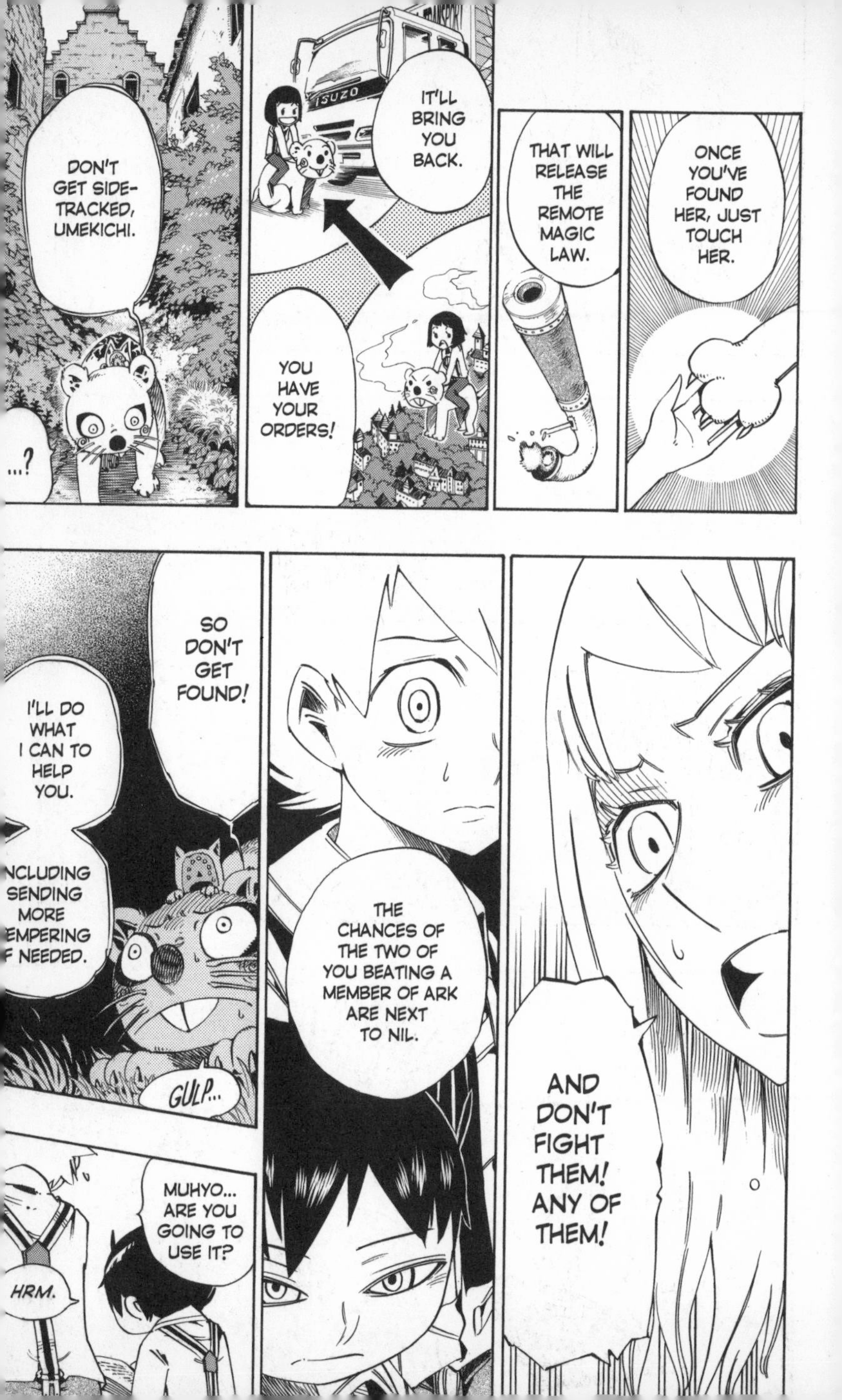
ONCE YOU'VE FOUND HER, JUST TOUCH HER.
THAT WILL RELEASE THE REMOTE MAGIC LAW.
IT'LL BRING YOU BACK.
YOU HAVE YOUR ORDERS!
ISUZO
DON'T GET SIDE-TRACKED, UMEKICHI.
...?
AND DON'T FIGHT THEM! ANY OF THEM!
THE CHANCES OF THE TWO OF YOU BEATING A MEMBER OF ARK ARE NEXT TO NIL.
SO DON'T GET FOUND!
I'LL DO WHAT I CAN TO HELP YOU.
NCLUDING SENDING MORE EMPERING F NEEDED.
GULP...
MUHYO... ARE YOU GOING TO USE IT?
HRM.

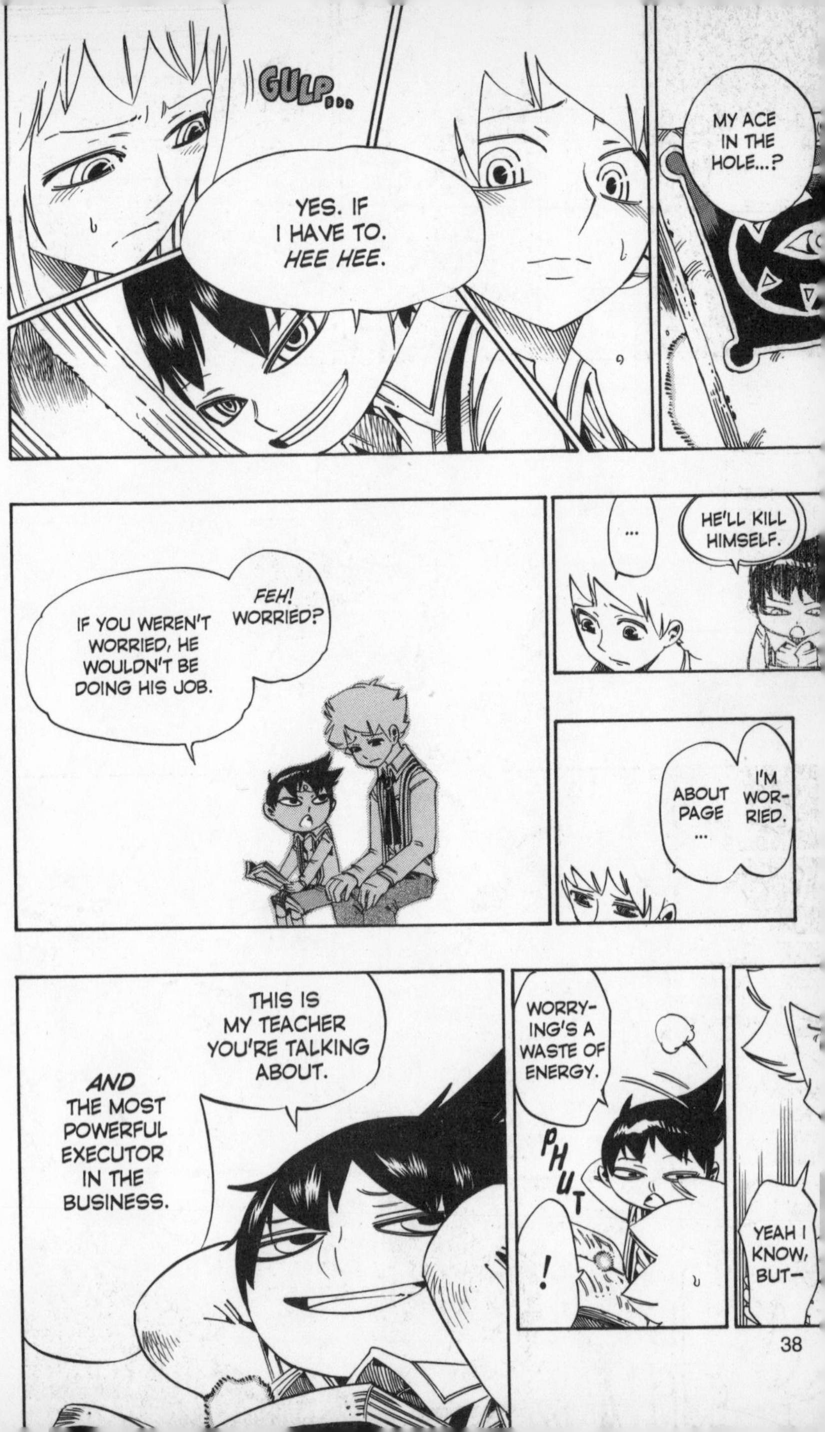
MY ACE IN THE HOLE...?
GULP...
YES. IF I HAVE TO. *HEE HEE.*
HE'LL KILL HIMSELF.
...
I'M WOR-RIED.
ABOUT PAGE ...
FEH! WORRIED?
IF YOU WEREN'T WORRIED, HE WOULDN'T BE DOING HIS JOB.
YEAH I KNOW, BUT—
WORRY-ING'S A WASTE OF ENERGY.
PHUT
!
THIS IS MY TEACHER YOU'RE TALKING ABOUT.
AND THE MOST POWERFUL EXECUTOR IN THE BUSINESS.

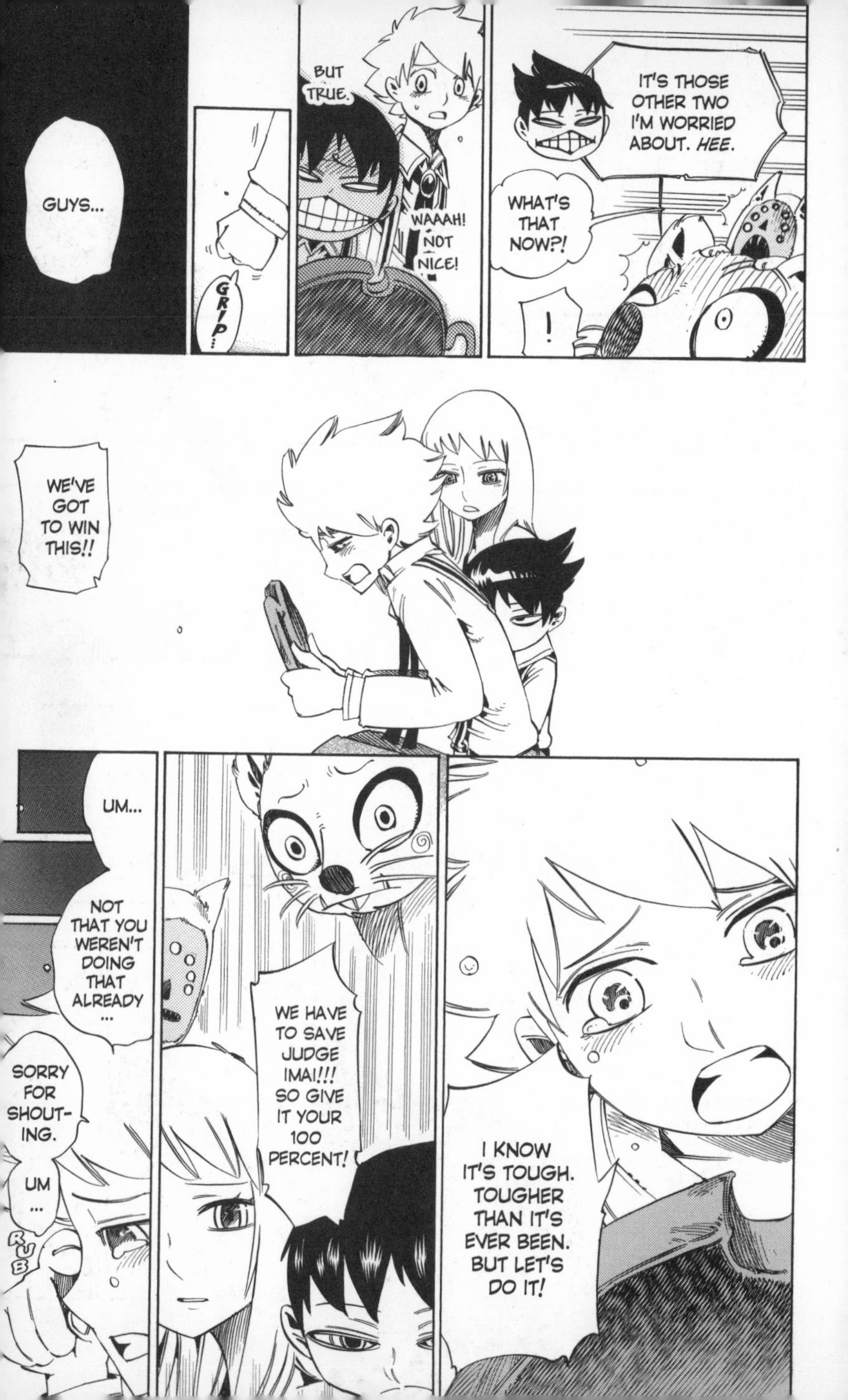
IT'S THOSE OTHER TWO I'M WORRIED ABOUT. HEE.
WHAT'S THAT NOW?!
!
BUT TRUE.
WAAAH! NOT NICE!
GRIP...
GUYS...
WE'VE GOT TO WIN THIS!!
I KNOW IT'S TOUGH. TOUGHER THAN IT'S EVER BEEN. BUT LET'S DO IT!
WE HAVE TO SAVE JUDGE IMAI!!! SO GIVE IT YOUR 100 PERCENT!
UM...
NOT THAT YOU WEREN'T DOING THAT ALREADY...
SORRY FOR SHOUTING.
UM...
RUB

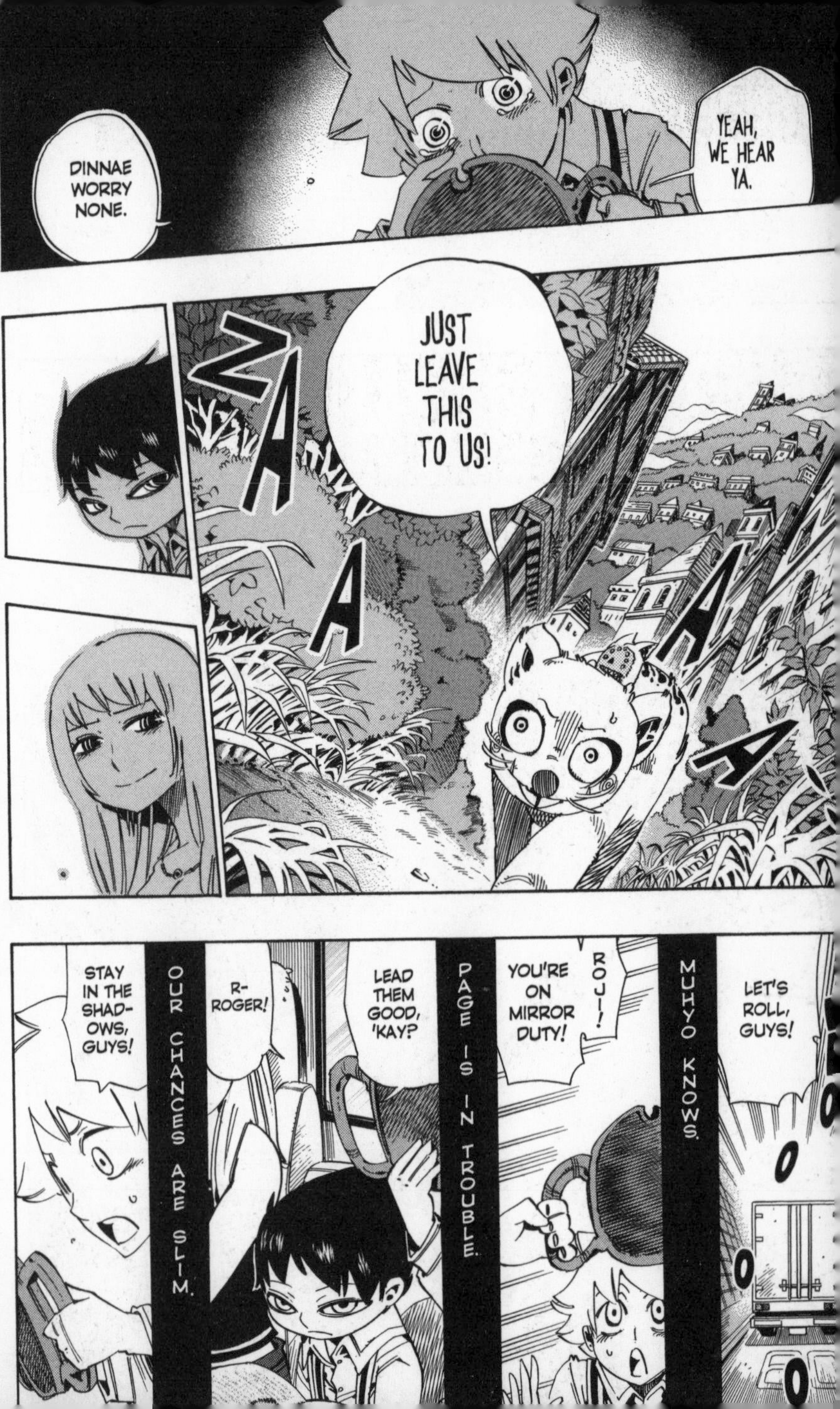
YEAH, WE HEAR YA.
DINNAE WORRY NONE.
JUST LEAVE THIS TO US!
ZAAAA
LET'S ROLL, GUYS!
MUHYO KNOWS.
ROJI!
YOU'RE ON MIRROR DUTY!
PAGE IS IN TROUBLE.
LEAD THEM GOOD, 'KAY?
R-ROGER!
OUR CHANCES ARE SLIM.
STAY IN THE SHADOWS, GUYS!

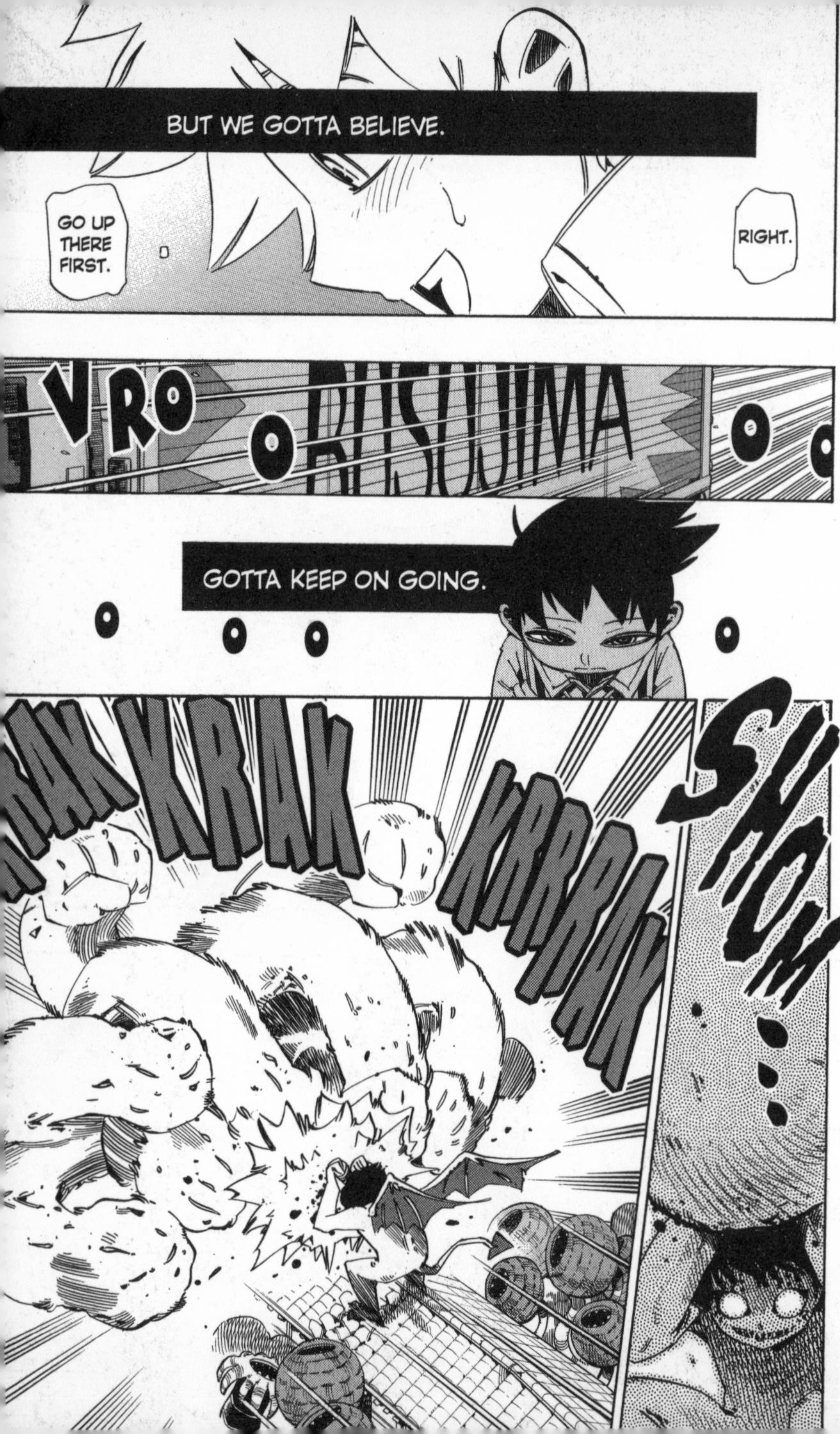
BUT WE GOTTA BELIEVE.
RIGHT.
GO UP THERE FIRST.
VRO
GOTTA KEEP ON GOING.
SHOOM...
KRRAK
KRAK
KRAK

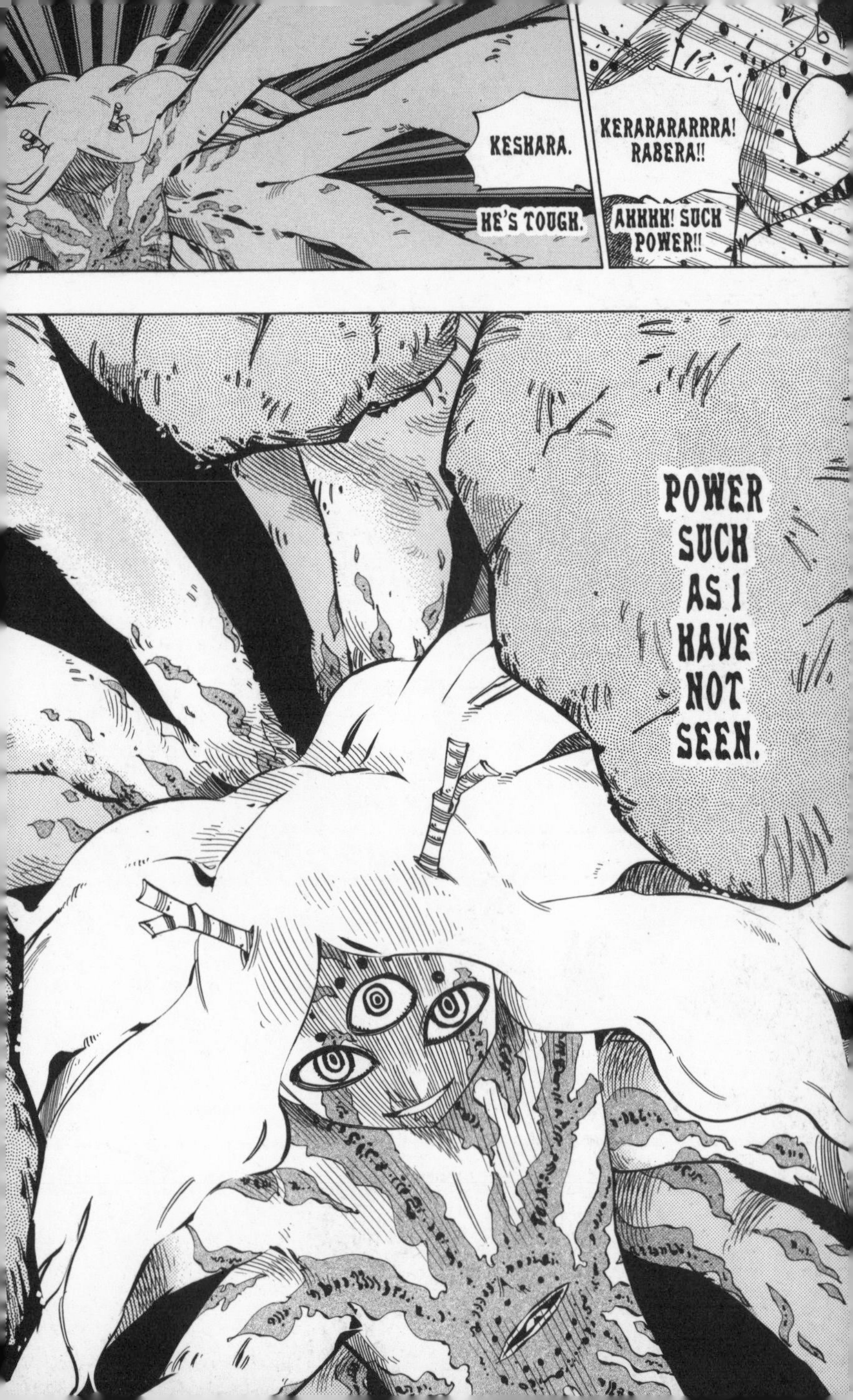
KERARARARRRA! RABERA!!
AHHHH! SUCH POWER!!
KESHARA.
HE'S TOUGH.
POWER SUCH AS I HAVE NOT SEEN.

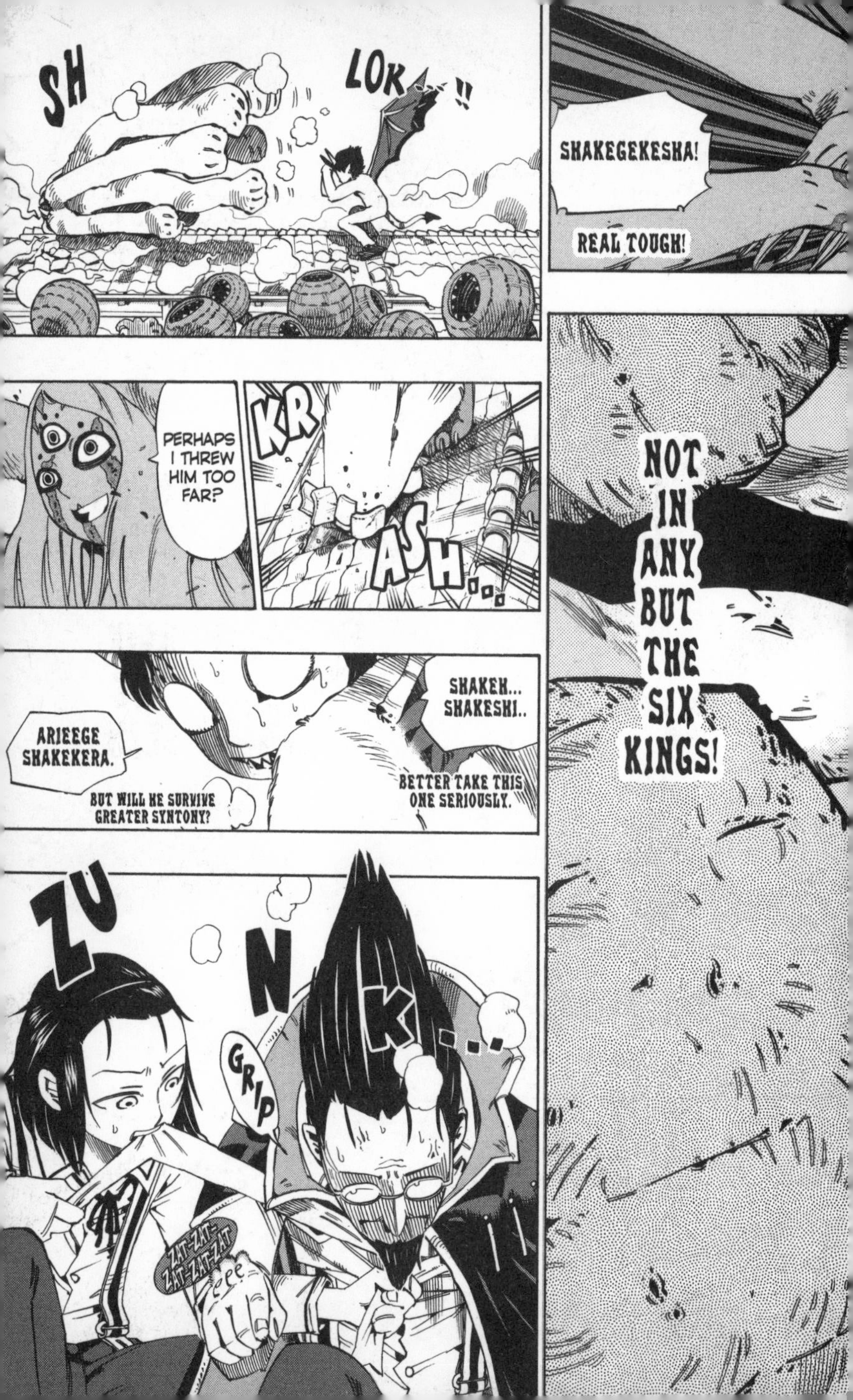
SHAKEGEKESHA!
REAL TOUGH!
NOT IN ANY BUT THE SIX KINGS!
SH LOK..!!
PERHAPS I THREW HIM TOO FAR?
KRASH...
SHAKEH... SHAKESHI..
BETTER TAKE THIS ONE SERIOUSLY.
ARIEEGE SHAKEKERA.
BUT WILL HE SURVIVE GREATER SYNTONY?
ZUNK...
GRIP

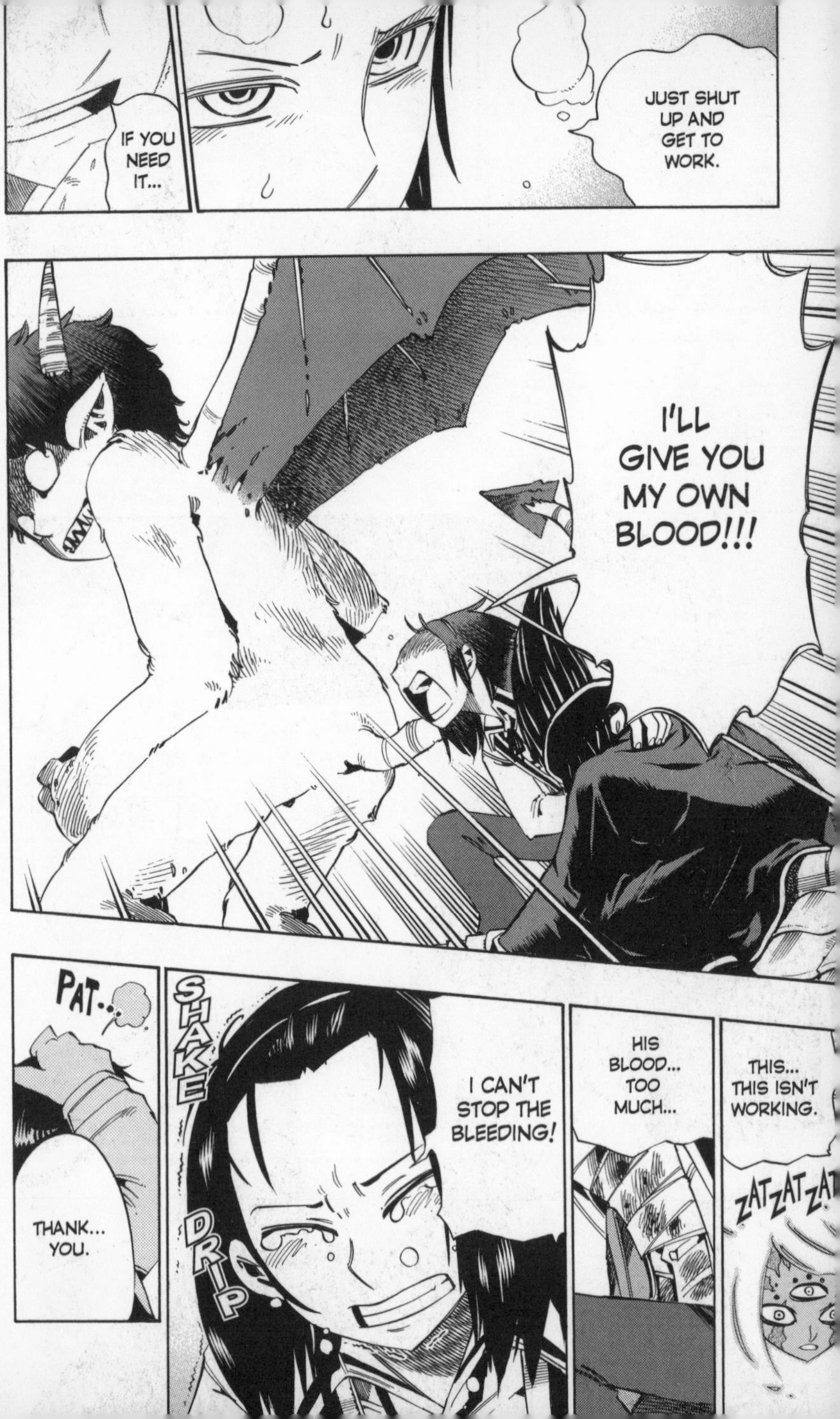
JUST SHUT UP AND GET TO WORK.
IF YOU NEED IT...
I'LL GIVE YOU MY OWN BLOOD!!!
THIS... THIS ISN'T WORKING.
ZAT ZAT ZAT
HIS BLOOD... TOO MUCH...
I CAN'T STOP THE BLEEDING!
SHAKE
DRIP
PAT...
THANK... YOU.

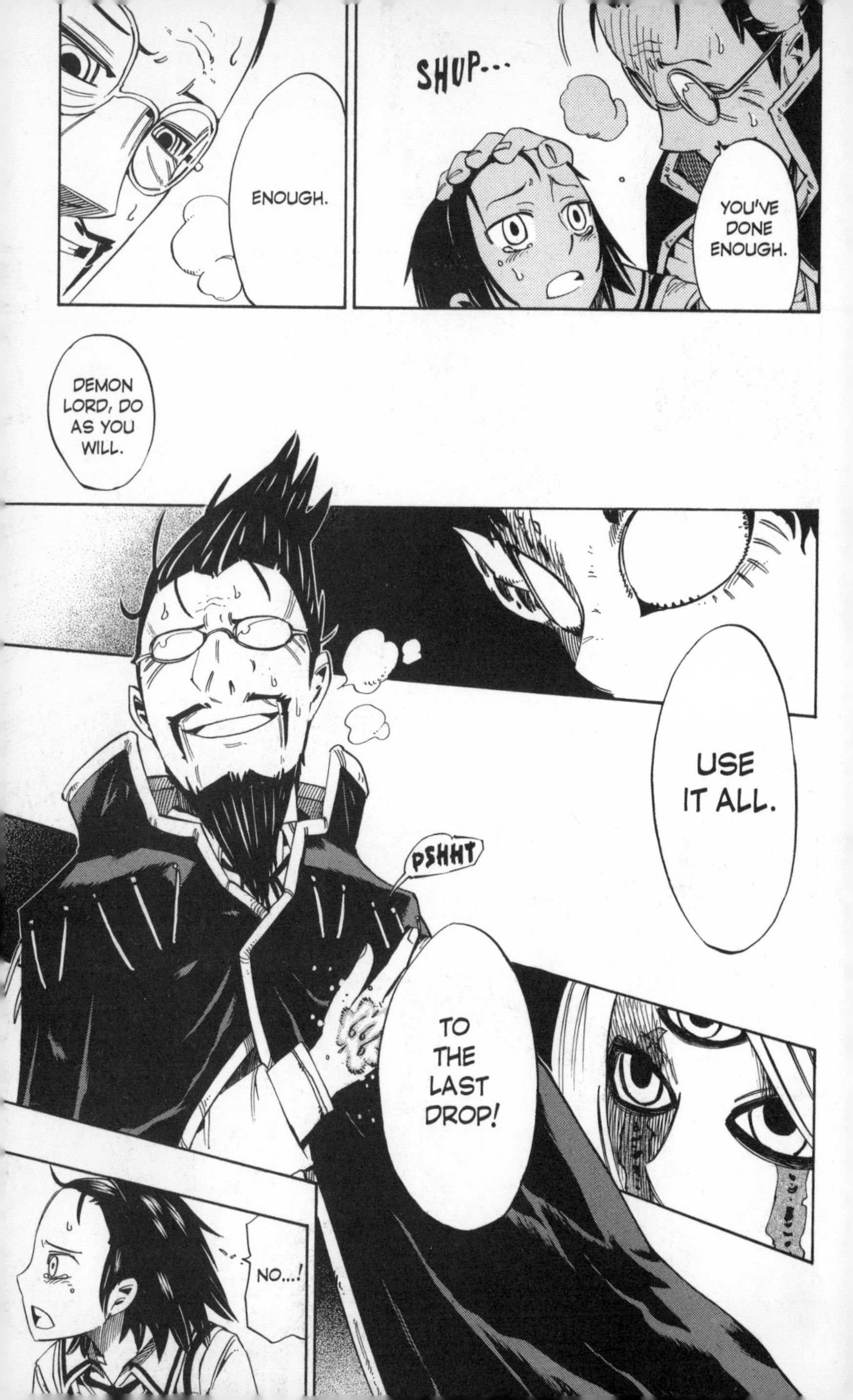
SHUP...
YOU'VE DONE ENOUGH.
ENOUGH.
DEMON LORD, DO AS YOU WILL.
USE IT ALL.
PSHHT
TO THE LAST DROP!
NO...!

FROM H.I., TOKUSHIMA PREFECTURE

Q: (1) WHEN YOU SAY PEOPLE WERE CLASSMATES AT M.L.S., THEY AREN'T NECESSARILY THE SAME AGE, RIGHT?

A: (1) NOT NECESSARILY. LIKE I SAID BEFORE, PEOPLE ENTER AT DIFFERENT AGES. I'M GUESSING THAT IF THEY'RE REALLY FAR APART IN AGE, THEY'D PUT THEM IN DIFFERENT CLASSROOMS THOUGH.

Q: (2) COULD ROJI ENTER THE M.L.S. NOW IF HE WANTED TO?

A: (2) WELL, MAYBE...NOT? HE'S KINDA BIG...

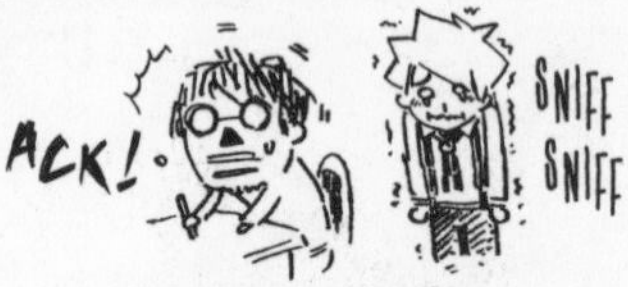

SNIFF SNIFF
ACK!

ERM, THAT IS... NO, I'M SURE HE COULD GET IN! NO PROBLEM! *EH HEH HEH...*

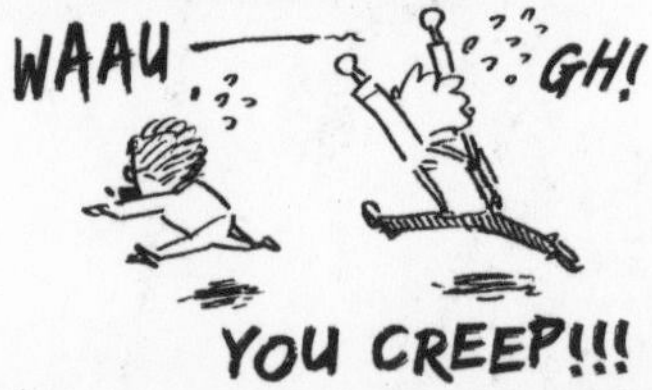

WAAU——GH!
YOU CREEP!!!

HUH, I GUESS HE WAS SERIOUS ABOUT THAT WHOLE M.L.S. THING AFTER ALL. AND HE WOULDN'T BE *THAT* OUT OF PLACE WITH ALL THE FIRST-YEAR KIDS ANYWAY...

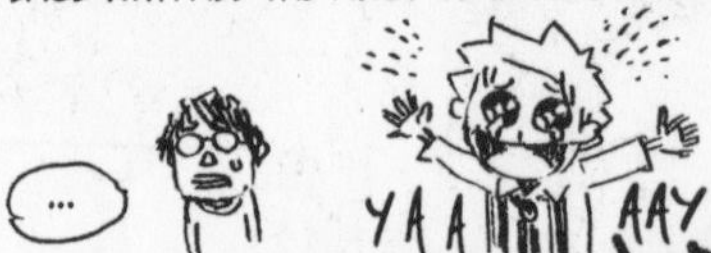

YAAAAY
...

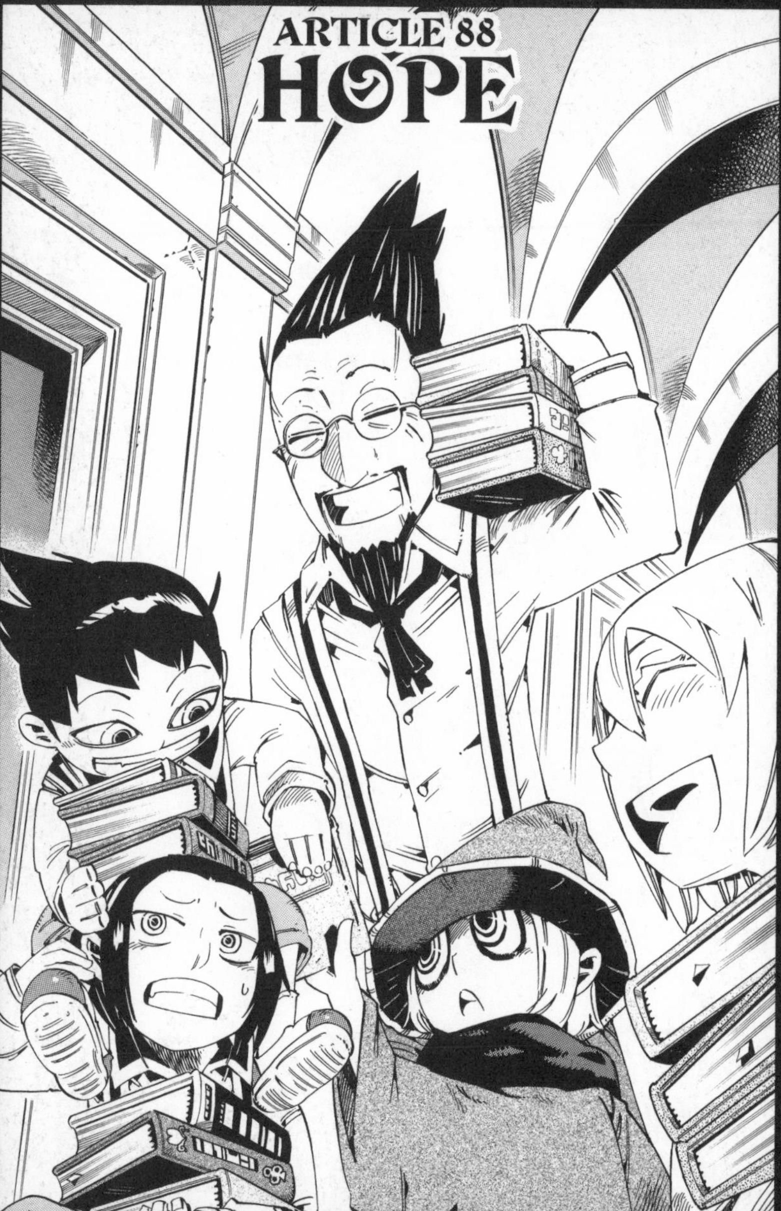
ARTICLE 88
HOPE

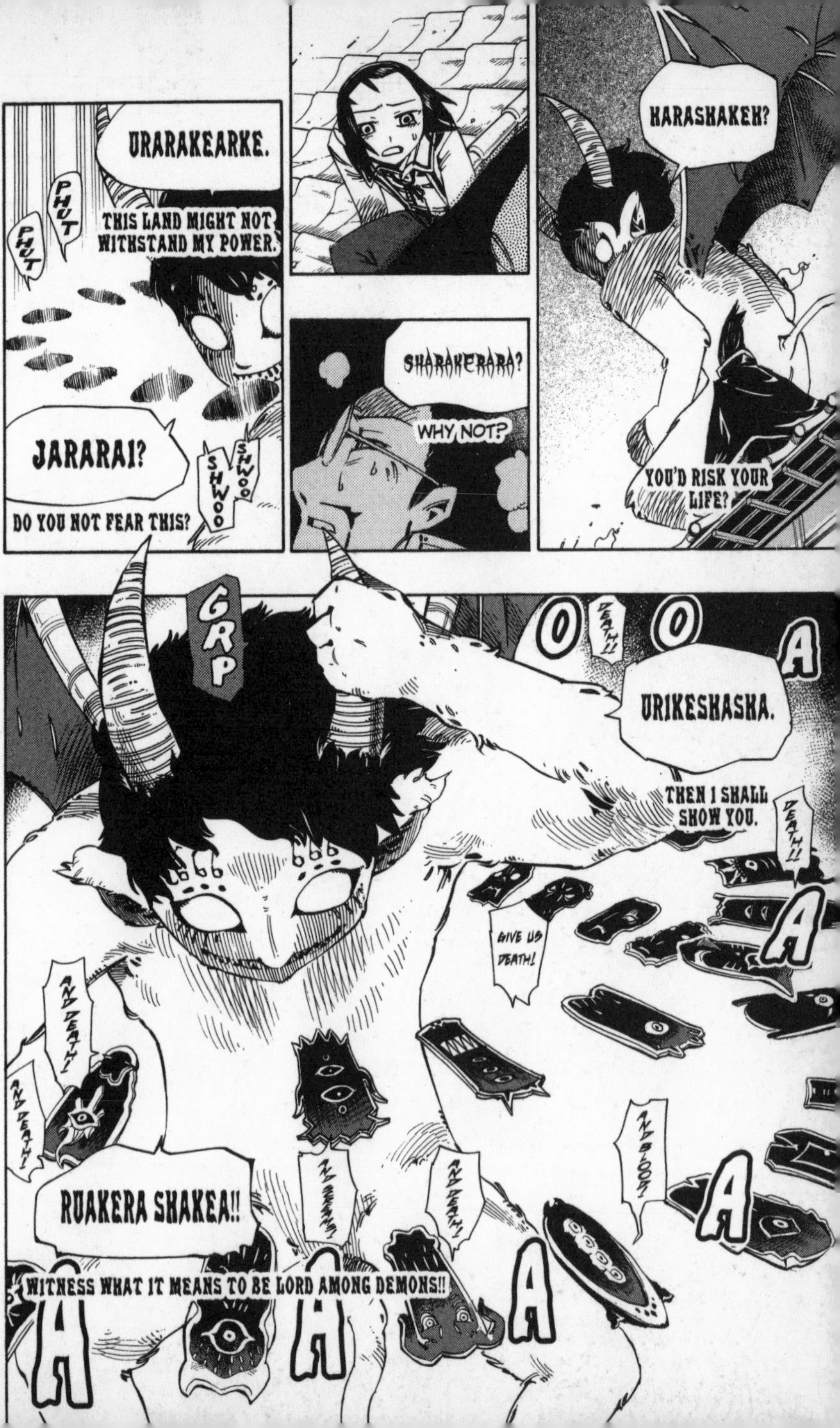
HARASHAKEH?
YOU'D RISK YOUR LIFE?
SHARAKERARA?
WHY NOT?
URARAKEARKE.
THIS LAND MIGHT NOT WITHSTAND MY POWER.
PHUT
PHUT
JARARAI?
DO YOU NOT FEAR THIS?
SHWOO
SHWOO
GRP
OOOA
DEATH!!
URIKESHASHA.
THEN I SHALL SHOW YOU.
DEATH!!
AAA
GIVE US DEATH!
AND BLOOD!
AND DEATH!
AND DEATH!
AND DEATH!
RUAKERA SHAKEA!!
WITNESS WHAT IT MEANS TO BE LORD AMONG DEMONS!!
AAAA

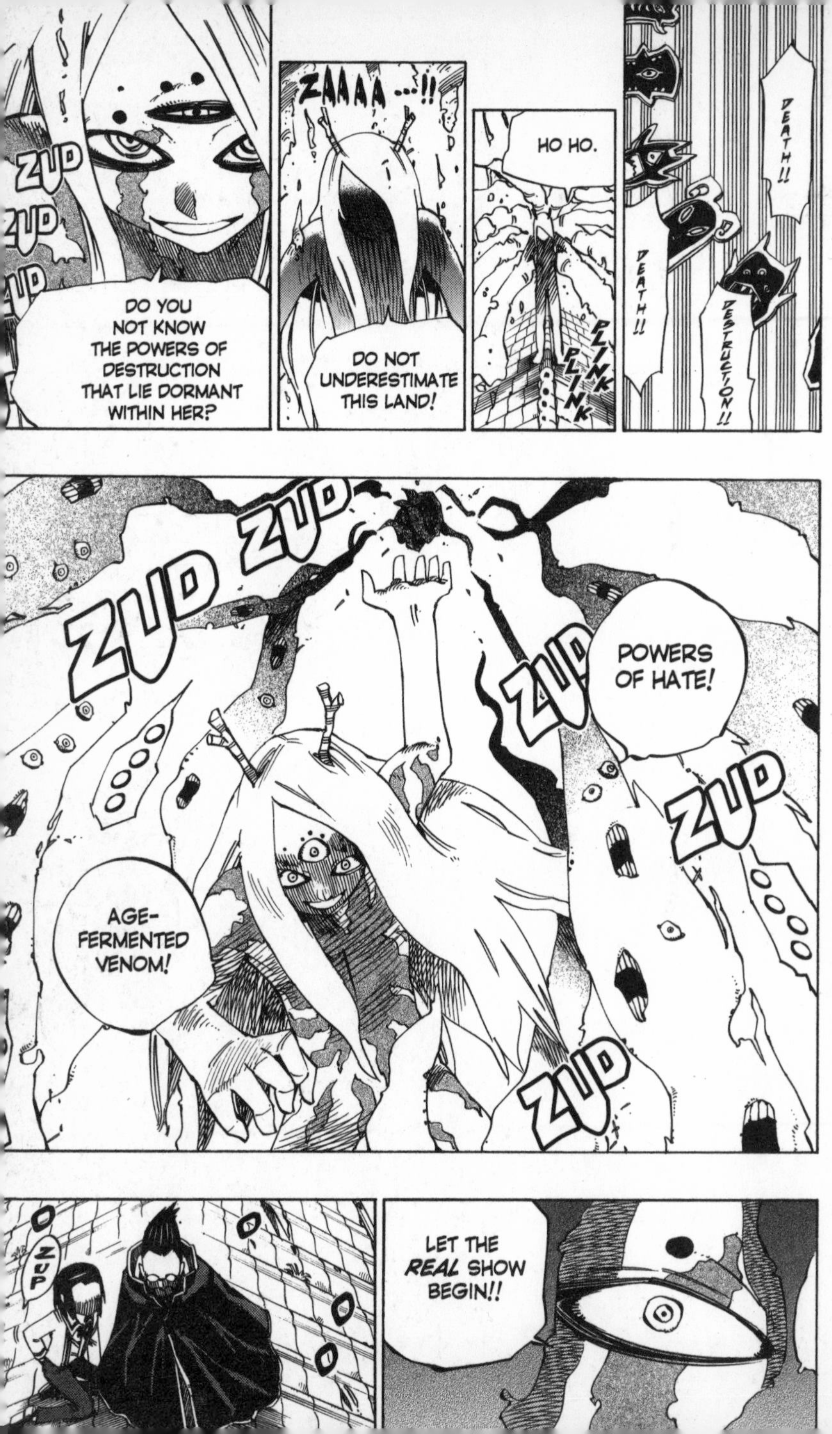

DEATH!!
DESTRUCTION!!
DEATH!!
HO HO.
PLINK
PLINK
PLINK
ZAAAA...!!
DO NOT UNDERESTIMATE THIS LAND!
ZUD
ZUD
ZUD
DO YOU NOT KNOW THE POWERS OF DESTRUCTION THAT LIE DORMANT WITHIN HER?
ZUD
ZUD
ZUD
POWERS OF HATE!
ZUD
ZUD
ZUD
AGE-FERMENTED VENOM!
ZUD
LET THE *REAL* SHOW BEGIN!!
ZUP

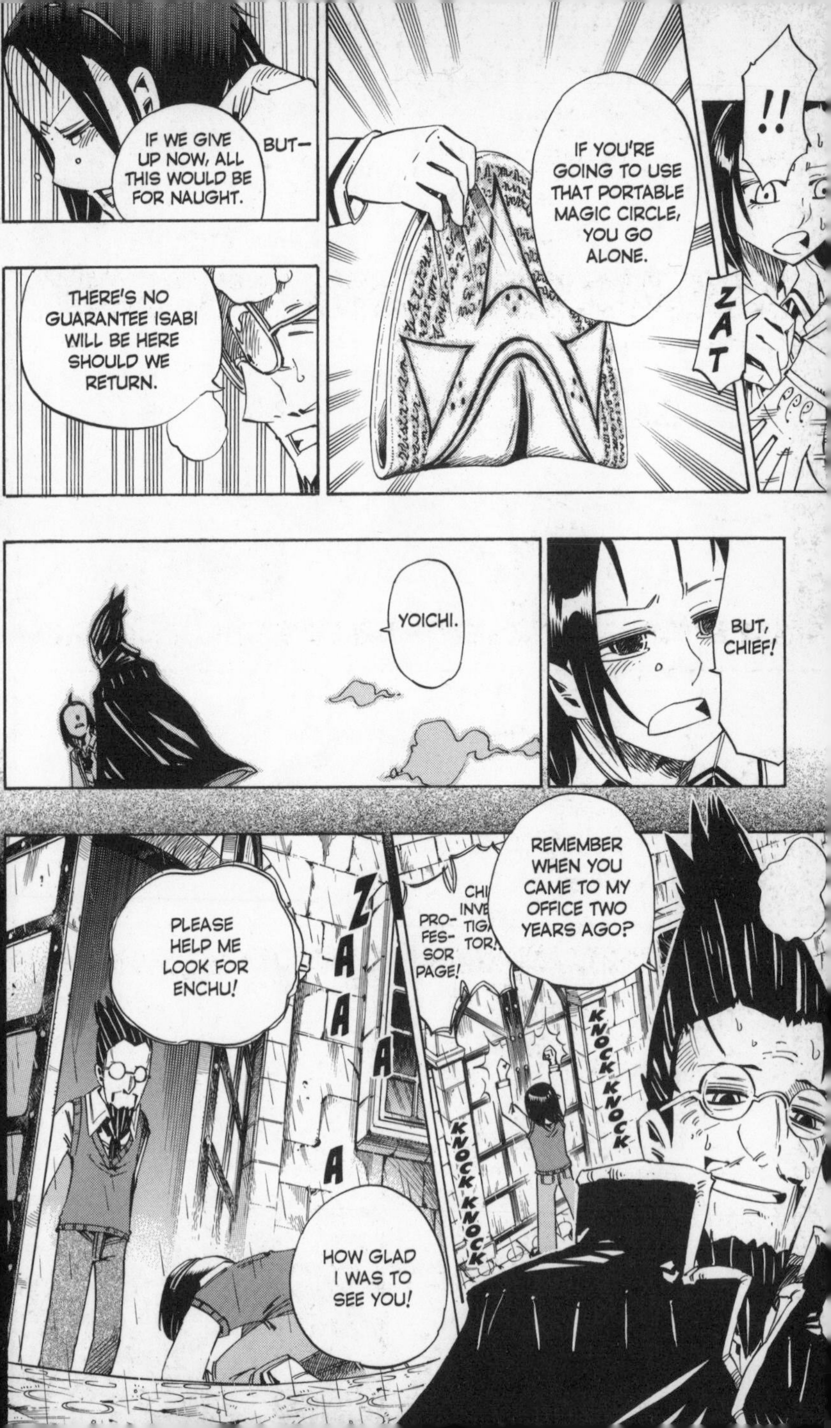
!!
ZAT
IF YOU'RE GOING TO USE THAT PORTABLE MAGIC CIRCLE, YOU GO ALONE.
BUT—
IF WE GIVE UP NOW, ALL THIS WOULD BE FOR NAUGHT.
THERE'S NO GUARANTEE ISABI WILL BE HERE SHOULD WE RETURN.
BUT, CHIEF!
YOICHI.
REMEMBER WHEN YOU CAME TO MY OFFICE TWO YEARS AGO?
KNOCK KNOCK
KNOCK KNOCK
CHI INVE TIGA TOR!
PROFESSOR PAGE!
ZAAAAA
PLEASE HELP ME LOOK FOR ENCHU!
HOW GLAD I WAS TO SEE YOU!

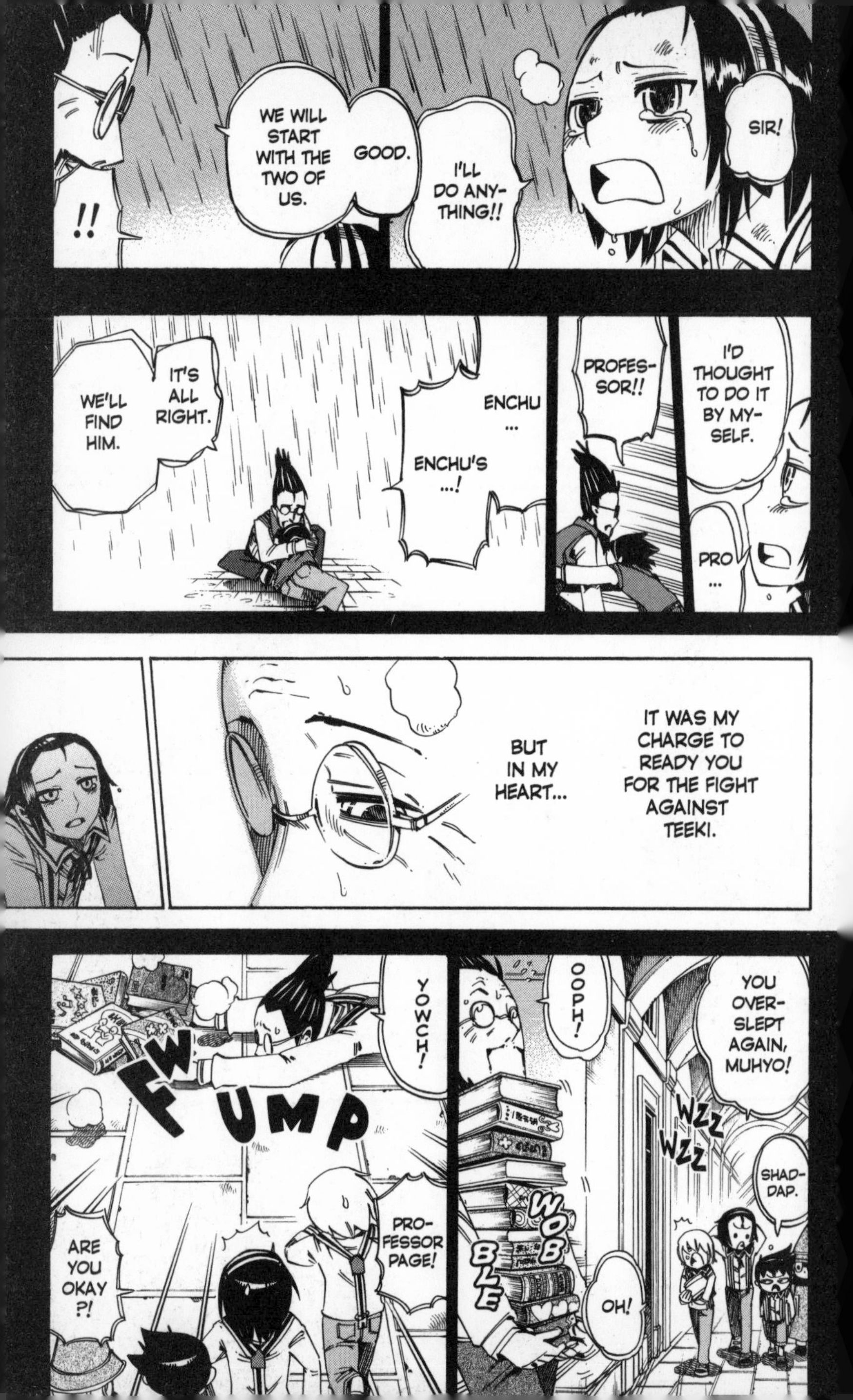

SIR!
I'LL DO ANY-THING!!
GOOD.
WE WILL START WITH THE TWO OF US.
!!
I'D THOUGHT TO DO IT BY MY-SELF.
PRO...
PROFES-SOR!!
ENCHU...
ENCHU'S...!
IT'S ALL RIGHT.
WE'LL FIND HIM.
IT WAS MY CHARGE TO READY YOU FOR THE FIGHT AGAINST TEEKI.
BUT IN MY HEART...
YOU OVER-SLEPT AGAIN, MUHYO!
WZZ WZZ
SHAD-DAP.
OOPH!
WOBBLE
OH!
YOWCH!
FWUMP
PRO-FESSOR PAGE!
ARE YOU OKAY?!

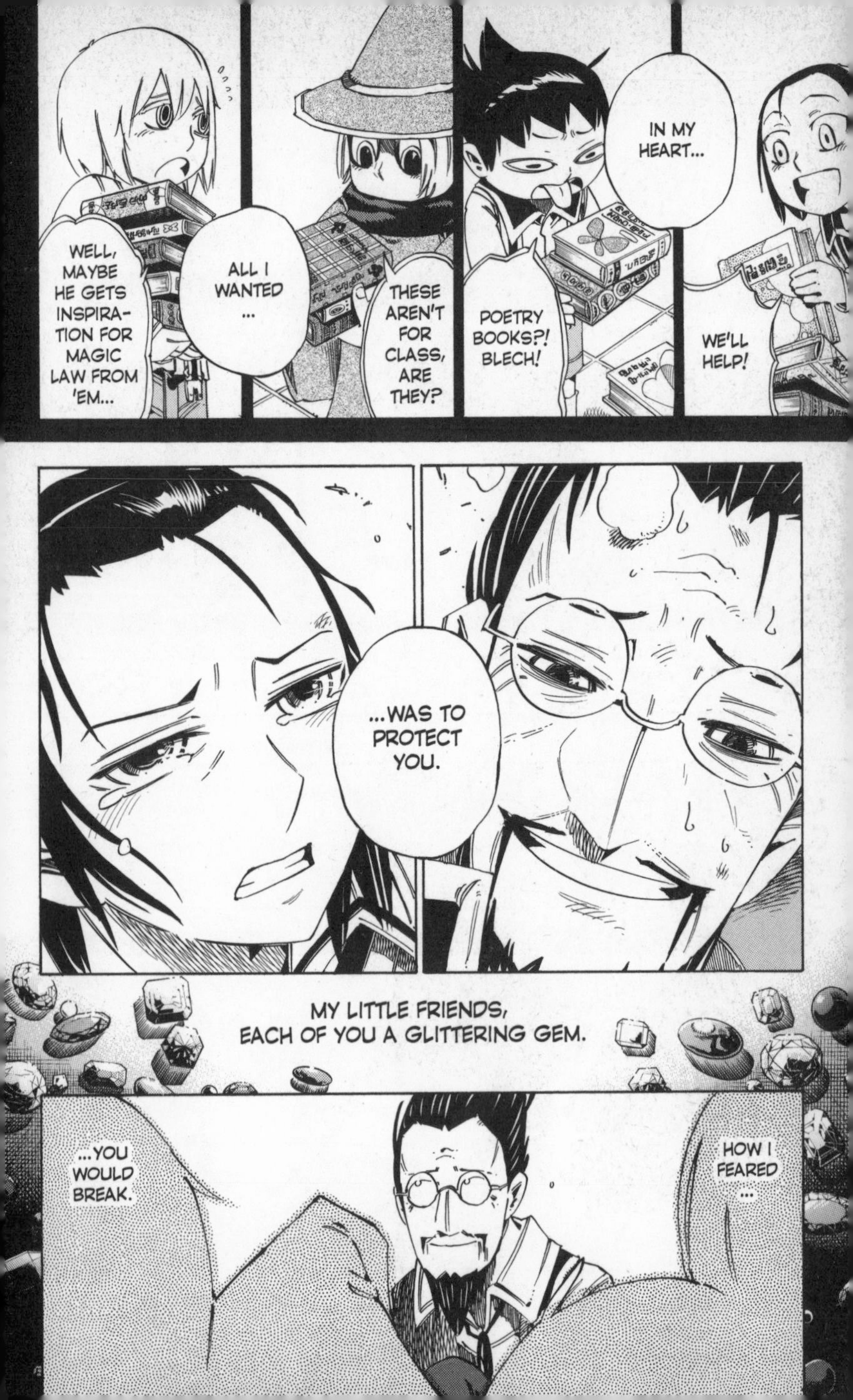
WE'LL HELP!
IN MY HEART...
POETRY BOOKS?! BLECH!
THESE AREN'T FOR CLASS, ARE THEY?
ALL I WANTED ...
WELL, MAYBE HE GETS INSPIRA-TION FOR MAGIC LAW FROM 'EM...
...WAS TO PROTECT YOU.
MY LITTLE FRIENDS, EACH OF YOU A GLITTERING GEM.
HOW I FEARED ...
...YOU WOULD BREAK.

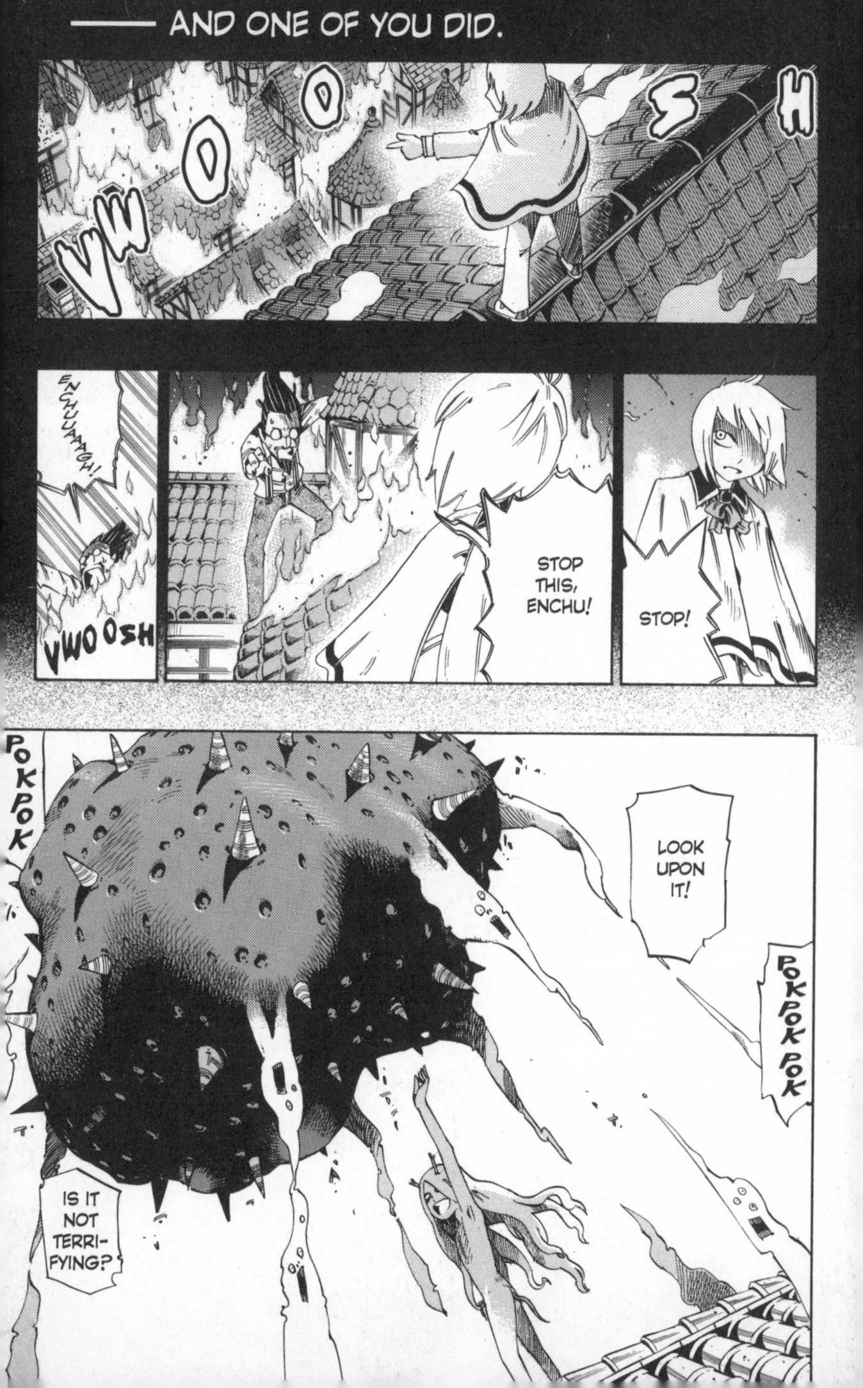
AND ONE OF YOU DID.
VWOOSH
STOP!
STOP THIS, ENCHU!
ENCHUAAAGH!
VWOOSH
POKPOKPOK
LOOK UPON IT!
POKPOK
IS IT NOT TERRI-FYING?

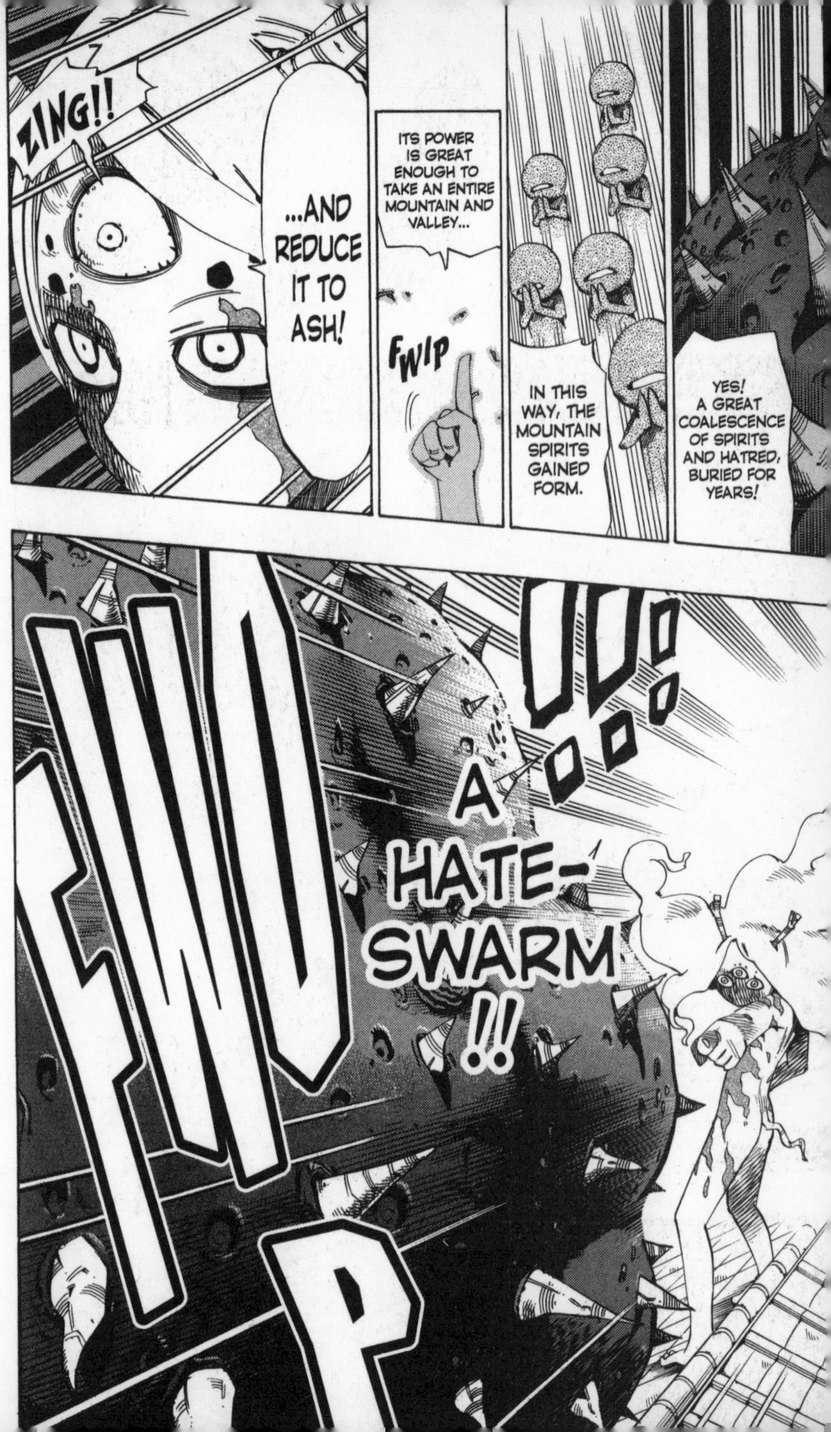
YES! A GREAT COALESCENCE OF SPIRITS AND HATRED, BURIED FOR YEARS!
IN THIS WAY, THE MOUNTAIN SPIRITS GAINED FORM.
ITS POWER IS GREAT ENOUGH TO TAKE AN ENTIRE MOUNTAIN AND VALLEY...
FWIP
ZING!!
...AND REDUCE IT TO ASH!
A HATE-SWARM!!

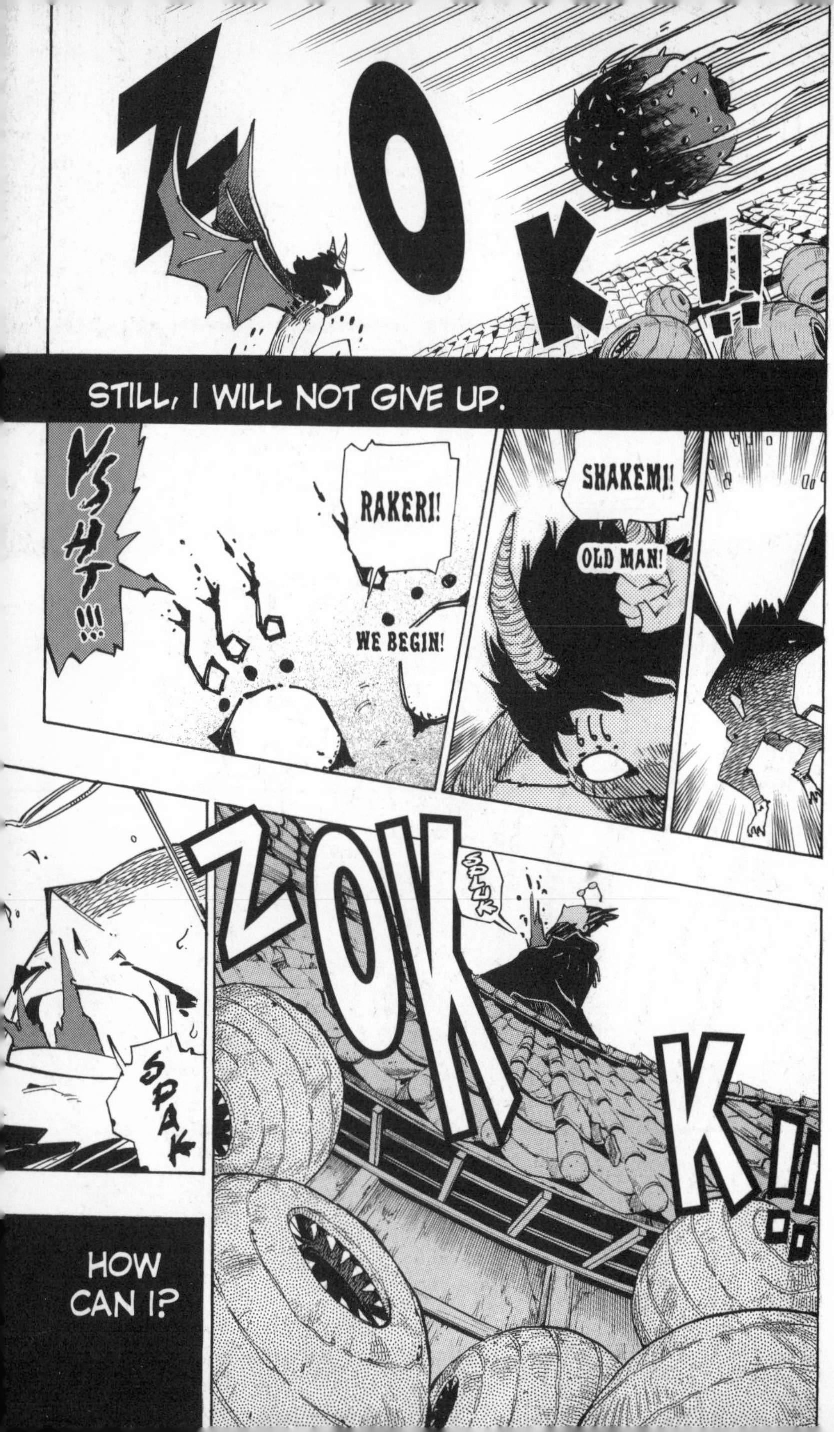
ZOK!!
STILL, I WILL NOT GIVE UP.
SHAKEMI!
OLD MAN!
RAKERI!
WE BEGIN!
VSHT!!!
ZOK
K!!
SPLUK
SPAK
HOW CAN I?

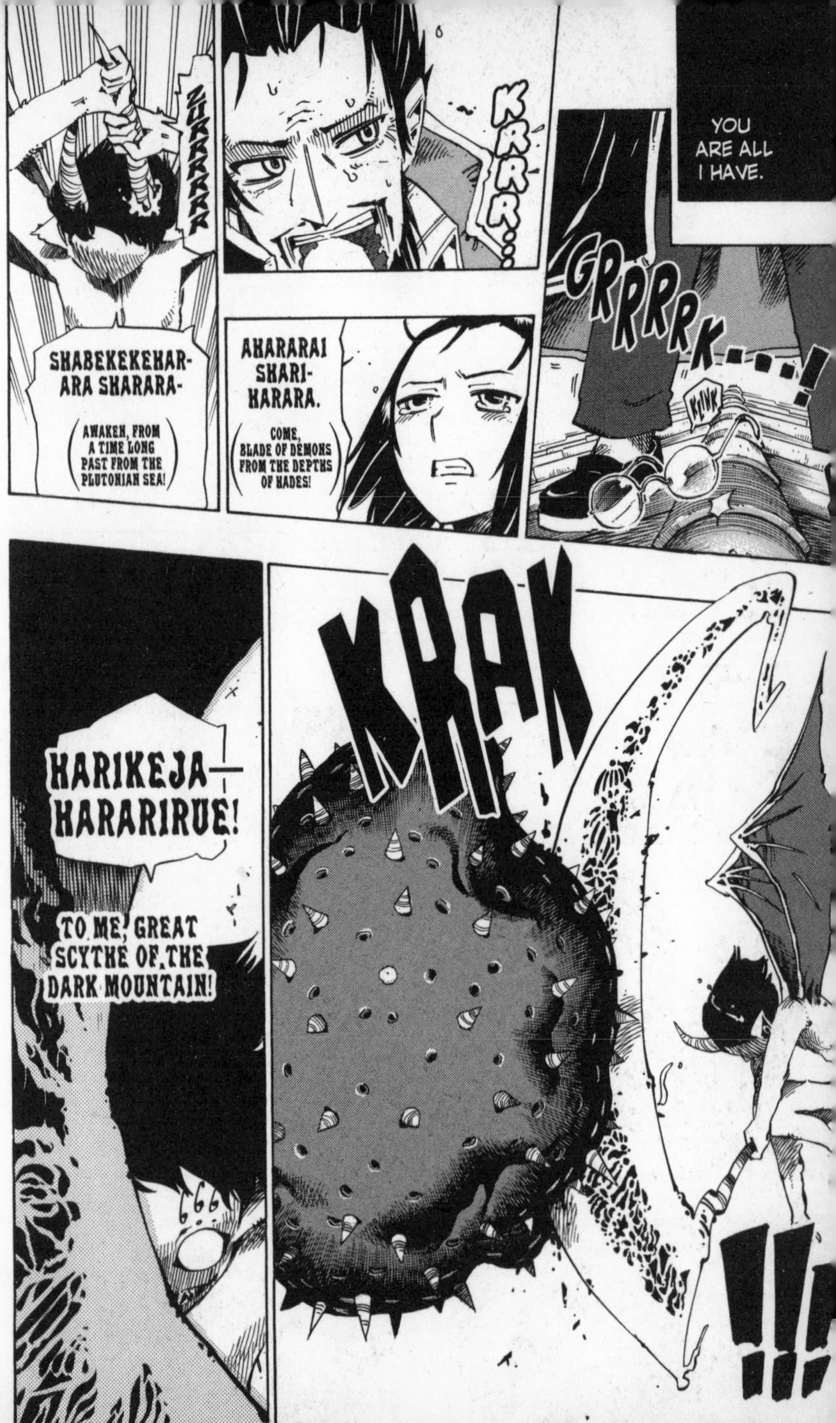
YOU ARE ALL I HAVE.
GRRRRK...!
KLINK
KRRR...
AHARARAI SHARI-HARARA.
(COME, BLADE OF DEMONS FROM THE DEPTHS OF HADES!)
ZURRRRRR
SHABEKEKEHAR-ARA SHARARA-
(AWAKEN, FROM A TIME LONG PAST FROM THE PLUTONIAN SEA!)
KRAK
!!!
HARIKEJA— HARARIRUE!
TO ME, GREAT SCYTHE OF THE DARK MOUNTAIN!

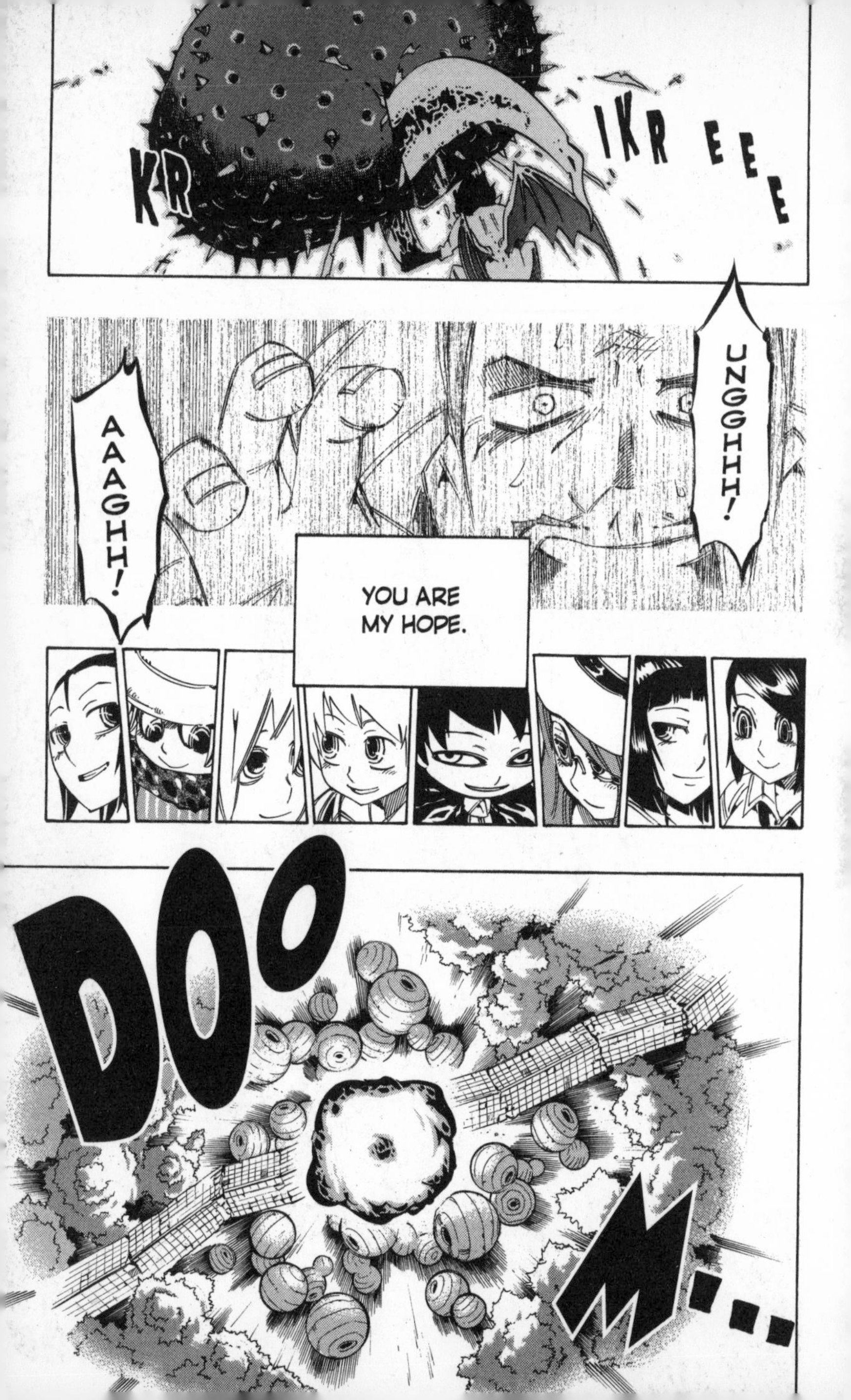
KR IKR EEEE
UNGGHHH!
AAAGHH!
YOU ARE MY HOPE.
DOOM...

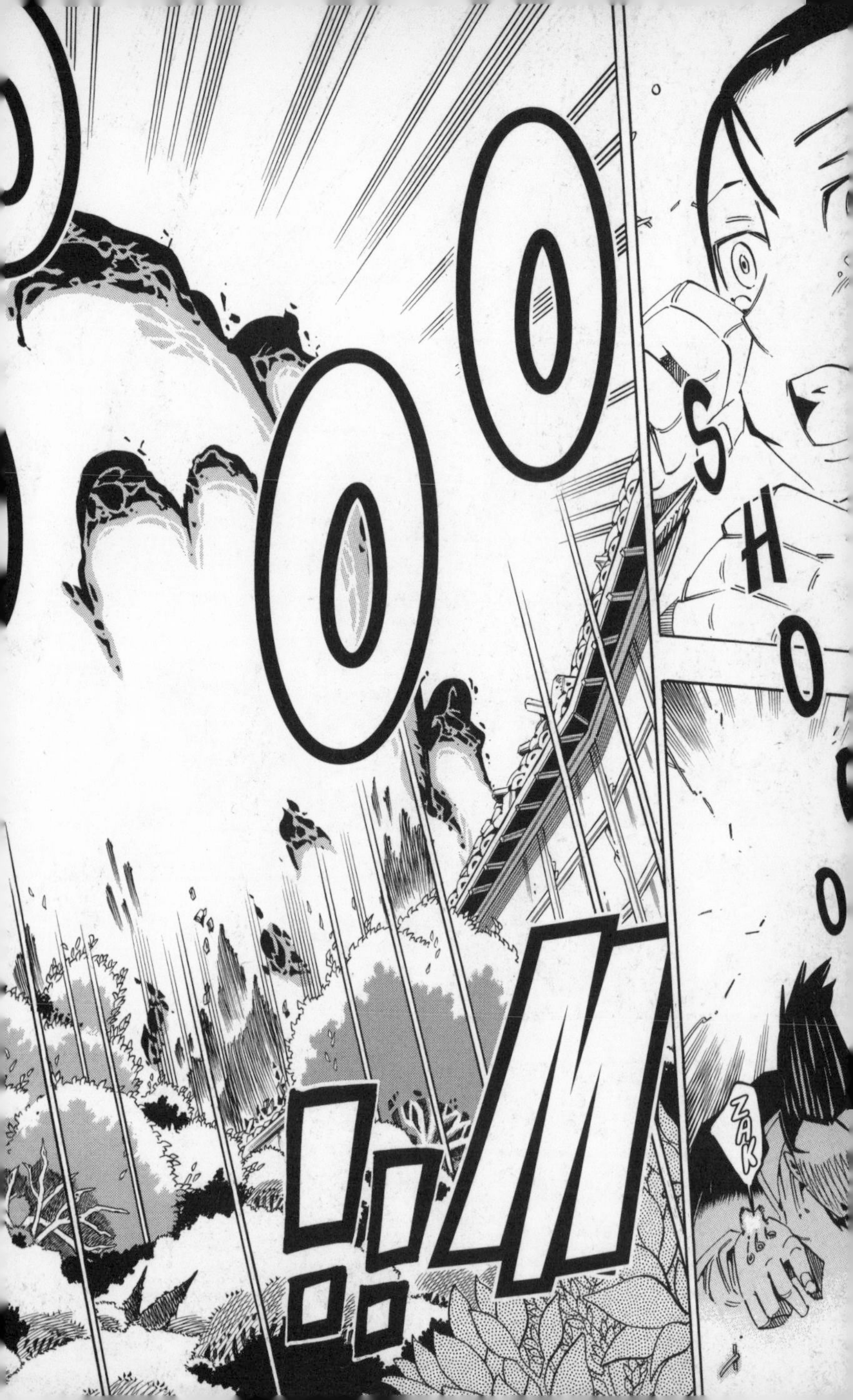

SHOOO
OOOO!!
NAK

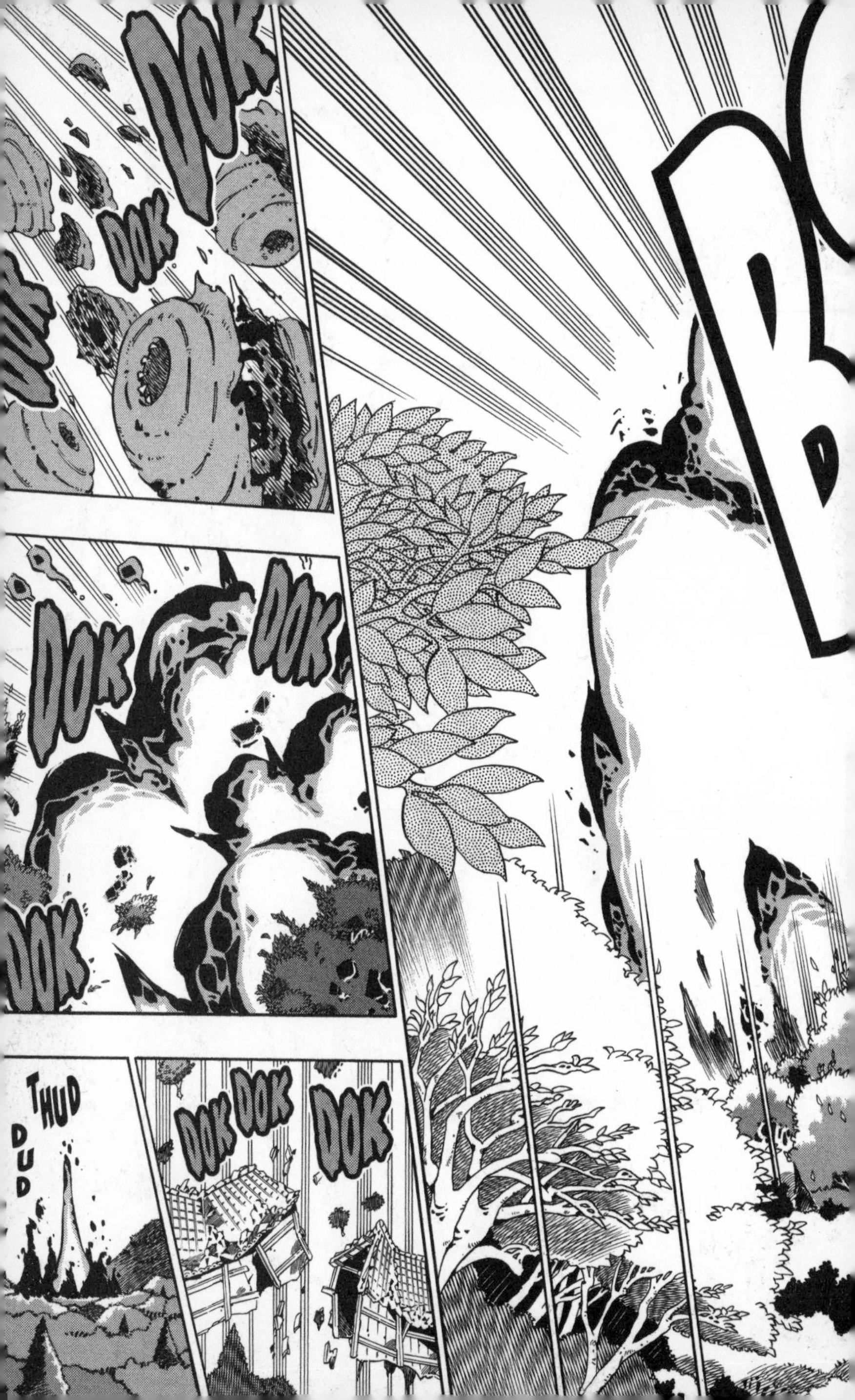
DOK
DOK
DOK
DOK
DOK
DOK
DOK
DOK
THUD
DUD

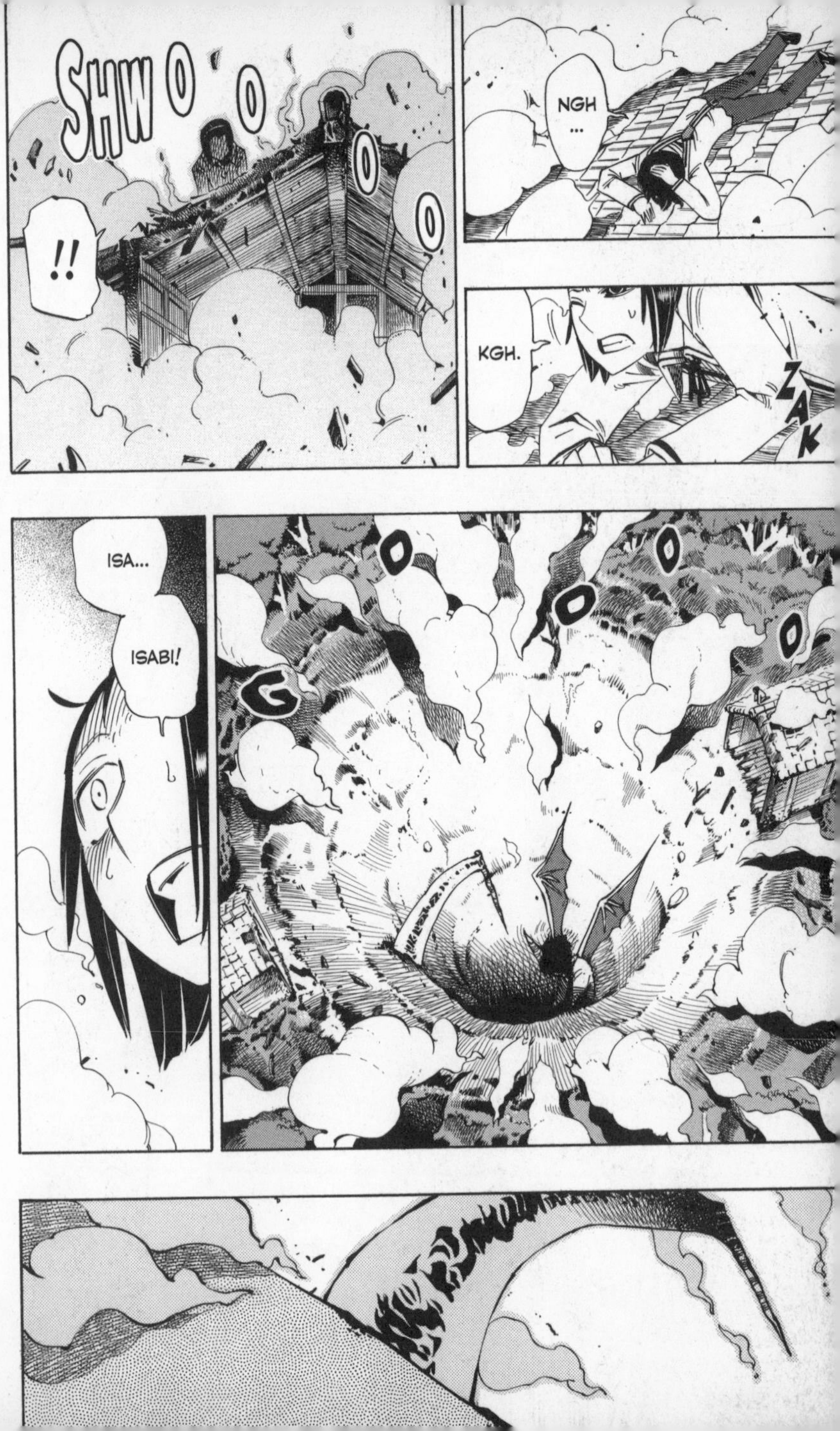
NGH...
KGH.
ZAK
SHWOOOO
!!
GOOOO
ISA...
ISABI!

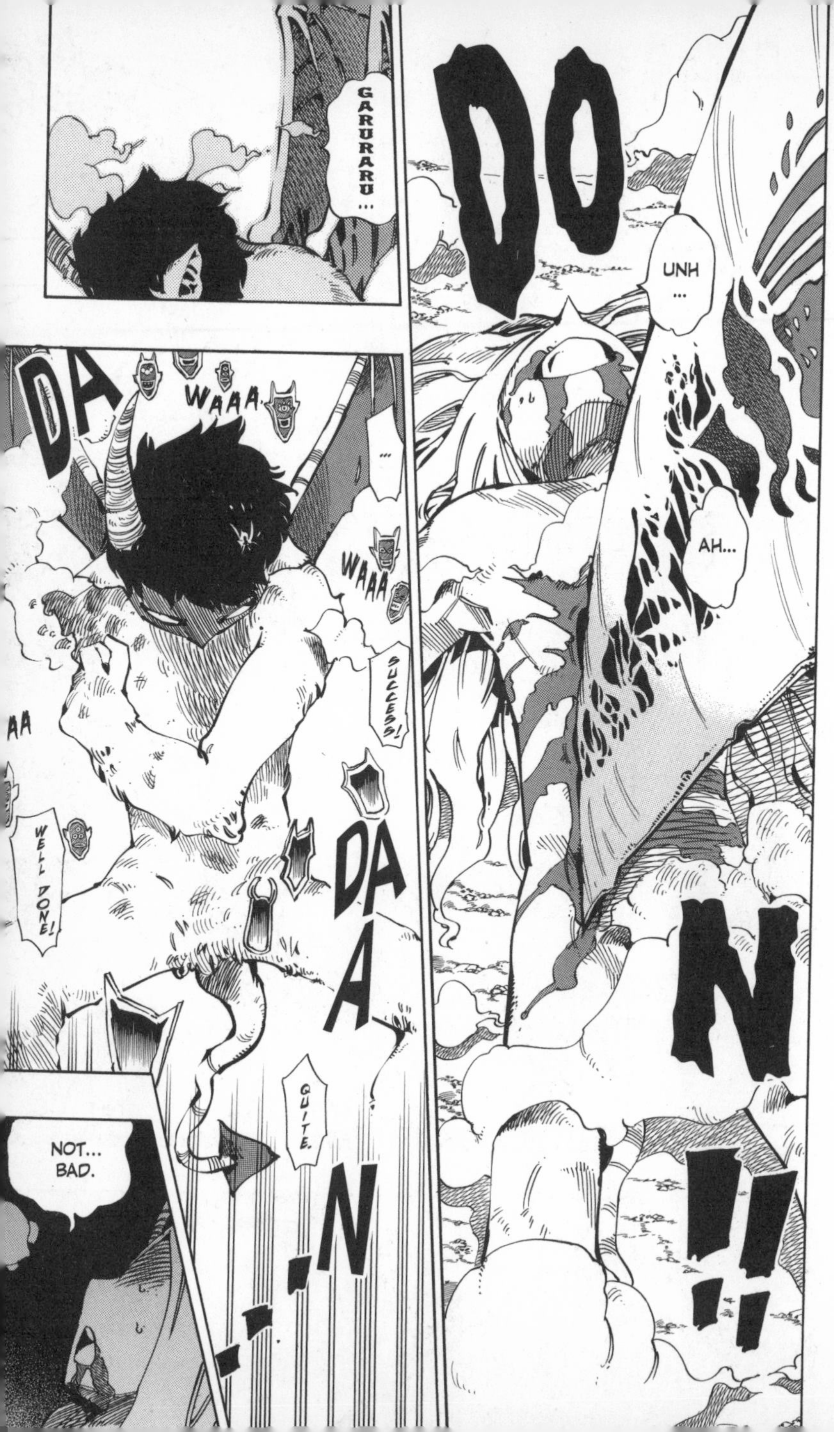
DO
UNH...
AH...
N!!
GARURARU...
DA
WAAA
...
WAAA
SUCCESS!
WELL DONE!
AA
DAA...N
QUITE.
NOT... BAD.

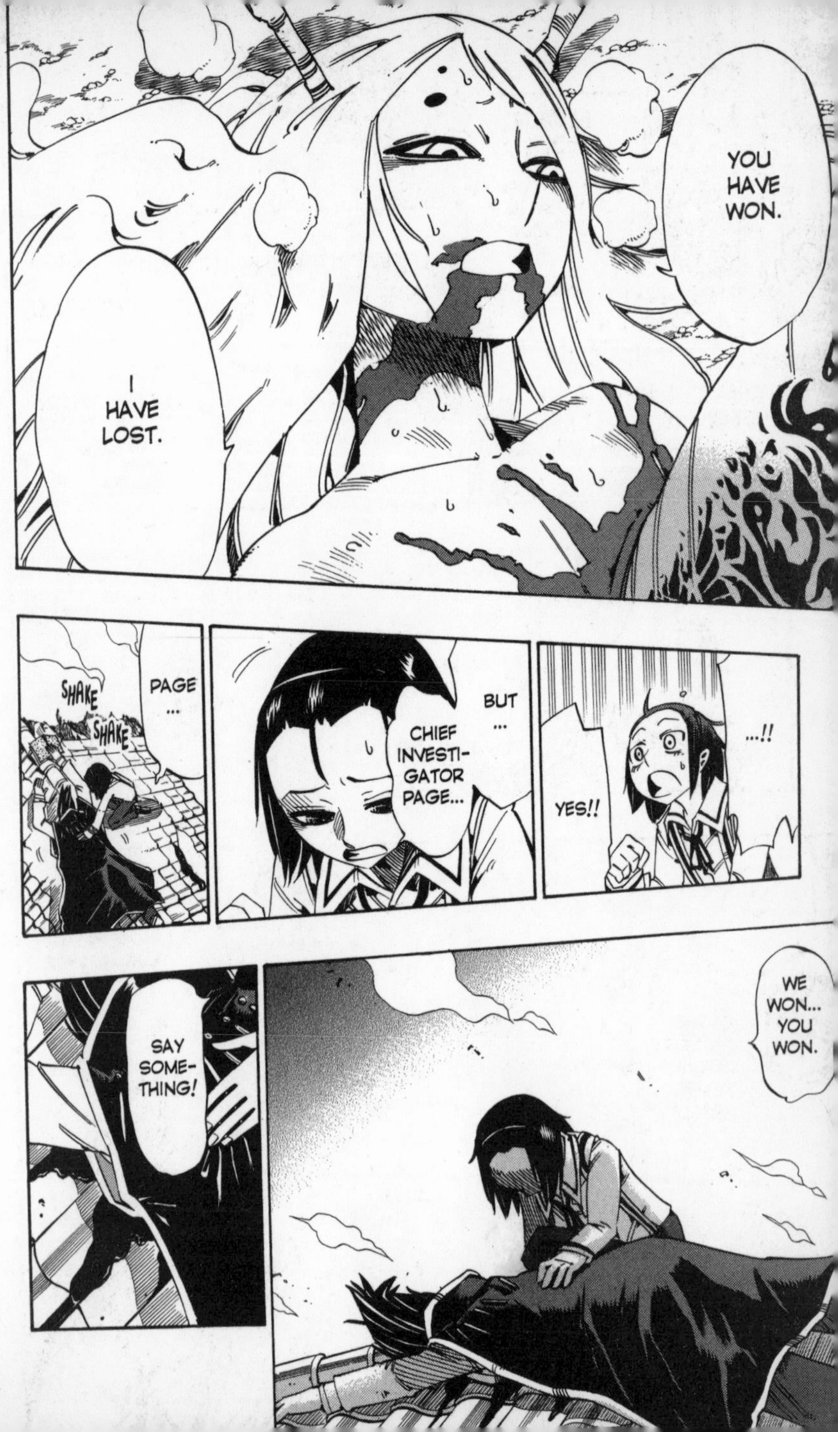
YOU HAVE WON.
I HAVE LOST.
...!!
YES!!
BUT ...
CHIEF INVESTI-GATOR PAGE...
PAGE ...
SHAKE
SHAKE
WE WON... YOU WON.
SAY SOME-THING!

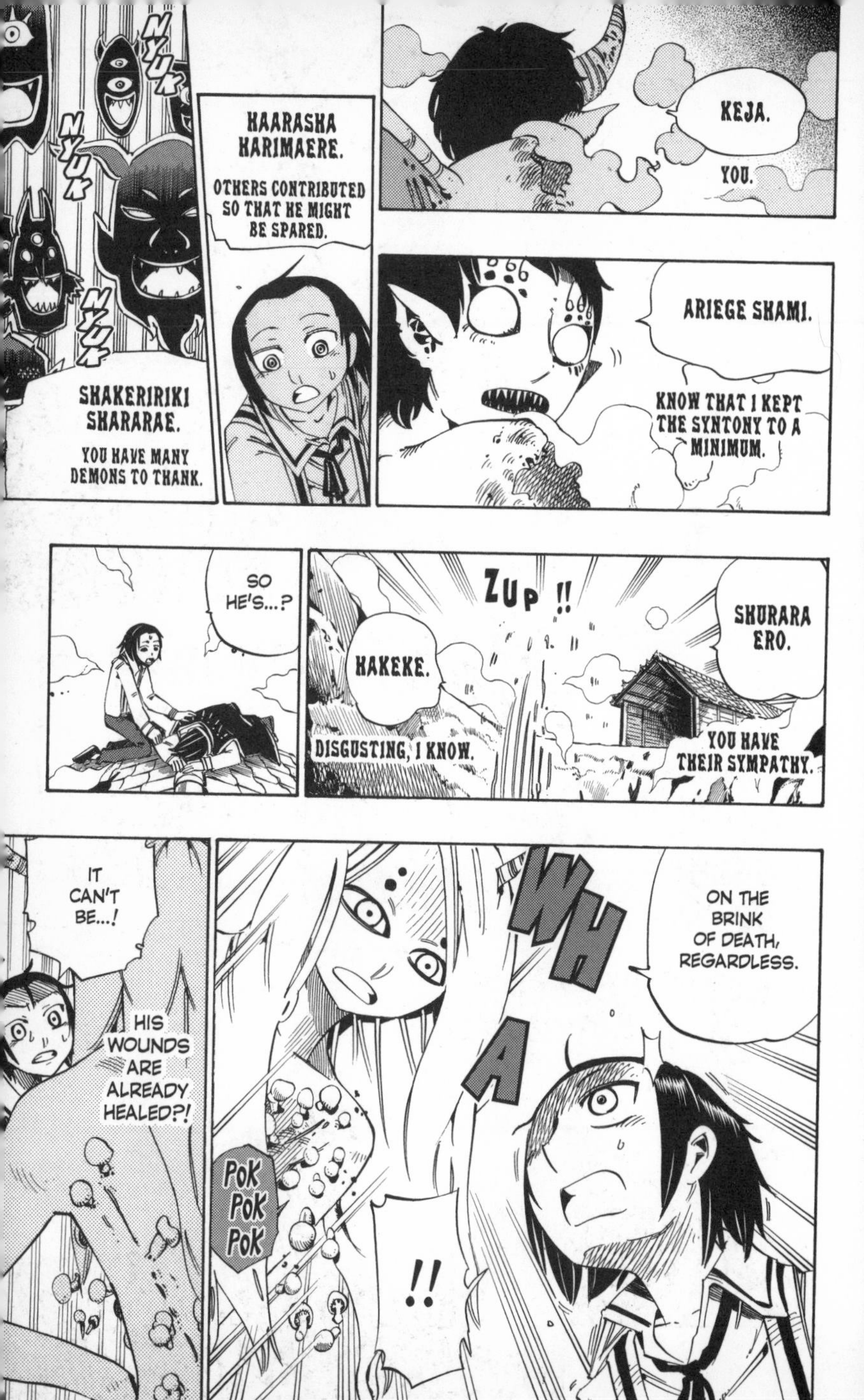
KEJA.
YOU.
ARIEGE SHAMI.
KNOW THAT I KEPT THE SYNTONY TO A MINIMUM.
HAARASHA HARIMAERE.
OTHERS CONTRIBUTED SO THAT HE MIGHT BE SPARED.
NYUK
NYUK
NYUK
SHAKERIRIKI SHARARAE.
YOU HAVE MANY DEMONS TO THANK.
SHURARA ERO.
YOU HAVE THEIR SYMPATHY.
ZUP !!
HAKEKE.
DISGUSTING, I KNOW.
SO HE'S...?
ON THE BRINK OF DEATH, REGARDLESS.
WHA
!!
POK POK POK
IT CAN'T BE...!
HIS WOUNDS ARE ALREADY HEALED?!

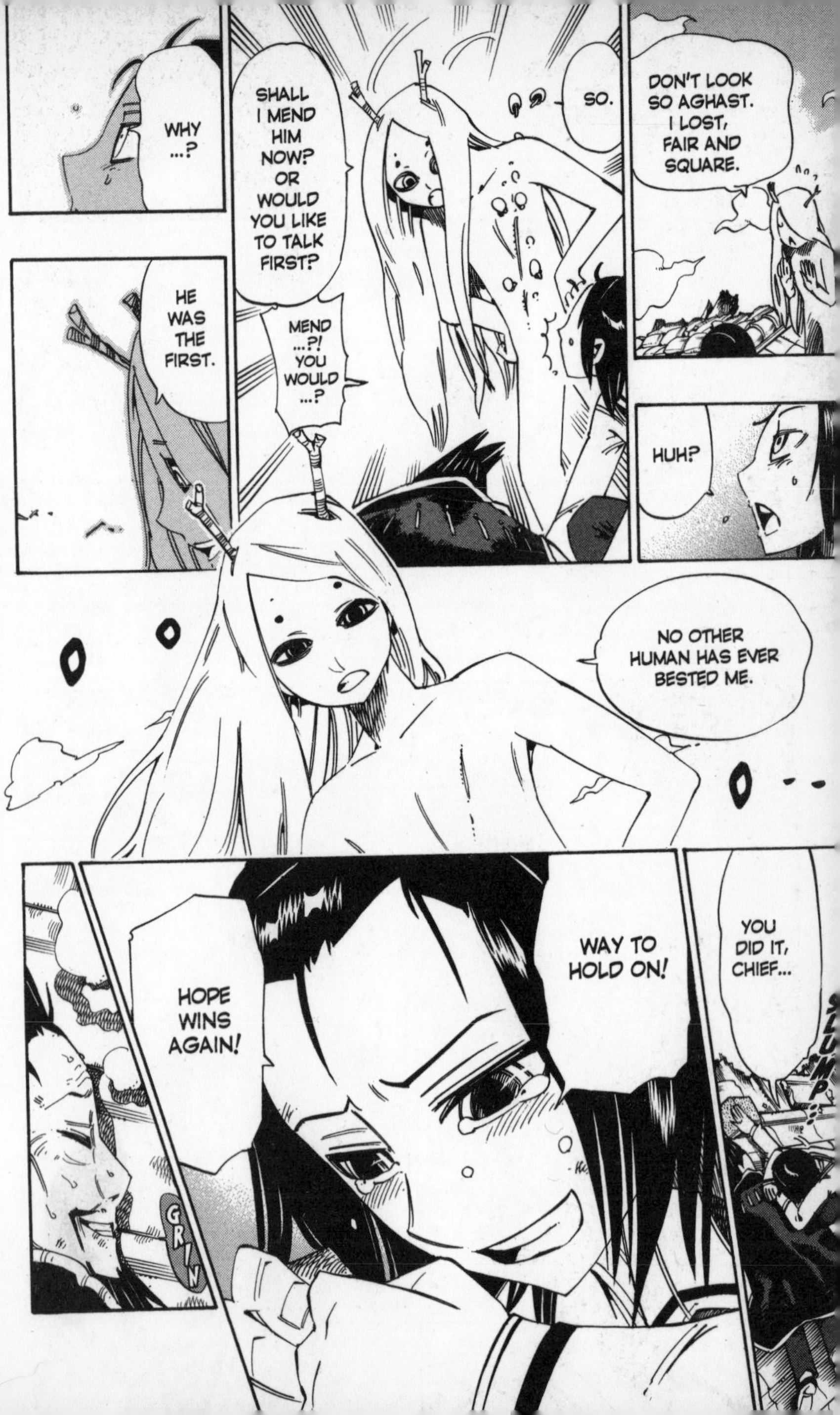
DON'T LOOK SO AGHAST. I LOST, FAIR AND SQUARE.
HUH?
SO.
SHALL I MEND HIM NOW? OR WOULD YOU LIKE TO TALK FIRST?
MEND ...?! YOU WOULD ...?
WHY ...?
HE WAS THE FIRST.
NO OTHER HUMAN HAS EVER BESTED ME.
YOU DID IT, CHIEF...
SLUMP
WAY TO HOLD ON!
HOPE WINS AGAIN!
GRIN

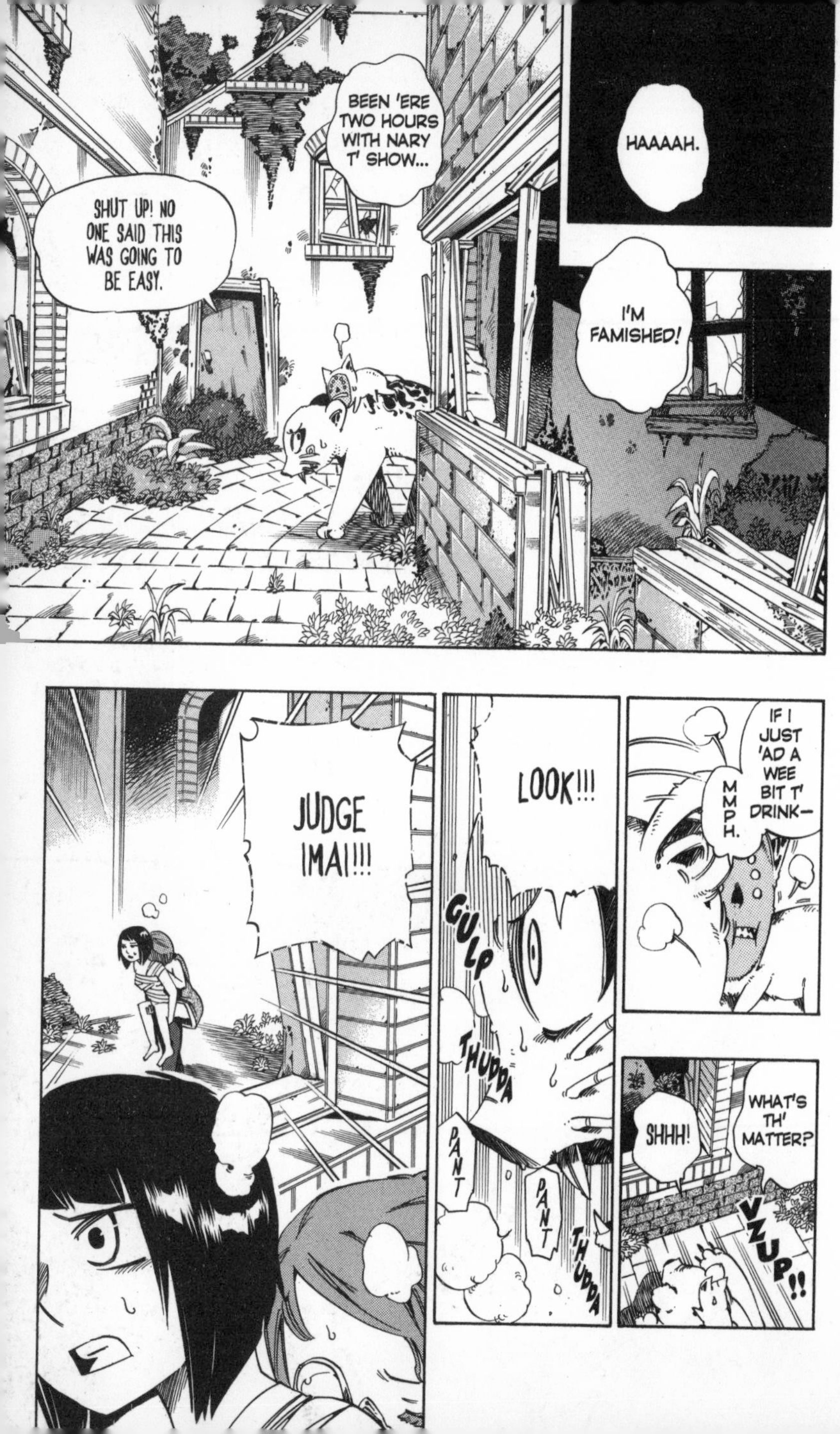
HAAAAH.
I'M FAMISHED!
BEEN 'ERE TWO HOURS WITH NARY T' SHOW...
SHUT UP! NO ONE SAID THIS WAS GOING TO BE EASY.
IF I JUST 'AD A WEE BIT T' DRINK—
MMPH.
WHAT'S TH' MATTER?
SHHH!
VZUP!!
LOOK!!!
GULP
THUDDA
PANT
PANT
THUDDA
JUDGE IMAI!!!

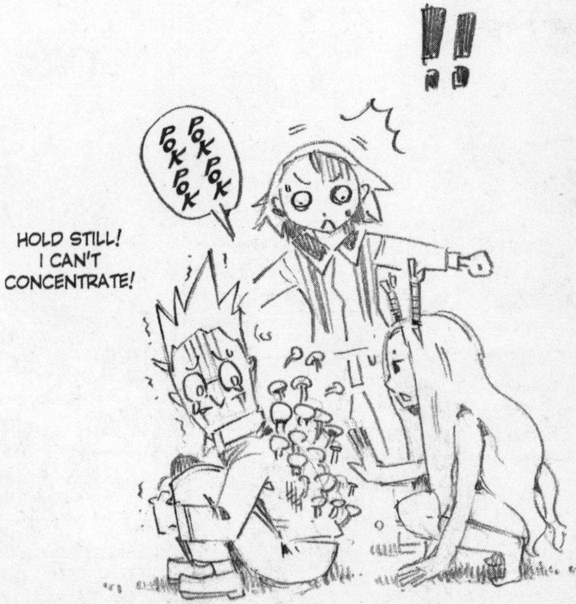
POK POK POK POK
HOLD STILL! I CAN'T CONCENTRATE!

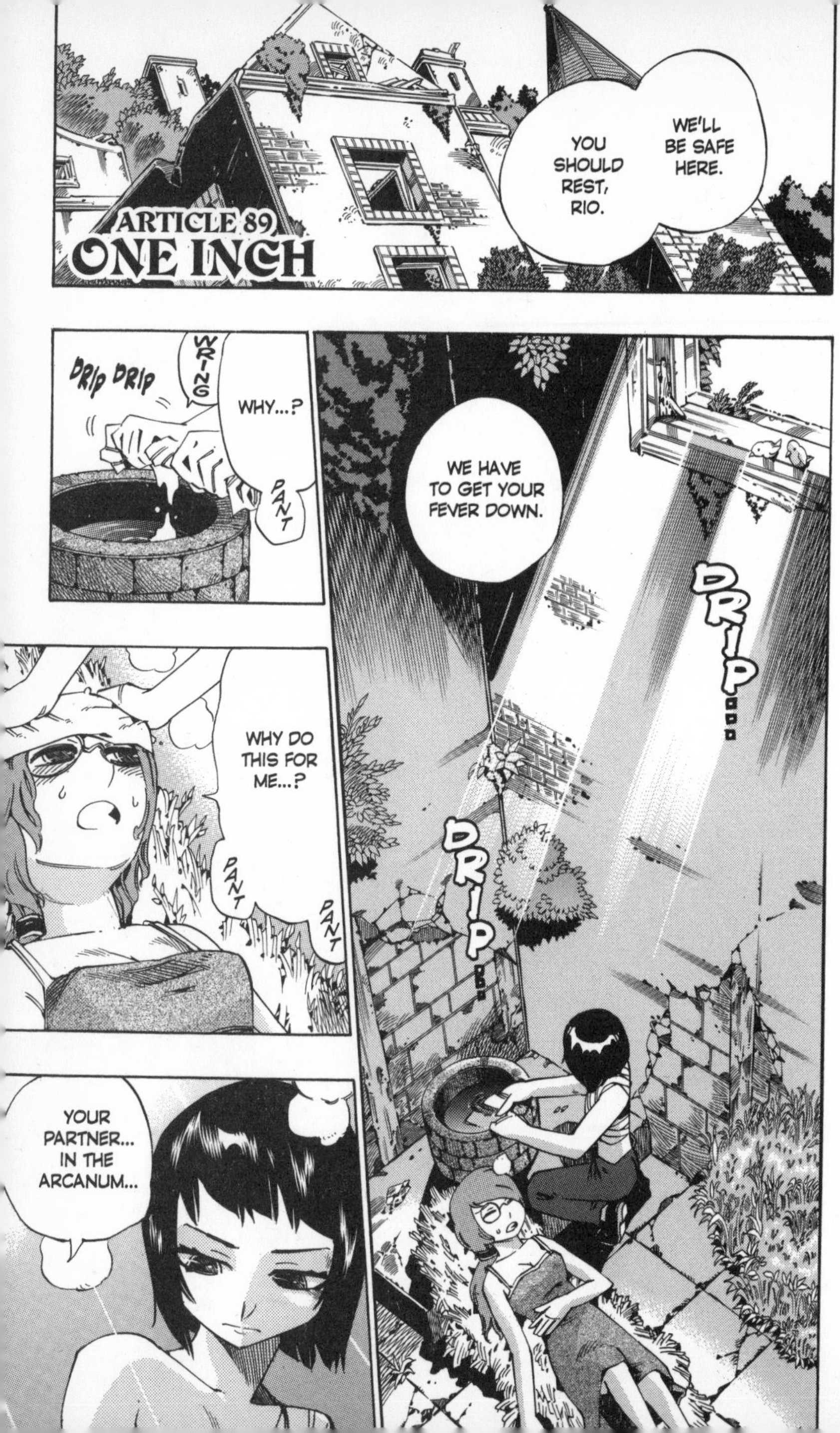
ARTICLE 89
ONE INCH
WE'LL BE SAFE HERE.
YOU SHOULD REST, RIO.
WE HAVE TO GET YOUR FEVER DOWN.
DRIP...
DRIP...
WRING
DRIP DRIP
WHY...?
PANT
WHY DO THIS FOR ME...?
PANT
PANT
YOUR PARTNER... IN THE ARCANUM...

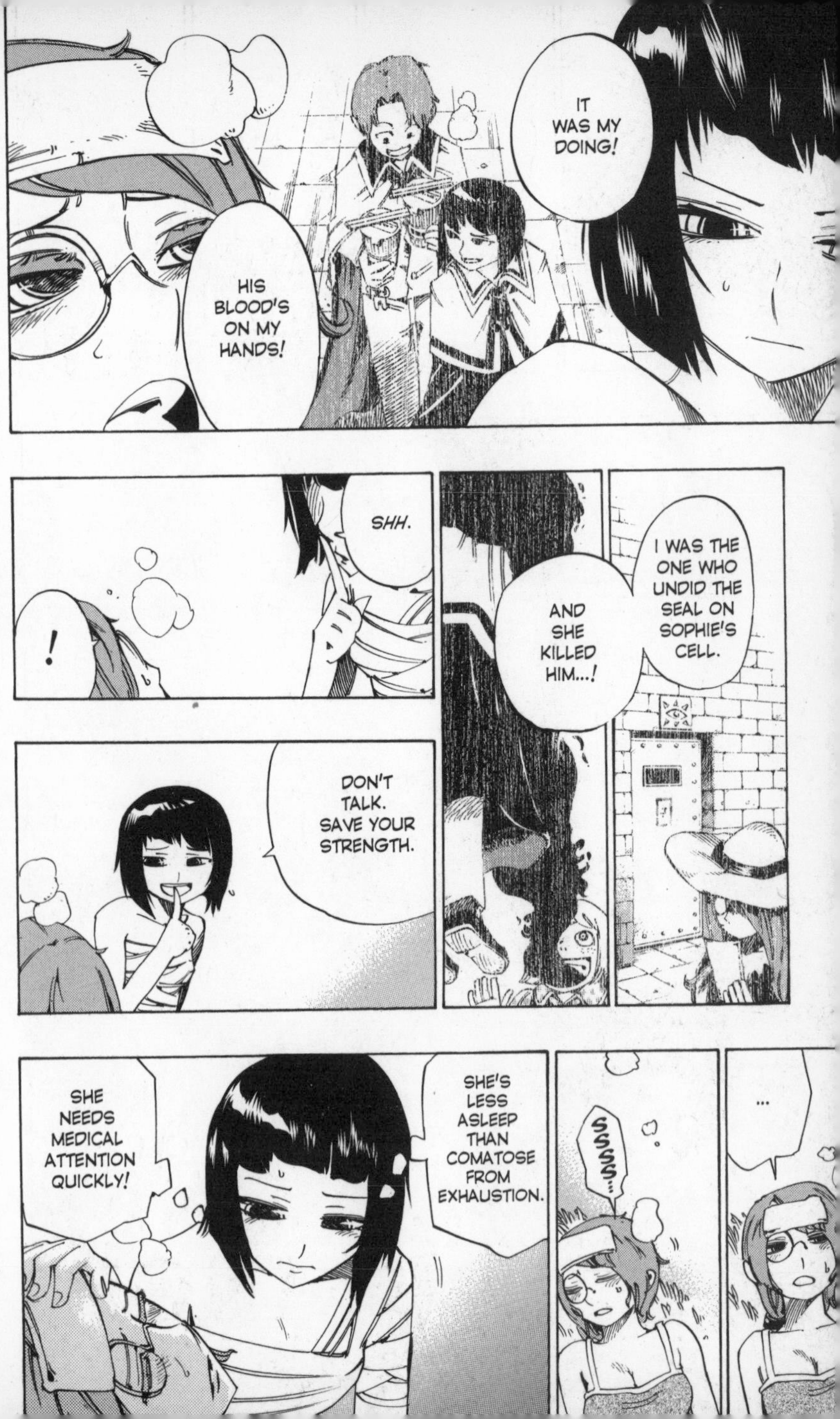
IT WAS MY DOING!
HIS BLOOD'S ON MY HANDS!
I WAS THE ONE WHO UNDID THE SEAL ON SOPHIE'S CELL.
AND SHE KILLED HIM...!
SHH.
!
DON'T TALK. SAVE YOUR STRENGTH.
...
SSSS...
SHE'S LESS ASLEEP THAN COMATOSE FROM EXHAUSTION.
SHE NEEDS MEDICAL ATTENTION QUICKLY!

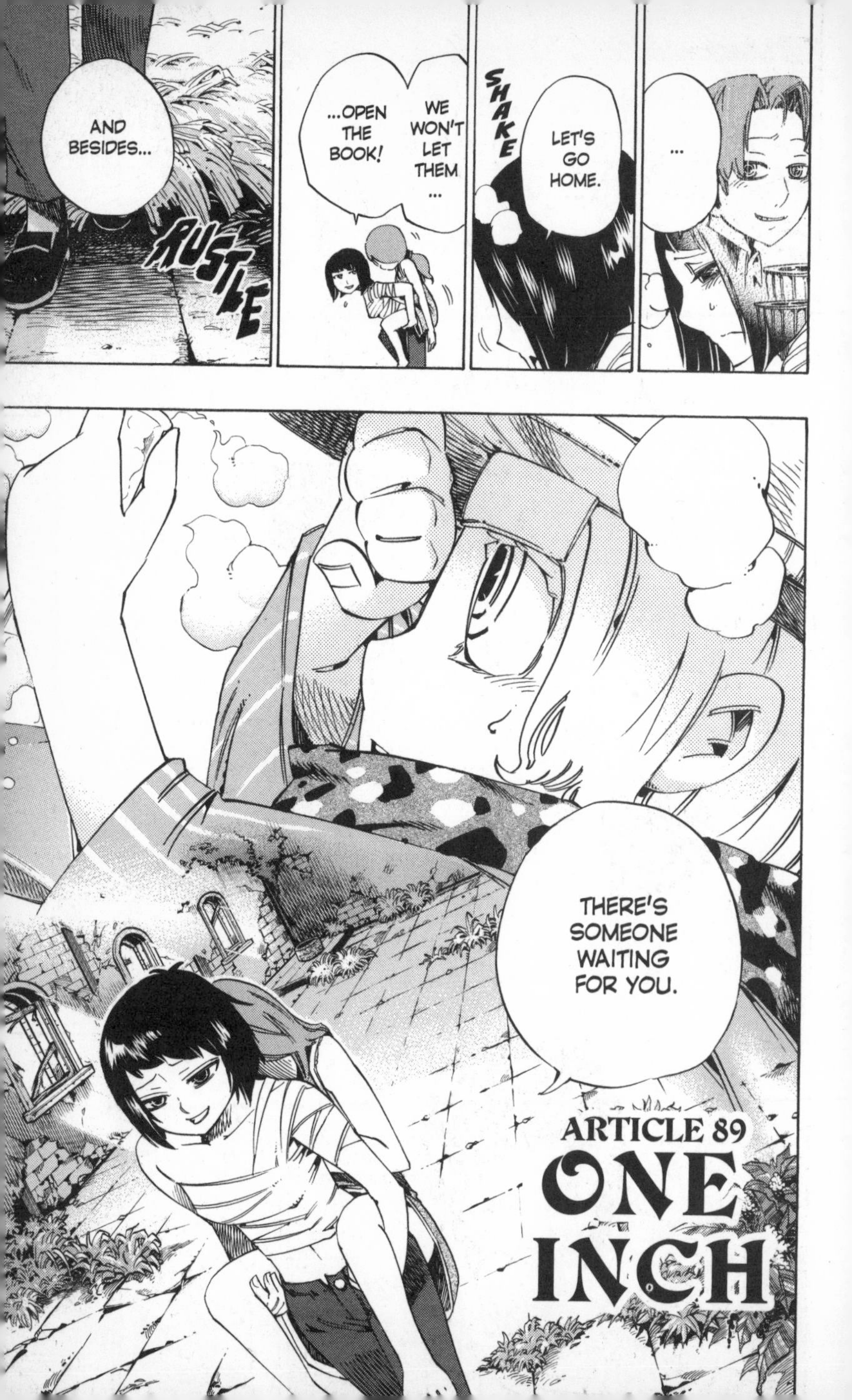
...
LET'S GO HOME.
SHAKE
WE WON'T LET THEM ...
...OPEN THE BOOK!
AND BESIDES...
RUSTLE
THERE'S SOMEONE WAITING FOR YOU.
ARTICLE 89
ONE INCH

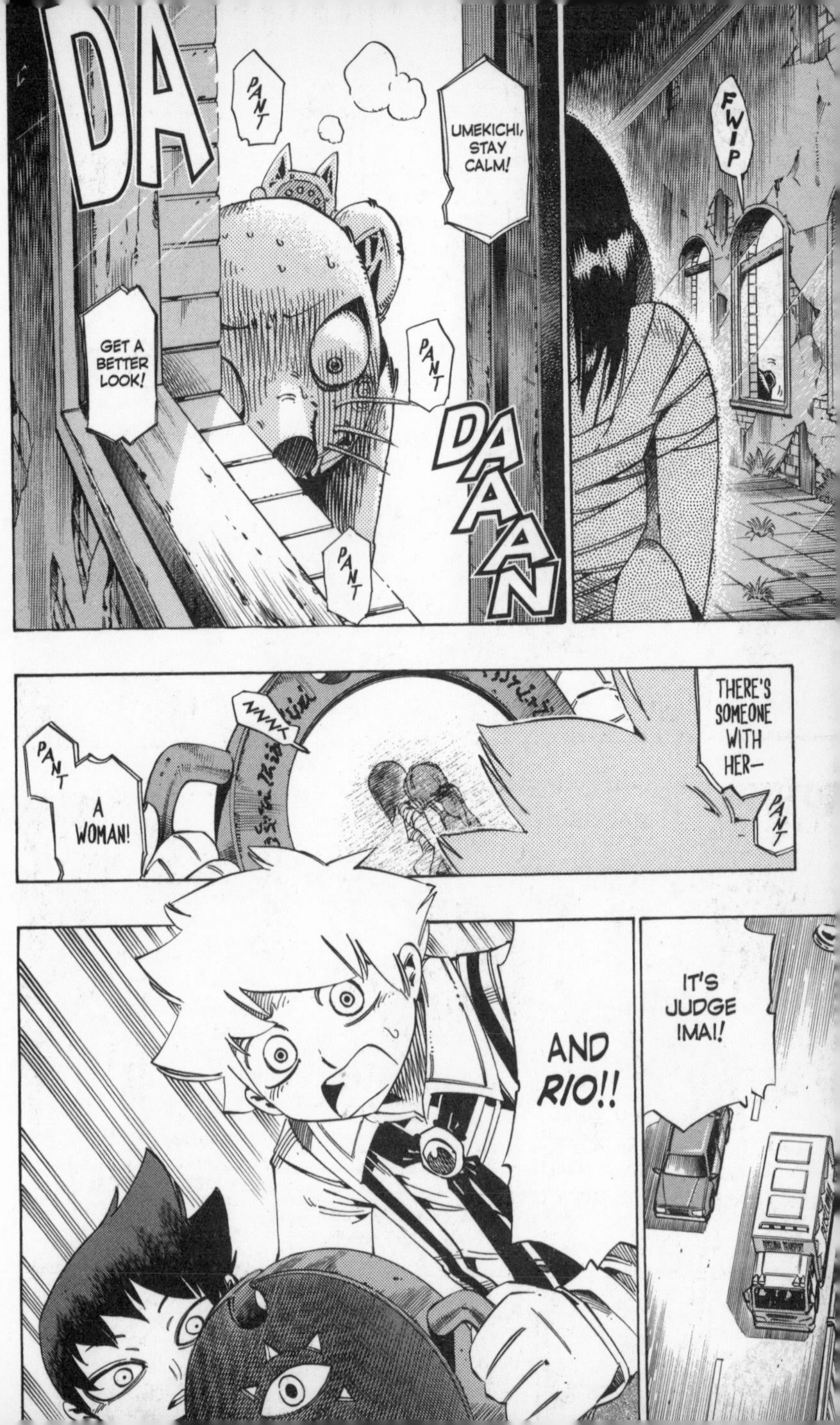

FWIP
UMEKICHI, STAY CALM!
PANT
DA
PANT
DAAAN
GET A BETTER LOOK!
PANT
THERE'S SOMEONE WITH HER—
PANT
NNNK
PANT
A WOMAN!
IT'S JUDGE IMAI!
AND RIO!!

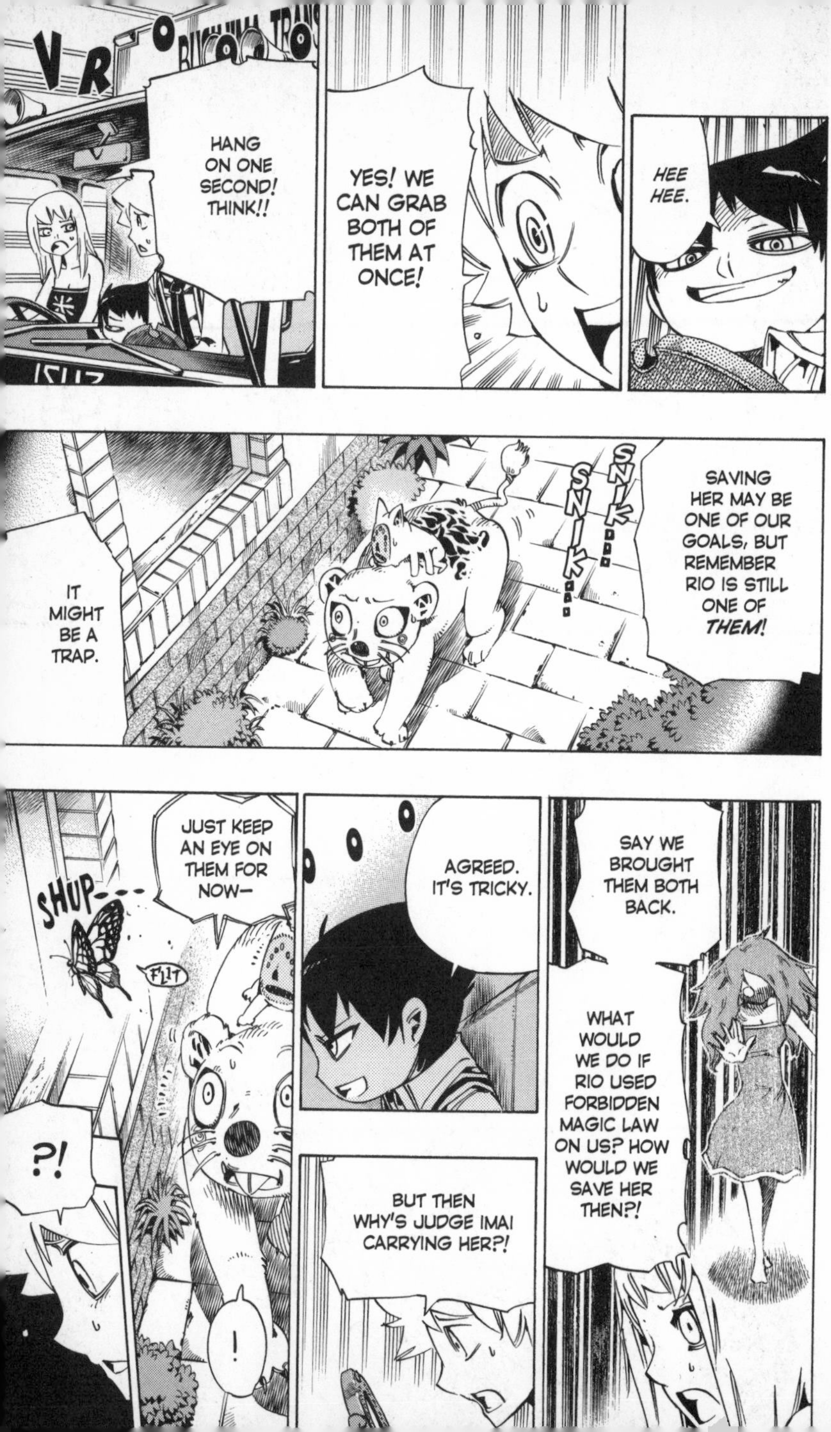
HEE HEE.
YES! WE CAN GRAB BOTH OF THEM AT ONCE!
HANG ON ONE SECOND! THINK!!
SAVING HER MAY BE ONE OF OUR GOALS, BUT REMEMBER RIO IS STILL ONE OF *THEM*!
SNIK...
SNIK...
IT MIGHT BE A TRAP.
SAY WE BROUGHT THEM BOTH BACK.
WHAT WOULD WE DO IF RIO USED FORBIDDEN MAGIC LAW ON US? HOW WOULD WE SAVE HER THEN?!
AGREED. IT'S TRICKY.
BUT THEN WHY'S JUDGE IMAI CARRYING HER?!
JUST KEEP AN EYE ON THEM FOR NOW—
SHUP...
FLIT
?!
!

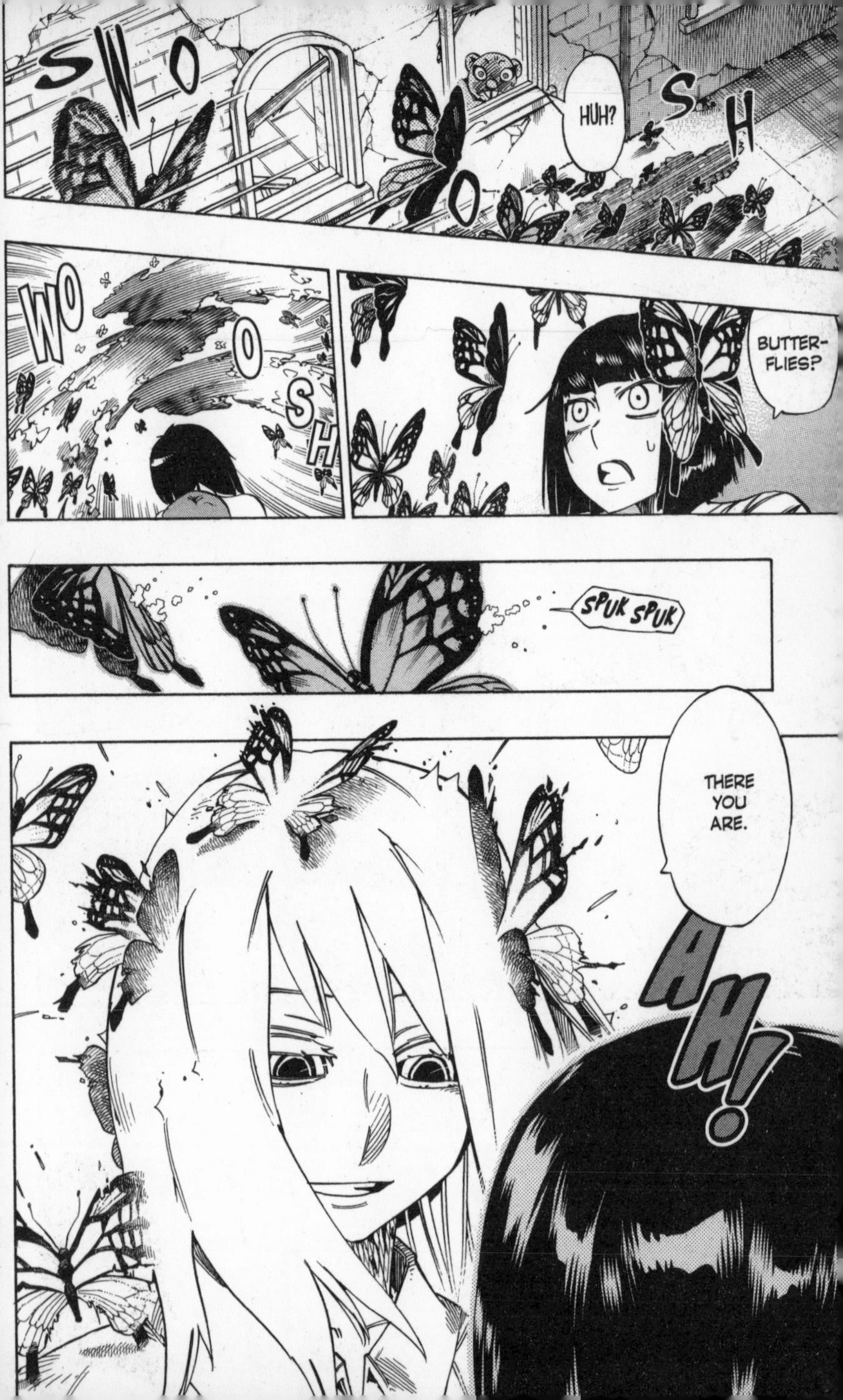

SH
HUH?
SWOOSH
BUTTER-FLIES?
WOOSH
SPUK SPUK
THERE YOU ARE.
AH!

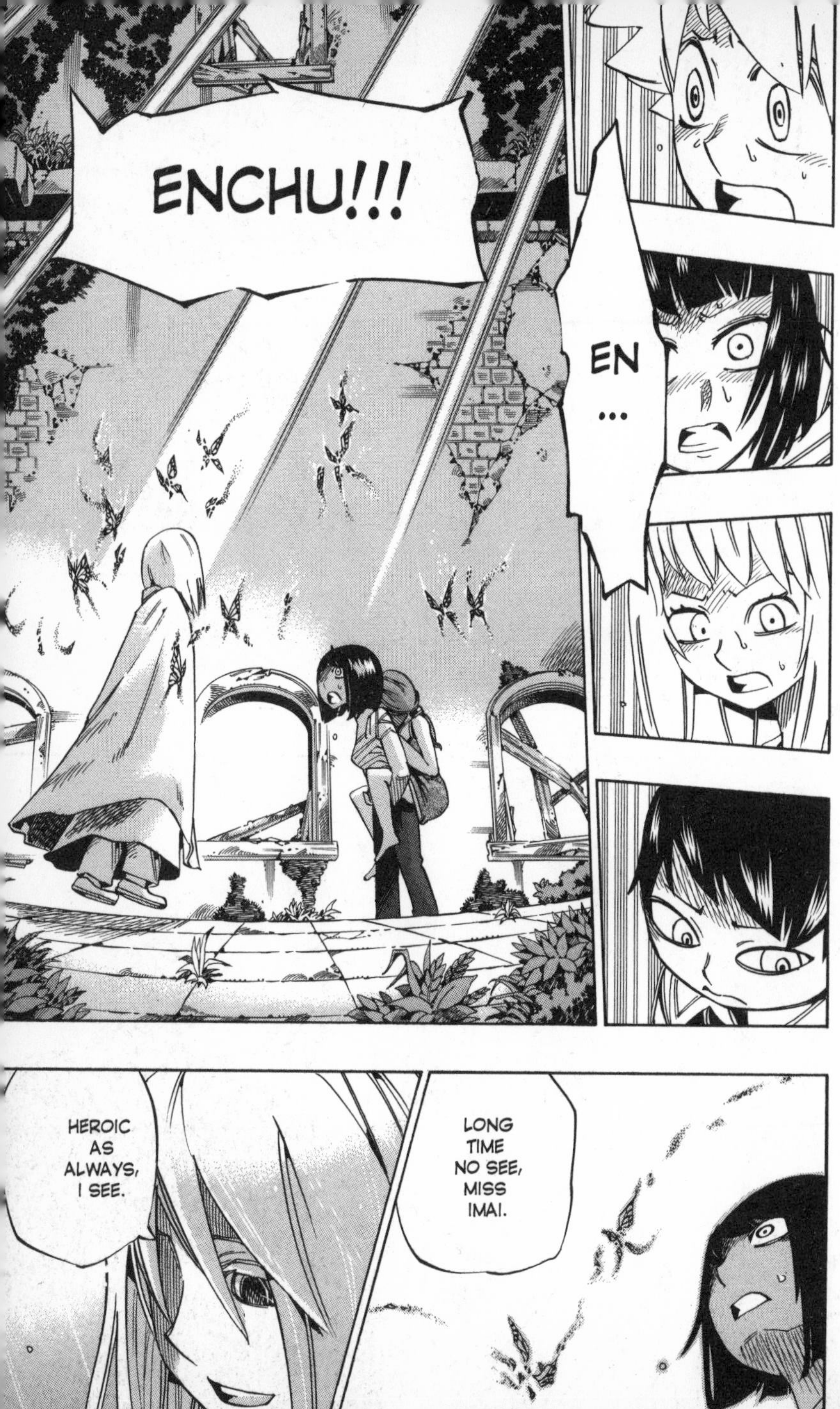
EN ...
ENCHU!!!
LONG TIME NO SEE, MISS IMAI.
HEROIC AS ALWAYS, I SEE.

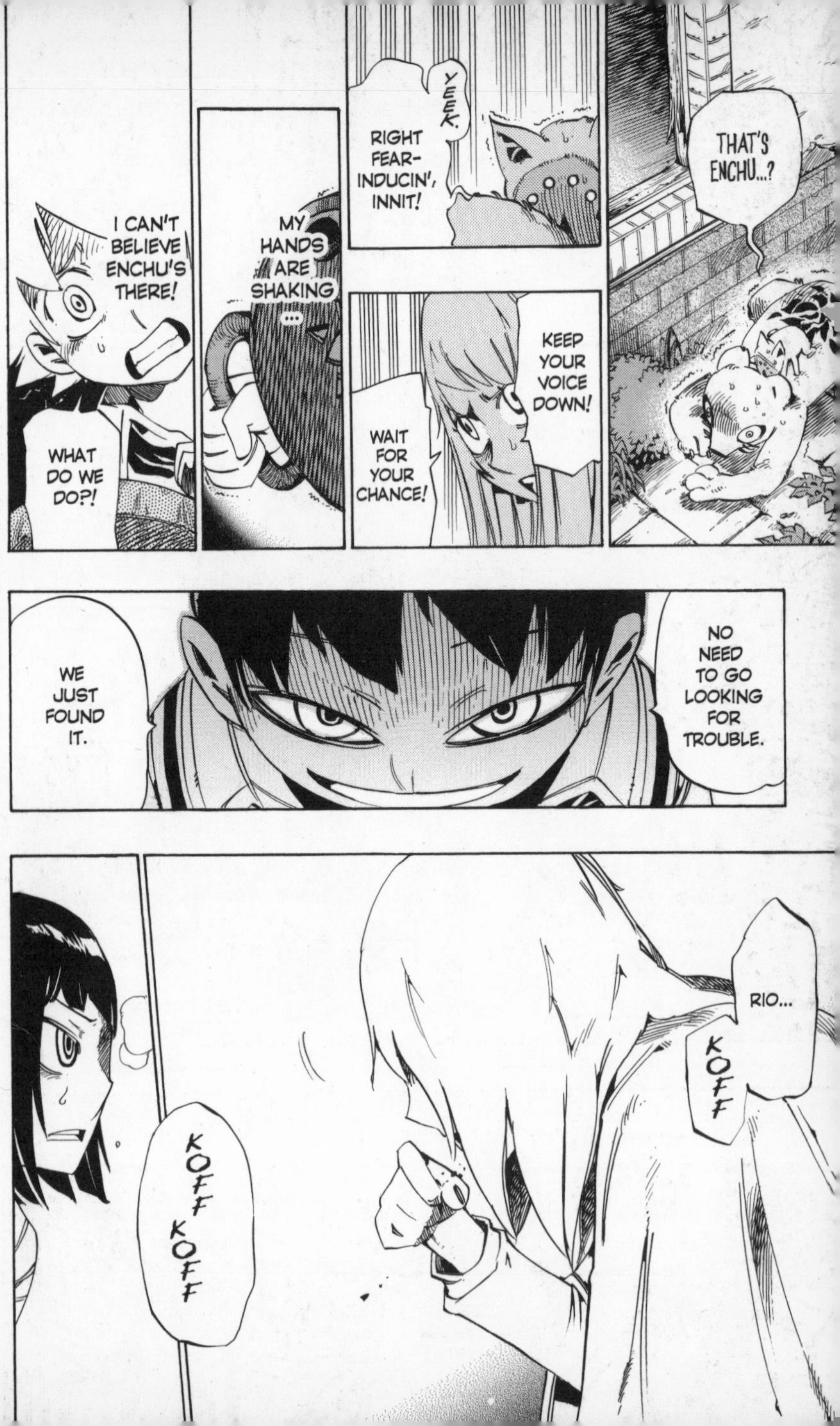
THAT'S ENCHU...?
YEEK.
RIGHT FEAR-INDUCIN', INNIT!
KEEP YOUR VOICE DOWN!
WAIT FOR YOUR CHANCE!
MY HANDS ARE SHAKING...
I CAN'T BELIEVE ENCHU'S THERE!
WHAT DO WE DO?!
NO NEED TO GO LOOKING FOR TROUBLE.
WE JUST FOUND IT.
RIO...
KOFF
KOFF KOFF

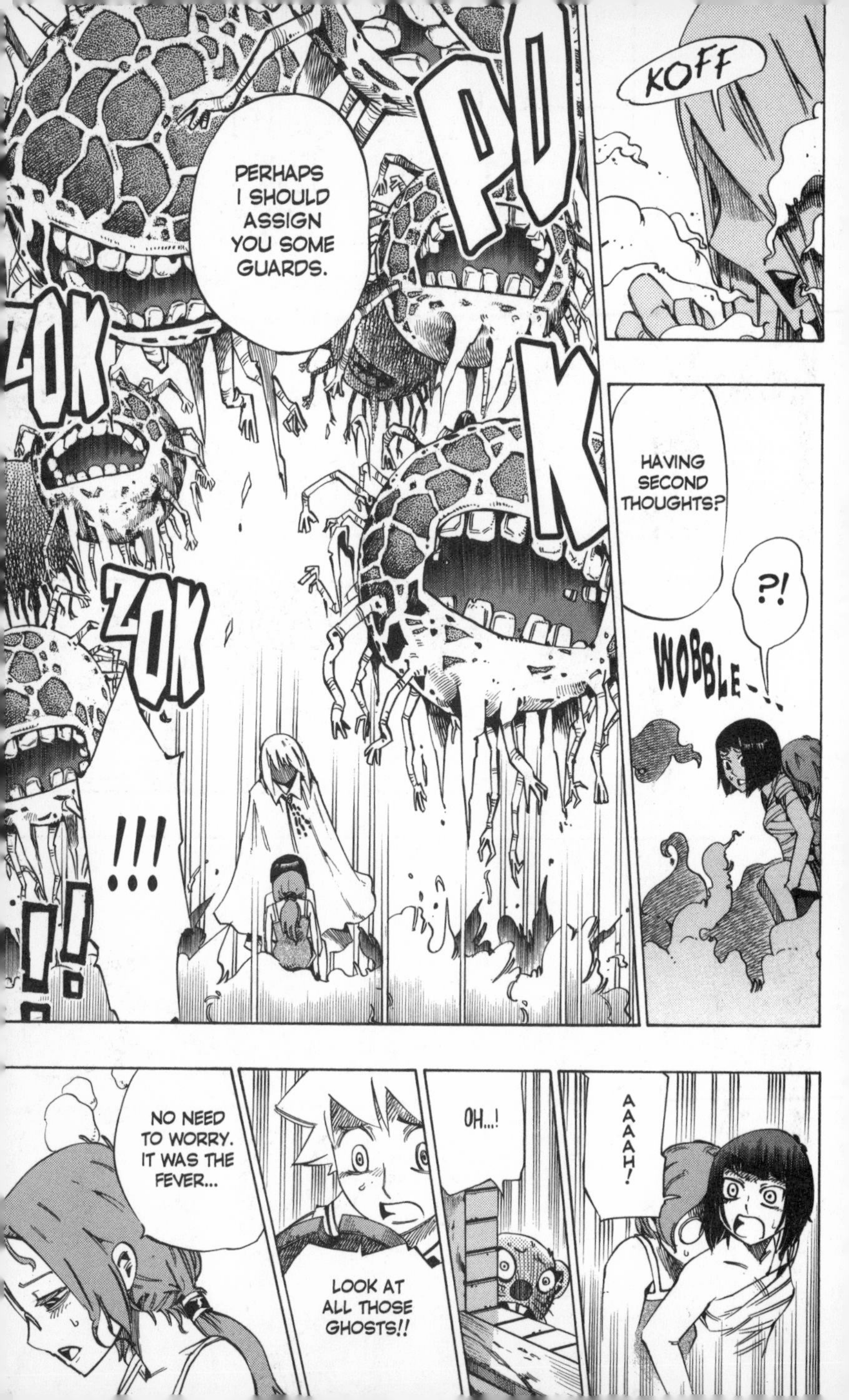

KOFF
HAVING SECOND THOUGHTS?
?!
WOBBLE...
PERHAPS I SHOULD ASSIGN YOU SOME GUARDS.
POK
ZOK
ZOK
!!!
!!
AAAAH!
OH...!
LOOK AT ALL THOSE GHOSTS!!
NO NEED TO WORRY. IT WAS THE FEVER...

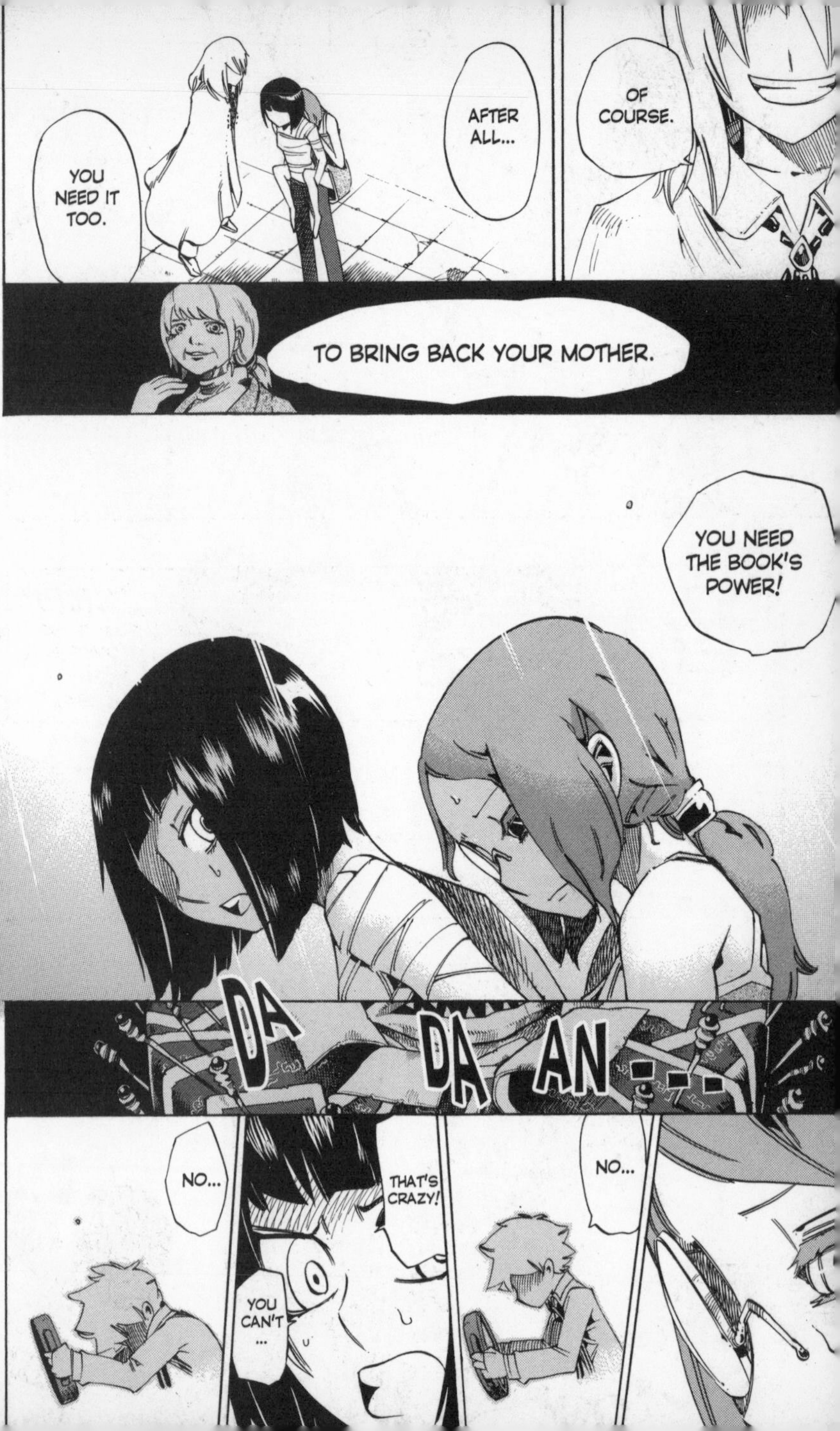
OF COURSE.
AFTER ALL...
YOU NEED IT TOO.
TO BRING BACK YOUR MOTHER.
YOU NEED THE BOOK'S POWER!
DA DA AN...
NO...
THAT'S CRAZY!
YOU CAN'T ...
NO...

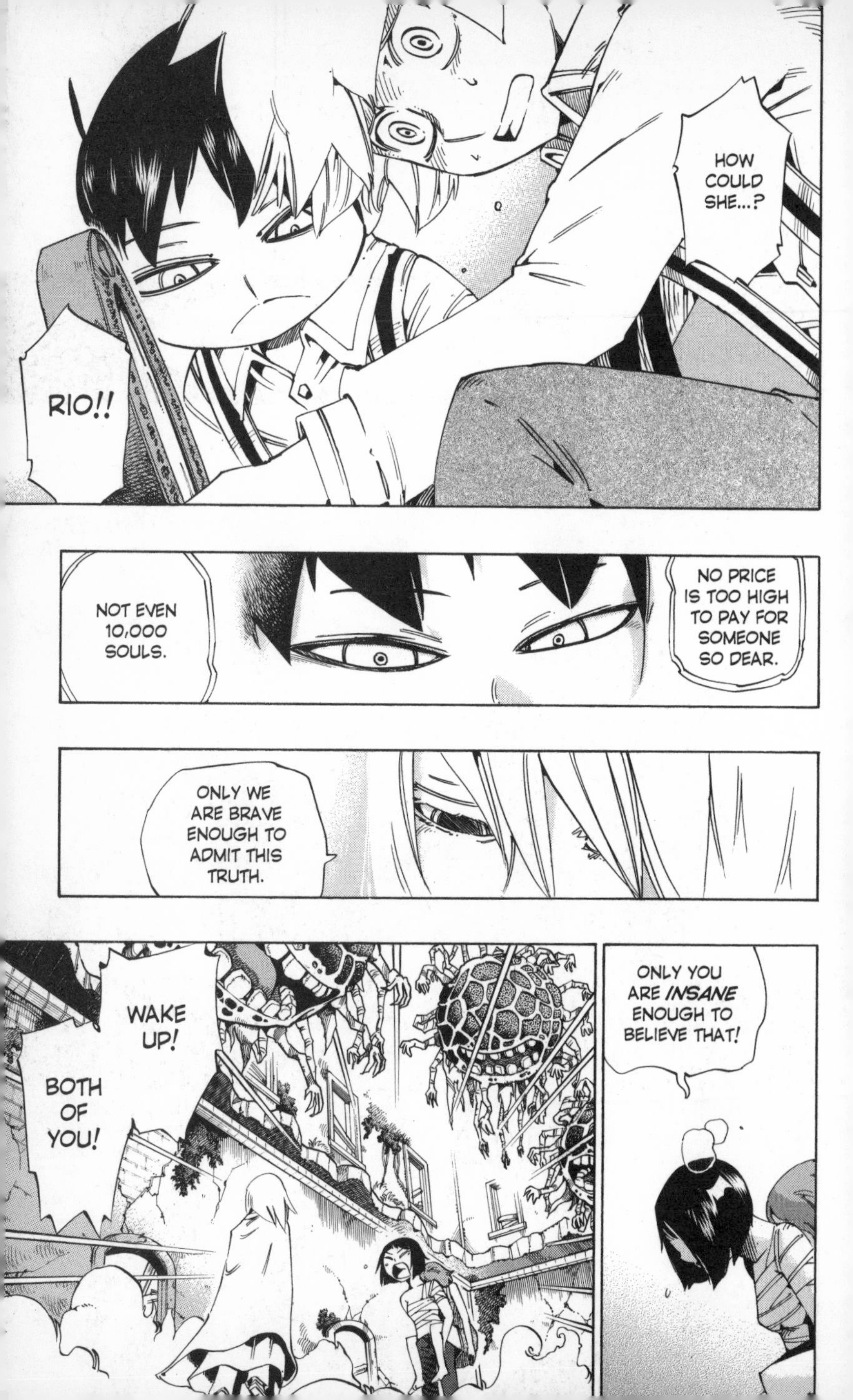

HOW COULD SHE...?
RIO!!
NO PRICE IS TOO HIGH TO PAY FOR SOMEONE SO DEAR.
NOT EVEN 10,000 SOULS.
ONLY WE ARE BRAVE ENOUGH TO ADMIT THIS TRUTH.
ONLY YOU ARE *INSANE* ENOUGH TO BELIEVE THAT!
WAKE UP!
BOTH OF YOU!

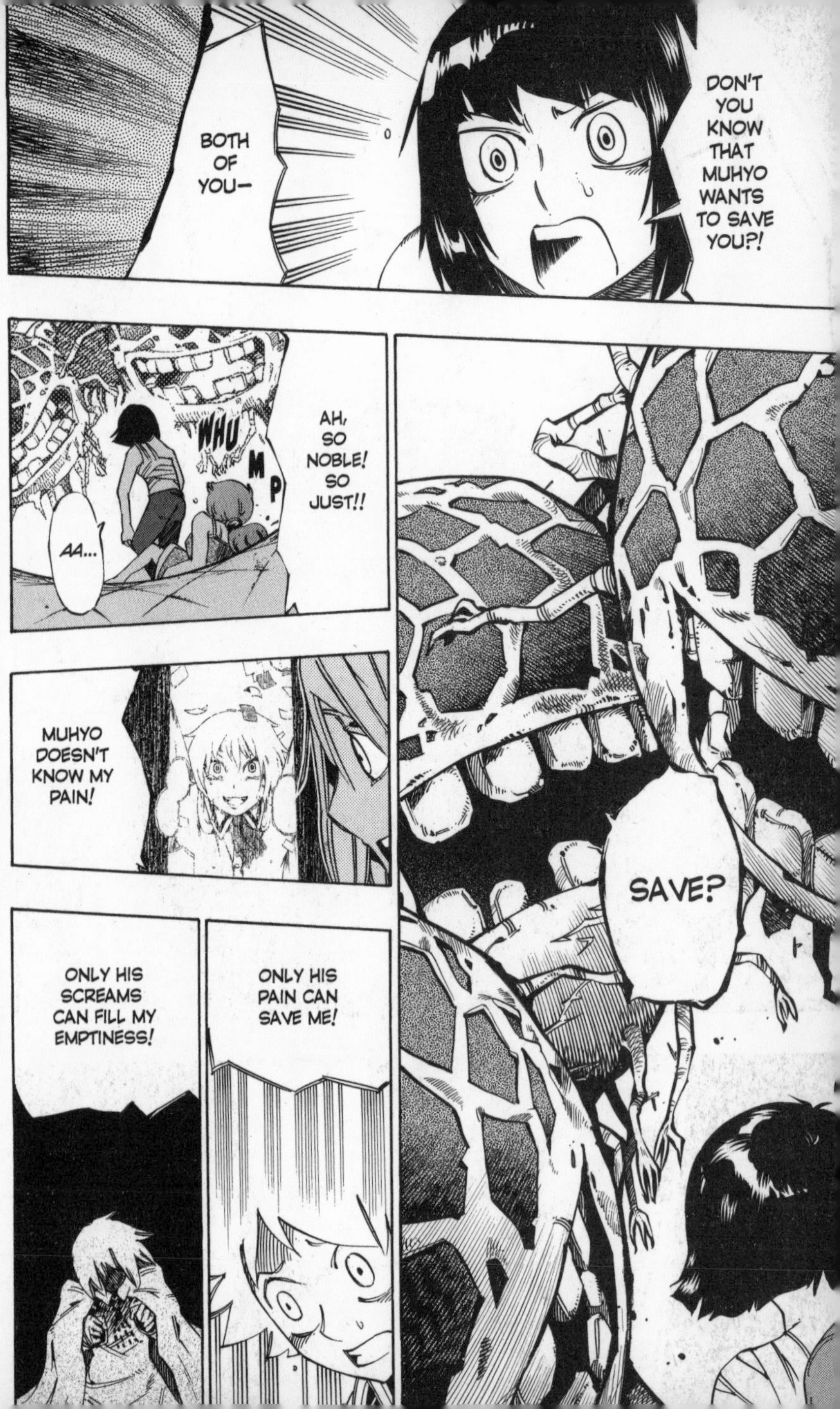
DON'T YOU KNOW THAT MUHYO WANTS TO SAVE YOU?!
BOTH OF YOU—
SAVE?
AH, SO NOBLE! SO JUST!!
WHUMP
AA...
MUHYO DOESN'T KNOW MY PAIN!
ONLY HIS PAIN CAN SAVE ME!
ONLY HIS SCREAMS CAN FILL MY EMPTINESS!

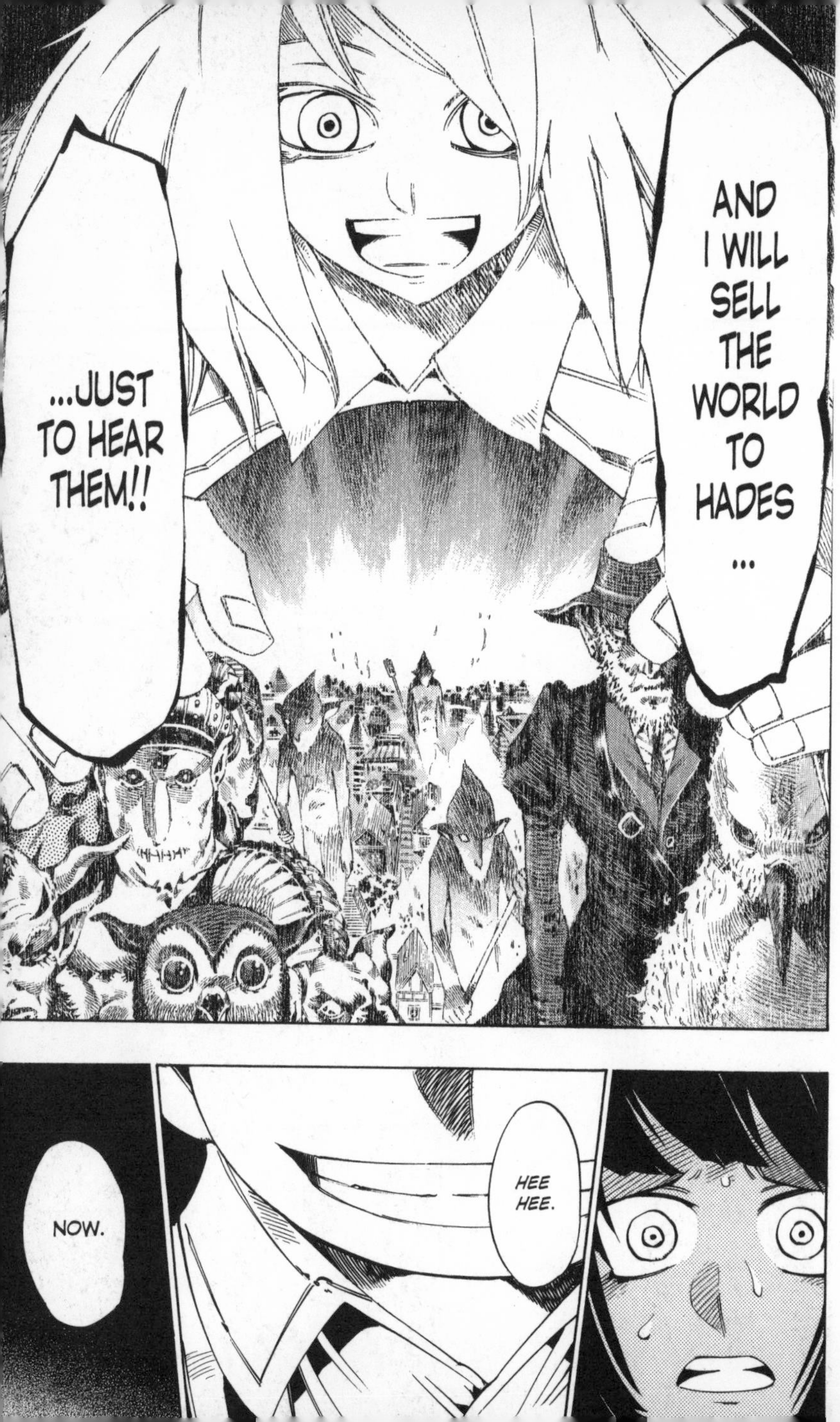
AND I WILL SELL THE WORLD TO HADES...
...JUST TO HEAR THEM!!
HEE HEE.
NOW.

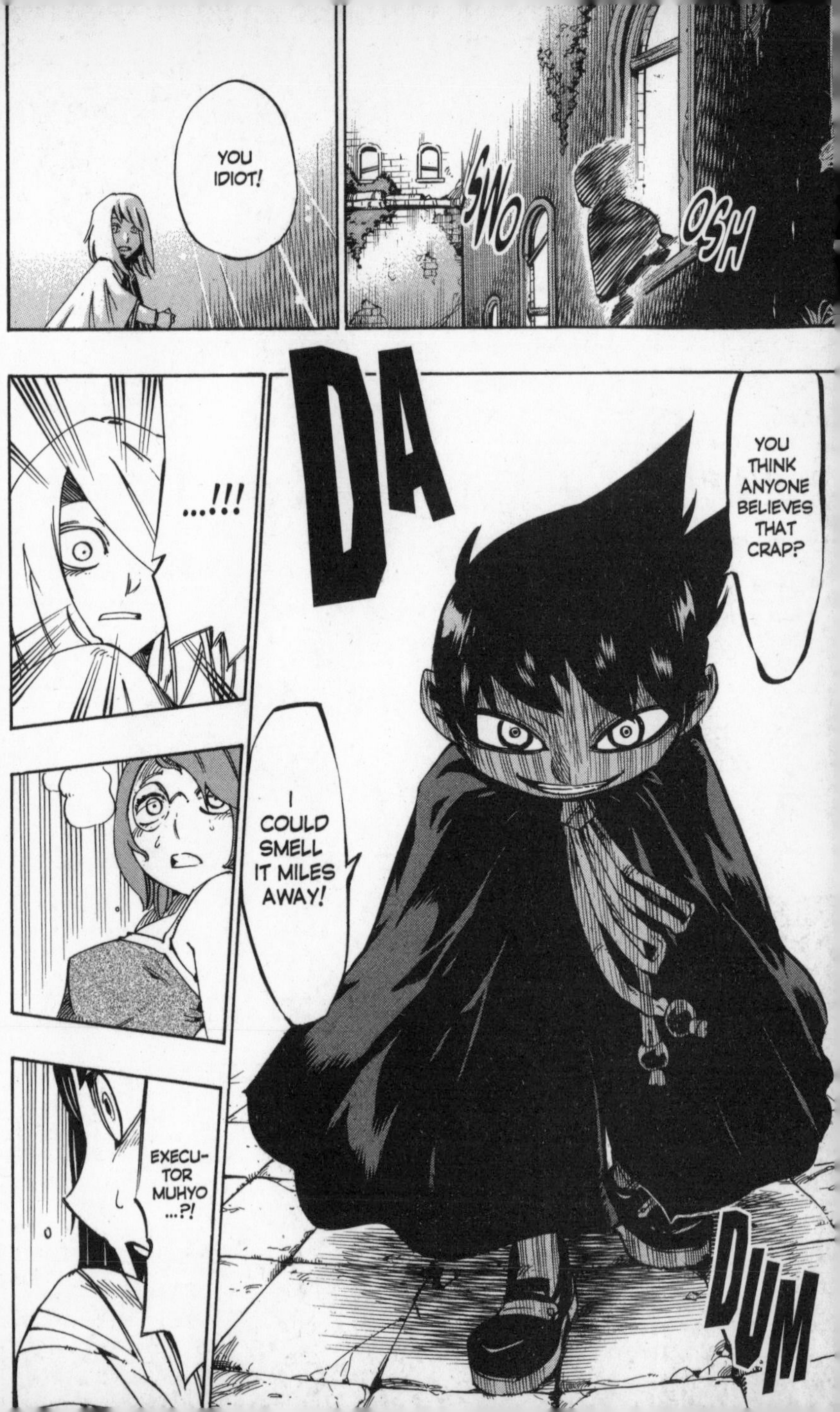
SWO
OSH
YOU IDIOT!
DA
YOU THINK ANYONE BELIEVES THAT CRAP?
I COULD SMELL IT MILES AWAY!
DUM
...!!!
EXECU-TOR MUHYO ...?!

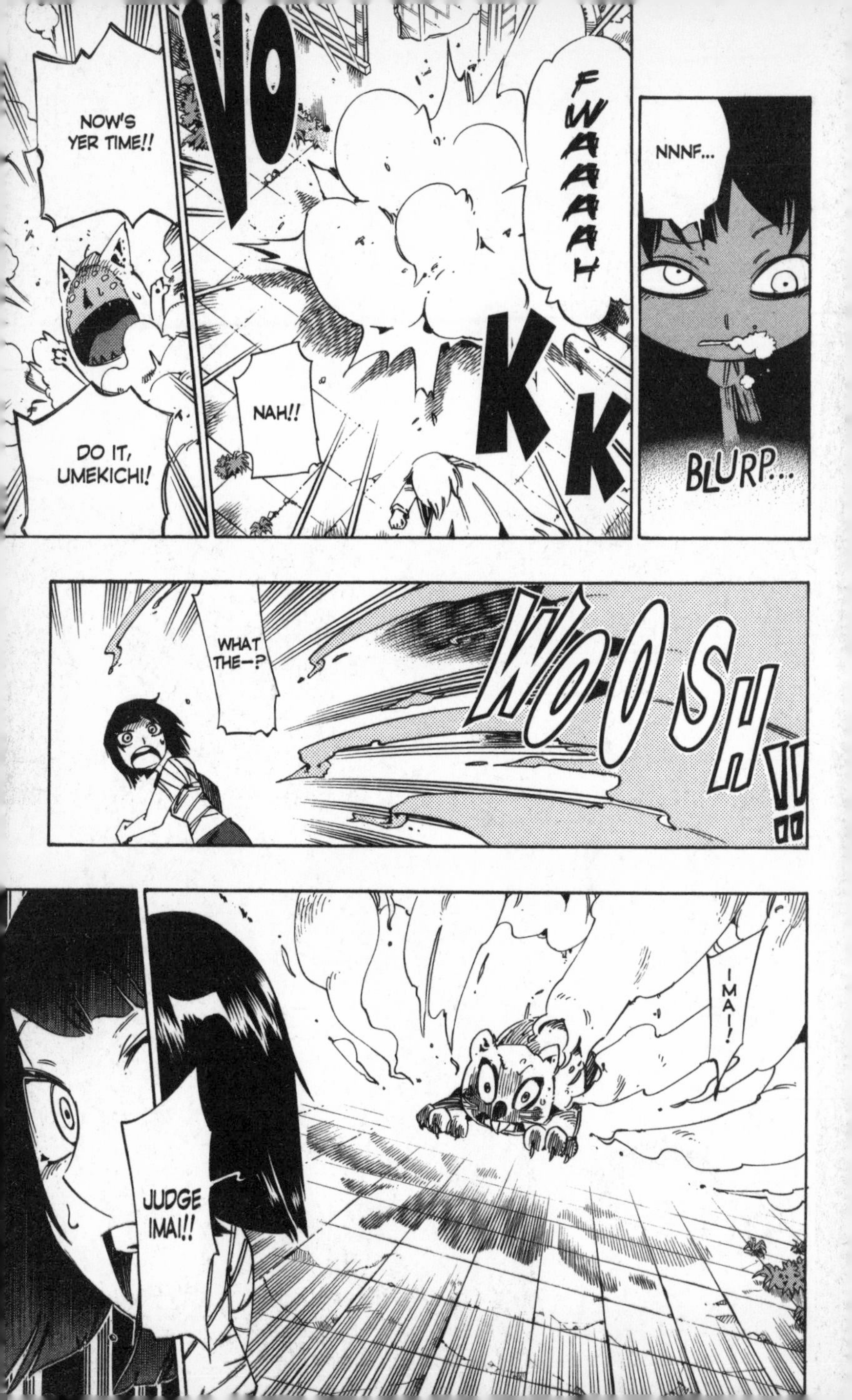
NNNF...
BLURP...
FWAAAAAH
VO
KK
NAH!!
NOW'S YER TIME!!
DO IT, UMEKICHI!
WHAT THE—?
WOOSH!!
IMAI!
JUDGE IMAI!!

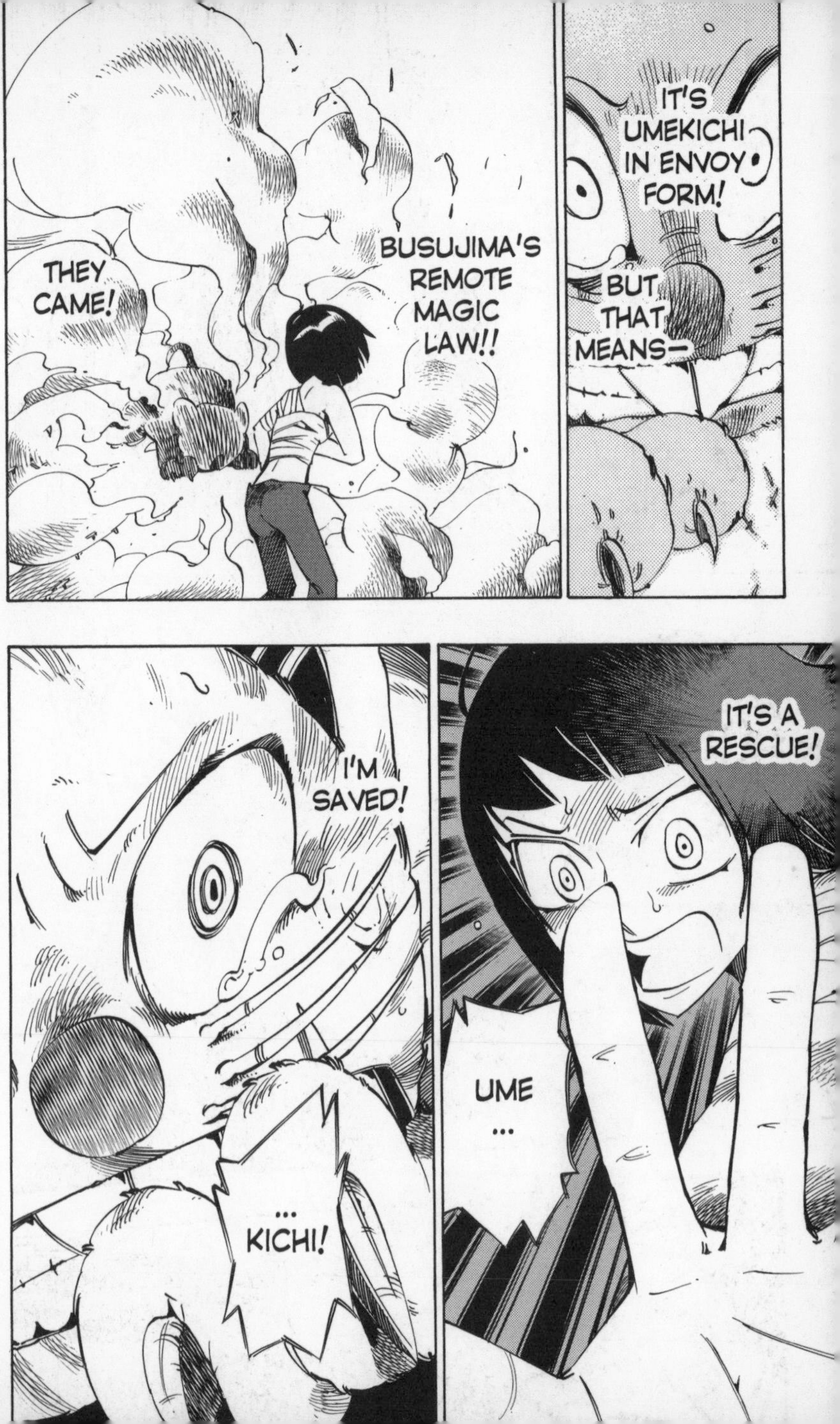
IT'S UMEKICHI IN ENVOY FORM!
BUT THAT MEANS—
BUSUJIMA'S REMOTE MAGIC LAW!!
THEY CAME!
IT'S A RESCUE!
UME ...
I'M SAVED!
... KICHI!

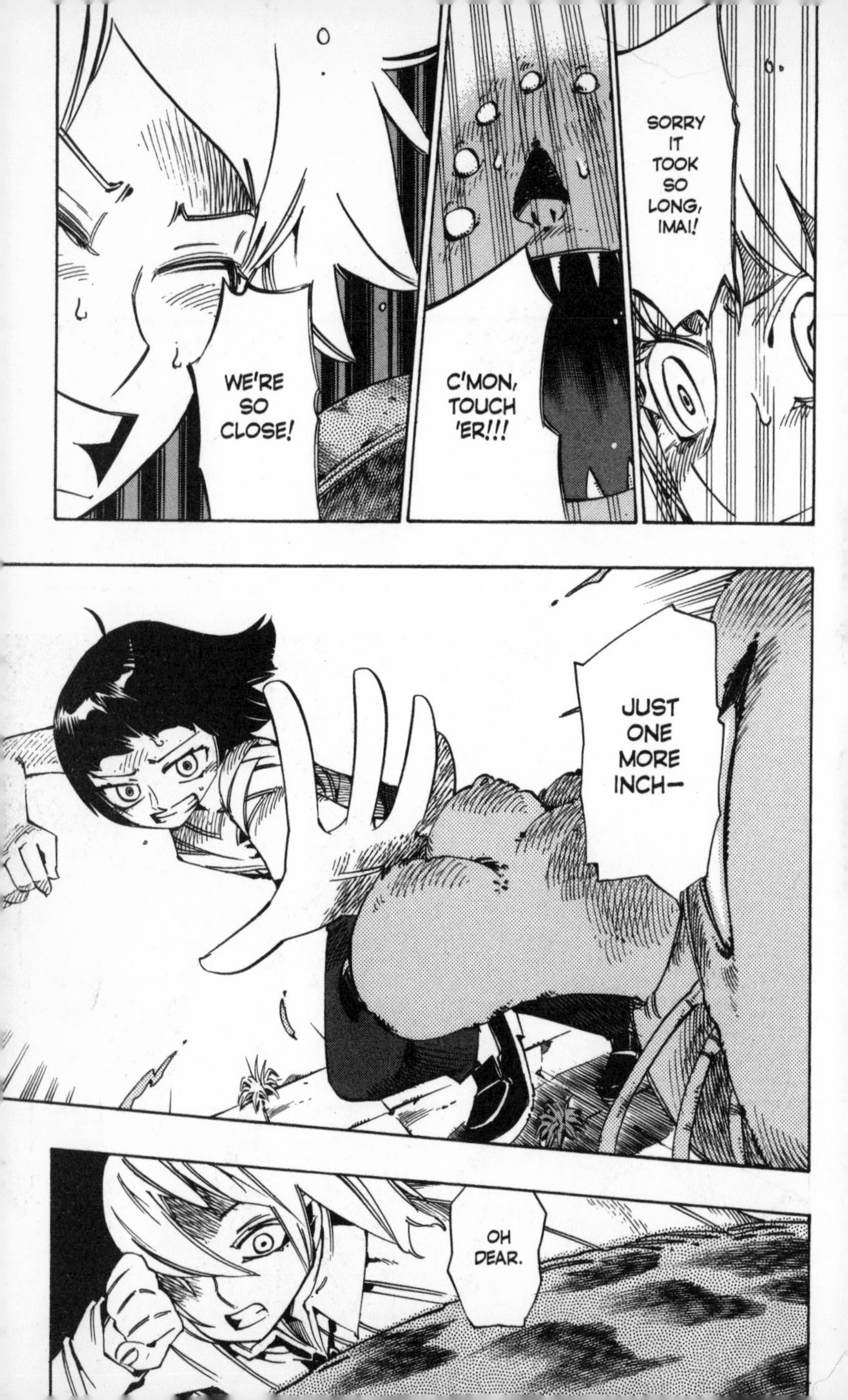
SORRY IT TOOK SO LONG, IMAI!
C'MON, TOUCH 'ER!!!
WE'RE SO CLOSE!
JUST ONE MORE INCH—
OH DEAR.

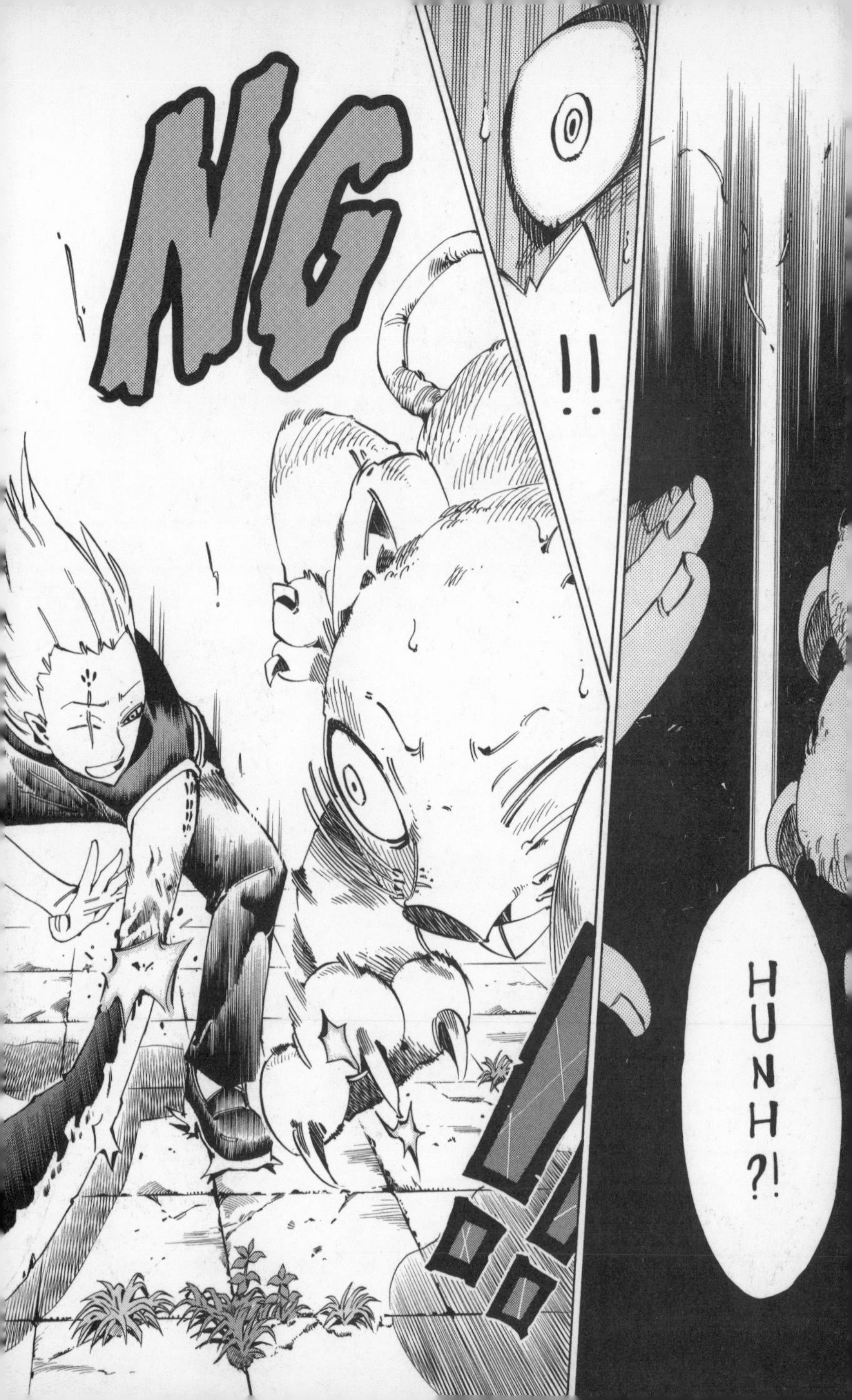
HUNH?!
!!
NG

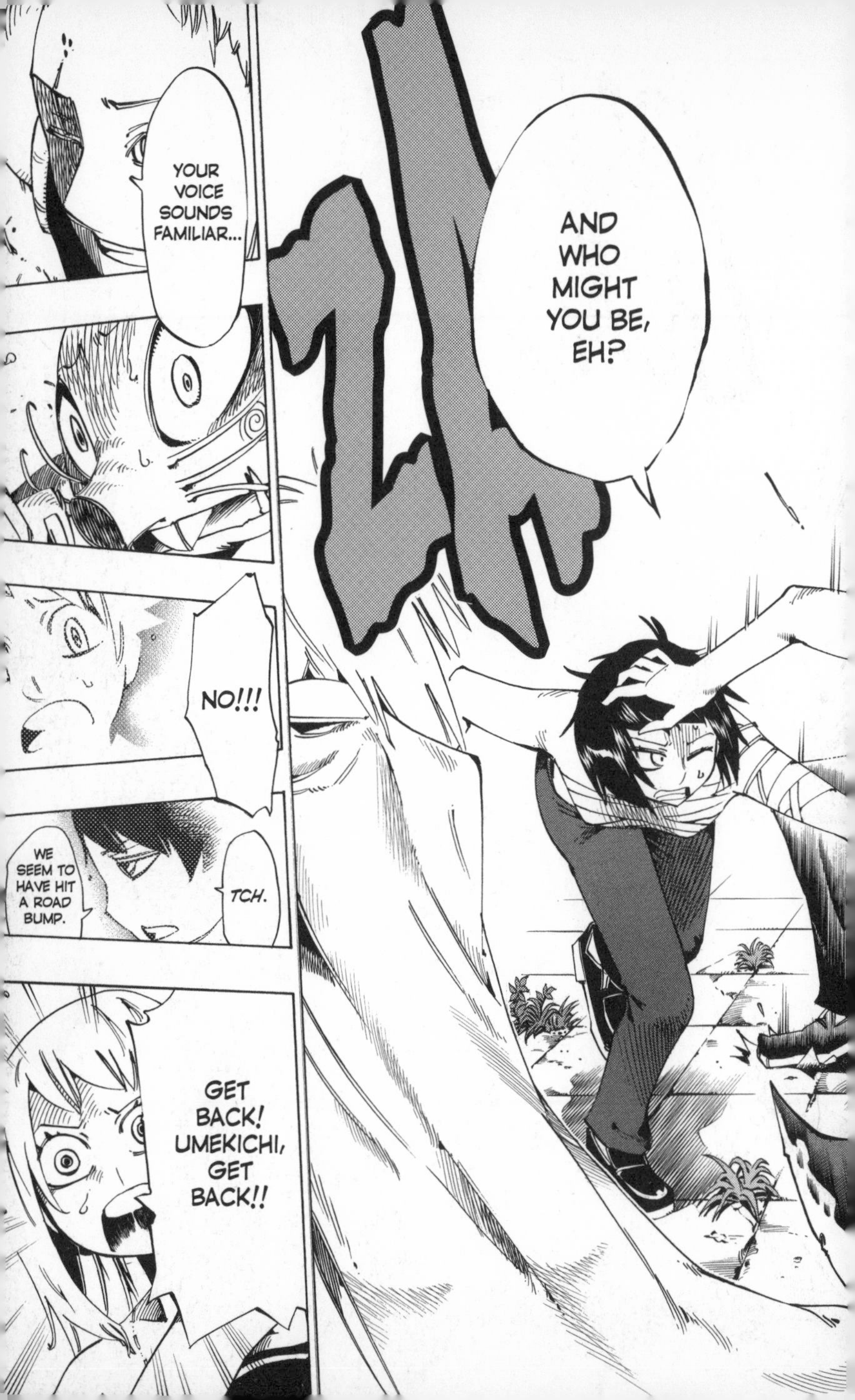
AND WHO MIGHT YOU BE, EH?
YOUR VOICE SOUNDS FAMILIAR...
NO!!!
TCH.
WE SEEM TO HAVE HIT A ROAD BUMP.
GET BACK! UMEKICHI, GET BACK!!

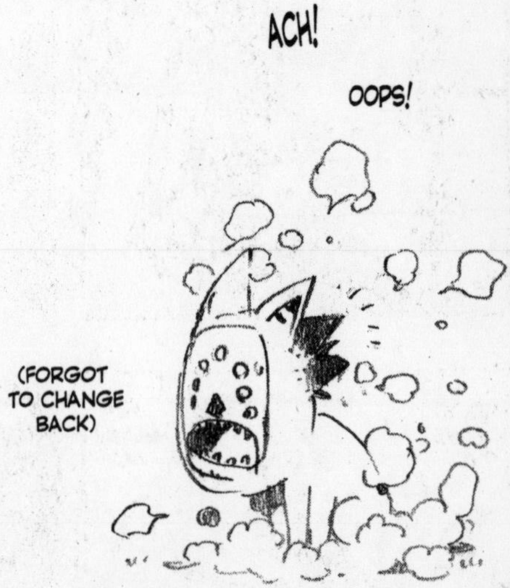
ACH!
OOPS!
(FORGOT TO CHANGE BACK)

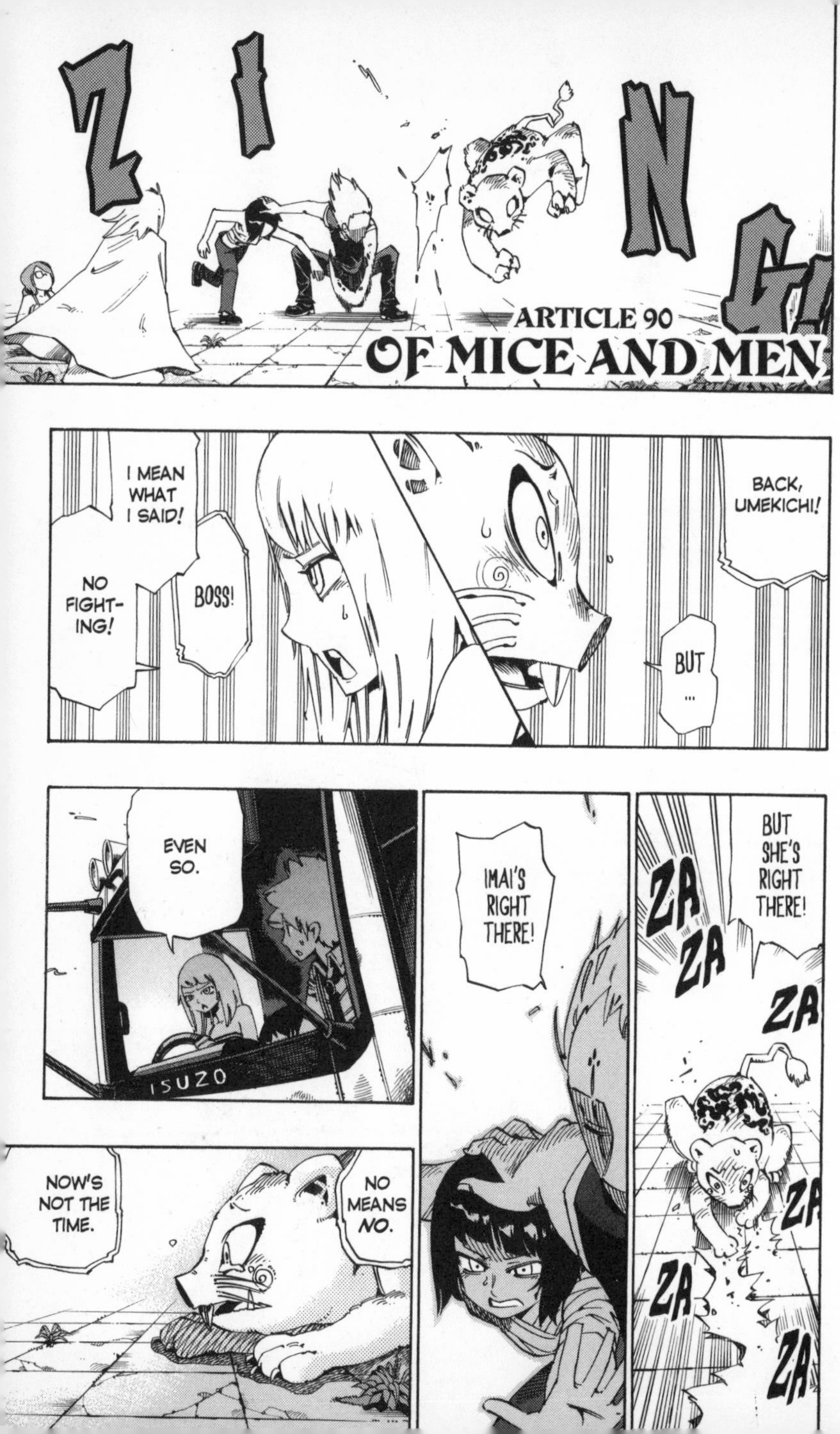
ZING
ARTICLE 90
OF MICE AND MEN
BACK, UMEKICHI!
BUT ...
BOSS!
I MEAN WHAT I SAID!
NO FIGHTING!
BUT SHE'S RIGHT THERE!
ZA ZA ZA
ZA
ZA
ZA
ZA
IMAI'S RIGHT THERE!
EVEN SO.
ISUZO
NO MEANS NO.
NOW'S NOT THE TIME.

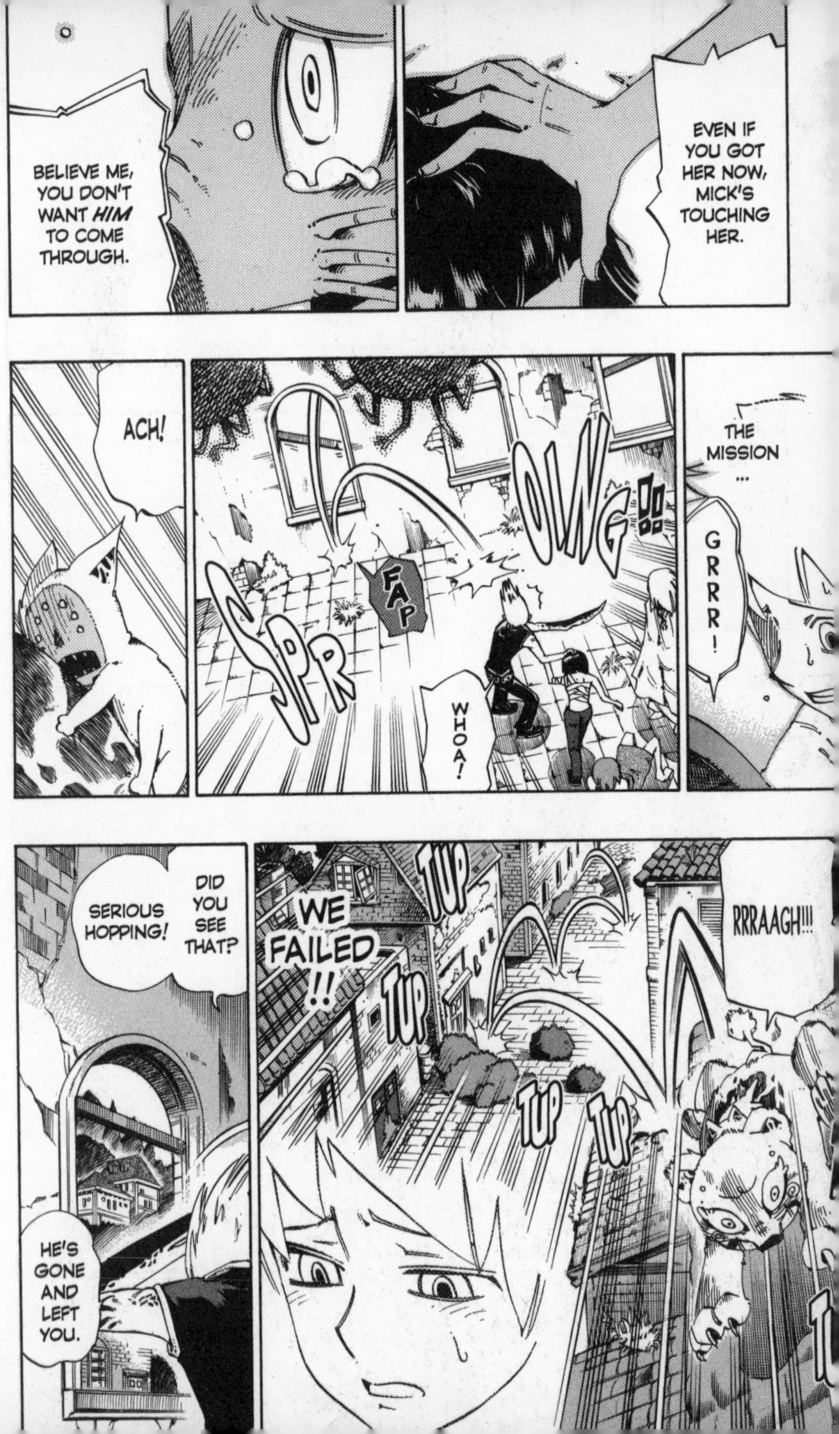
EVEN IF YOU GOT HER NOW, MICK'S TOUCHING HER.
BELIEVE ME, YOU DON'T WANT *HIM* TO COME THROUGH.
THE MISSION ...
GRRR!
OWNG!!
FAP
SPPR
WHOA!
ACH!
RRRAAGH!!!
TUP
TUP
WE FAILED!!
TUP
TUP
TUP
DID YOU SEE THAT?
SERIOUS HOPPING!
HE'S GONE AND LEFT YOU.

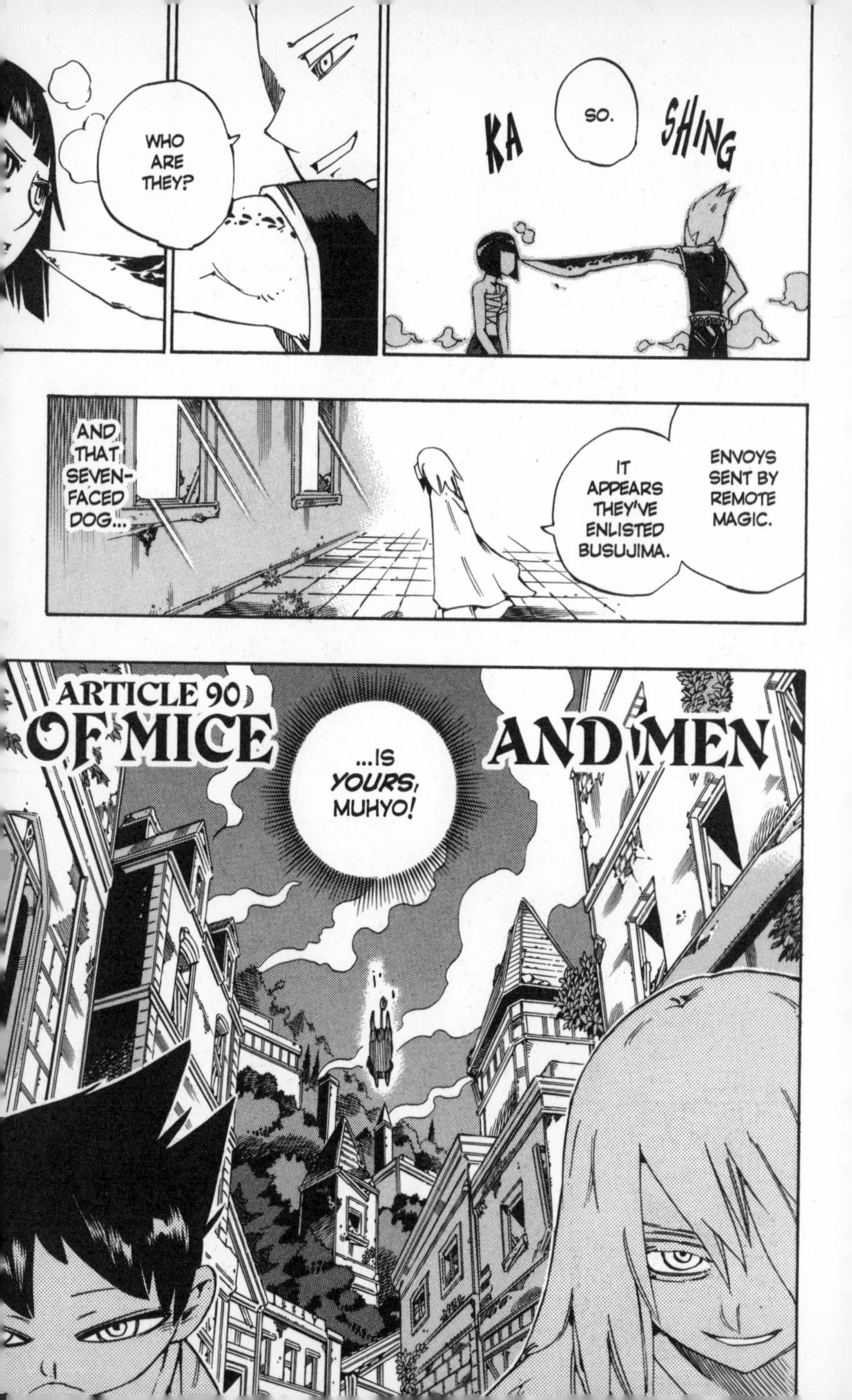
SO.
KA SHING
WHO ARE THEY?
ENVOYS SENT BY REMOTE MAGIC.
IT APPEARS THEY'VE ENLISTED BUSUJIMA.
AND THAT SEVEN-FACED DOG...
ARTICLE 90 OF MICE AND MEN
...IS YOURS, MUHYO!

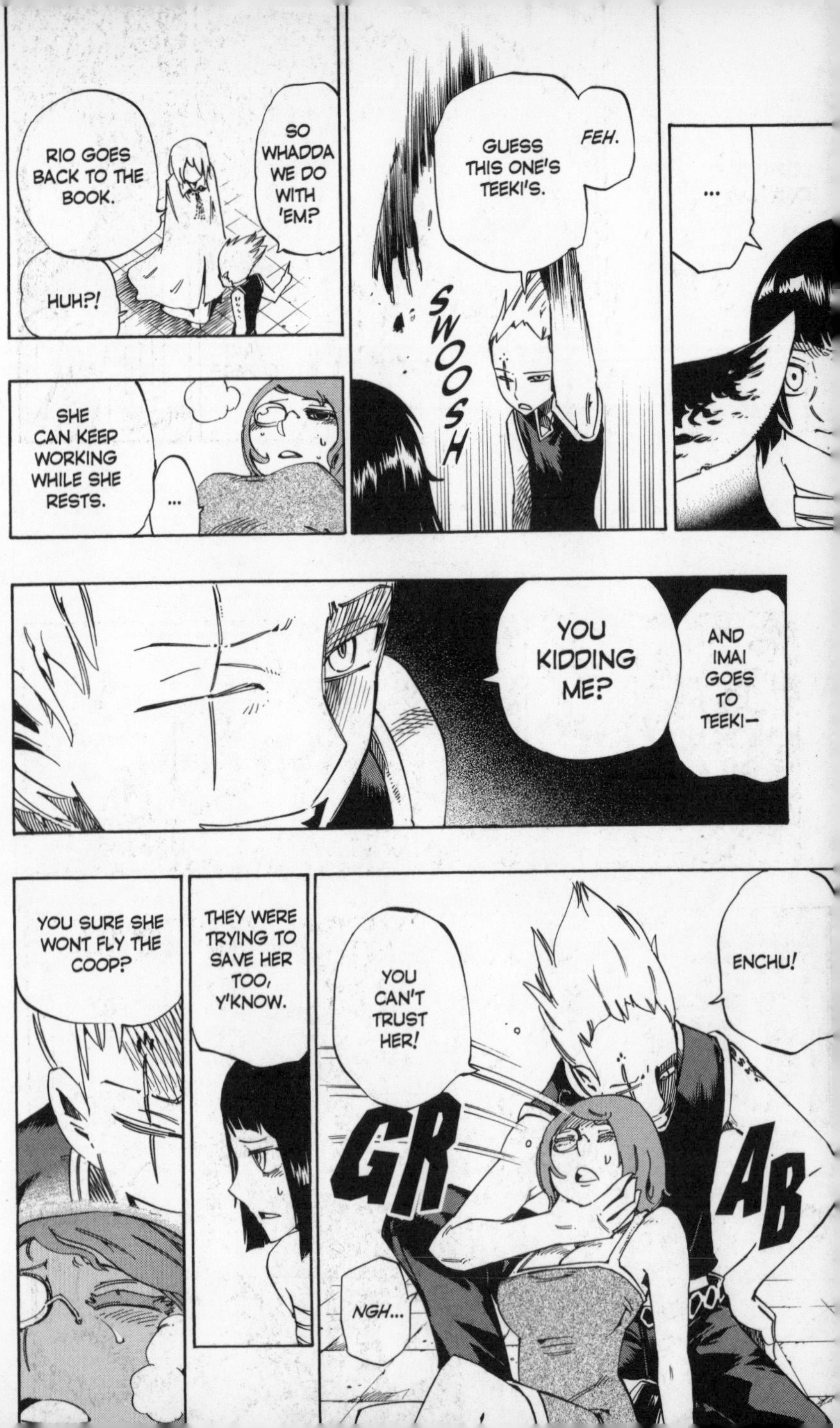
...
FEH.
GUESS THIS ONE'S TEEKI'S.
SWOOSH
SO WHADDA WE DO WITH 'EM?
RIO GOES BACK TO THE BOOK.
HUH?!
SHE CAN KEEP WORKING WHILE SHE RESTS.
...
AND IMAI GOES TO TEEKI—
YOU KIDDING ME?
ENCHU!
YOU CAN'T TRUST HER!
GRAB
NGH...
THEY WERE TRYING TO SAVE HER TOO, Y'KNOW.
YOU SURE SHE WONT FLY THE COOP?

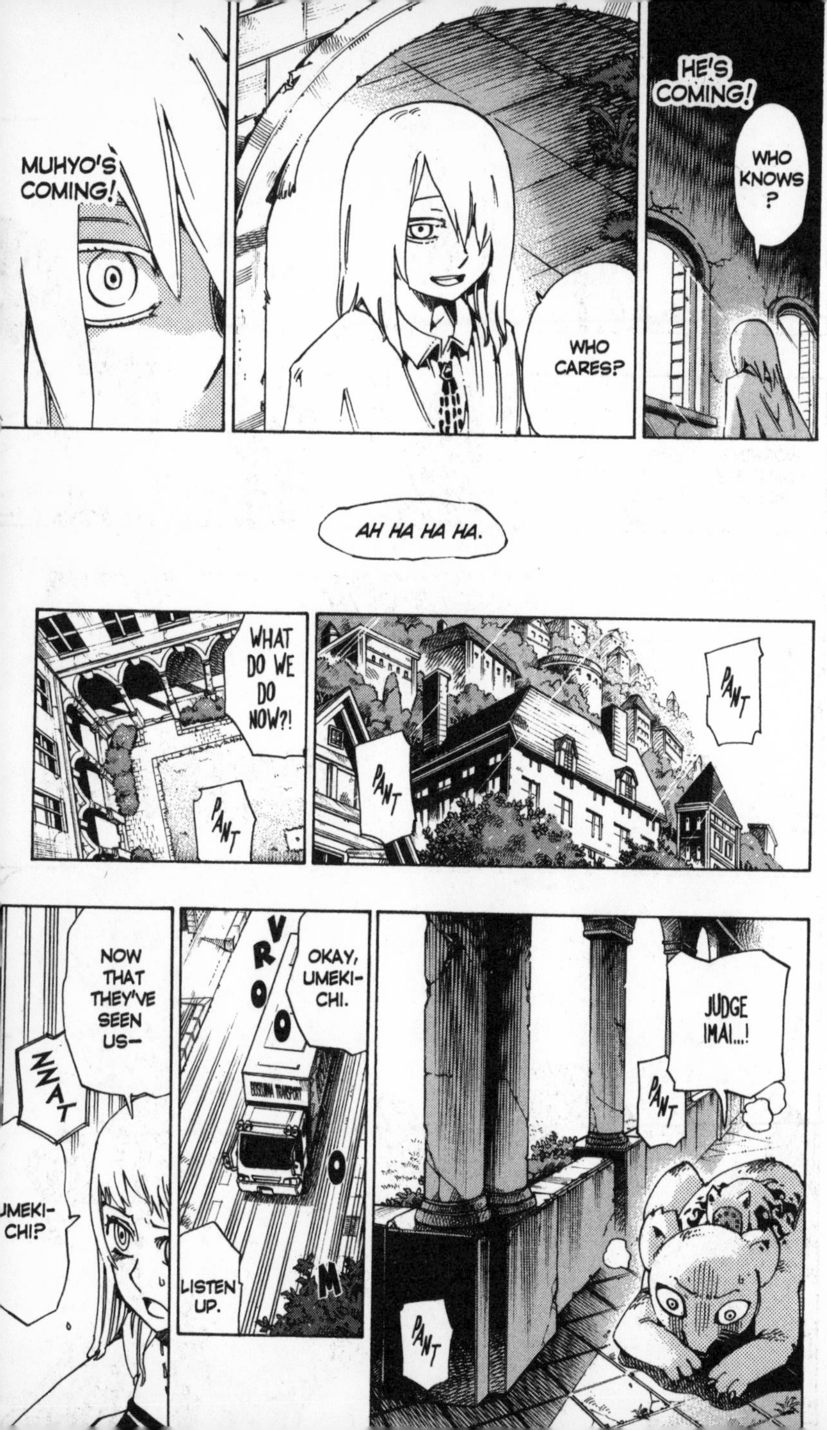
HE'S COMING!
WHO KNOWS?
WHO CARES?
MUHYO'S COMING!
AH HA HA HA.
PANT
PANT
WHAT DO WE DO NOW?!
PANT
JUDGE IMAI...!
PANT
PANT
VROOOM
OKAY, UMEKI-CHI.
LISTEN UP.
NOW THAT THEY'VE SEEN US—
ZZAT
UMEKI-CHI?

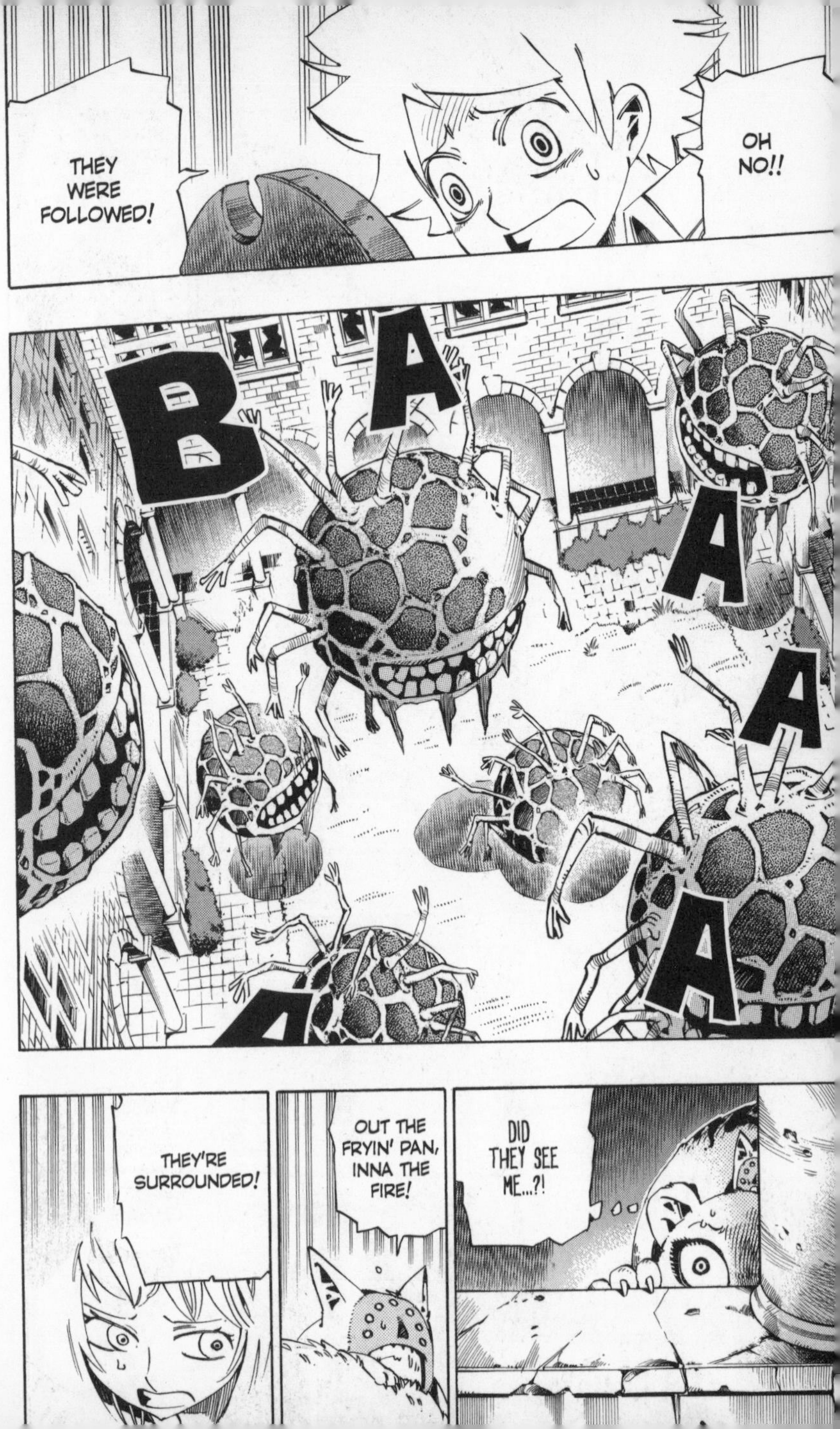
OH NO!!
THEY WERE FOLLOWED!
BAAAAA
DID THEY SEE ME...?!
OUT THE FRYIN' PAN, INNA THE FIRE!
THEY'RE SURROUNDED!

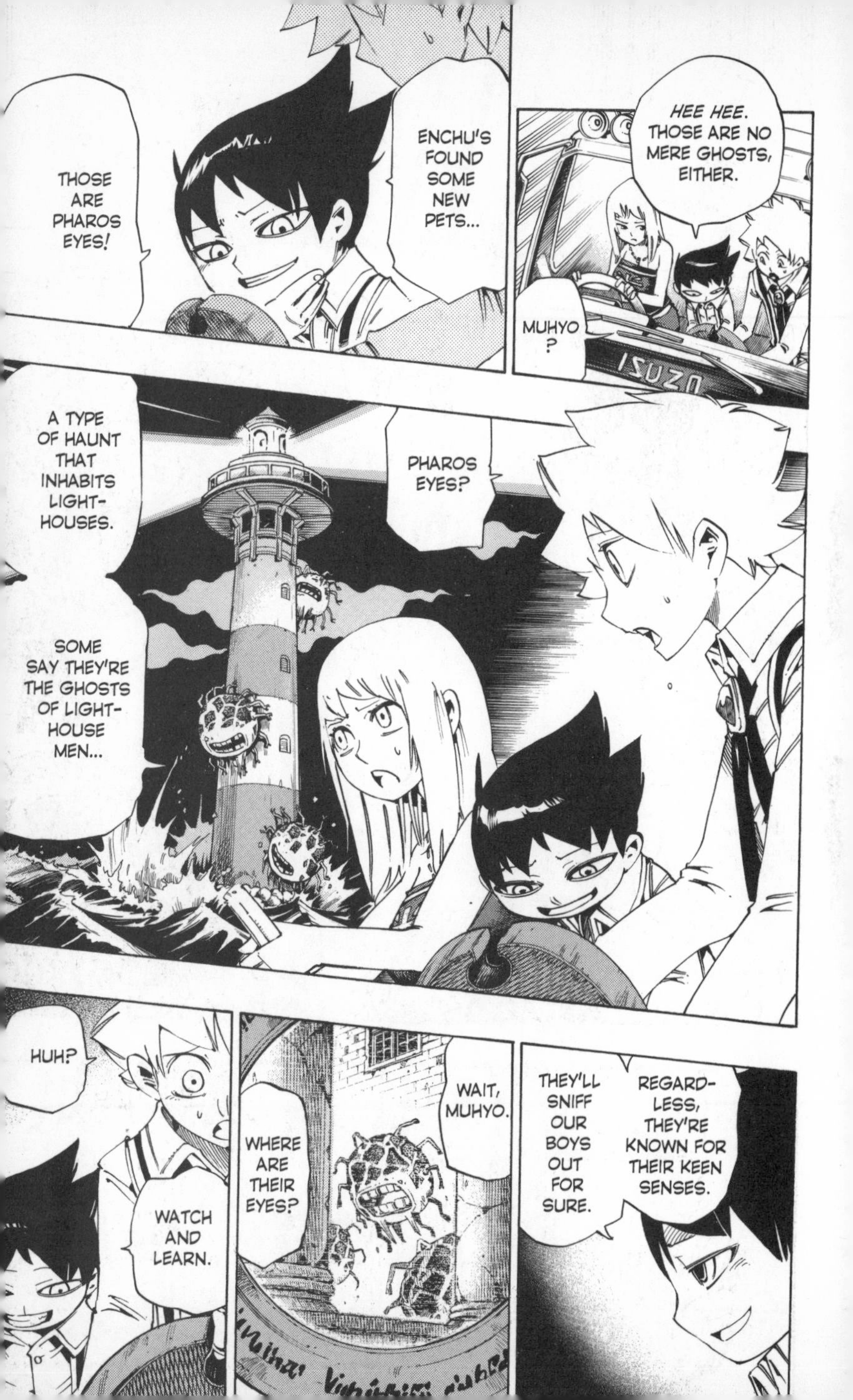
HEE HEE. THOSE ARE NO MERE GHOSTS, EITHER.
MUHYO?
ENCHU'S FOUND SOME NEW PETS...
THOSE ARE PHAROS EYES!
PHAROS EYES?
A TYPE OF HAUNT THAT INHABITS LIGHT-HOUSES.
SOME SAY THEY'RE THE GHOSTS OF LIGHT-HOUSE MEN...
REGARD-LESS, THEY'RE KNOWN FOR THEIR KEEN SENSES.
THEY'LL SNIFF OUR BOYS OUT FOR SURE.
WAIT, MUHYO.
WHERE ARE THEIR EYES?
HUH?
WATCH AND LEARN.

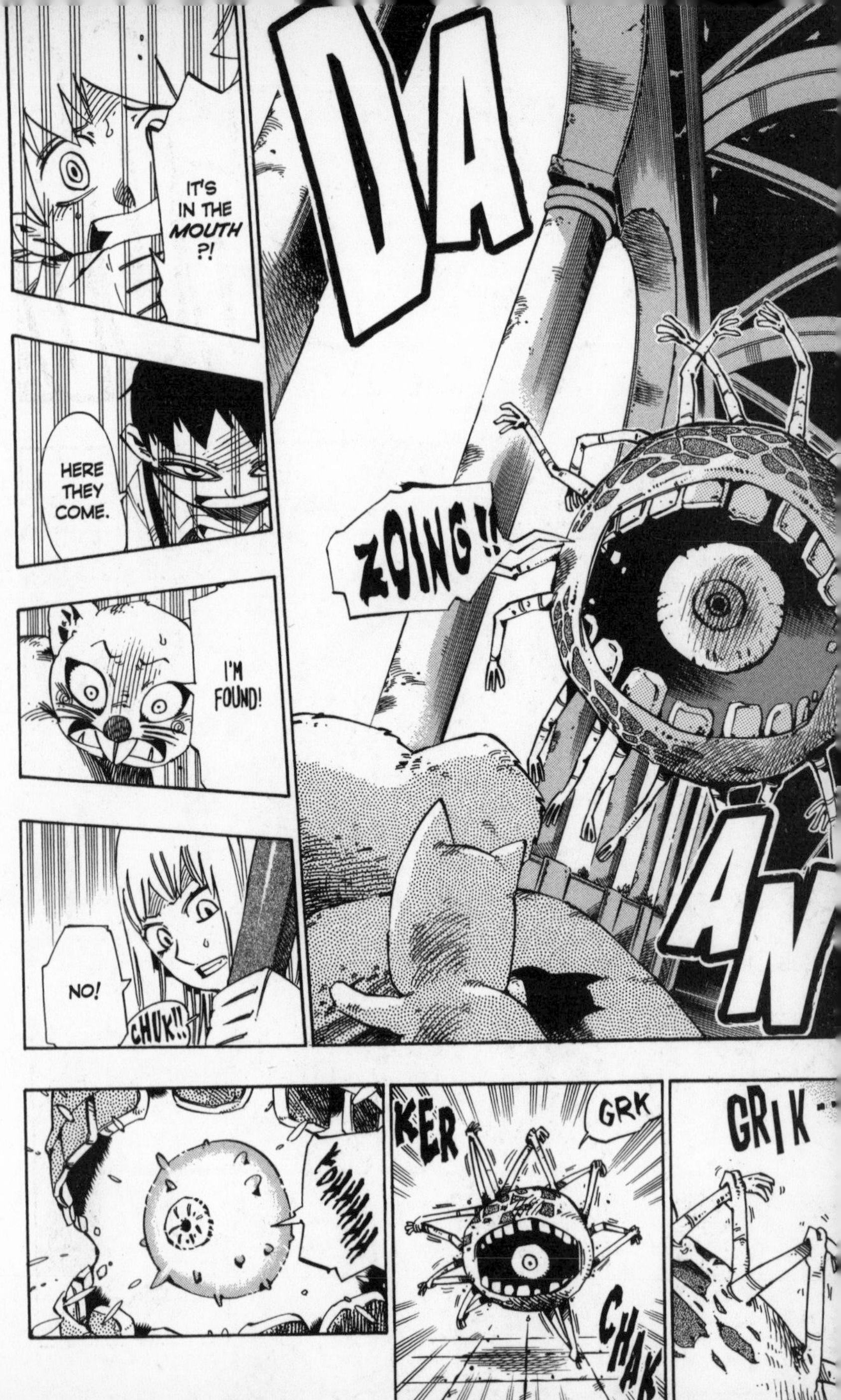
DA
ZOING!!
AN
IT'S IN THE MOUTH?!
HERE THEY COME.
I'M FOUND!
NO!
CHUK!!
GRIK...
KER
GRK
CHAK

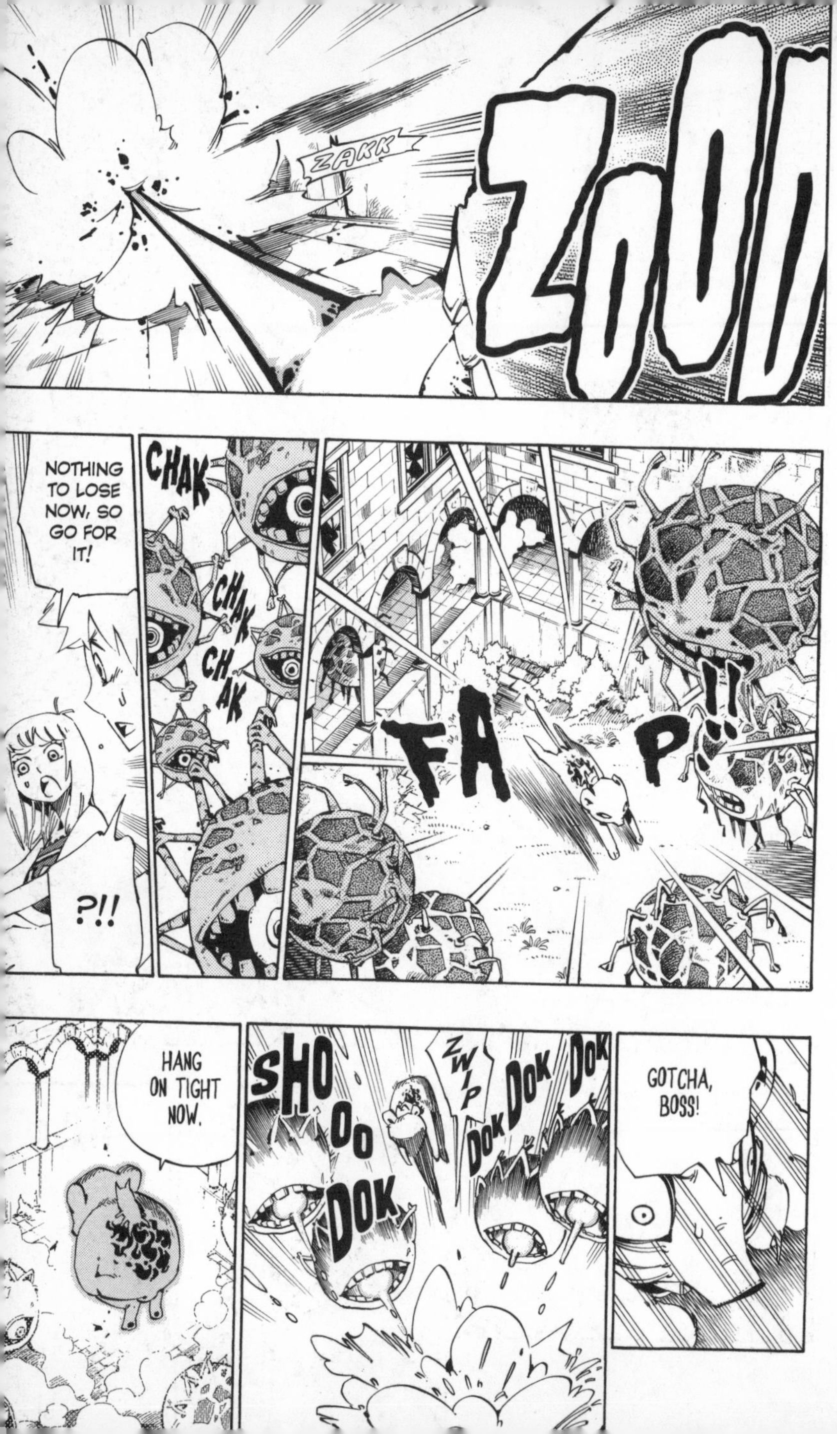
ZAKK
ZOO
FAP!!
CHAK
CHAK
CHAK
NOTHING TO LOSE NOW, SO GO FOR IT!
?!!
GOTCHA, BOSS!
DOK
DOK
DOK
ZWIP
DOK
SHOOO
DOK
HANG ON TIGHT NOW.

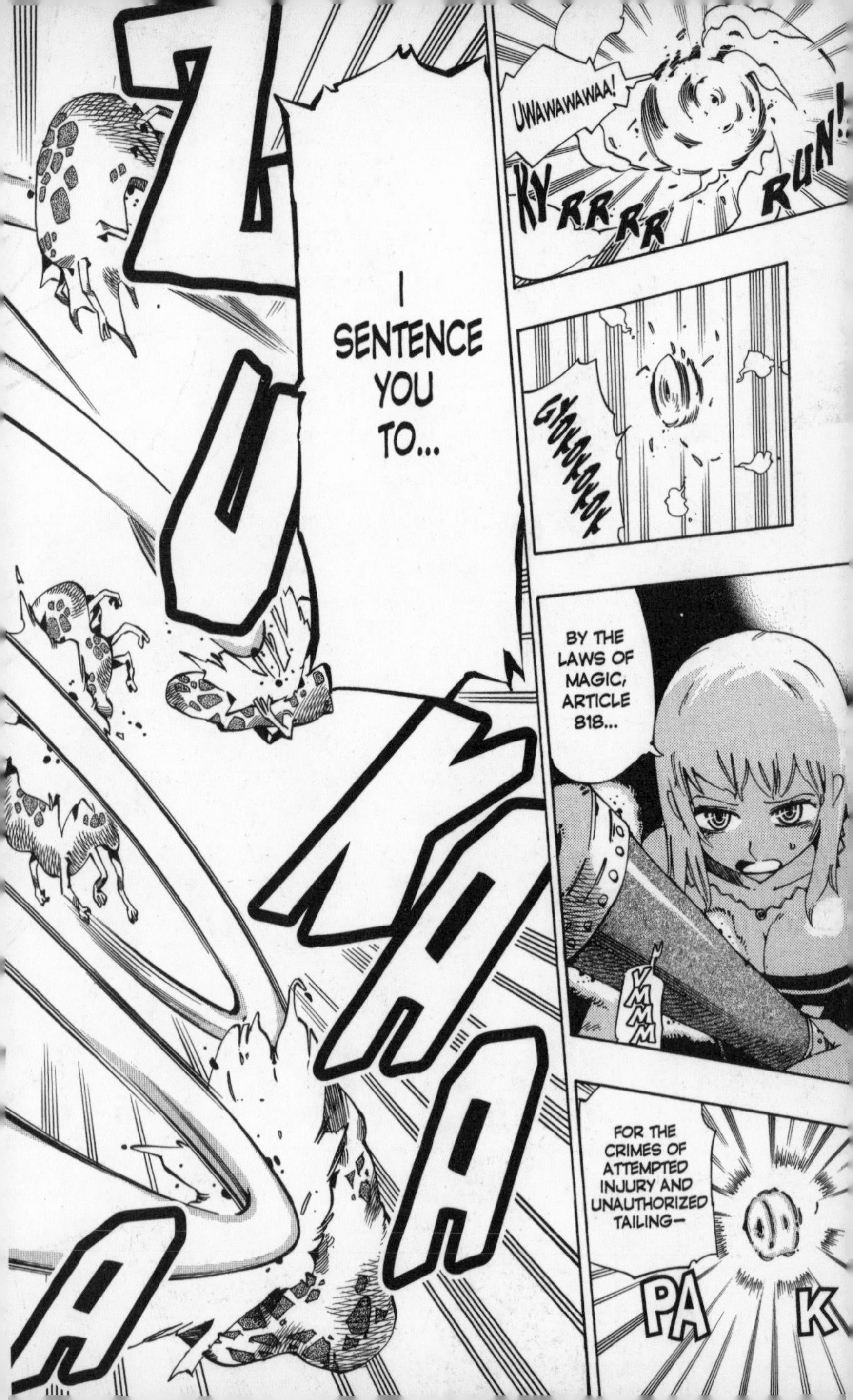
UWAWAWAWAA!
KYRRRRR RUN!
GYOKOKOKOK
BY THE LAWS OF MAGIC, ARTICLE 818...
VMMM
FOR THE CRIMES OF ATTEMPTED INJURY AND UNAUTHORIZED TAILING—
PAK
I SENTENCE YOU TO...

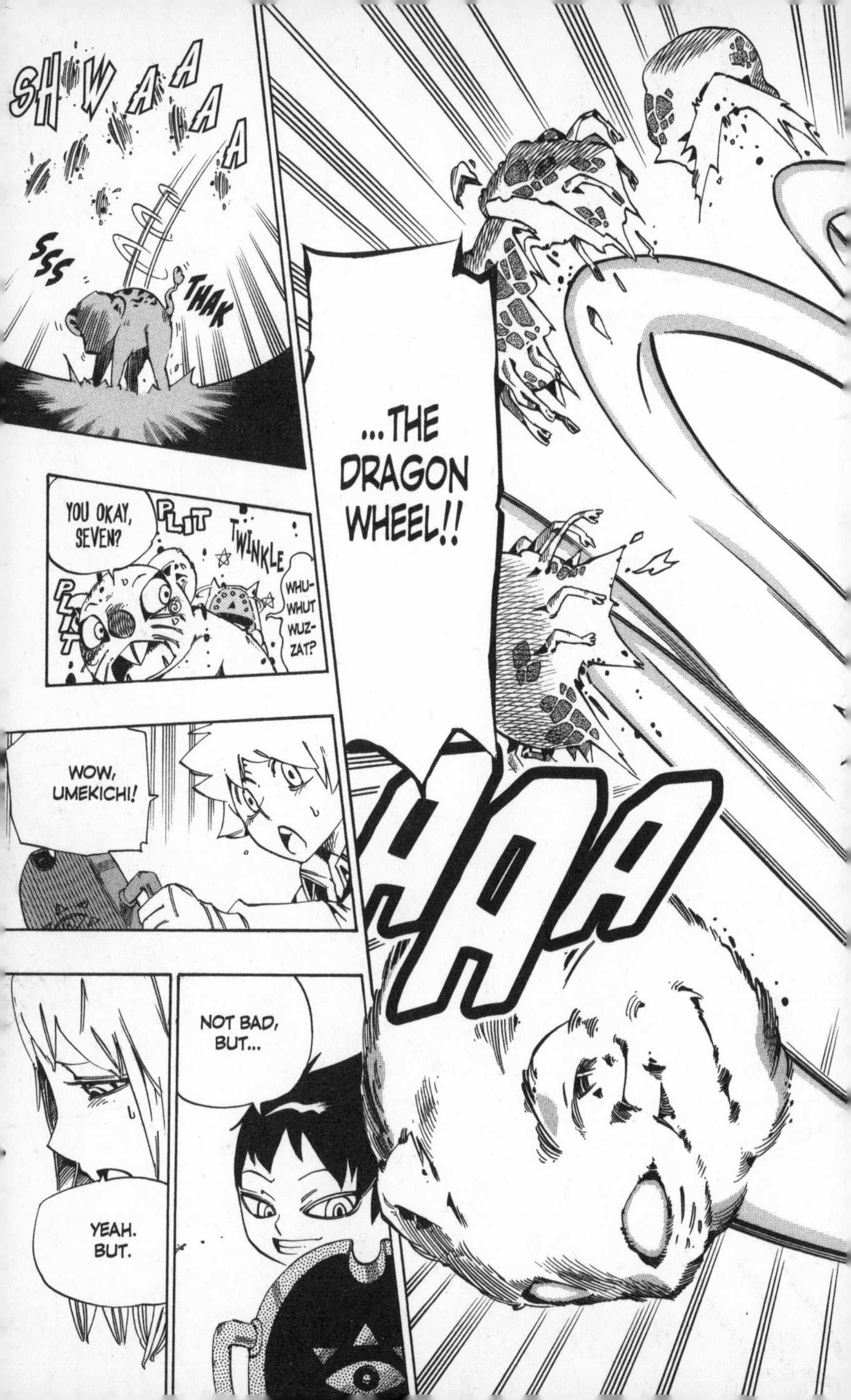
...THE DRAGON WHEEL!!
HAA
SHWAAAAA
SSS
THAK
YOU OKAY, SEVEN?
PLIT
TWINKLE
WHU-WHUT WUZ-ZAT?
PLIT
WOW, UMEKICHI!
NOT BAD, BUT...
YEAH. BUT.

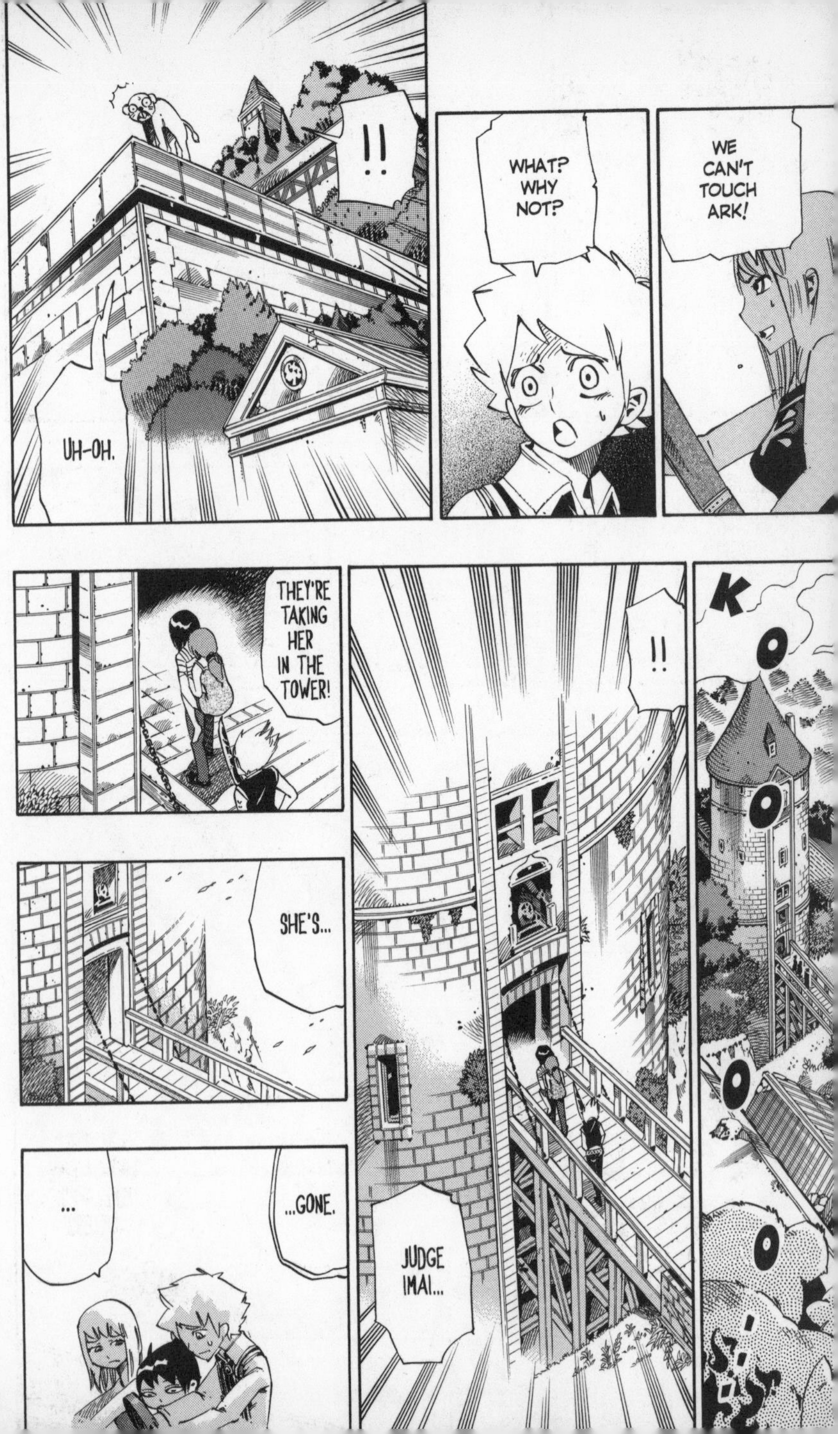
WE CAN'T TOUCH ARK!
WHAT? WHY NOT?
!!
UH-OH.
KOOOO
!!
JUDGE IMAI...
THEY'RE TAKING HER IN THE TOWER!
SHE'S...
...GONE.
...

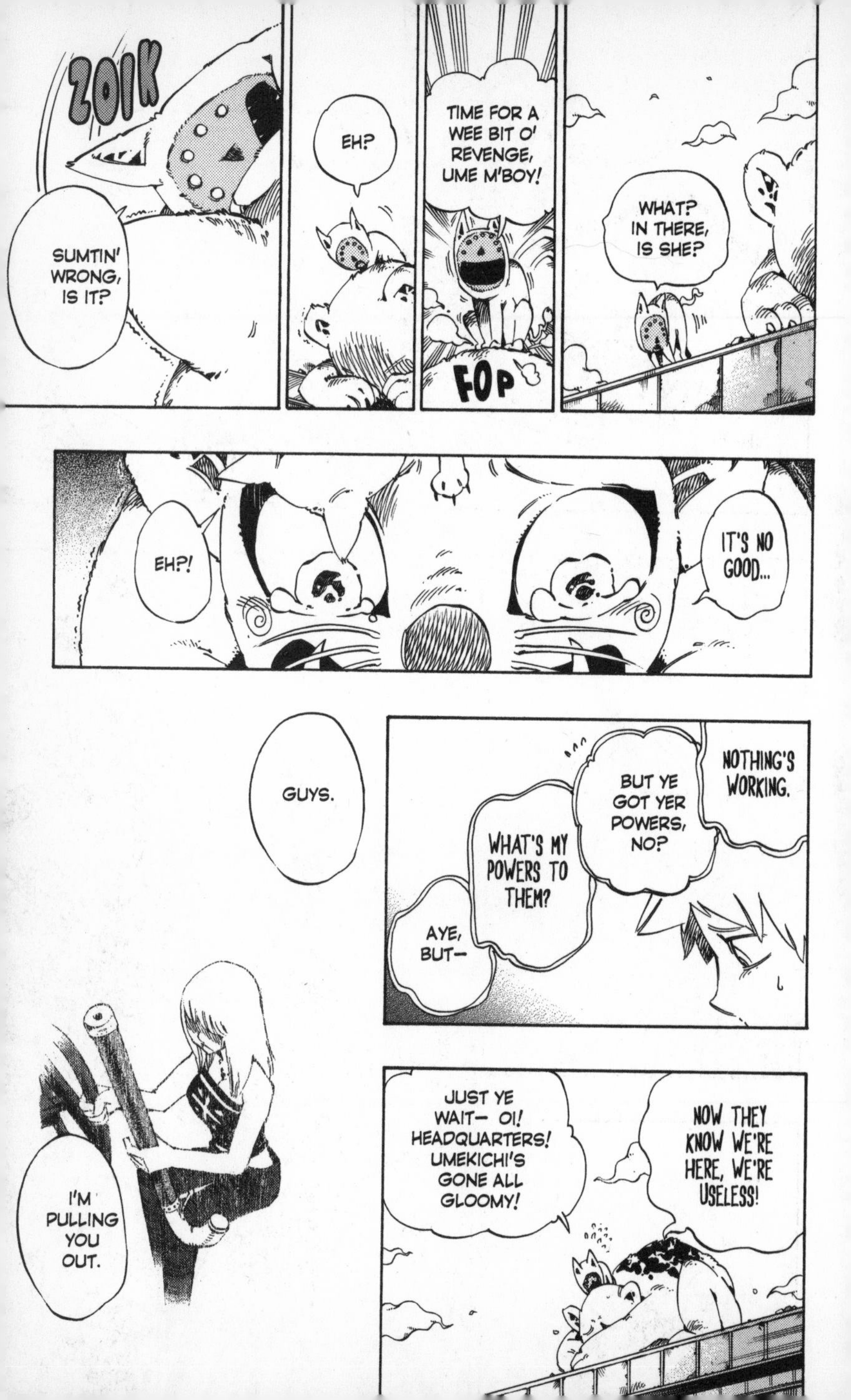
WHAT? IN THERE, IS SHE?
TIME FOR A WEE BIT O' REVENGE, UME M'BOY!
FOP
EH?
ZOIK
SUMTIN' WRONG, IS IT?
IT'S NO GOOD...
EH?!
NOTHING'S WORKING.
BUT YE GOT YER POWERS, NO?
WHAT'S MY POWERS TO THEM?
AYE, BUT—
NOW THEY KNOW WE'RE HERE, WE'RE USELESS!
JUST YE WAIT— OI! HEADQUARTERS! UMEKICHI'S GONE ALL GLOOMY!
GUYS.
I'M PULLING YOU OUT.

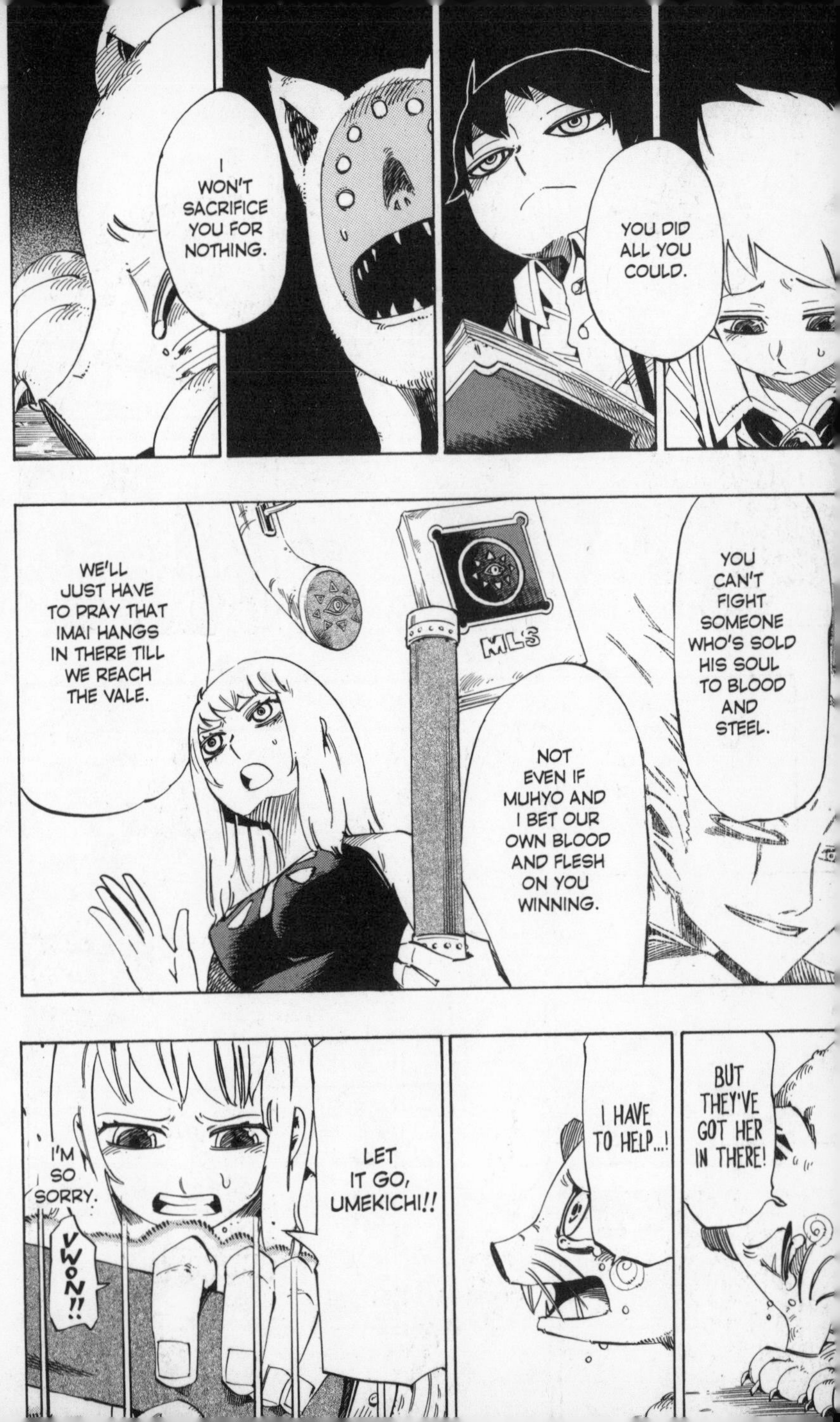
YOU DID ALL YOU COULD.
I WON'T SACRIFICE YOU FOR NOTHING.
YOU CAN'T FIGHT SOMEONE WHO'S SOLD HIS SOUL TO BLOOD AND STEEL.
NOT EVEN IF MUHYO AND I BET OUR OWN BLOOD AND FLESH ON YOU WINNING.
WE'LL JUST HAVE TO PRAY THAT IMAI HANGS IN THERE TILL WE REACH THE VALE.
MLS
BUT THEY'VE GOT HER IN THERE!
I HAVE TO HELP...!
LET IT GO, UMEKICHI!!
I'M SO SORRY.
VWON!!

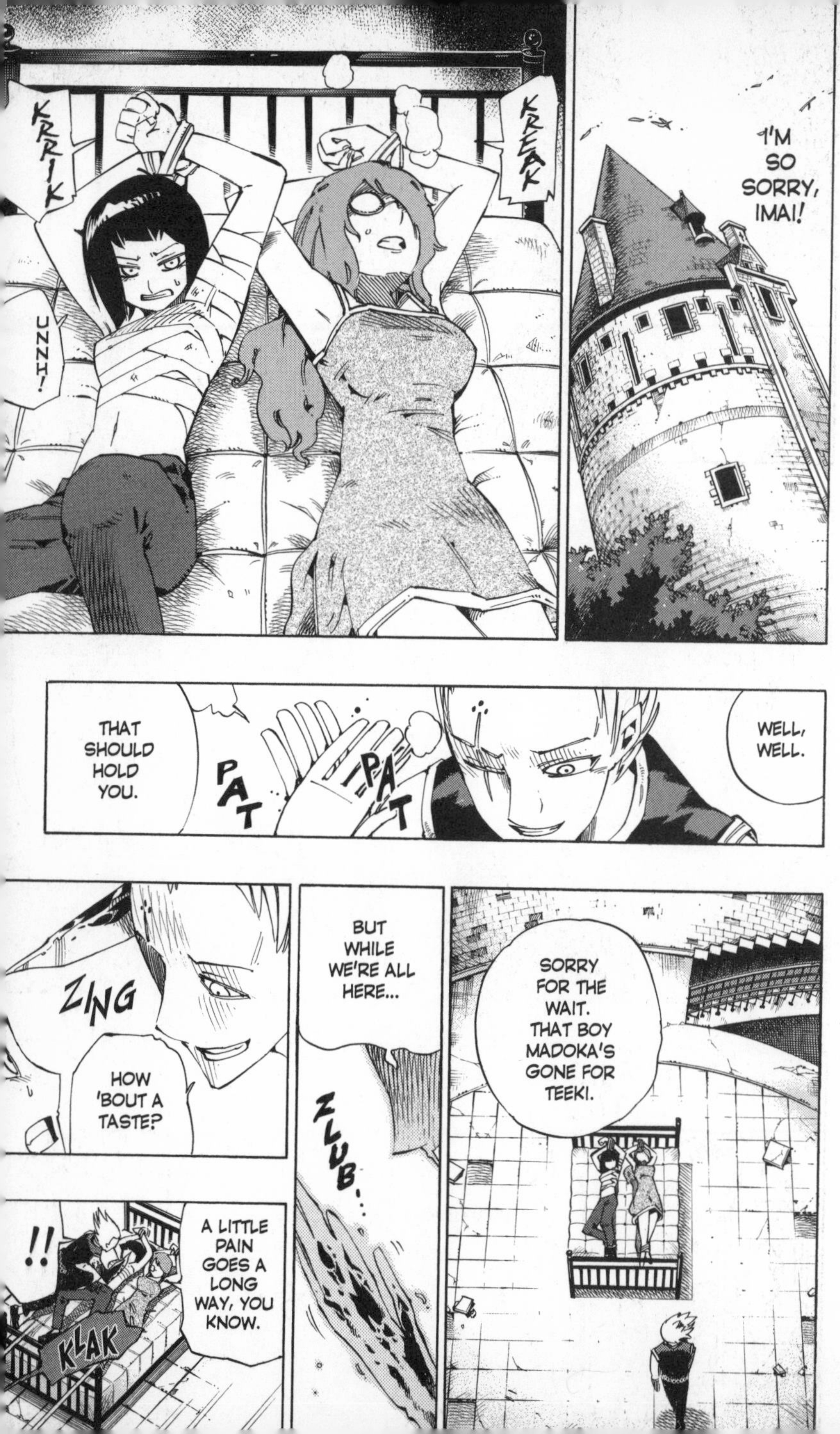
I'M SO SORRY, IMAI!
KREAK
KRRIK
UNNH!
WELL, WELL.
PAT
PAT
PAT
THAT SHOULD HOLD YOU.
SORRY FOR THE WAIT. THAT BOY MADOKA'S GONE FOR TEEKI.
BUT WHILE WE'RE ALL HERE...
ZLUB...
ZING
HOW 'BOUT A TASTE?
A LITTLE PAIN GOES A LONG WAY, YOU KNOW.
!!
KLAK

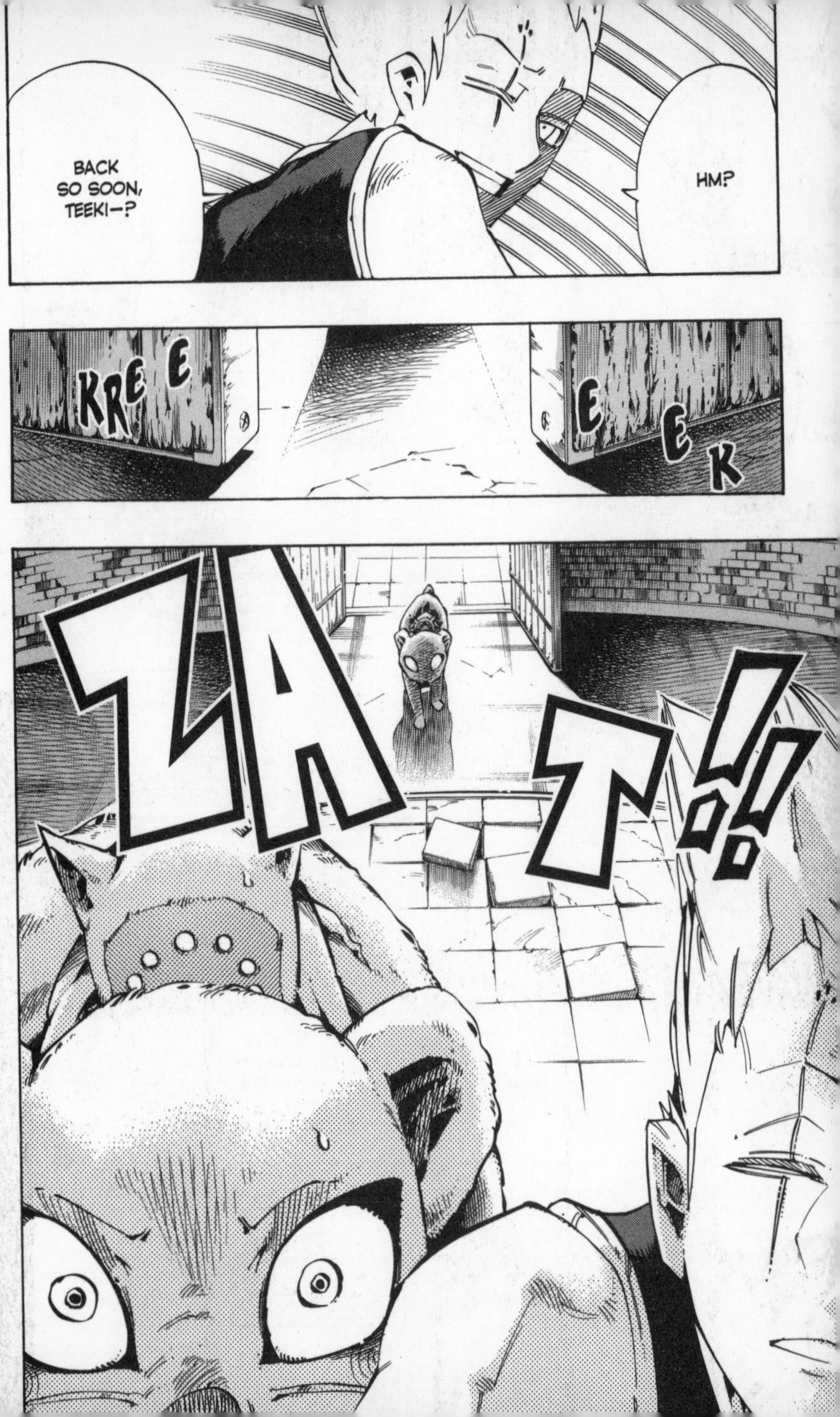
HM?
BACK SO SOON, TEEKI—?
KREEEEK
ZAT!!

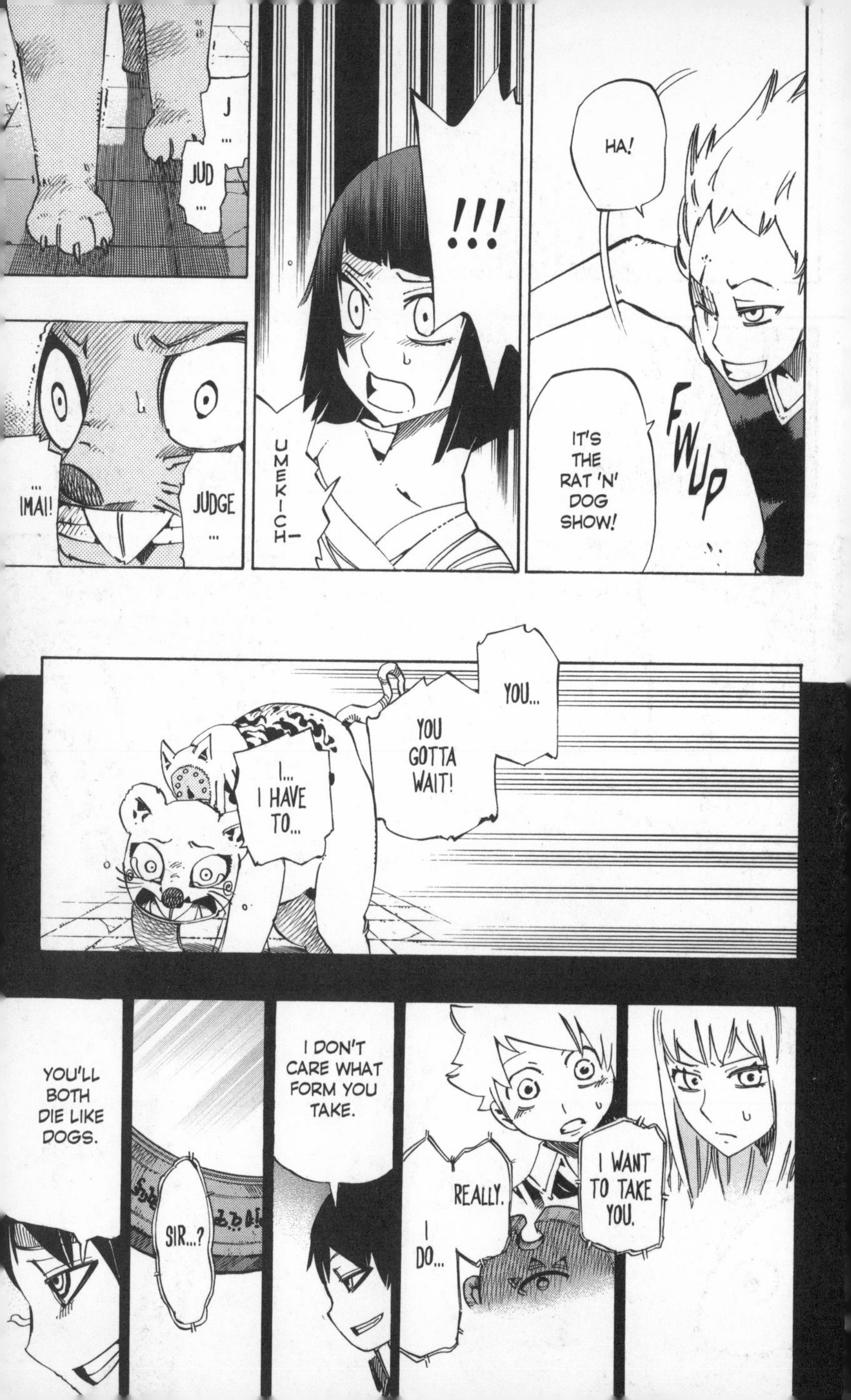
HA!
IT'S THE RAT 'N' DOG SHOW!
FWUP
!!!
UMEKICH—
J...
JUD...
JUDGE...
...IMAI!
YOU...
YOU GOTTA WAIT!
I... I HAVE TO...
I WANT TO TAKE YOU.
REALLY.
I DO...
I DON'T CARE WHAT FORM YOU TAKE.
SIR...?
YOU'LL BOTH DIE LIKE DOGS.

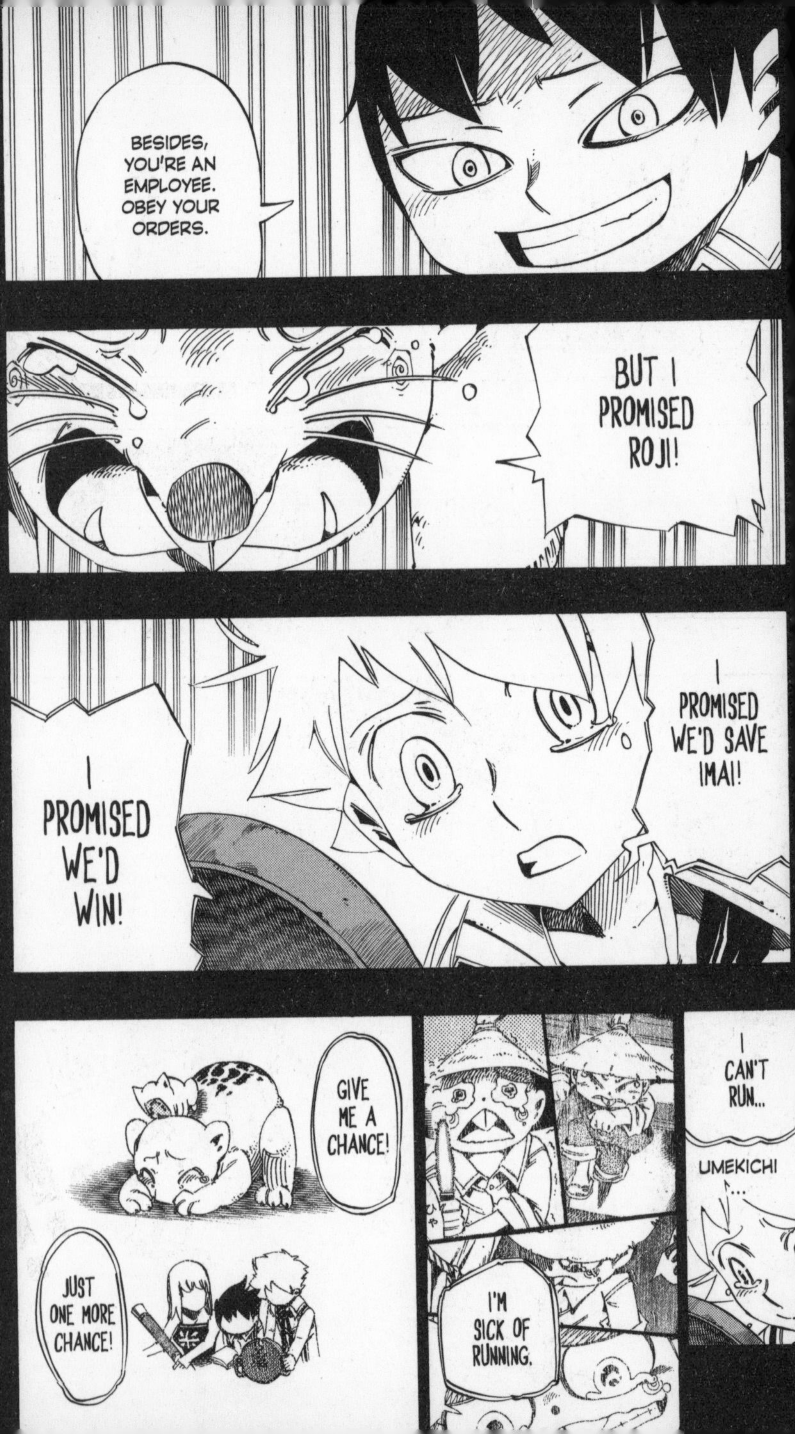
BESIDES, YOU'RE AN EMPLOYEE. OBEY YOUR ORDERS.
BUT I PROMISED ROJI!
I PROMISED WE'D SAVE IMAI!
I PROMISED WE'D WIN!
I CAN'T RUN...
UMEKICHI...
I'M SICK OF RUNNING.
GIVE ME A CHANCE!
JUST ONE MORE CHANCE!

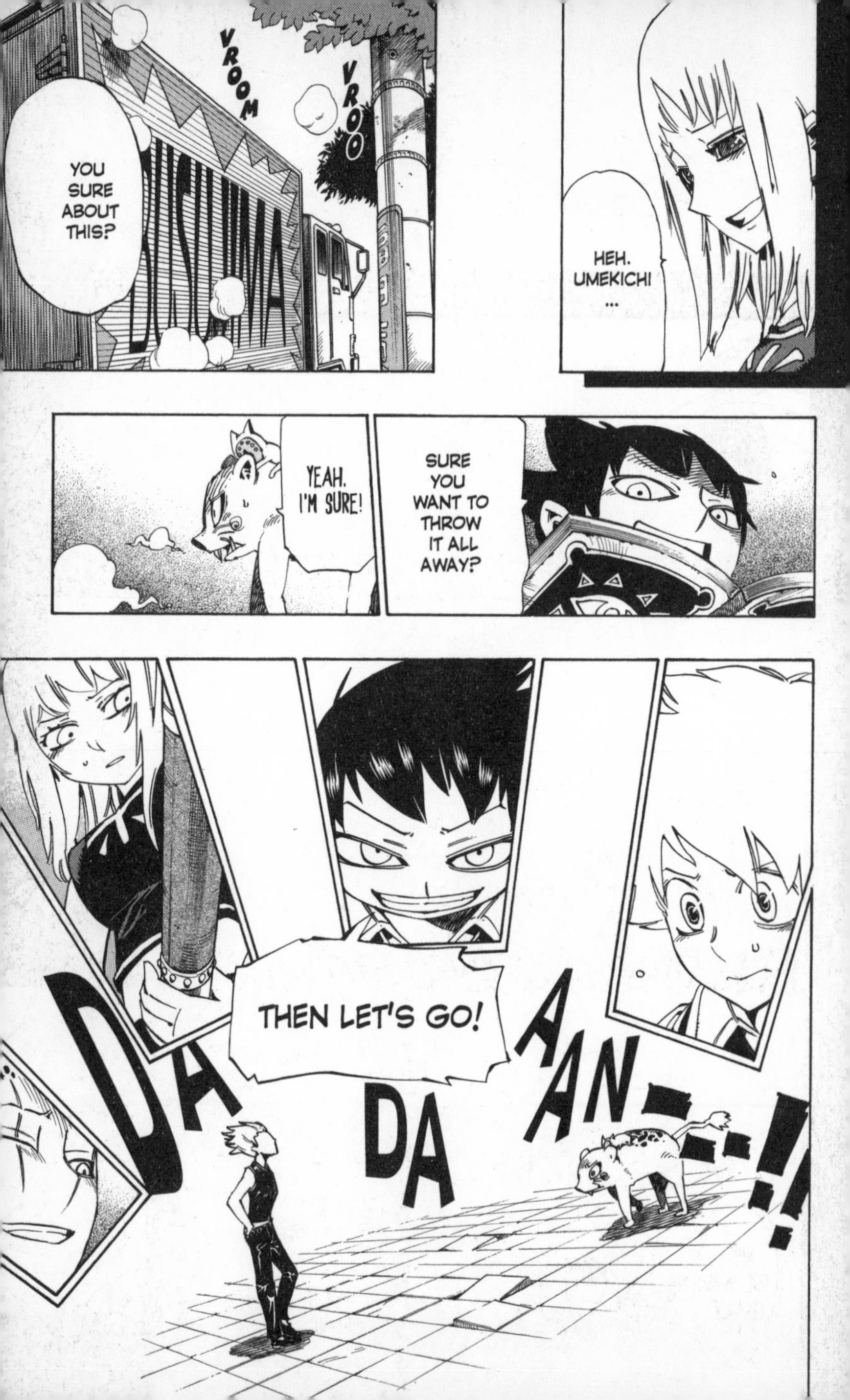
HEH. UMEKICHI ...
VROOM
VROO
YOU SURE ABOUT THIS?
SURE YOU WANT TO THROW IT ALL AWAY?
YEAH. I'M SURE!
THEN LET'S GO!
DA DA AAN--!!

Q: WHAT DOES NANA WEAR WHEN SHE'S NOT IN UNIFORM?

-H.I., TOKUSHIMA PREFECTURE

A: I ALWAYS THINK I'M GOING TO GET A CHANCE TO DRAW HER IN HER OWN CLOTHES, AND THEN I ALWAYS END UP FORGETTING... SHE'S BEEN IN HER SCHOOL UNIFORM THE WHOLE TIME, HASN'T SHE? I'M GUESSING SHE'S PRETTY FRUGAL, IN ANY CASE. SHE PROBABLY WEARS HER GRANDMA'S OLD STUFF OR SOMETHING FROM A FLEA MARKET WHEN SHE'S AT HOME.

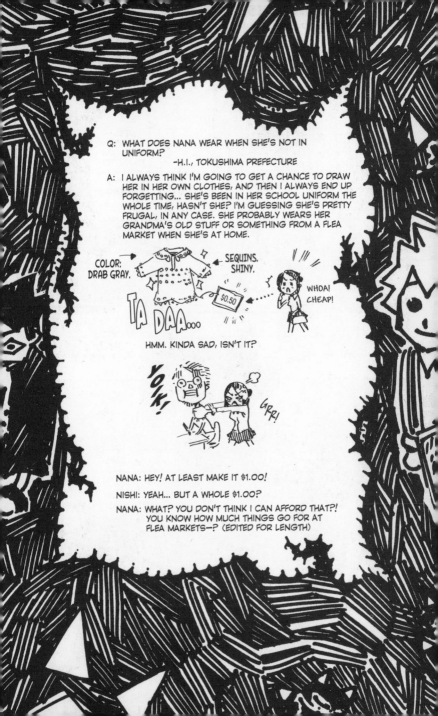

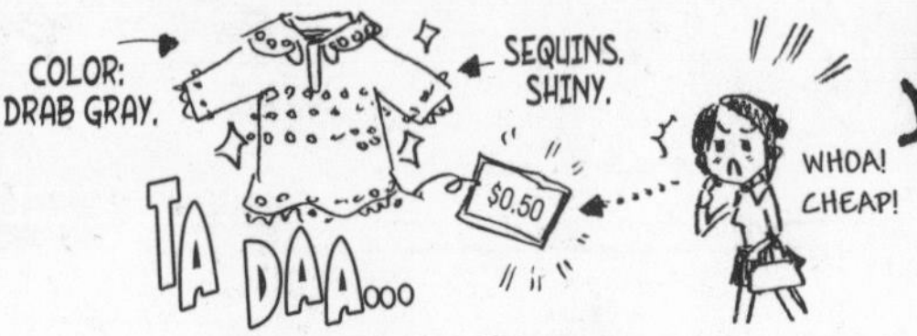
COLOR: DRAB GRAY.
SEQUINS. SHINY.
$0.50
TA DAA...
WHOA! CHEAP!

HMM. KINDA SAD, ISN'T IT?

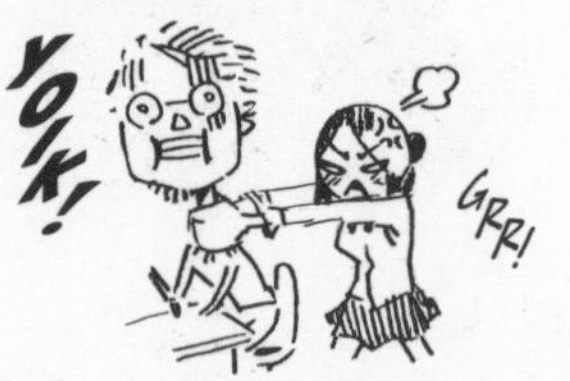
YOIK!
GRR!

NANA: HEY! AT LEAST MAKE IT $1.00!

NISHI: YEAH... BUT A WHOLE $1.00?

NANA: WHAT? YOU DON'T THINK I CAN AFFORD THAT?! YOU KNOW HOW MUCH THINGS GO FOR AT FLEA MARKETS—? (EDITED FOR LENGTH)

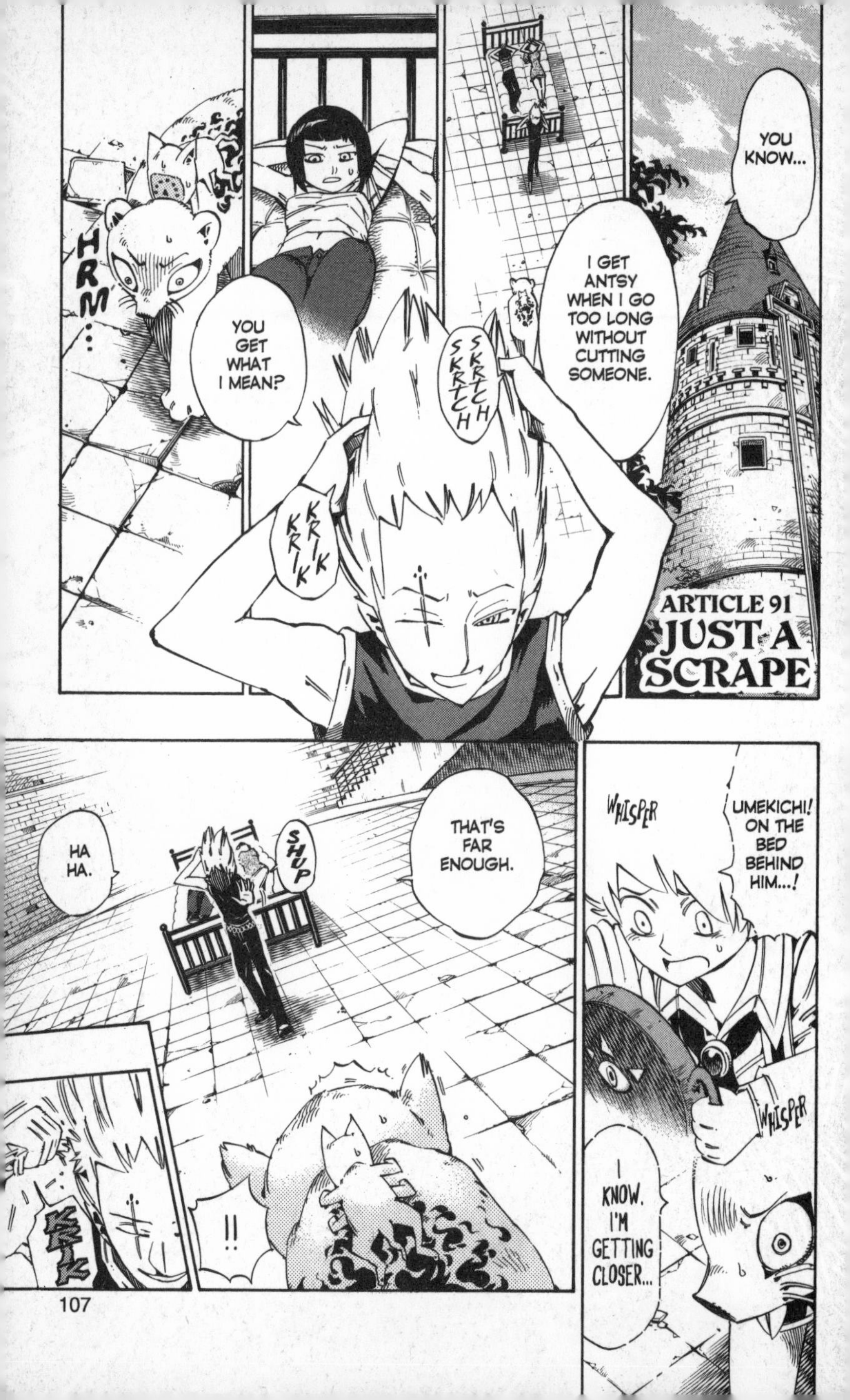
YOU KNOW...
I GET ANTSY WHEN I GO TOO LONG WITHOUT CUTTING SOMEONE.
ARTICLE 91
JUST A SCRAPE
HRM...
SKRTCH SKRTCH
YOU GET WHAT I MEAN?
KRIK KRIK
WHISPER
UMEKICHI! ON THE BED BEHIND HIM...!
WHISPER
I KNOW. I'M GETTING CLOSER...
THAT'S FAR ENOUGH.
SHUP
HA HA.
!!
KRIK

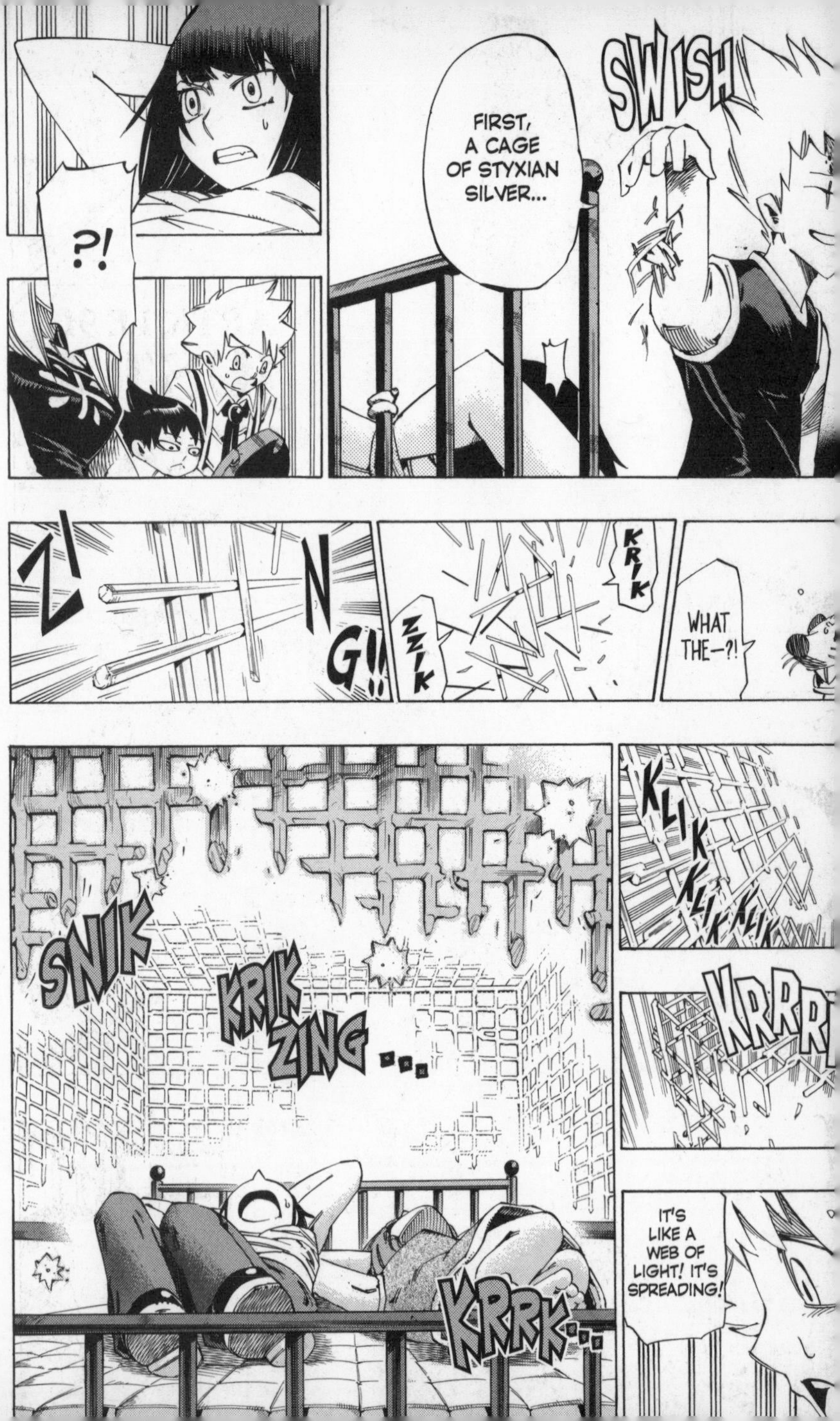
SWISH
FIRST, A CAGE OF STYXIAN SILVER...
?!
WHAT THE—?!
KRIK
ZZIK
ZNG!!
KLIK KLIK KLIK KLIK
KRRR
IT'S LIKE A WEB OF LIGHT! IT'S SPREADING!
KRIK ZING...
SNIK
KRRK...

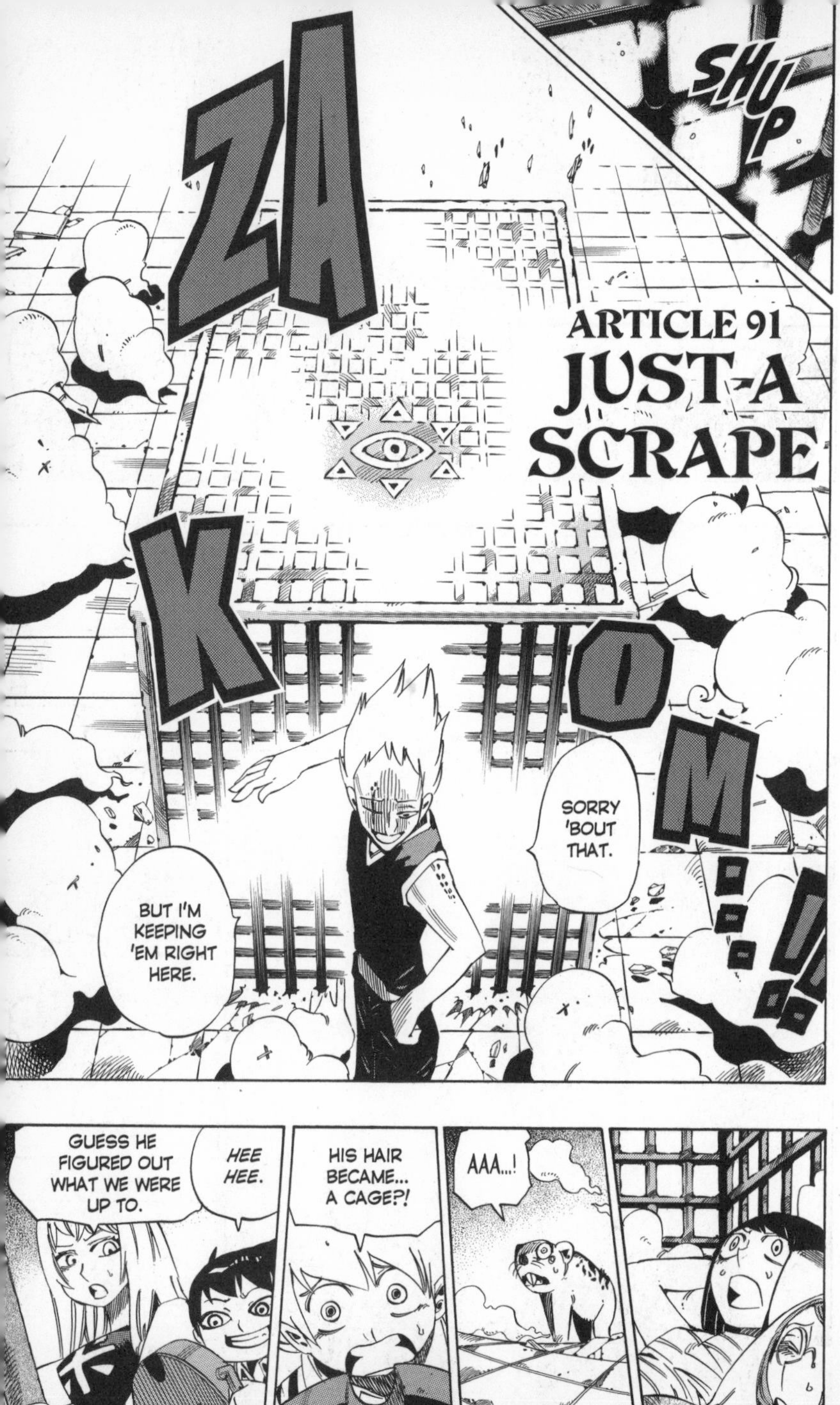
SHUP
ZAKOM!!
ARTICLE 91
JUST A SCRAPE
SORRY 'BOUT THAT.
BUT I'M KEEPING 'EM RIGHT HERE.
AAA...!
HIS HAIR BECAME... A CAGE?!
HEE HEE.
GUESS HE FIGURED OUT WHAT WE WERE UP TO.

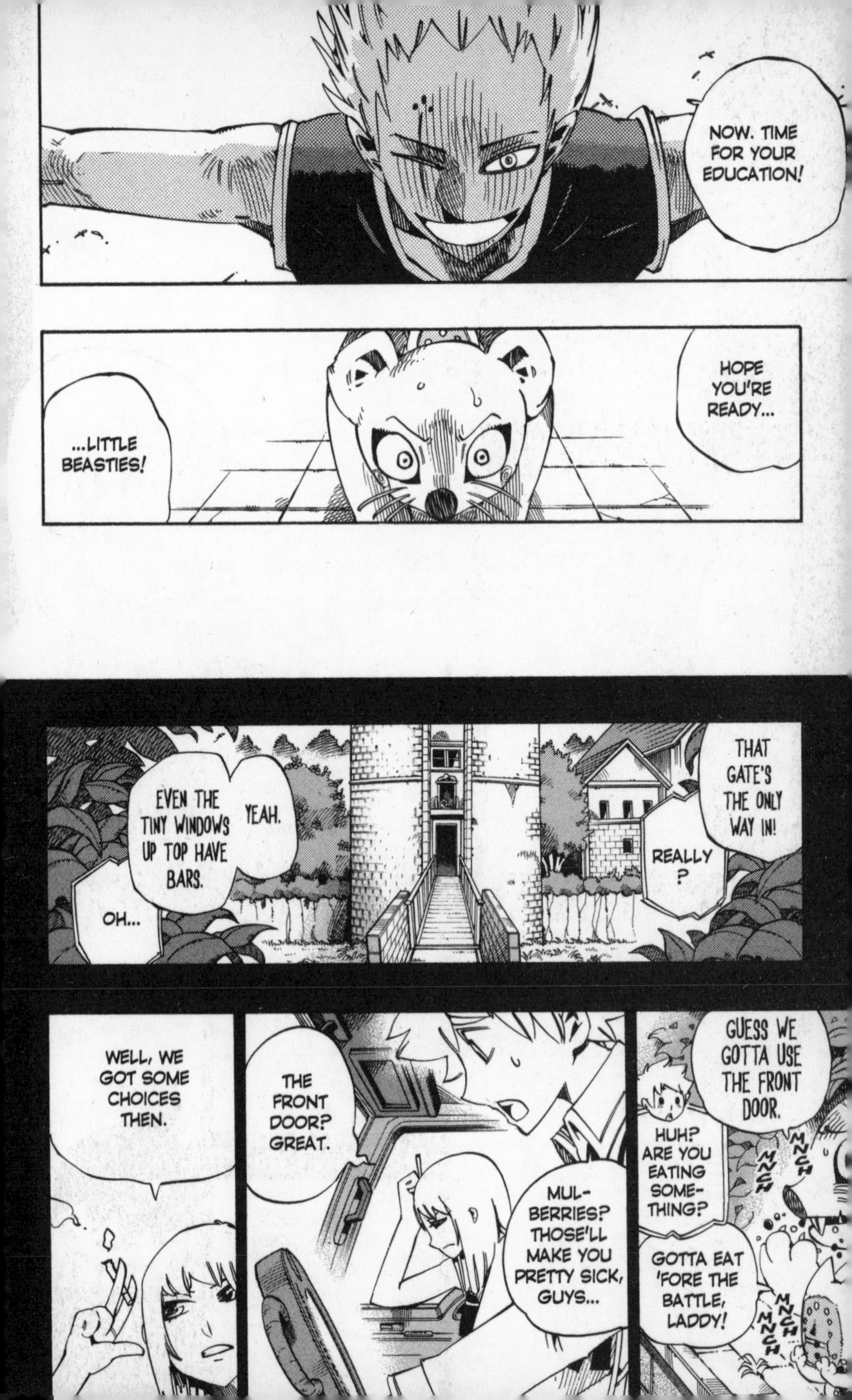
NOW. TIME FOR YOUR EDUCATION!
HOPE YOU'RE READY...
...LITTLE BEASTIES!
THAT GATE'S THE ONLY WAY IN!
REALLY?
YEAH.
EVEN THE TINY WINDOWS UP TOP HAVE BARS.
OH...
GUESS WE GOTTA USE THE FRONT DOOR.
MNCH MNCH
HUH? ARE YOU EATING SOMETHING?
GOTTA EAT 'FORE THE BATTLE, LADDY!
MNCH MNCH
THE FRONT DOOR? GREAT.
MUL-BERRIES? THOSE'LL MAKE YOU PRETTY SICK, GUYS...
WELL, WE GOT SOME CHOICES THEN.

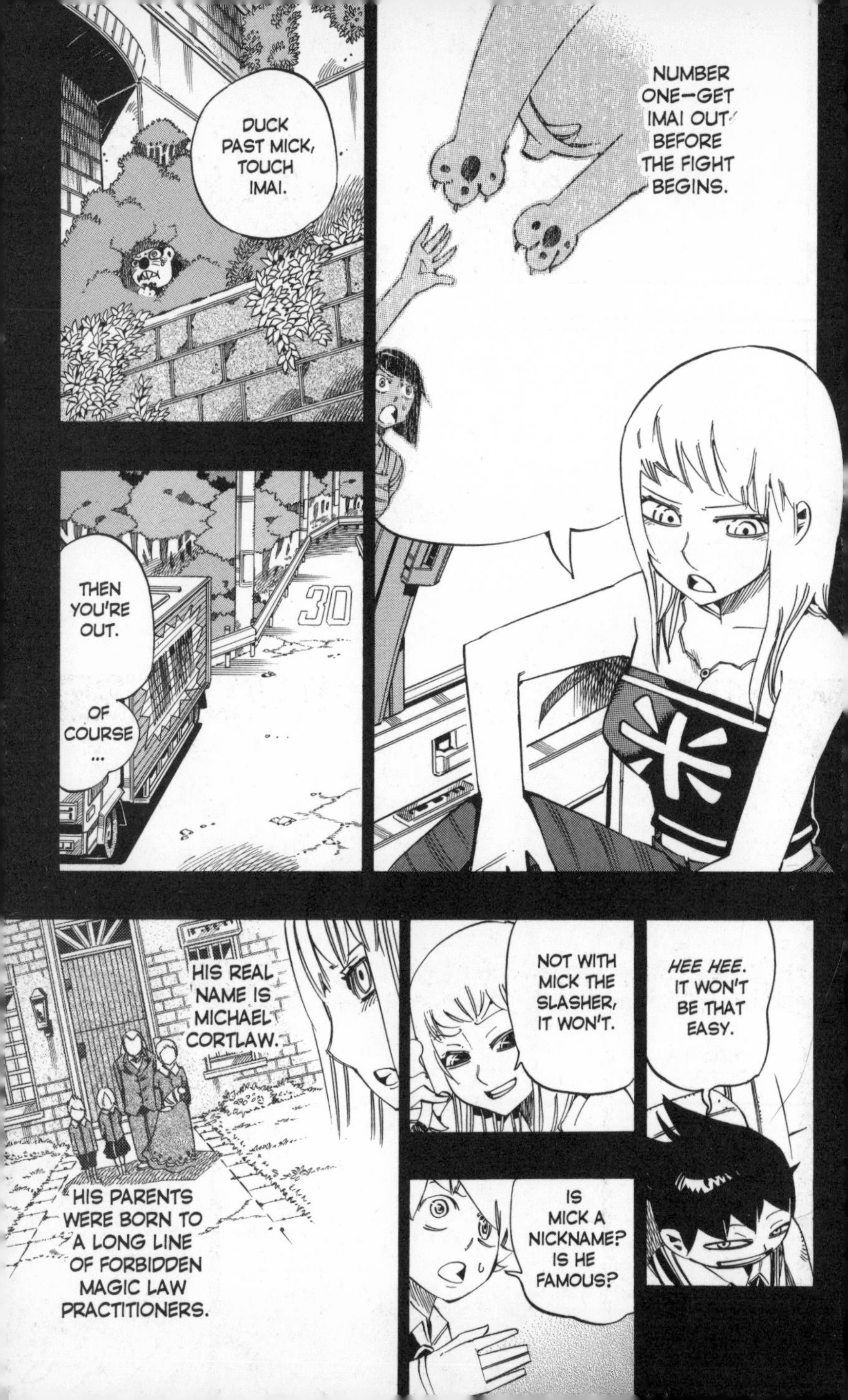
NUMBER ONE—GET IMAI OUT BEFORE THE FIGHT BEGINS.
DUCK PAST MICK, TOUCH IMAI.
THEN YOU'RE OUT.
OF COURSE ...
HEE HEE. IT WON'T BE THAT EASY.
NOT WITH MICK THE SLASHER, IT WON'T.
IS MICK A NICKNAME? IS HE FAMOUS?
HIS REAL NAME IS MICHAEL CORTLAW.
HIS PARENTS WERE BORN TO A LONG LINE OF FORBIDDEN MAGIC LAW PRACTITIONERS.

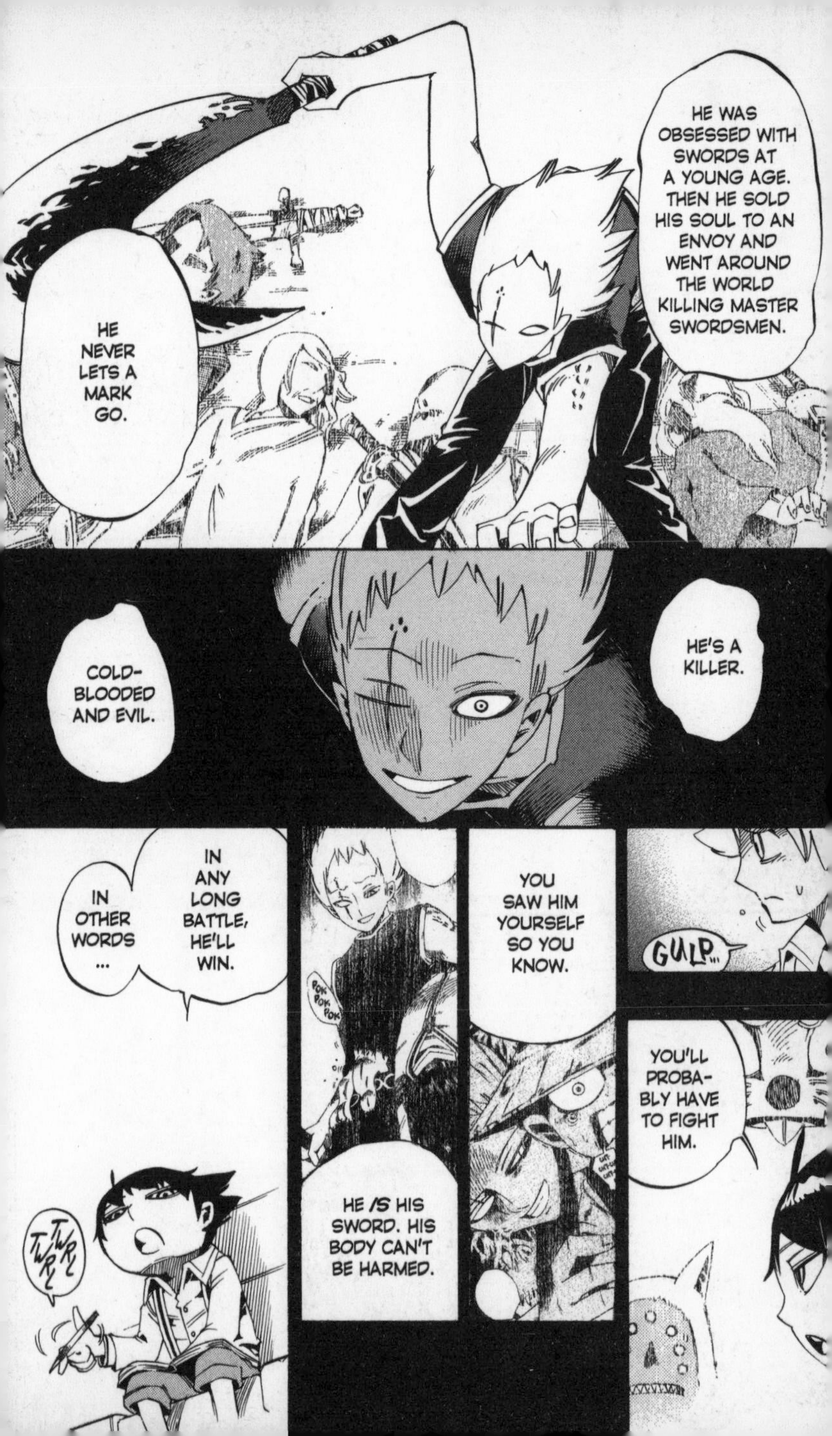
HE WAS OBSESSED WITH SWORDS AT A YOUNG AGE. THEN HE SOLD HIS SOUL TO AN ENVOY AND WENT AROUND THE WORLD KILLING MASTER SWORDSMEN.
HE NEVER LETS A MARK GO.
HE'S A KILLER.
COLD-BLOODED AND EVIL.
GULP...
YOU SAW HIM YOURSELF SO YOU KNOW.
POK POK POK
HE IS HIS SWORD. HIS BODY CAN'T BE HARMED.
YOU'LL PROBA-BLY HAVE TO FIGHT HIM.
IN ANY LONG BATTLE, HE'LL WIN.
IN OTHER WORDS ...
TWRL TWRL

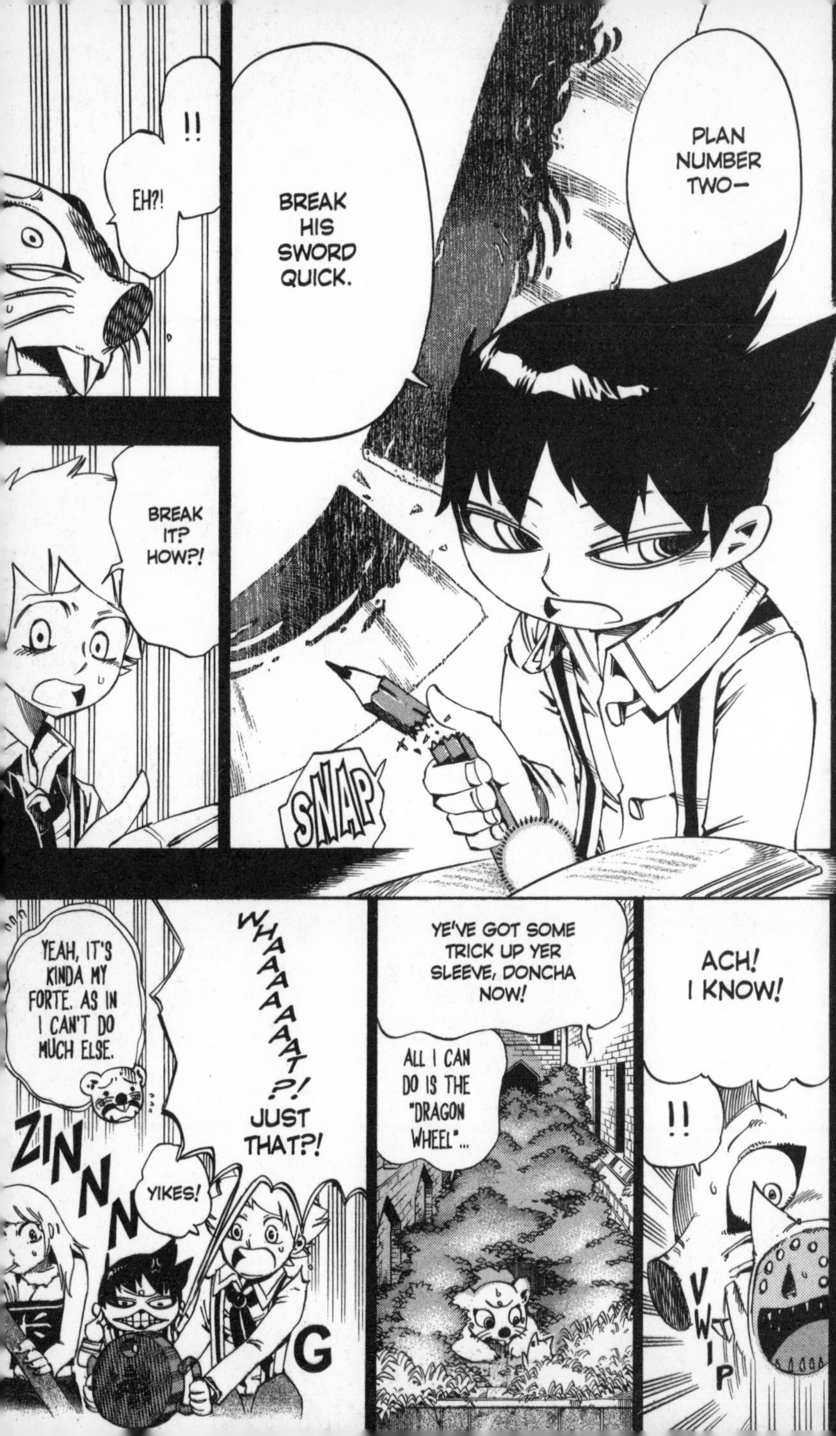
PLAN NUMBER TWO—
BREAK HIS SWORD QUICK.
SNAP
!!
EH?!
BREAK IT? HOW?!
ACH! I KNOW!
!!
VWIP
YE'VE GOT SOME TRICK UP YER SLEEVE, DONCHA NOW!
ALL I CAN DO IS THE "DRAGON WHEEL"...
WHAAAAAAAT?! JUST THAT?!
YEAH, IT'S KINDA MY FORTE. AS IN I CAN'T DO MUCH ELSE.
YIKES!
ZINNNG

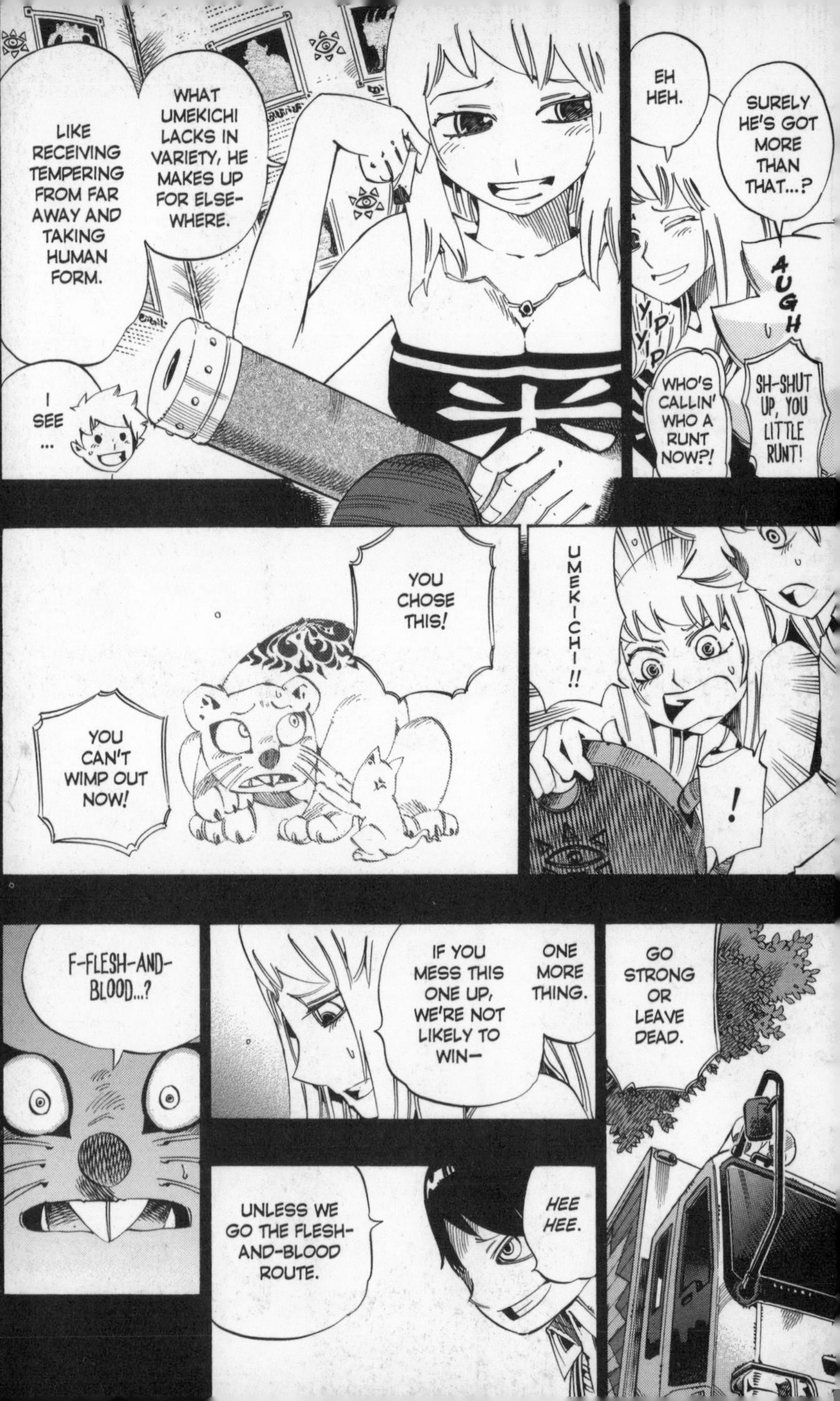
SURELY HE'S GOT MORE THAN THAT...?
EH HEH.
AUGH
SH-SHUT UP, YOU LITTLE RUNT!
YIP YIP
WHO'S CALLIN' WHO A RUNT NOW?!
WHAT UMEKICHI LACKS IN VARIETY, HE MAKES UP FOR ELSE-WHERE.
LIKE RECEIVING TEMPERING FROM FAR AWAY AND TAKING HUMAN FORM.
I SEE...
UMEKICHI!!
!
YOU CHOSE THIS!
YOU CAN'T WIMP OUT NOW!
GO STRONG OR LEAVE DEAD.
ONE MORE THING.
IF YOU MESS THIS ONE UP, WE'RE NOT LIKELY TO WIN—
HEE HEE.
UNLESS WE GO THE FLESH-AND-BLOOD ROUTE.
F-FLESH-AND-BLOOD...?

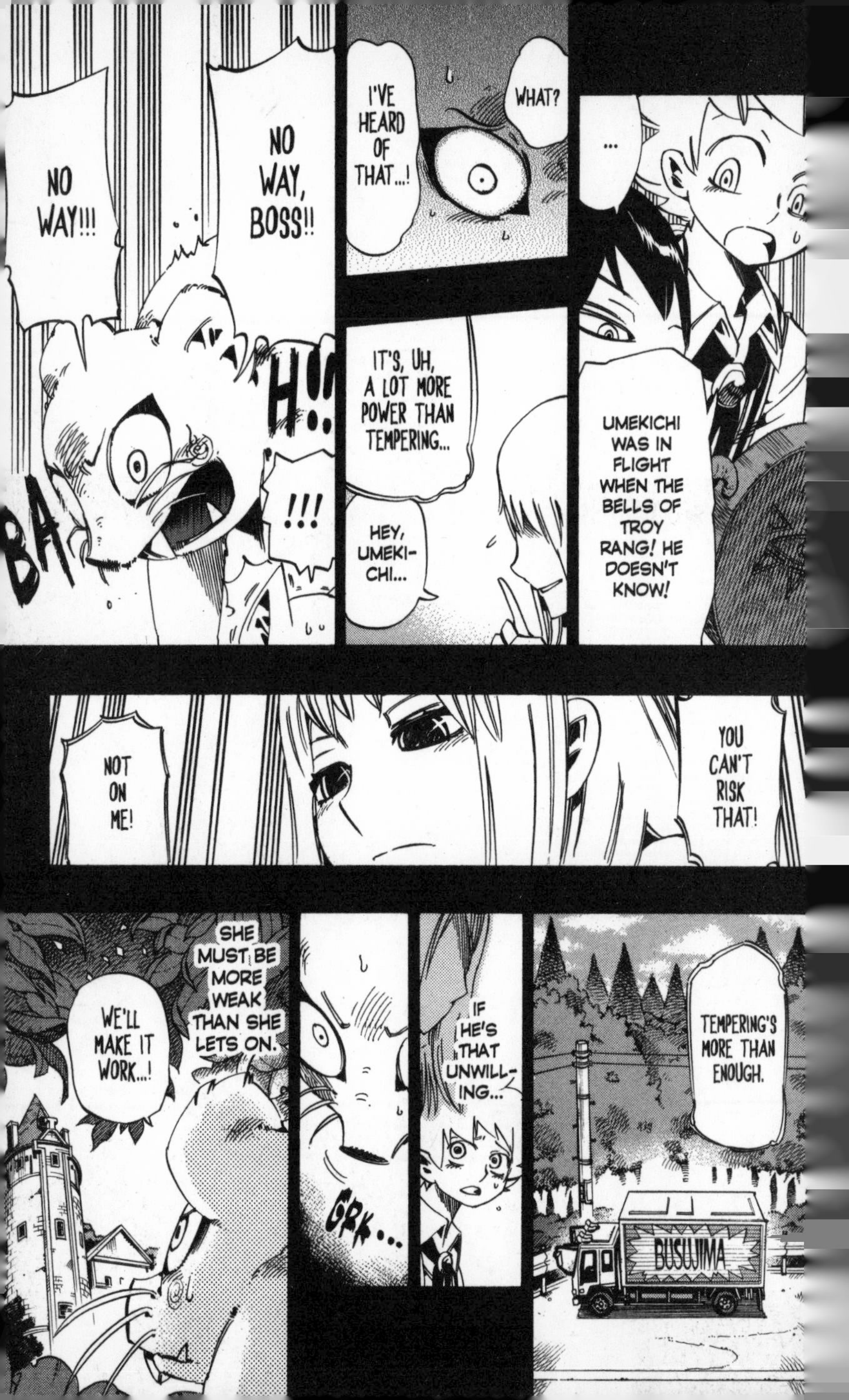
...
UMEKICHI WAS IN FLIGHT WHEN THE BELLS OF TROY RANG! HE DOESN'T KNOW!
WHAT?
I'VE HEARD OF THAT...!
IT'S, UH, A LOT MORE POWER THAN TEMPERING...
HEY, UMEKI-CHI...
NO WAY, BOSS!!
NO WAY!!!
BAH!!
!!!
YOU CAN'T RISK THAT!
NOT ON ME!
TEMPERING'S MORE THAN ENOUGH.
BUSUJIMA
IF HE'S THAT UNWILL-ING...
GRK...
SHE MUST BE MORE WEAK THAN SHE LETS ON.
WE'LL MAKE IT WORK...!

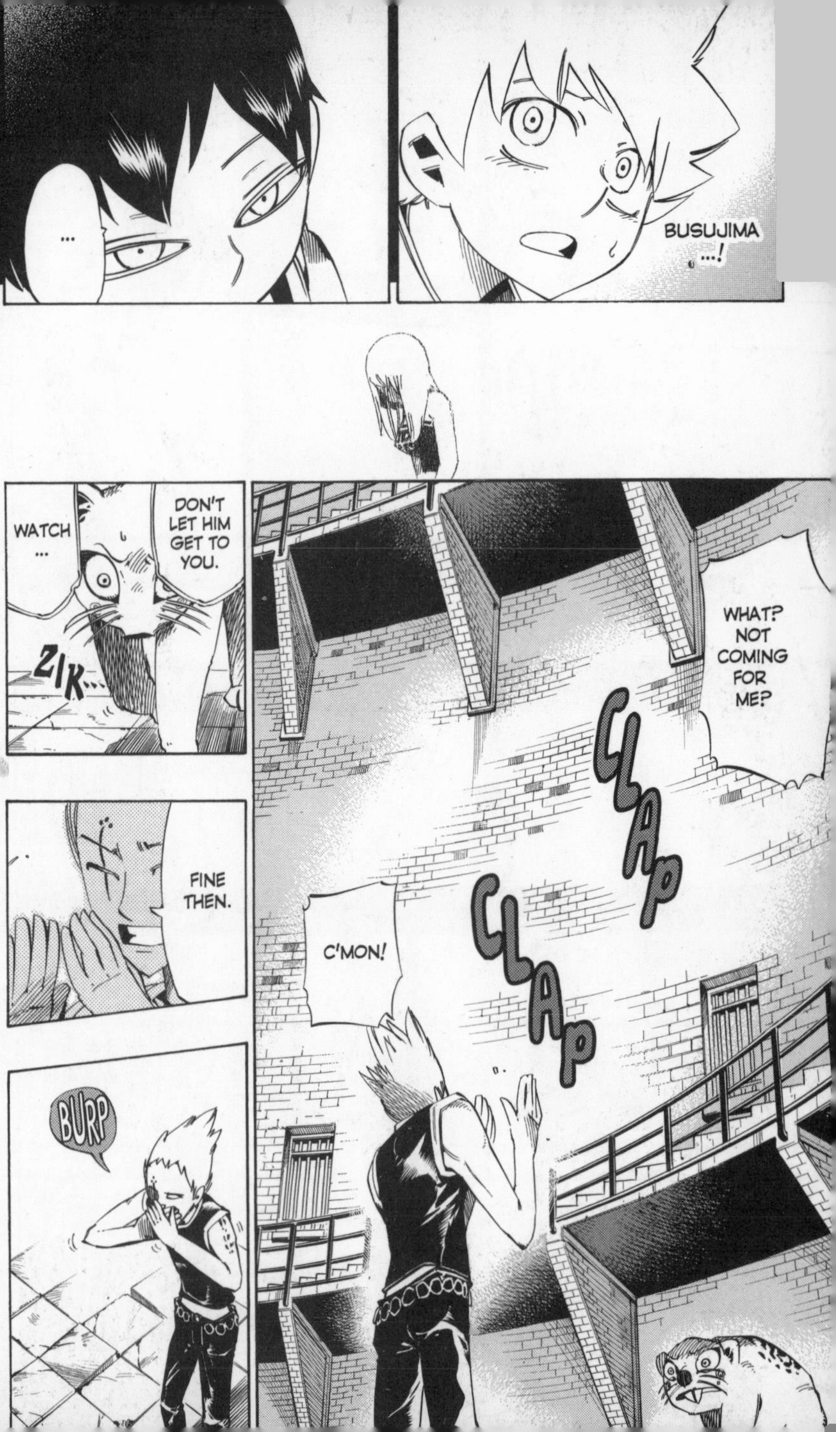

BUSUJIMA ...!
...
WHAT? NOT COMING FOR ME?
CLAP
CLAP
C'MON!
DON'T LET HIM GET TO YOU.
WATCH ...
ZIK...
FINE THEN.
BURP

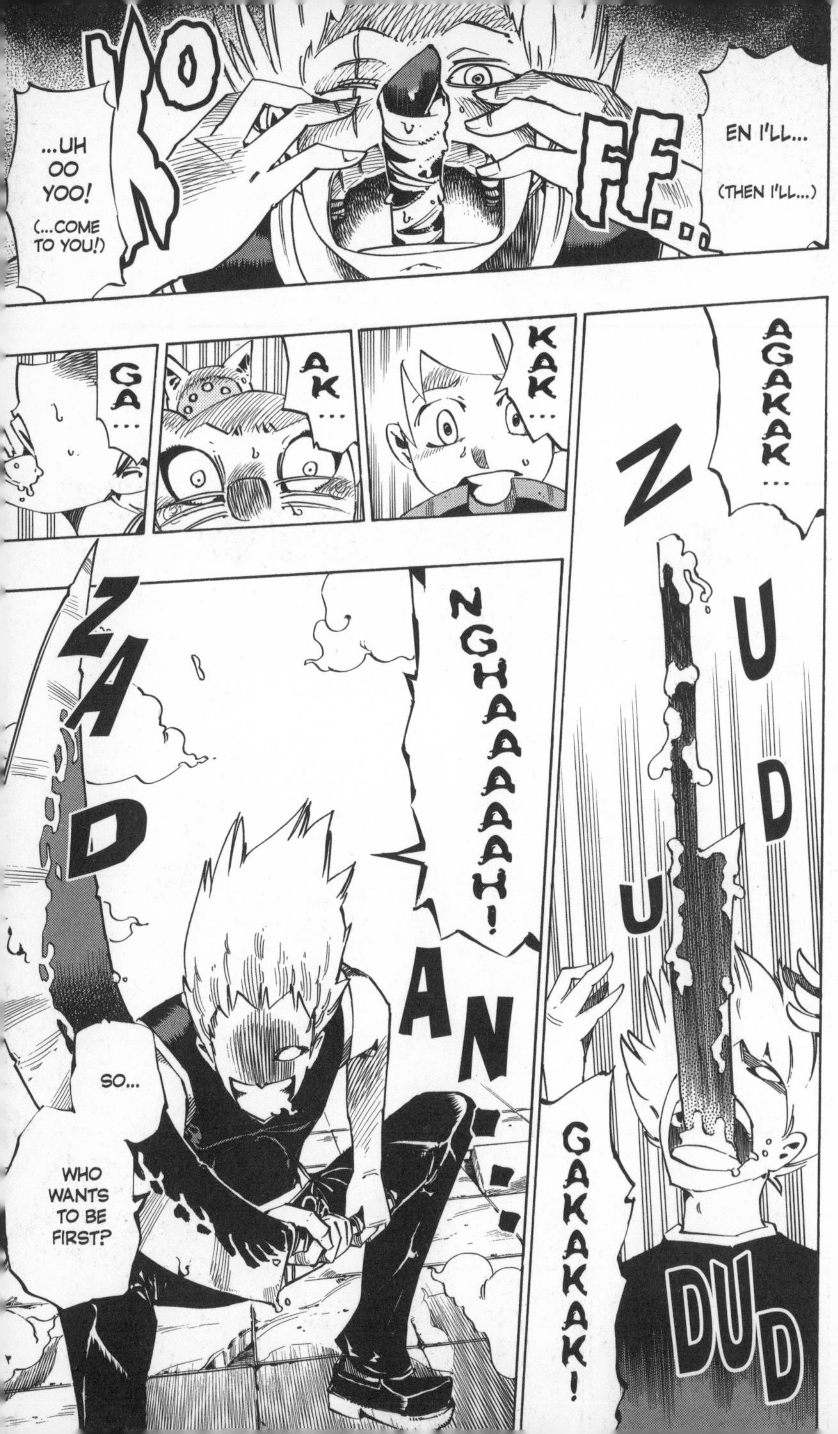
EN I'LL...
(THEN I'LL...)
KOFF...
...UH OO YOO!
(...COME TO YOU!)
AGAKAK...
ZUUD
GAKAKAK!
DUD
KAK...
AK...
GA...
NGHAAAAAAAH!
ZADAN..
SO...
WHO WANTS TO BE FIRST?

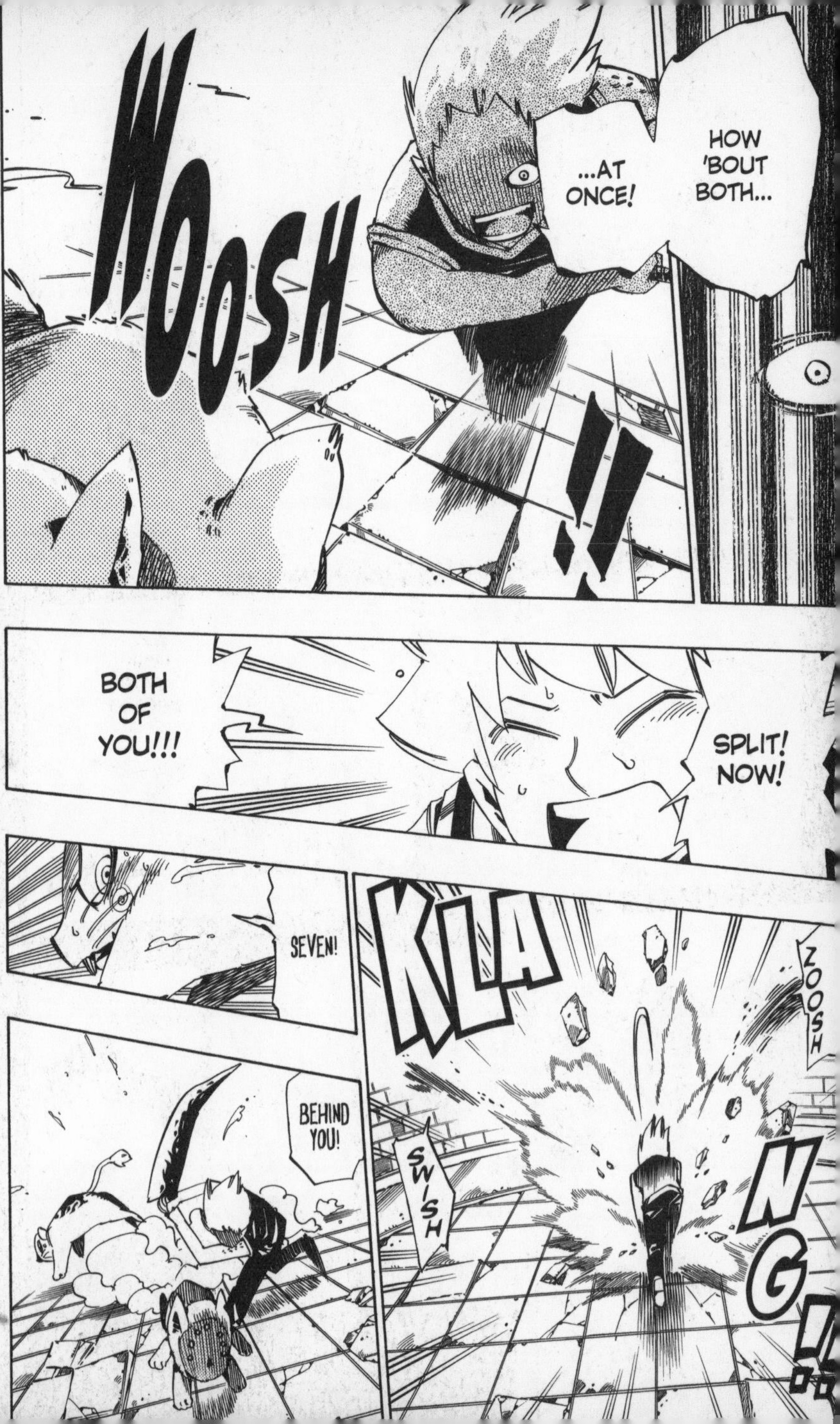
HOW 'BOUT BOTH...
...AT ONCE!
WOOSH
!!
SPLIT! NOW!
BOTH OF YOU!!!
KLANG!!
ZOOSH
SWISH
SEVEN!
BEHIND YOU!

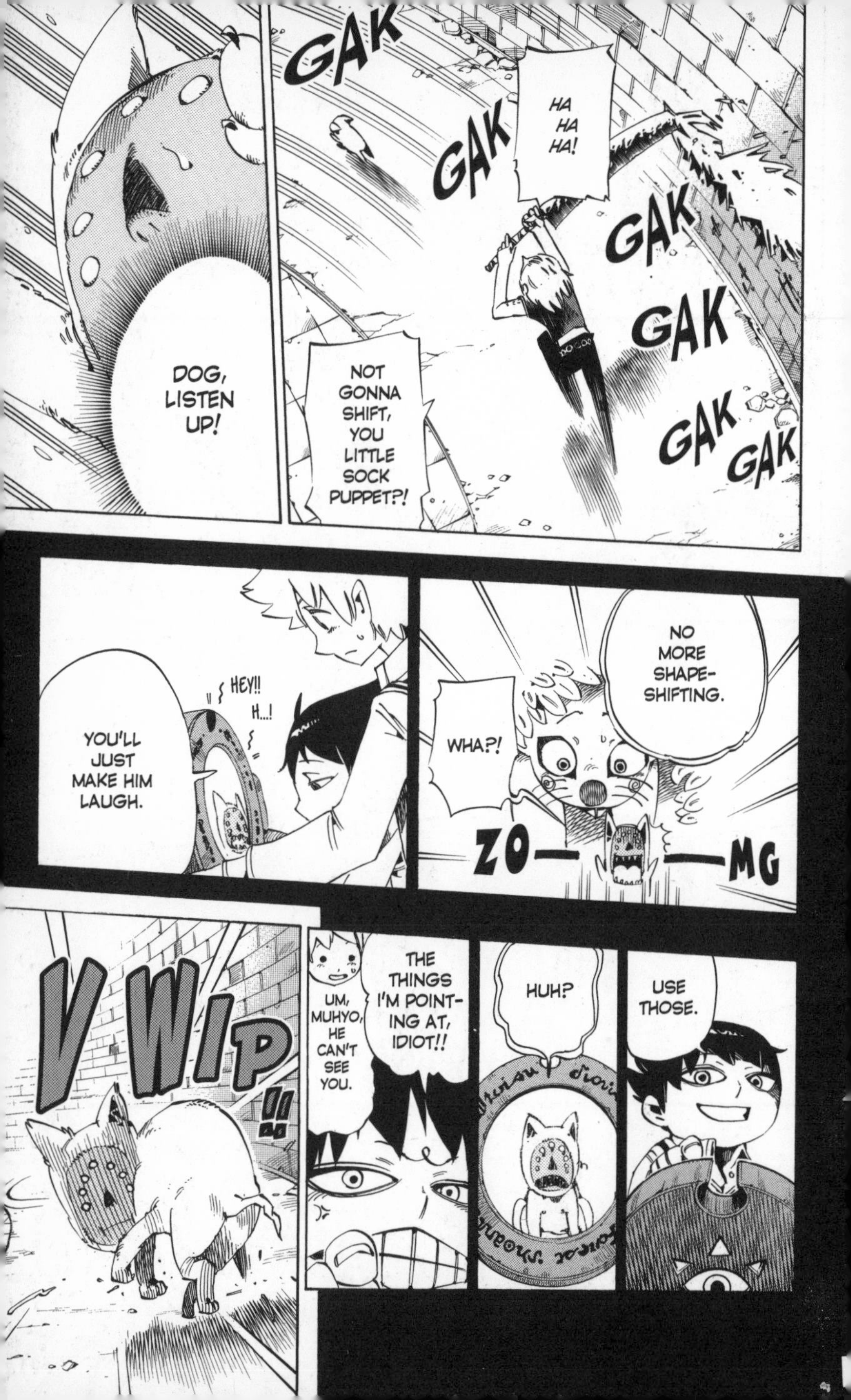
GAK
GAK
HA HA HA!
GAK
GAK
GAK
GAK
NOT GONNA SHIFT, YOU LITTLE SOCK PUPPET?!
DOG, LISTEN UP!
NO MORE SHAPE-SHIFTING.
WHA?!
ZO— —MG
HEY!!
H...!
YOU'LL JUST MAKE HIM LAUGH.
USE THOSE.
HUH?
THE THINGS I'M POINTING AT, IDIOT!!
UM, MUHYO, HE CAN'T SEE YOU.
V WIP!!

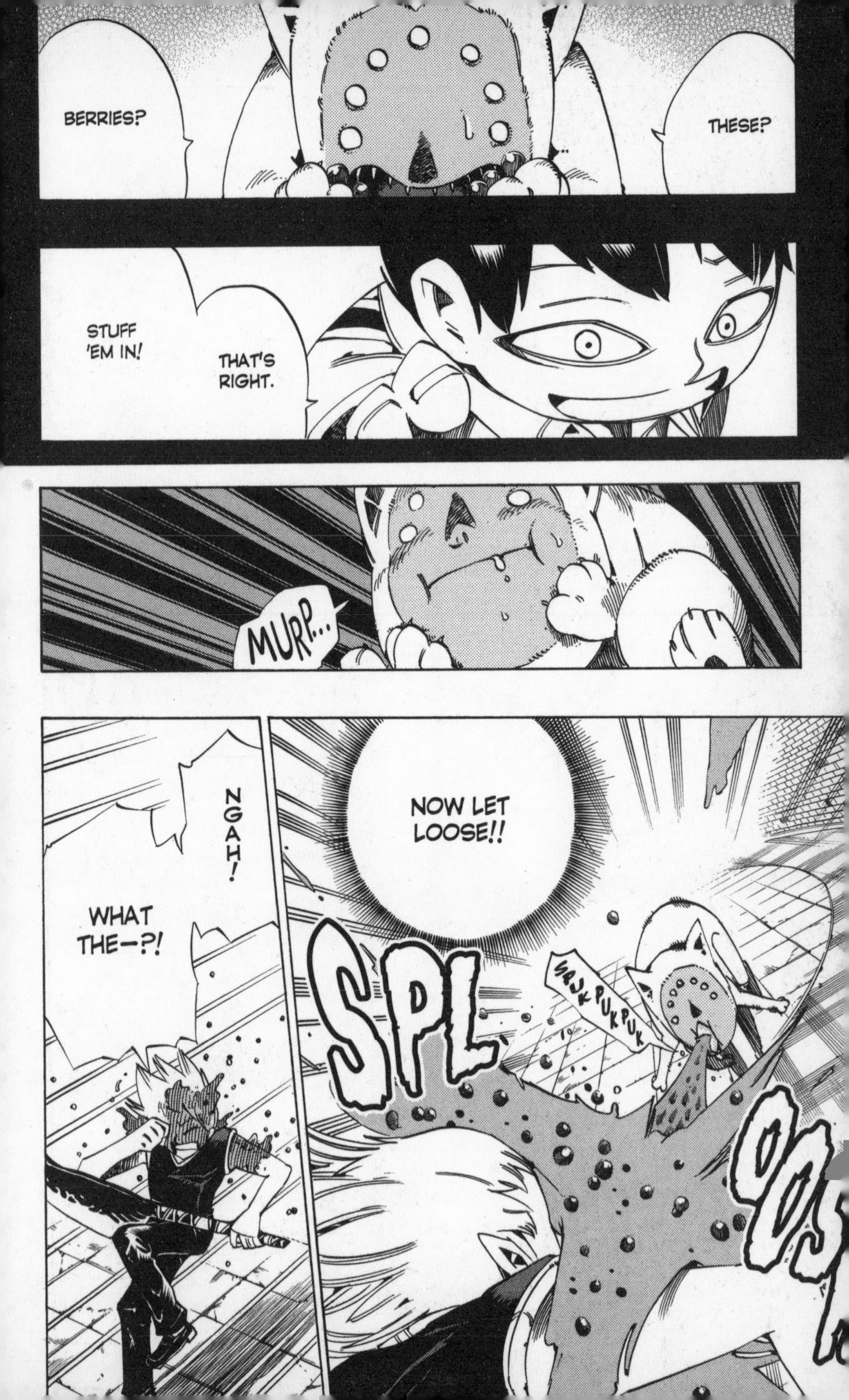
THESE?
BERRIES?
THAT'S RIGHT.
STUFF 'EM IN!
MURP...
NOW LET LOOSE!!
SPL
SPUK PUKPUK
NGAH!
WHAT THE—?!

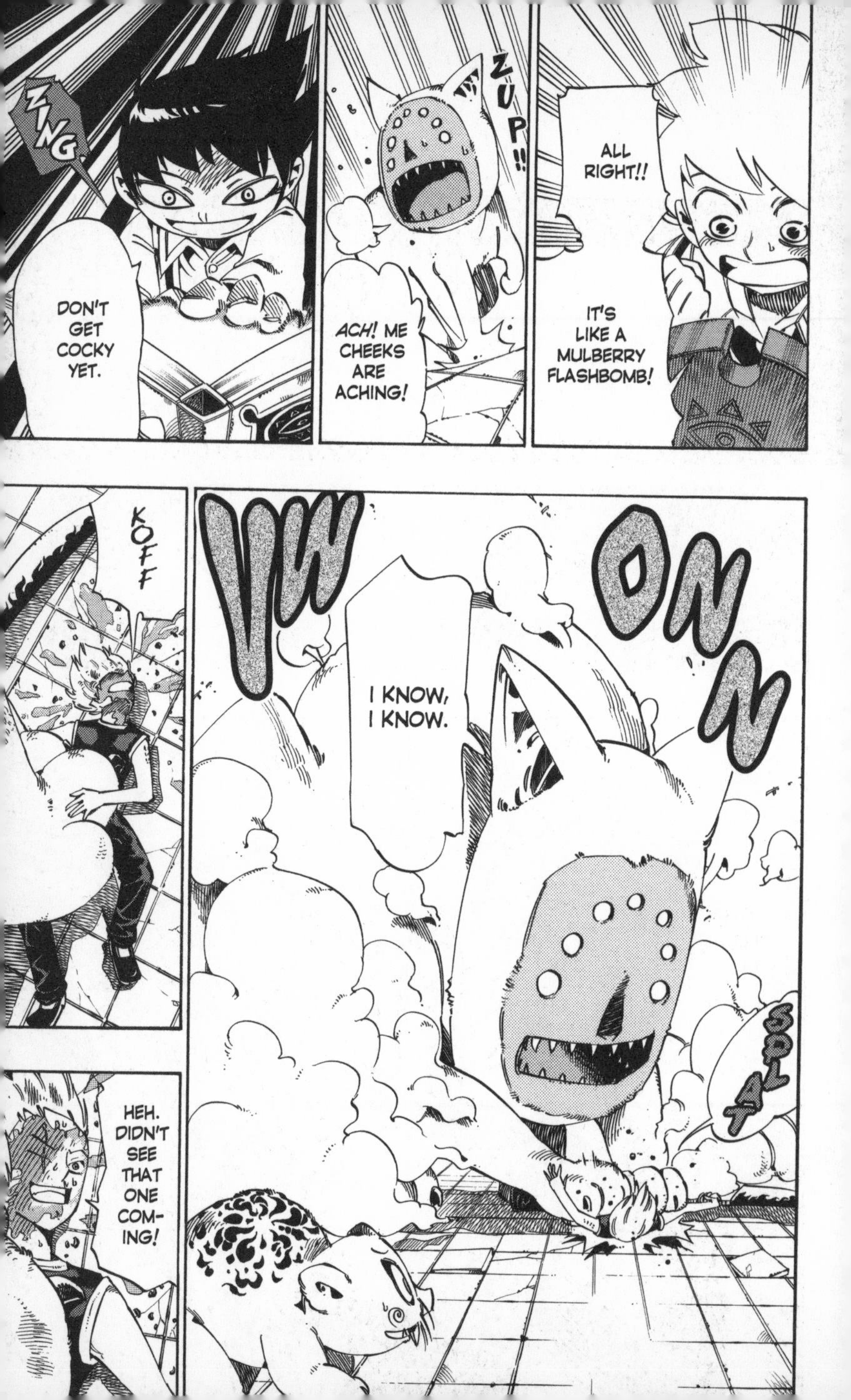
ALL RIGHT!!
IT'S LIKE A MULBERRY FLASHBOMB!
ZUP!!
ACH! ME CHEEKS ARE ACHING!
ZING
DON'T GET COCKY YET.
VWONN
I KNOW, I KNOW.
TAPS
KOFF
HEH. DIDN'T SEE THAT ONE COMING!

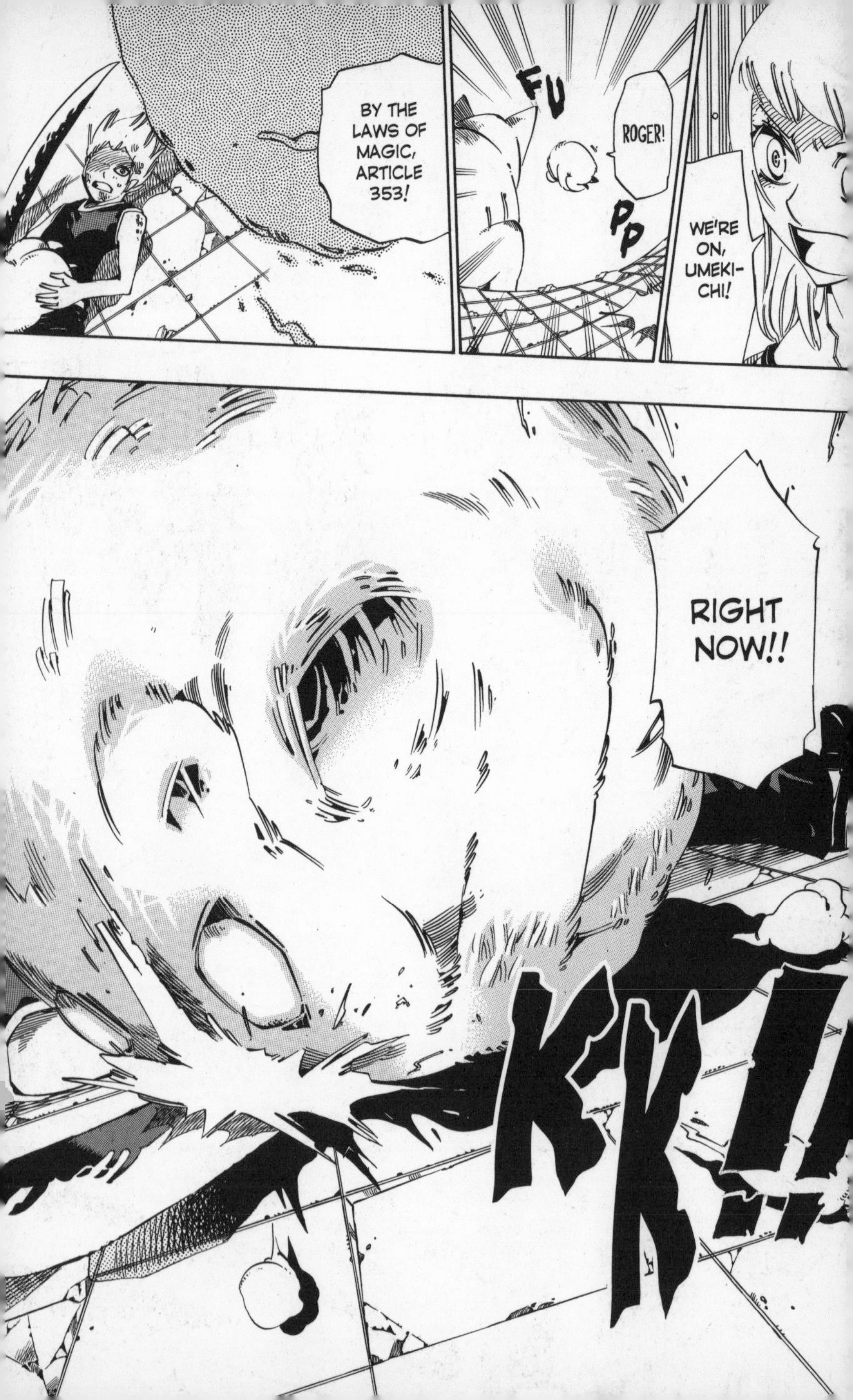
WE'RE ON, UMEKI-CHI!
FU
ROGER!
PP
BY THE LAWS OF MAGIC, ARTICLE 353!
RIGHT NOW!!
KK!!

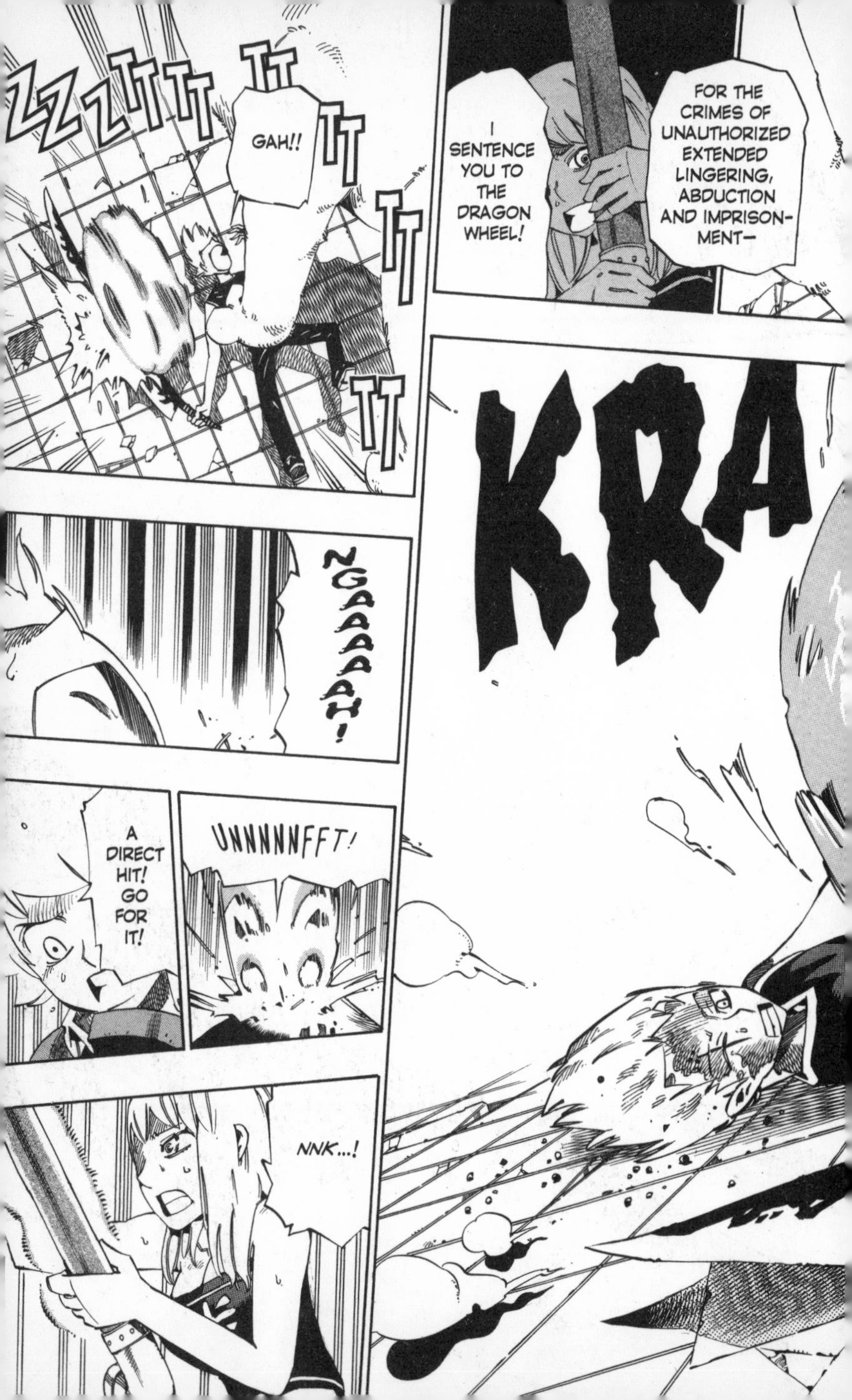
FOR THE CRIMES OF UNAUTHORIZED EXTENDED LINGERING, ABDUCTION AND IMPRISONMENT—
I SENTENCE YOU TO THE DRAGON WHEEL!
KRA
ZZZTTTT TTTTT
GAH!!
NGAAAAAAH!
UNNNNNFFT!
A DIRECT HIT! GO FOR IT!
NNK...!

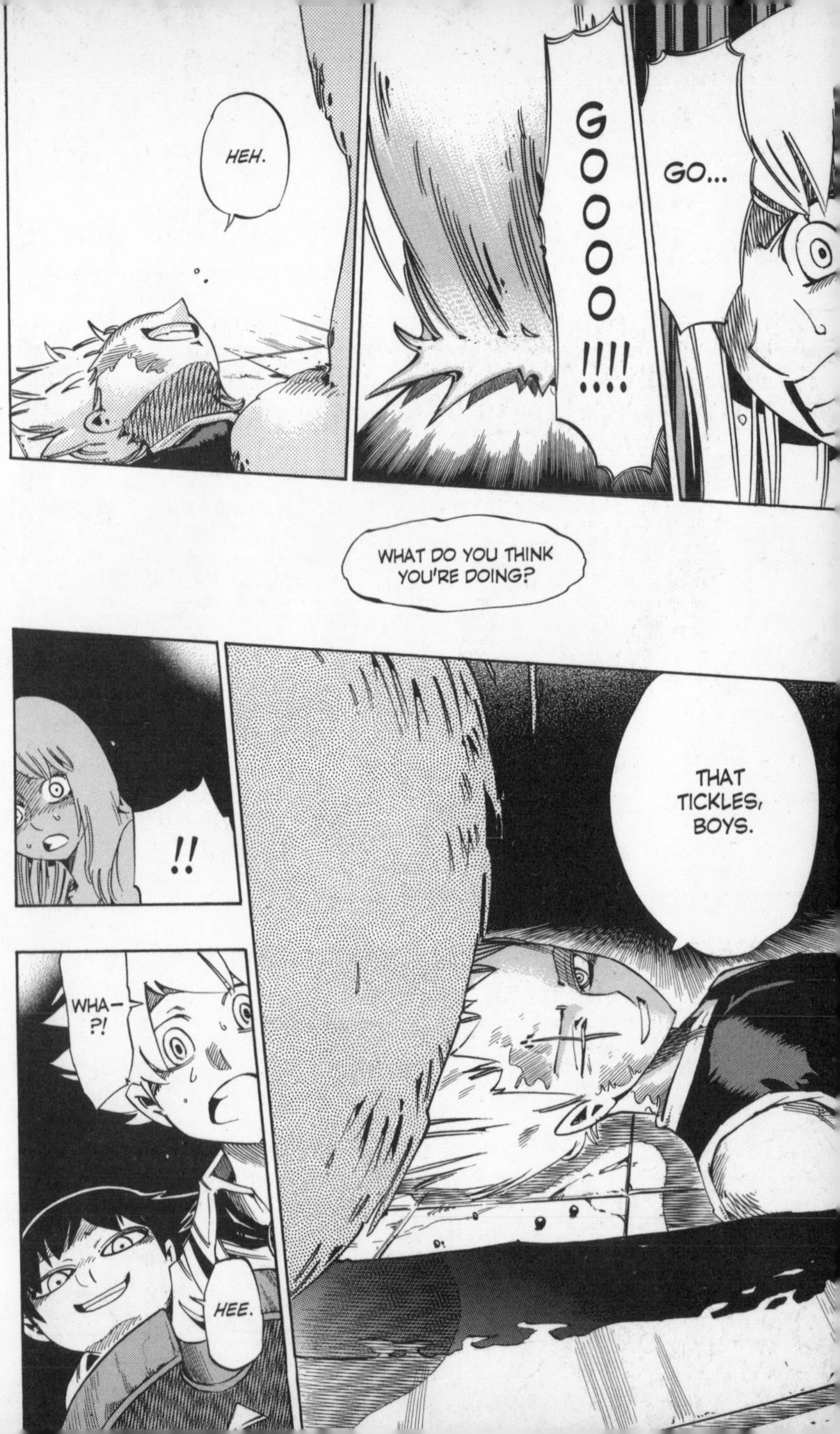
GO...
GOOOO!!!!
HEH.
WHAT DO YOU THINK YOU'RE DOING?
THAT TICKLES, BOYS.
!!
WHA—?!
HEE.

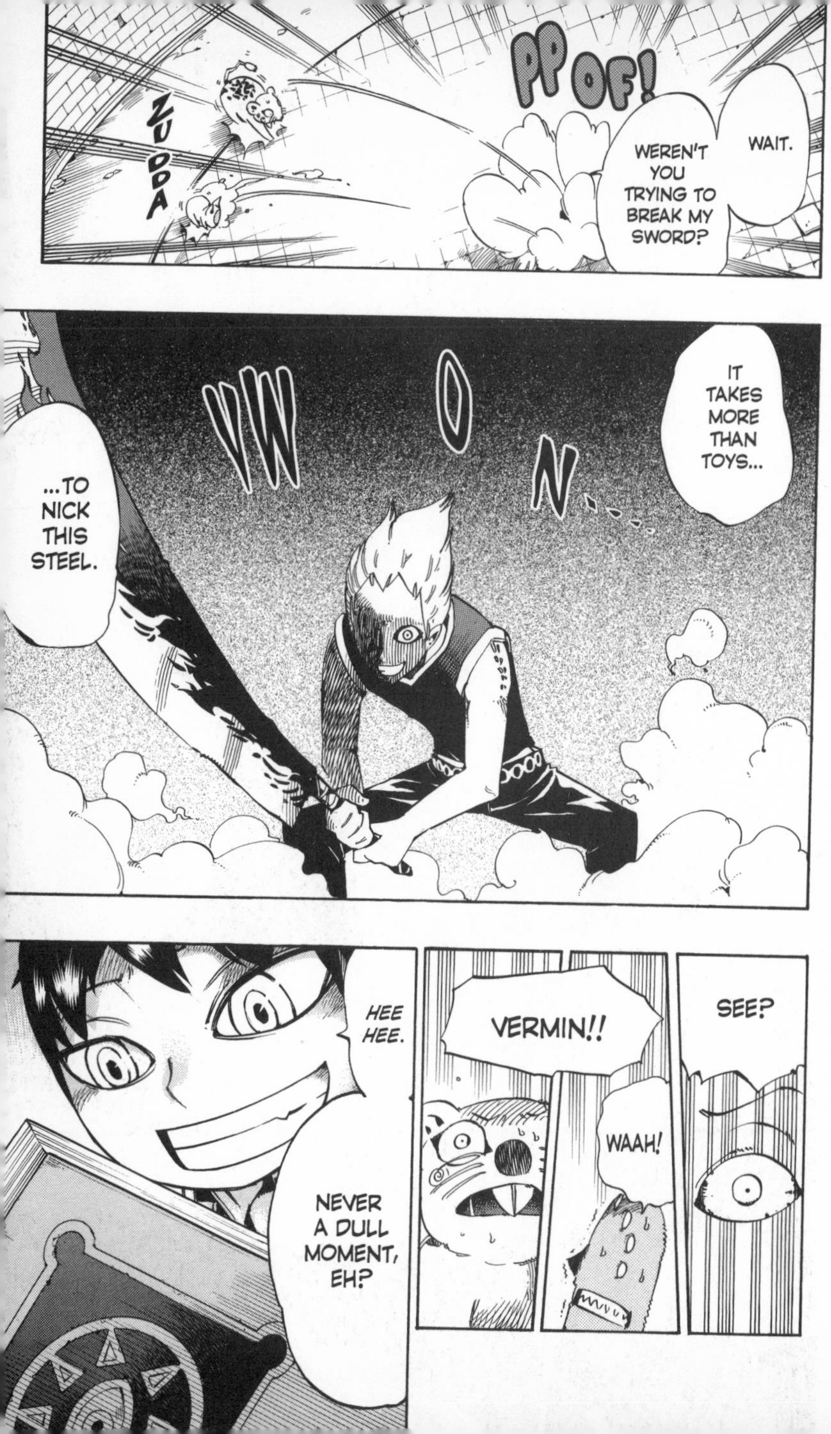
WAIT.
WEREN'T YOU TRYING TO BREAK MY SWORD?
PPOF!
ZUDDA
IT TAKES MORE THAN TOYS...
VWON...
...TO NICK THIS STEEL.
SEE?
VERMIN!!
WAAH!
HEE HEE.
NEVER A DULL MOMENT, EH?

ISABI
BIRTHDAY: UNKNOWN
HEIGHT: 175 CM TO 5 METERS

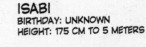

LIKES: SAKE
        FISHING
        GARDENING
        TOYING WITH
          MOUNTAIN SPIRITS

TALENTS: MAKING SAKE IN HIS
            SECRET STILL
          COUNTING CLOUDS
          COUNTING LEAVES

NOT GOOD WITH: SWEET SAKE
                REMEMBERING
                  THINGS

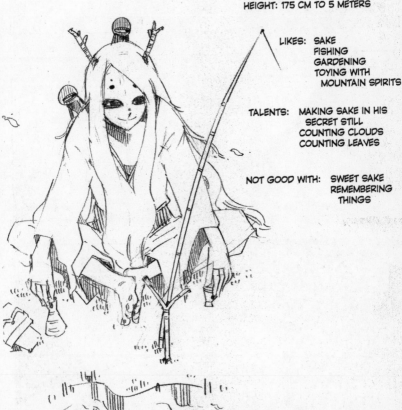

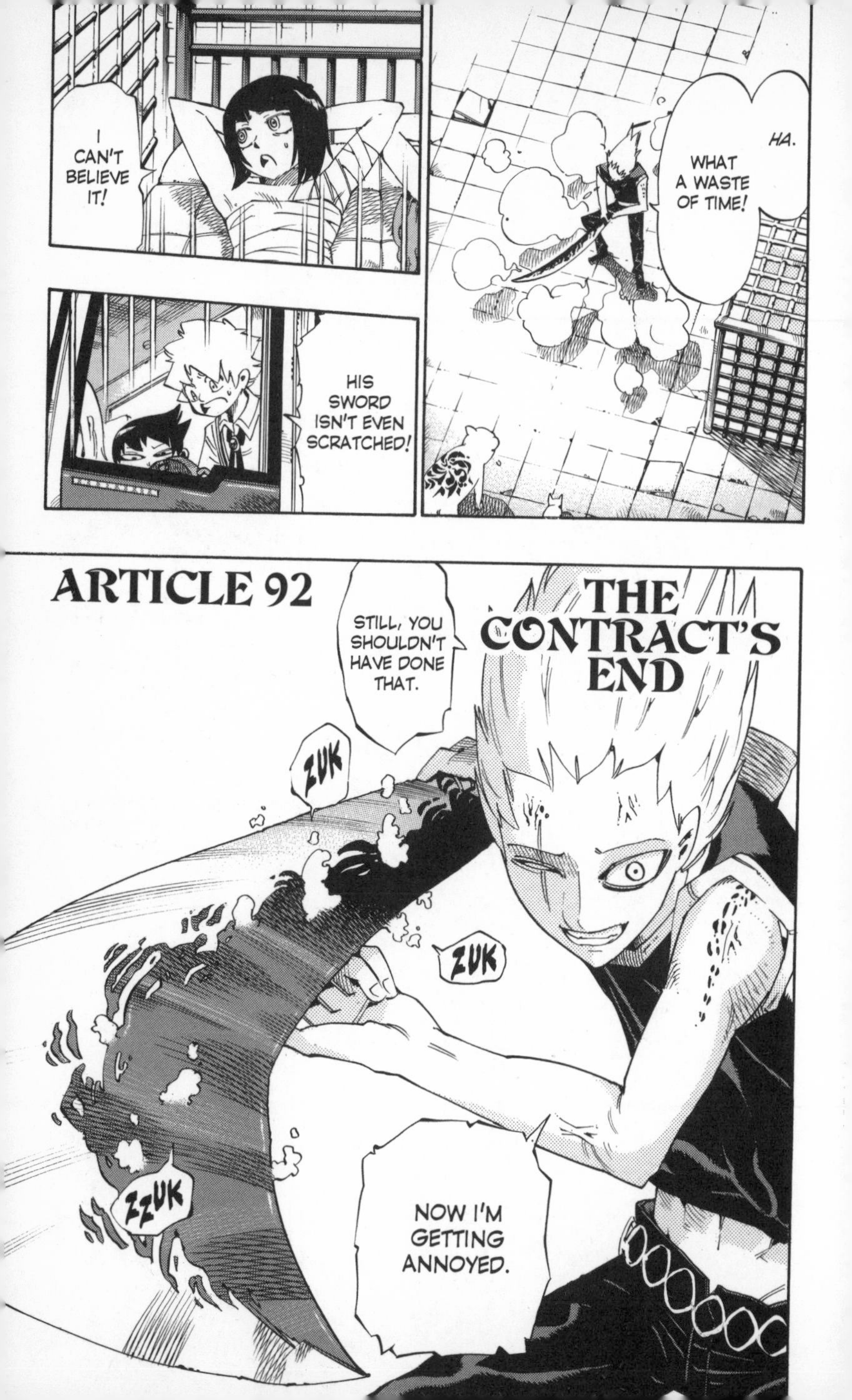

HA.
WHAT A WASTE OF TIME!
I CAN'T BELIEVE IT!
HIS SWORD ISN'T EVEN SCRATCHED!
THE CONTRACT'S END
ARTICLE 92
STILL, YOU SHOULDN'T HAVE DONE THAT.
ZUK
ZUK
NOW I'M GETTING ANNOYED.
ZZUK

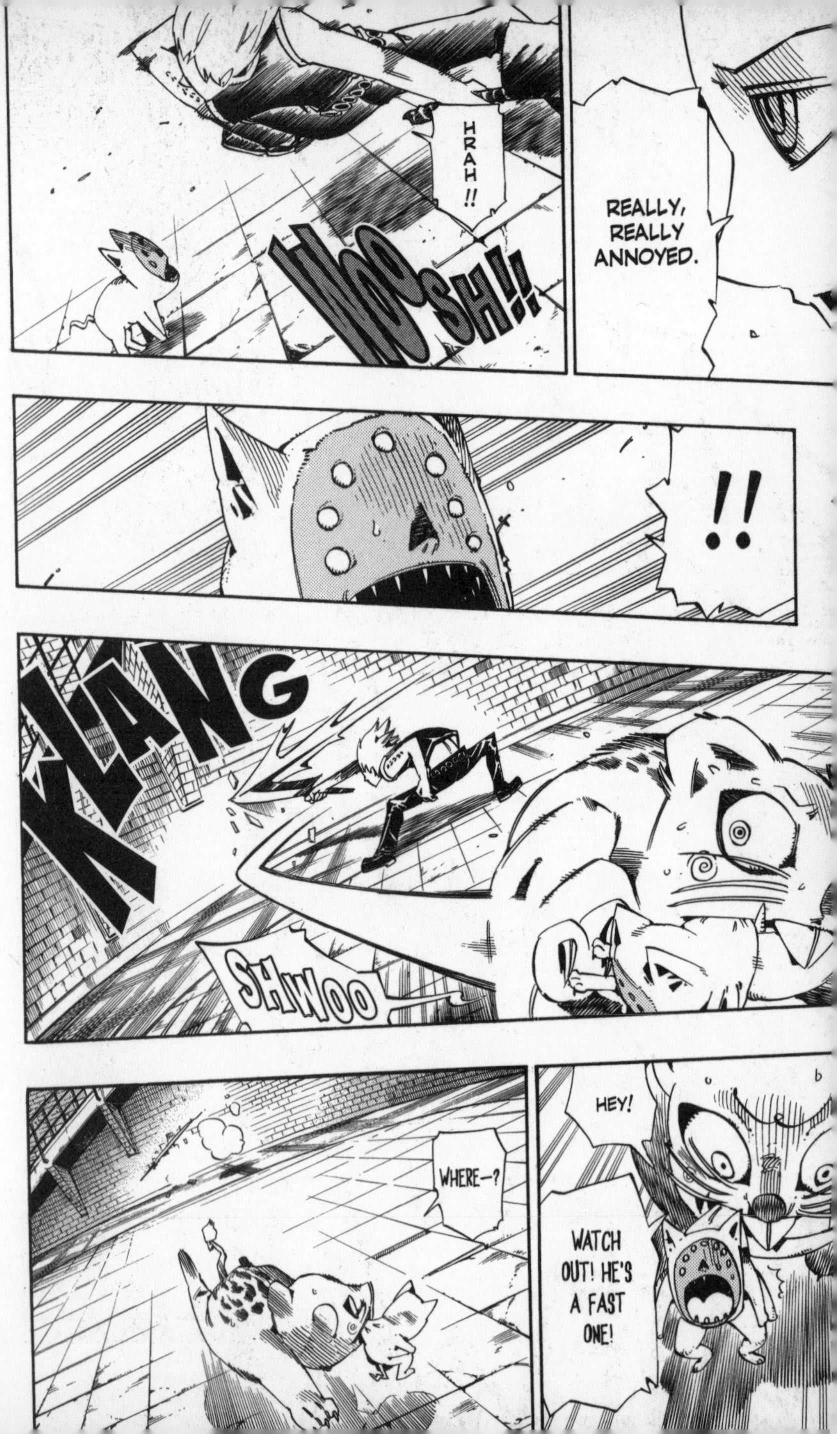
REALLY, REALLY ANNOYED.
HRAH!!
WHOOSH!!
!!
KLANG
SHWOO
HEY!
WATCH OUT! HE'S A FAST ONE!
WHERE–?

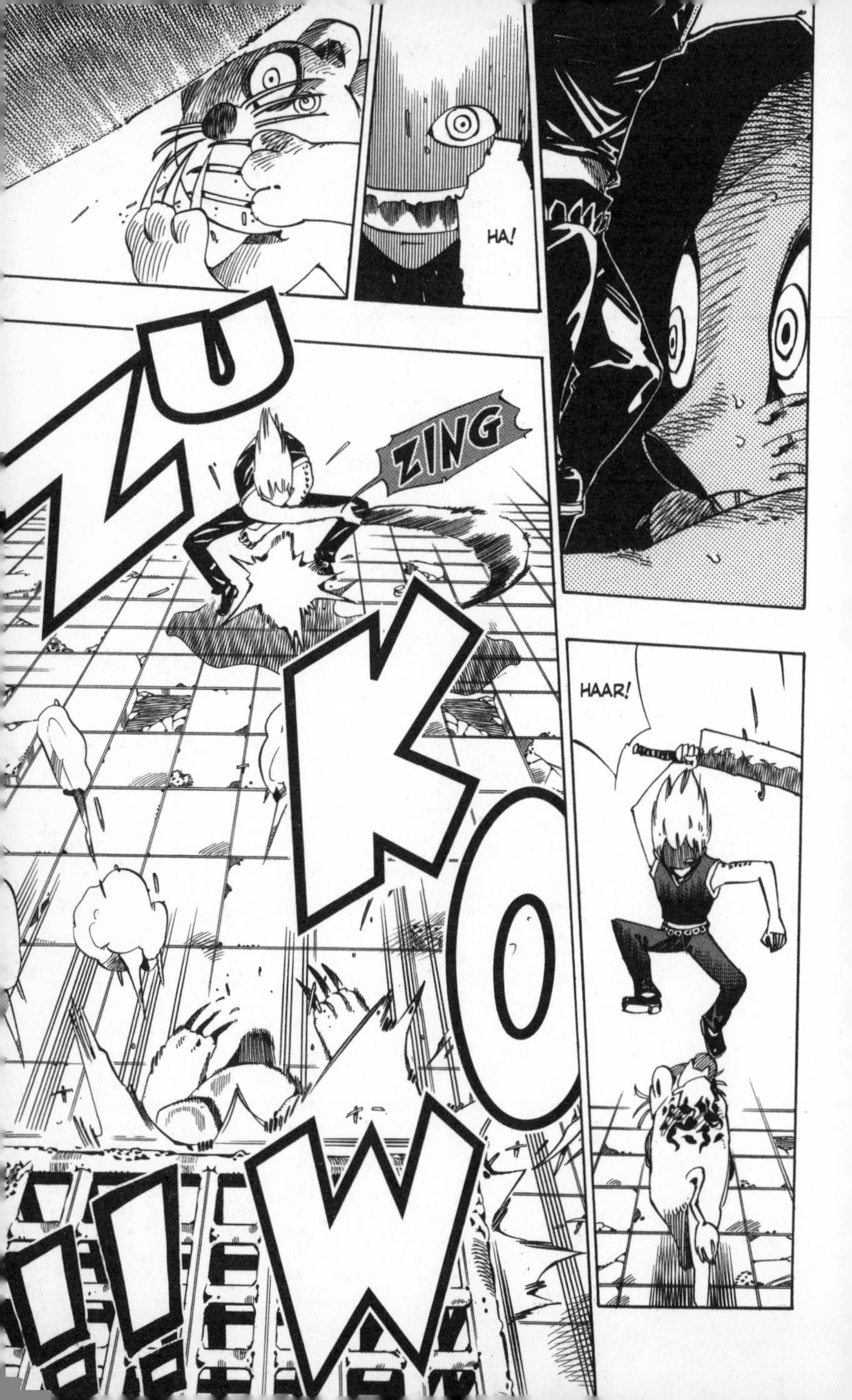
HA!
ZŪ
ZING
KOW!!
HAAR!

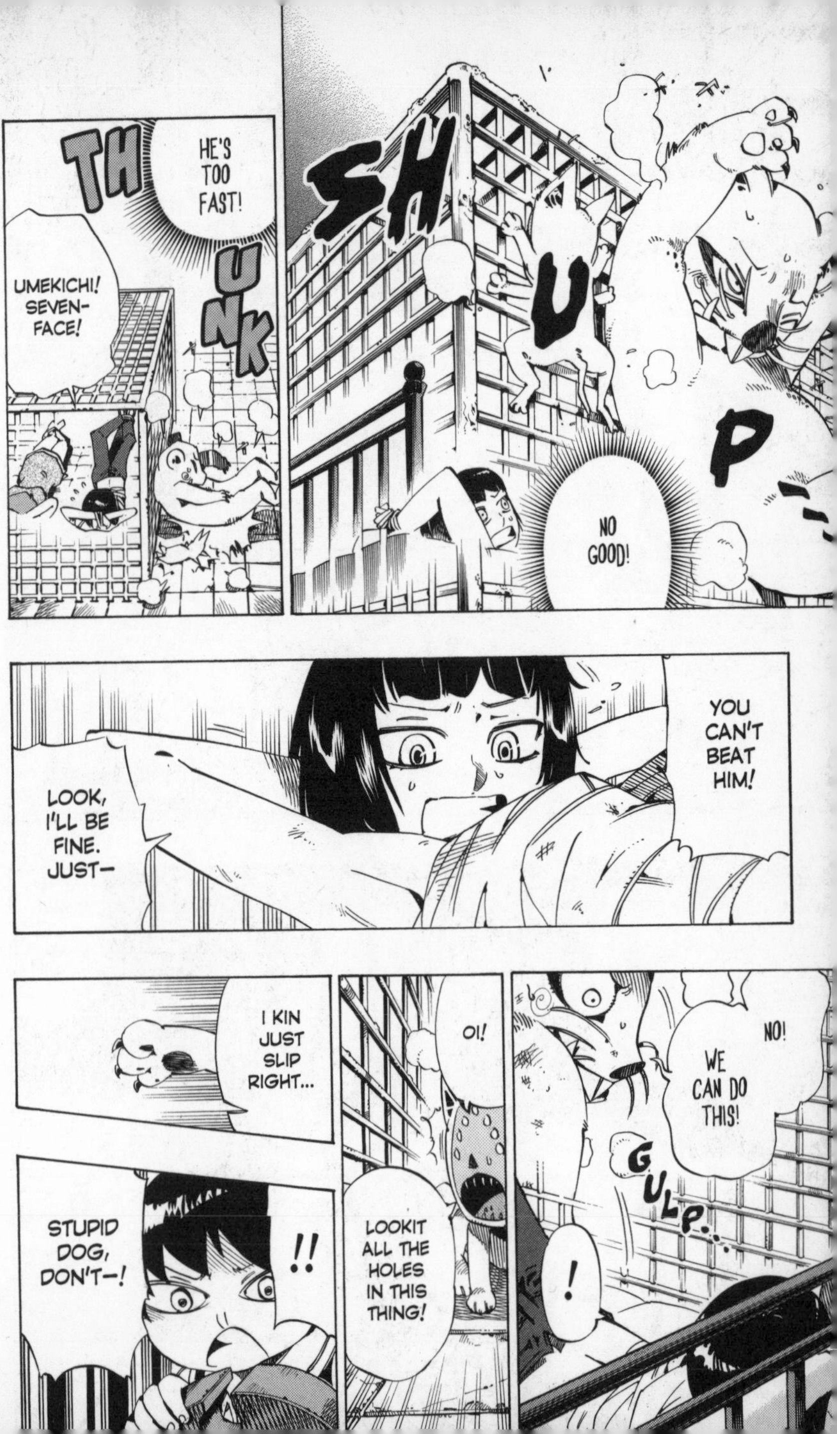
SHUP
NO GOOD!
HE'S TOO FAST!
THUNK
UMEKICHI! SEVEN-FACE!
YOU CAN'T BEAT HIM!
LOOK, I'LL BE FINE. JUST—
NO!
WE CAN DO THIS!
GULP...
!
OI!
LOOKIT ALL THE HOLES IN THIS THING!
I KIN JUST SLIP RIGHT...
STUPID DOG, DON'T—!
!!

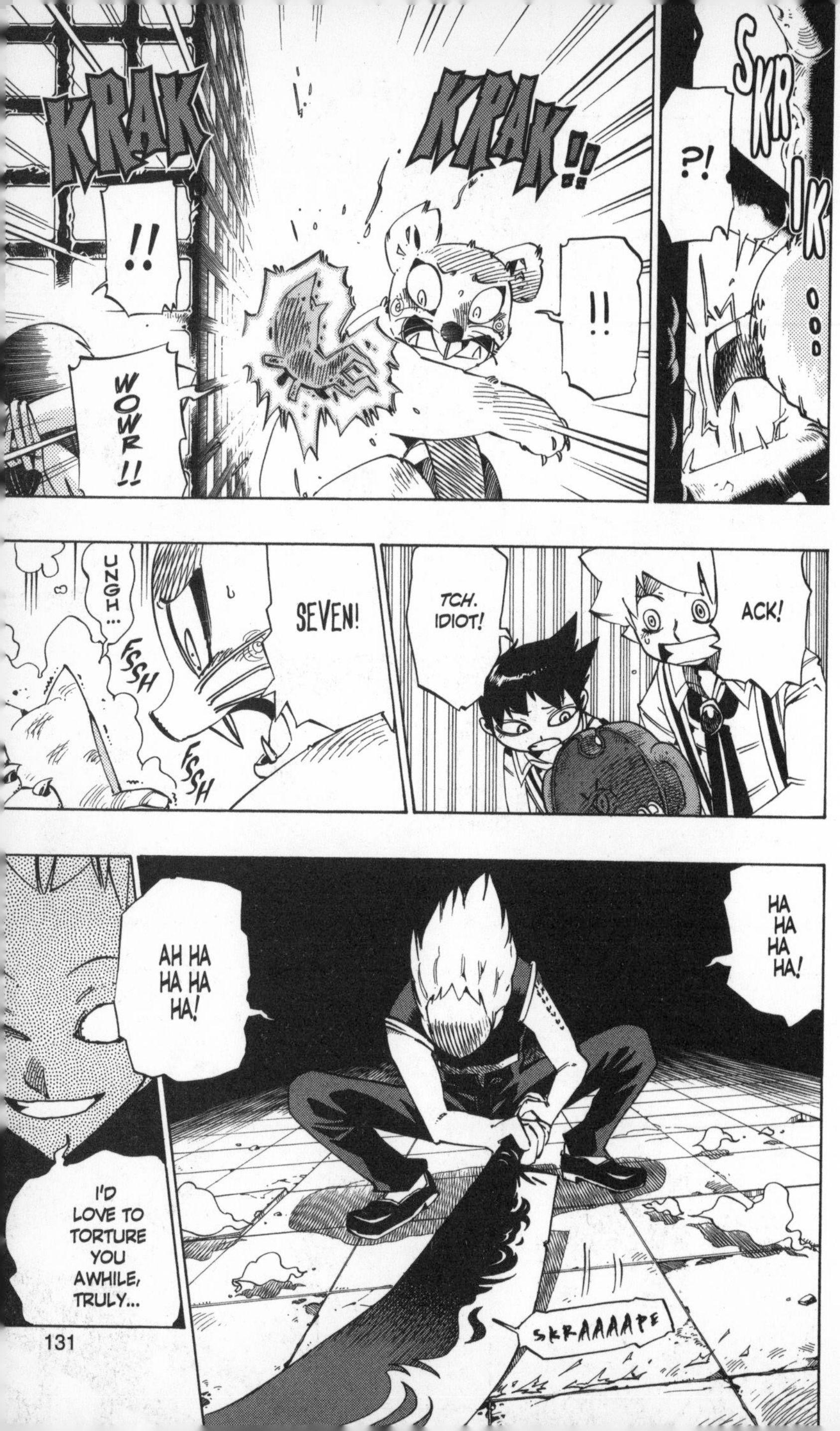
SKRIK
?!
KRAK!!
!!
KRAK
!!
WOWR!!
ACK!
TCH. IDIOT!
SEVEN!
UNGH...
FSSH
FSSH
HA HA HA HA!
AH HA HA HA HA!
I'D LOVE TO TORTURE YOU AWHILE, TRULY...
SKRAAAAPE

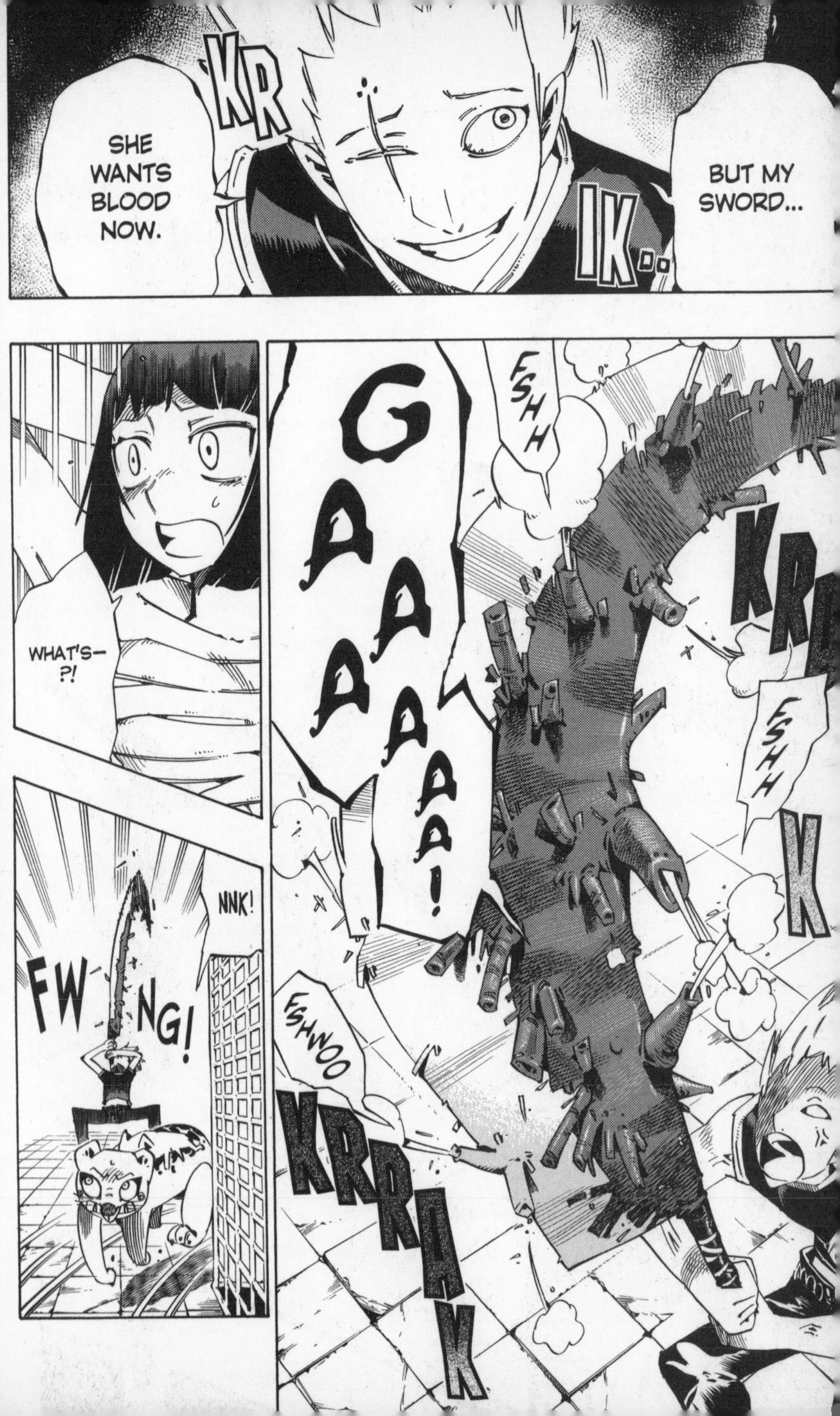
BUT MY SWORD...
KR
IK..
SHE WANTS BLOOD NOW.
FSHH
GAAAAAAAA!
KRR
FSHH
K
FSHWOO
KRRRAK
WHAT'S— ?!
NNK!
FW NG!

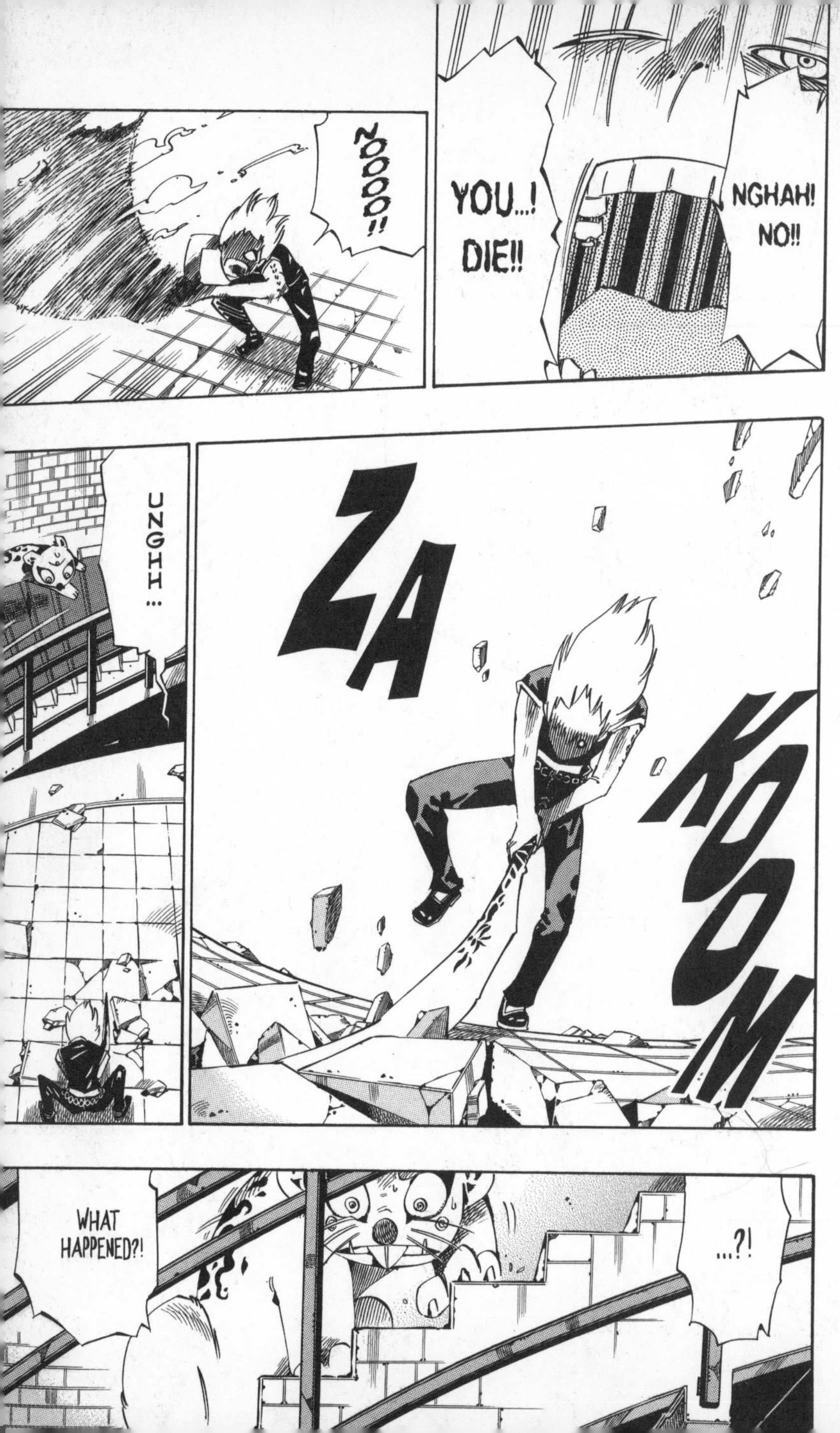
NGHAH! NO!!
YOU...! DIE!!
NOOOO!!
ZA
KOOM
UNGHH...
...?!
WHAT HAPPENED?!

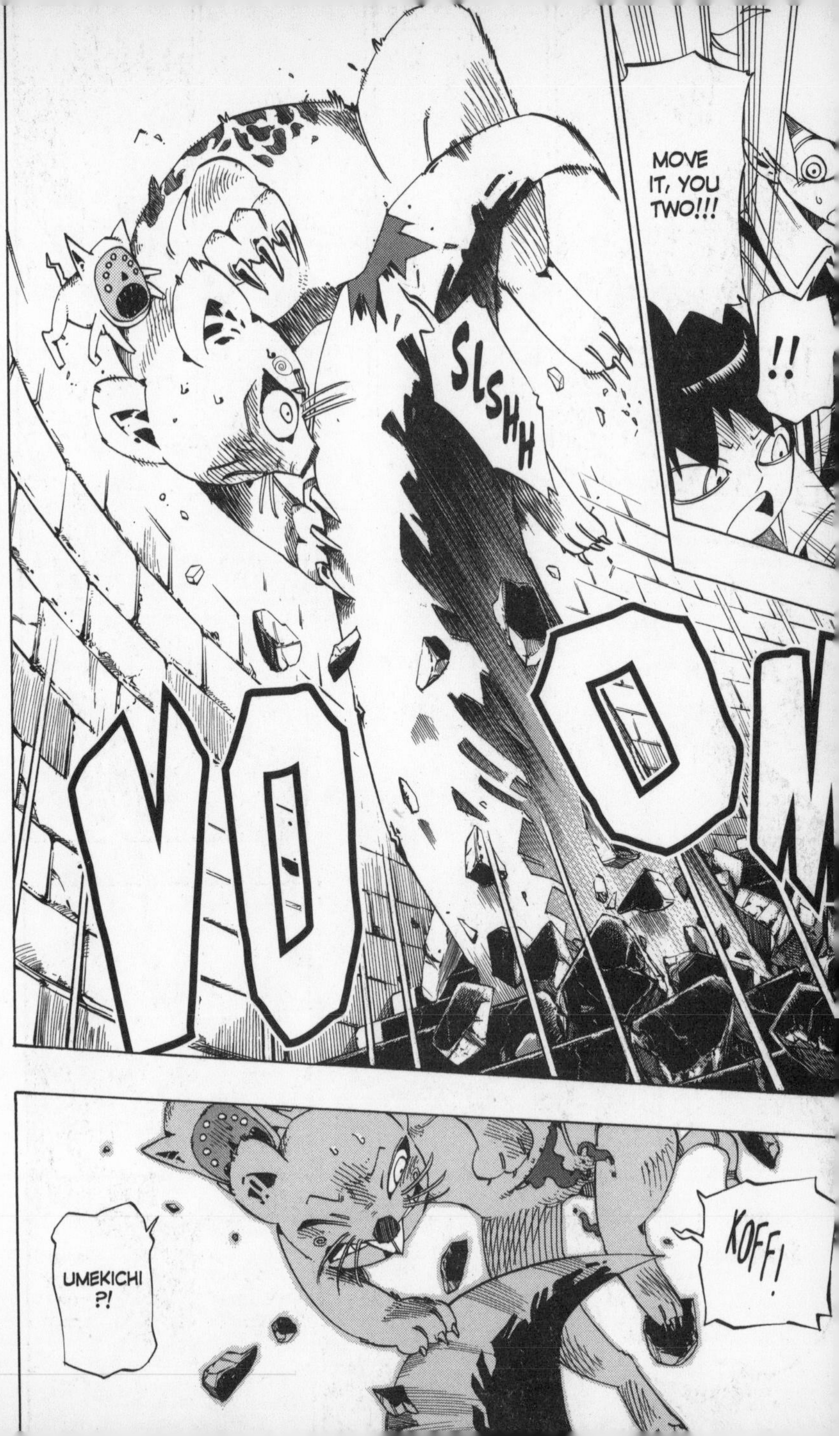
MOVE IT, YOU TWO!!!
!!
SLSHH
VOOOM
KOFF!
UMEKICHI ?!

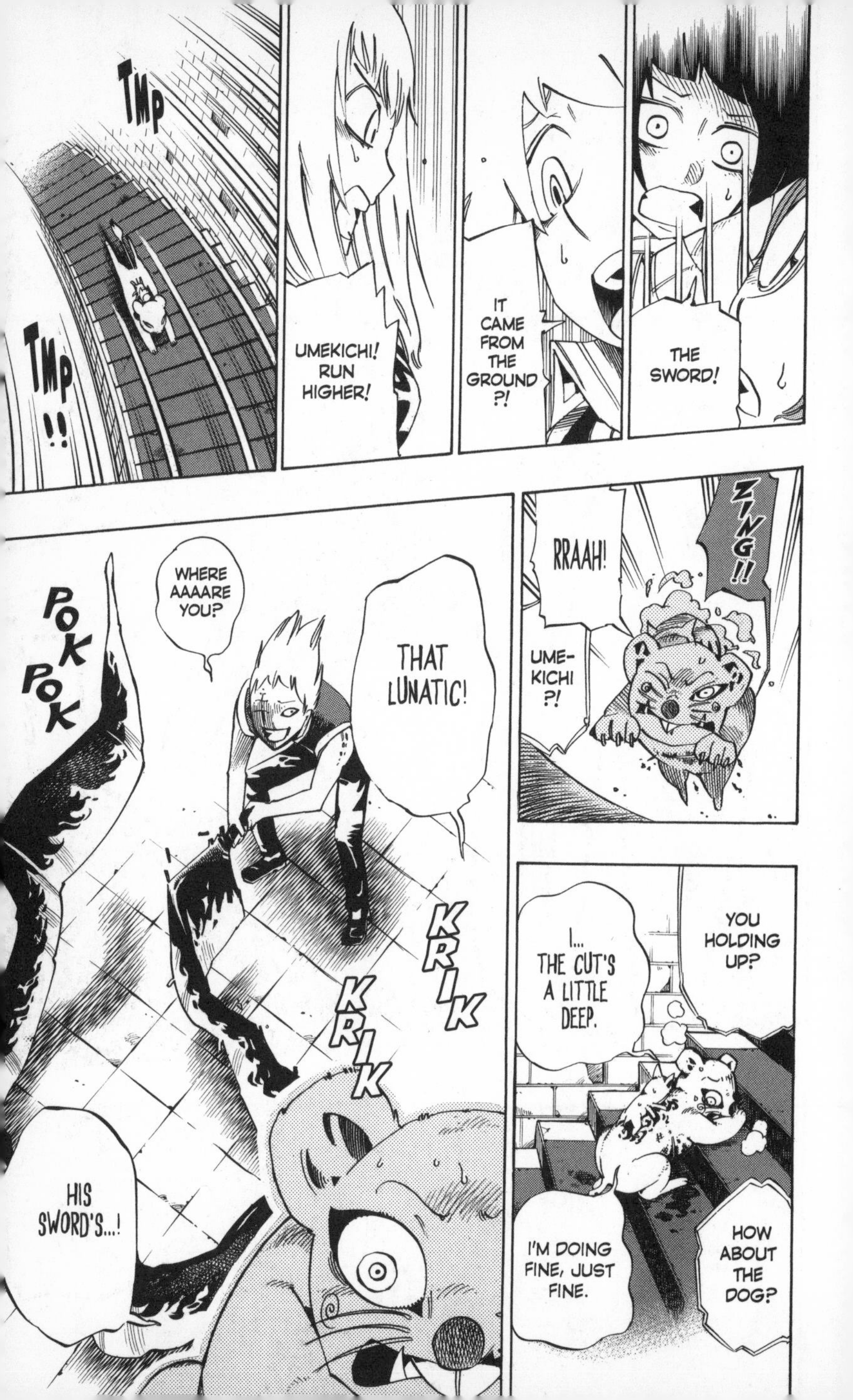
THE SWORD!
IT CAME FROM THE GROUND?!
UMEKICHI! RUN HIGHER!
TMP
TMP!!
ZING!!
RRAAH!
UME-KICHI?!
YOU HOLDING UP?
I... THE CUT'S A LITTLE DEEP.
HOW ABOUT THE DOG?
I'M DOING FINE, JUST FINE.
THAT LUNATIC!
WHERE AAAARE YOU?
POK POK
KRIK
KRIK
HIS SWORD'S...!

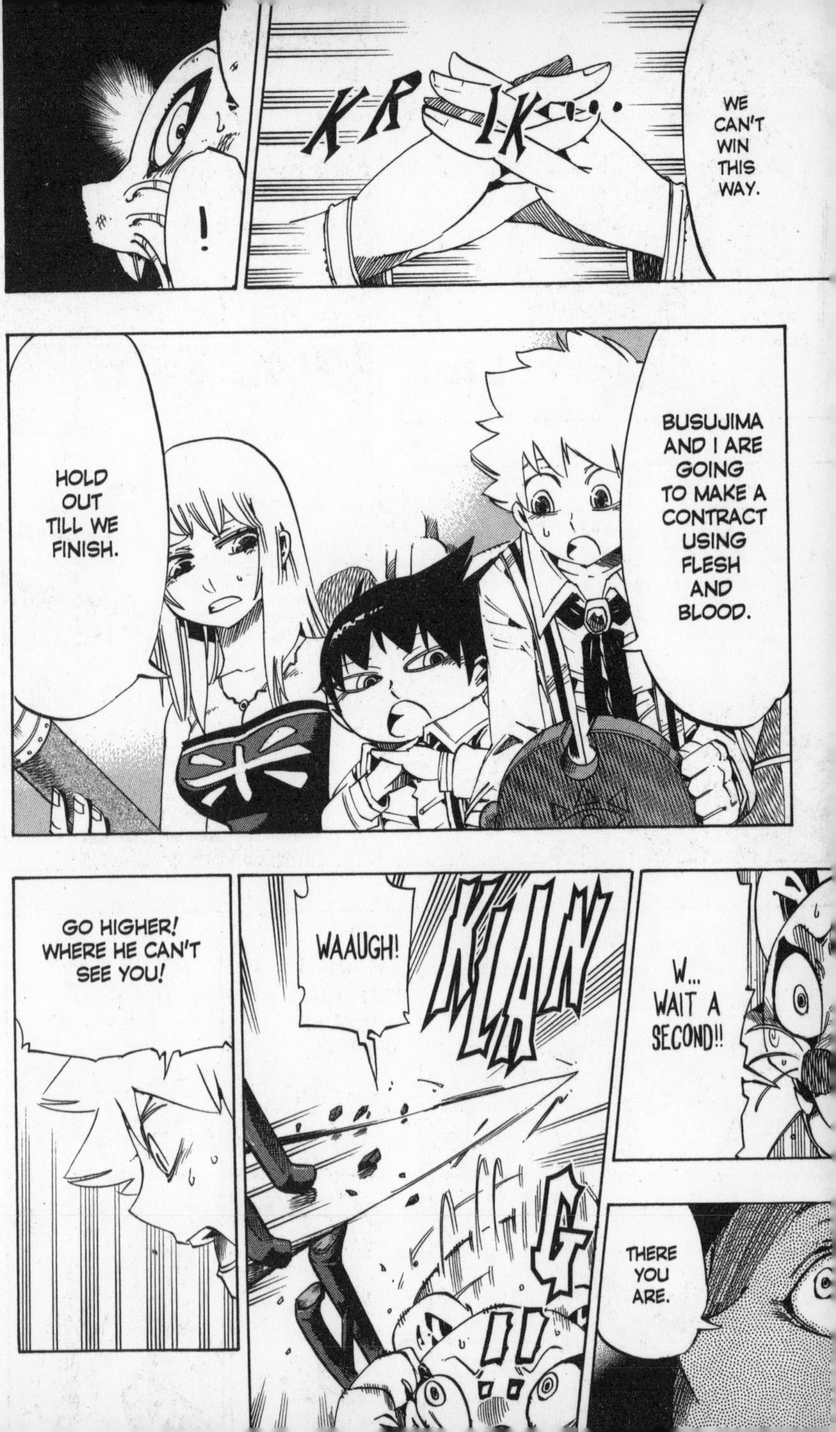
WE CAN'T WIN THIS WAY.
KRIK...
!
BUSUJIMA AND I ARE GOING TO MAKE A CONTRACT USING FLESH AND BLOOD.
HOLD OUT TILL WE FINISH.
W... WAIT A SECOND!!
THERE YOU ARE.
KLAN
WAAUGH!
G
GO HIGHER! WHERE HE CAN'T SEE YOU!

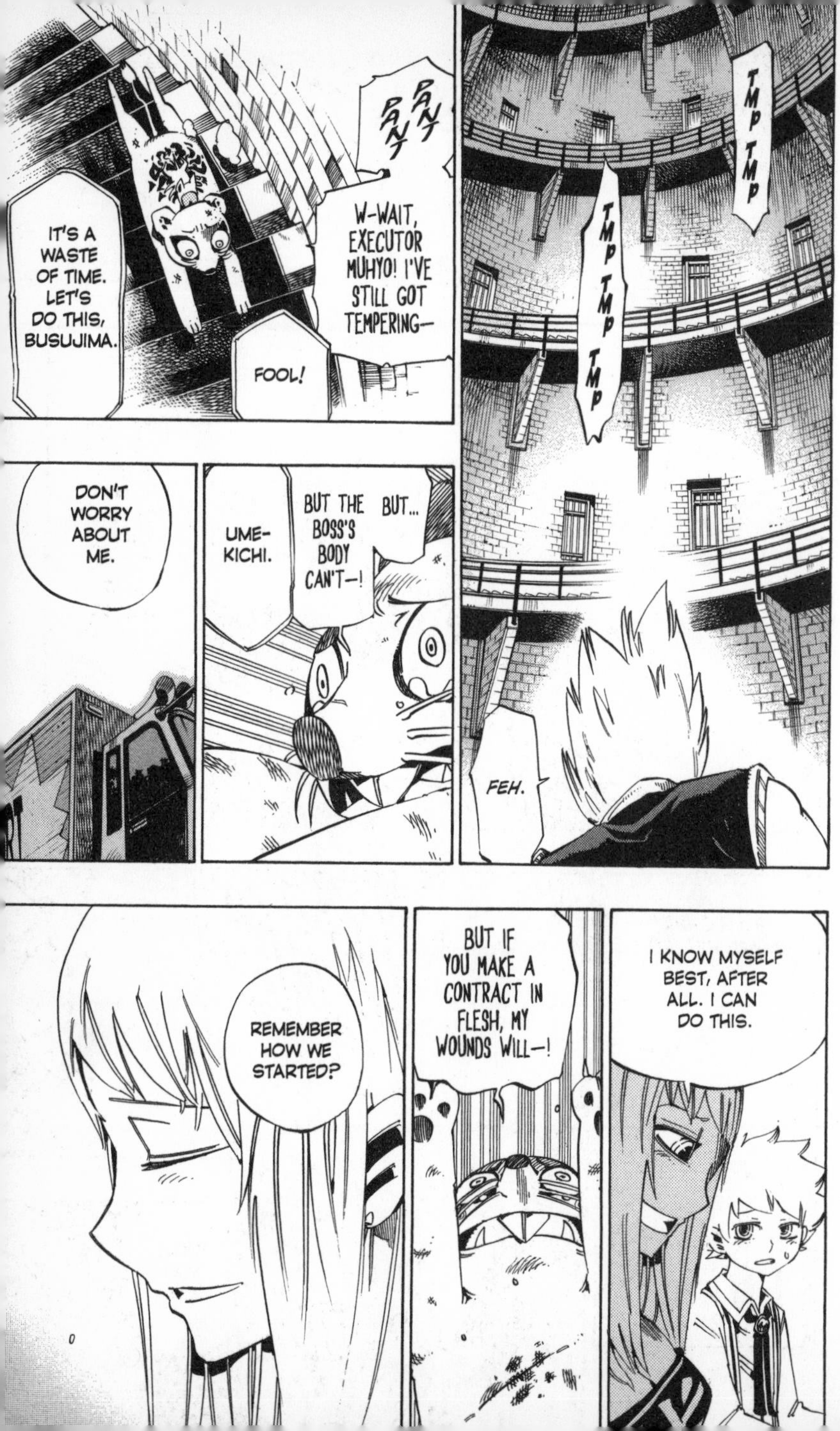

TMP TMP
TMP TMP TMP TMP
FEH.
PANT PANT
W-WAIT, EXECUTOR MUHYO! I'VE STILL GOT TEMPERING—
FOOL!
IT'S A WASTE OF TIME. LET'S DO THIS, BUSUJIMA.
BUT...
BUT THE BOSS'S BODY CAN'T—!
UME-KICHI.
DON'T WORRY ABOUT ME.
I KNOW MYSELF BEST, AFTER ALL. I CAN DO THIS.
BUT IF YOU MAKE A CONTRACT IN FLESH, MY WOUNDS WILL—!
REMEMBER HOW WE STARTED?

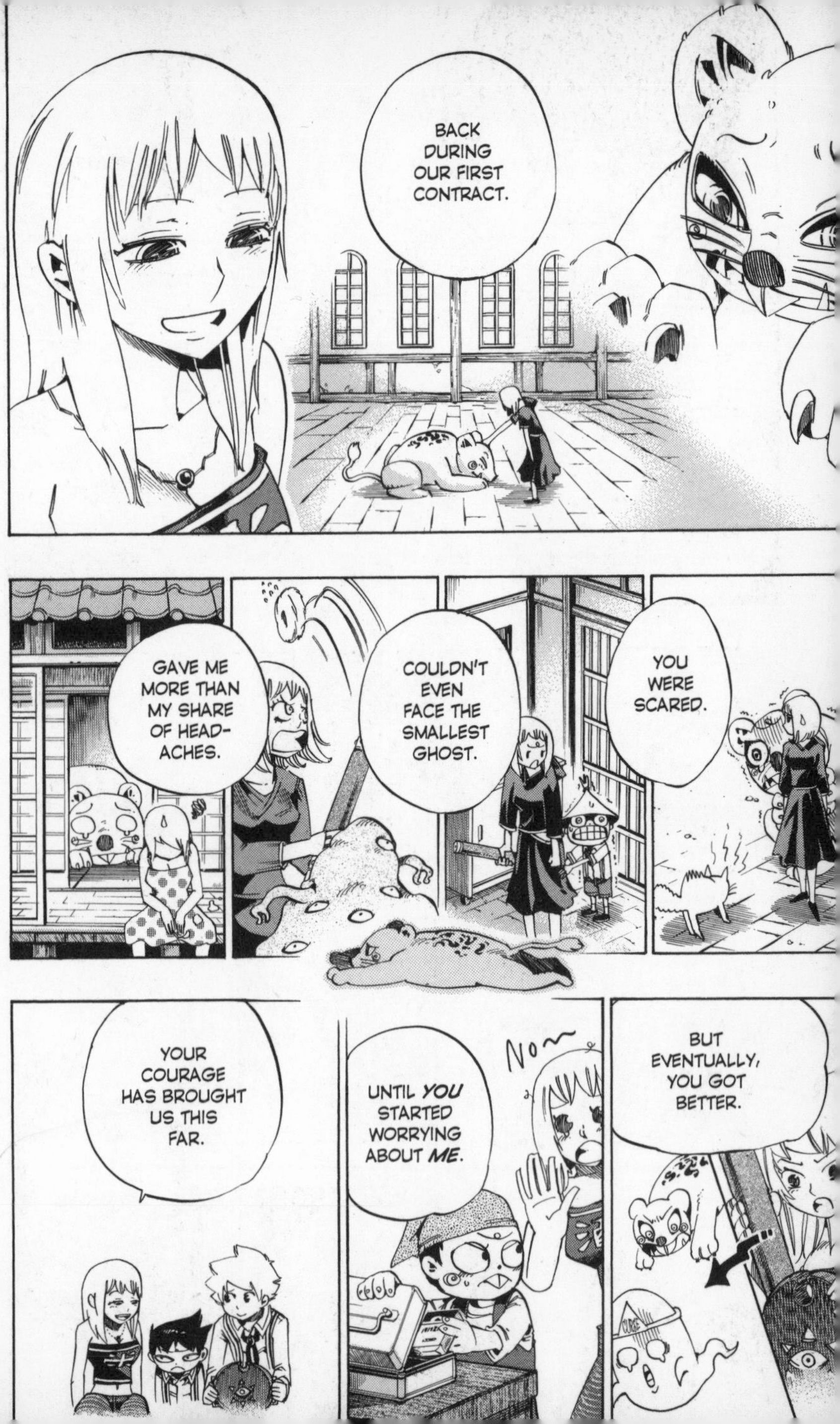
BACK DURING OUR FIRST CONTRACT.
YOU WERE SCARED.
COULDN'T EVEN FACE THE SMALLEST GHOST.
GAVE ME MORE THAN MY SHARE OF HEAD-ACHES.
BUT EVENTUALLY, YOU GOT BETTER.
CURSE
No~
UNTIL *YOU* STARTED WORRYING ABOUT *ME*.
YOUR COURAGE HAS BROUGHT US THIS FAR.

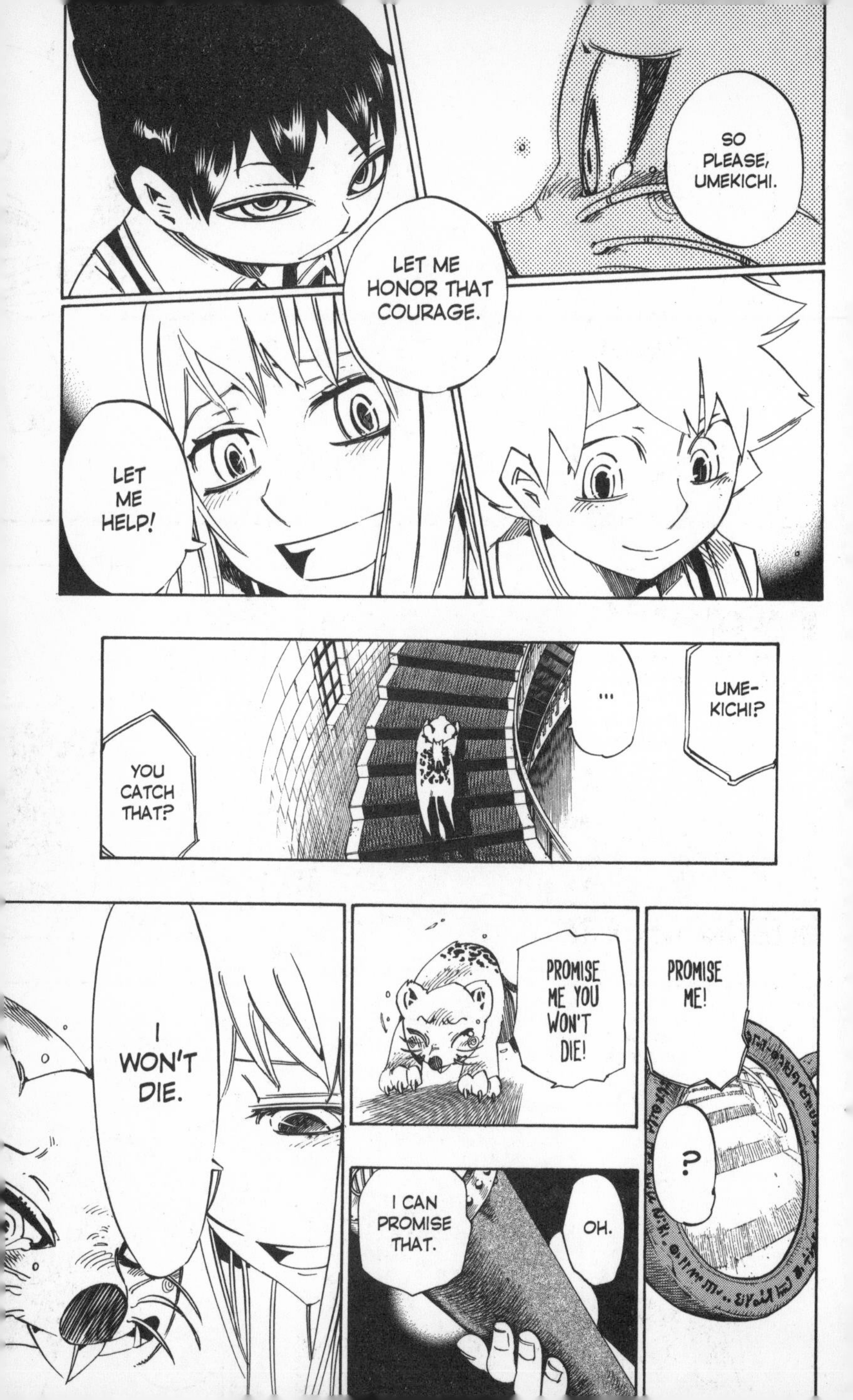
SO PLEASE, UMEKICHI.
LET ME HONOR THAT COURAGE.
LET ME HELP!
UME-KICHI?
...
YOU CATCH THAT?
PROMISE ME!
?
PROMISE ME YOU WON'T DIE!
OH.
I CAN PROMISE THAT.
I WON'T DIE.

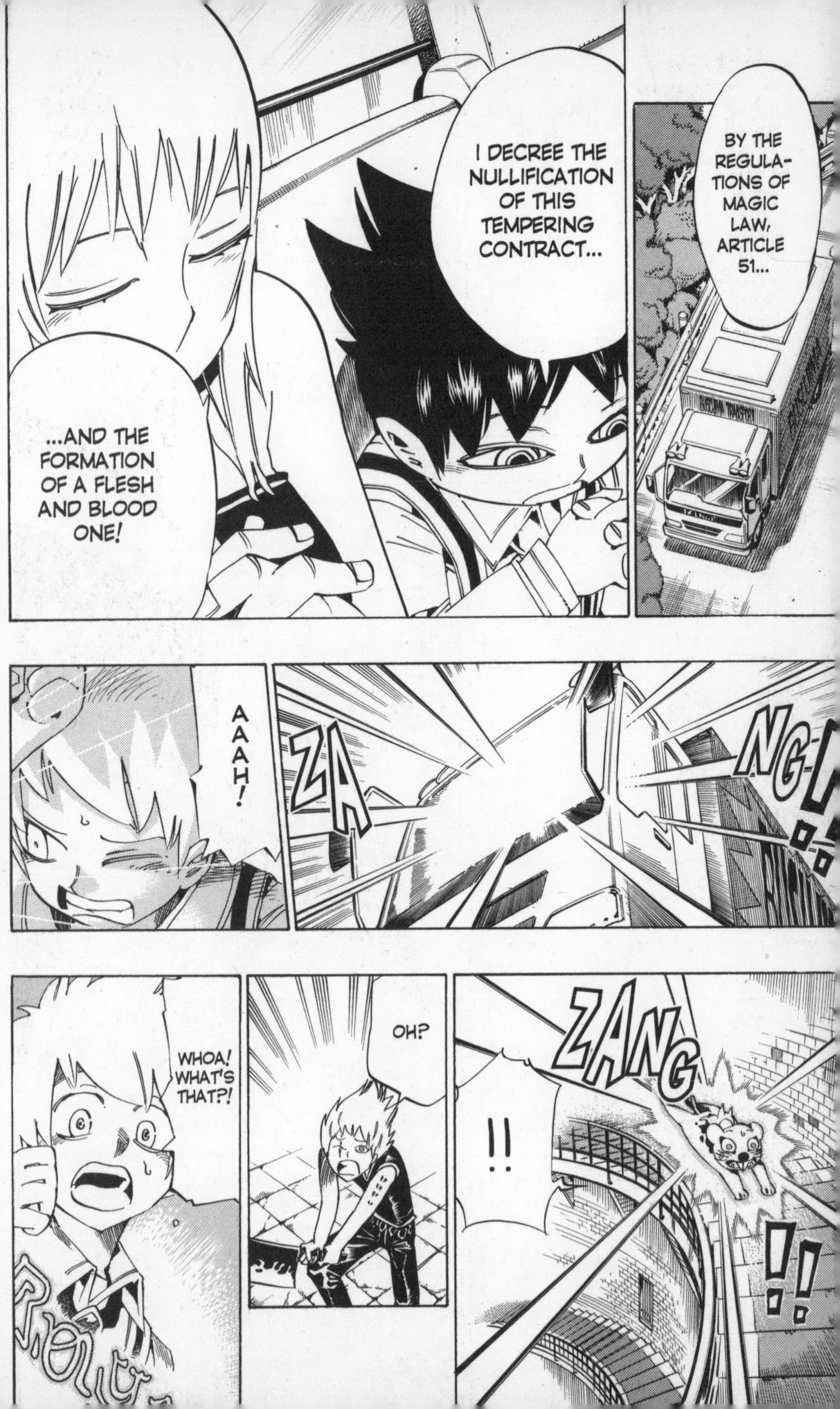
BY THE REGULATIONS OF MAGIC LAW, ARTICLE 51...
I DECREE THE NULLIFICATION OF THIS TEMPERING CONTRACT...
...AND THE FORMATION OF A FLESH AND BLOOD ONE!
ZA
NG!!
AAAH!
ZANG
!!
!!
OH?
WHOA! WHAT'S THAT?!

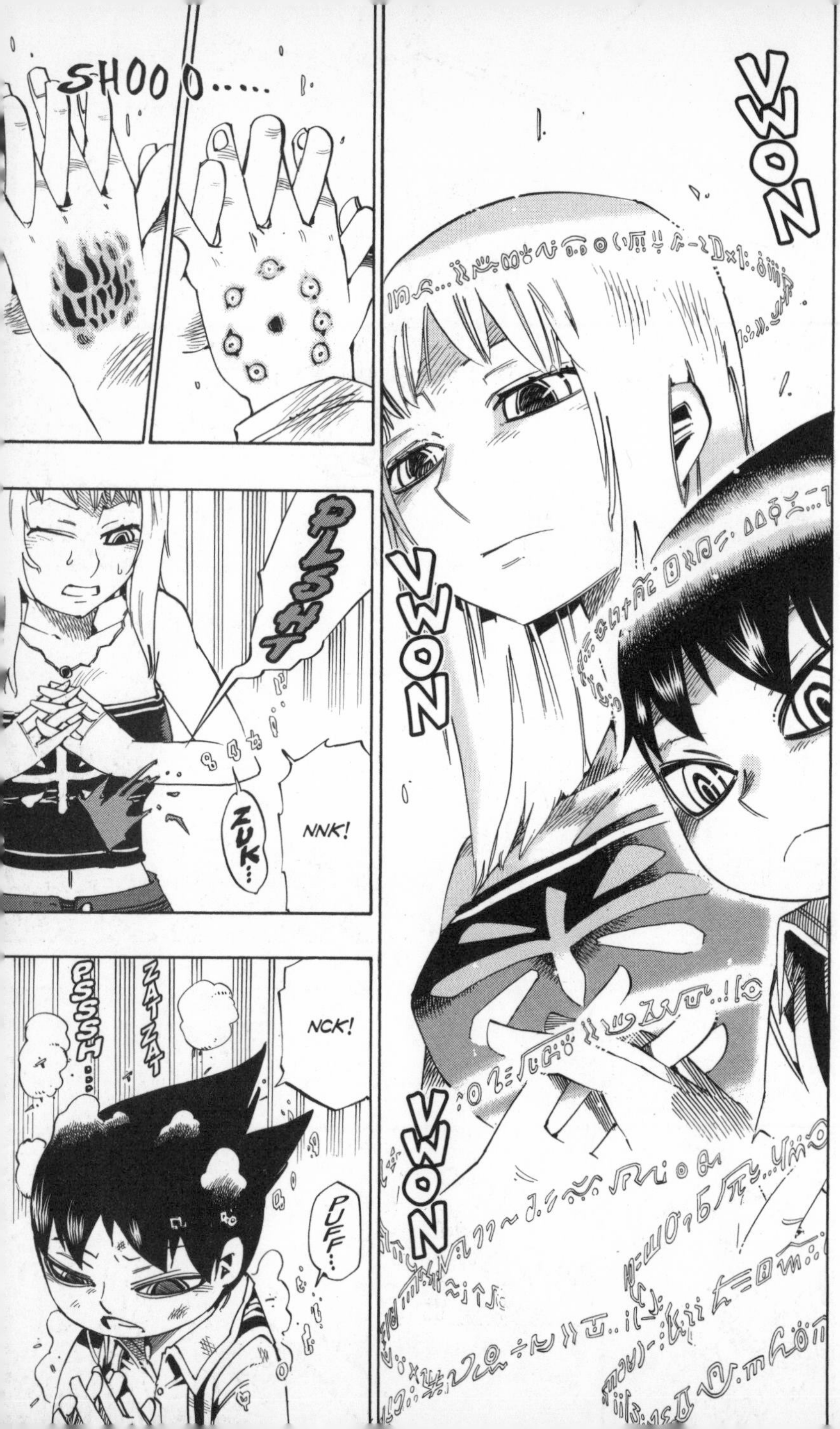

VWON
VWON
VWON
SHOOO.....
PISHT
NNK!
ZUK...
NCK!
ZATZAT
PSSSH...
PUFF...

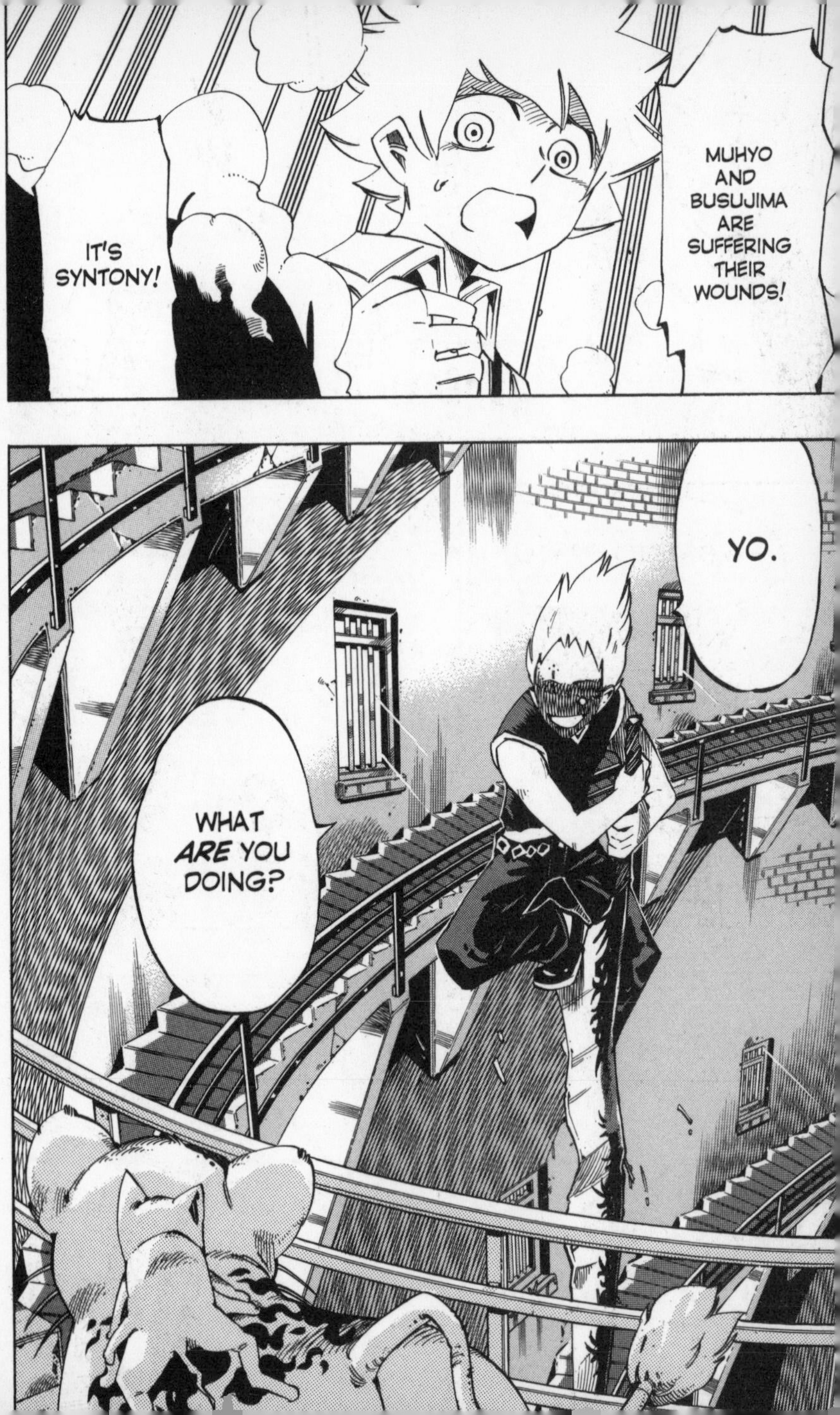
MUHYO AND BUSUJIMA ARE SUFFERING THEIR WOUNDS!
IT'S SYNTONY!
YO.
WHAT *ARE* YOU DOING?

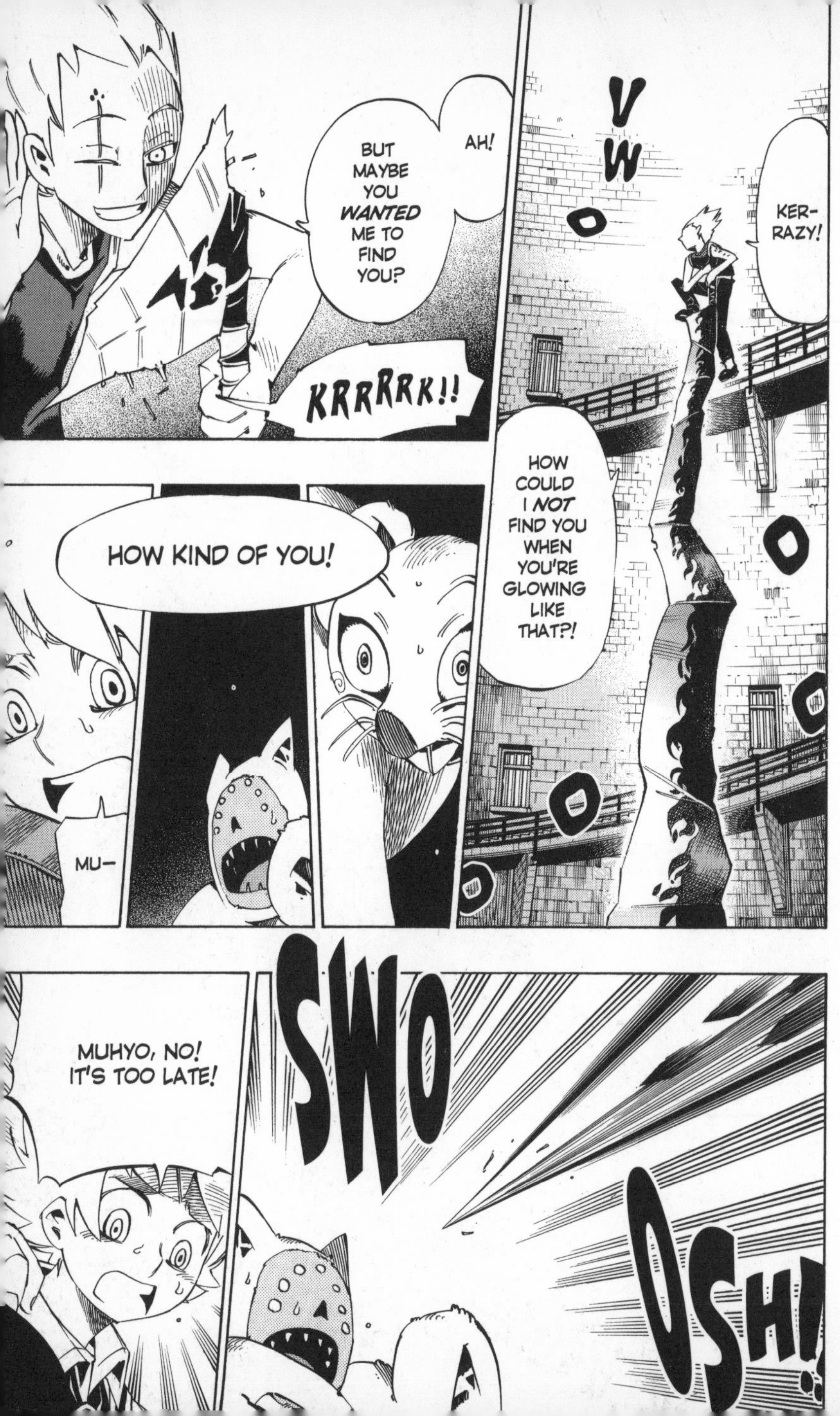
VWO
KER-RAZY!
HOW COULD I *NOT* FIND YOU WHEN YOU'RE GLOWING LIKE THAT?!
AH!
BUT MAYBE YOU *WANTED* ME TO FIND YOU?
KRRRRK!!
HOW KIND OF YOU!
MU—
SWOOSH!
MUHYO, NO! IT'S TOO LATE!

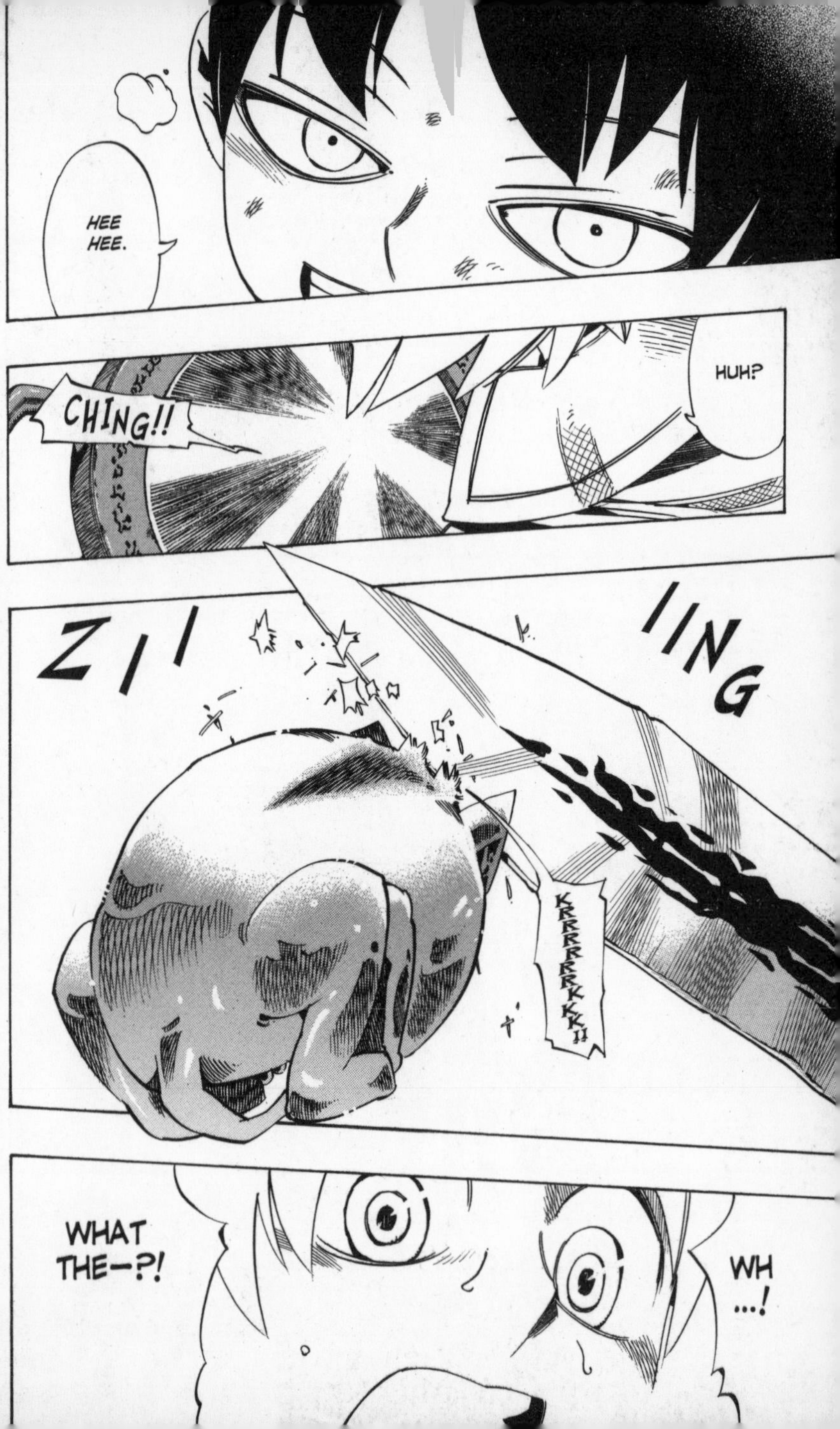
HEE HEE.
HUH?
CHING!!
ZIIIING
KRRRRRKKK!!
WH...!
WHAT THE–?!

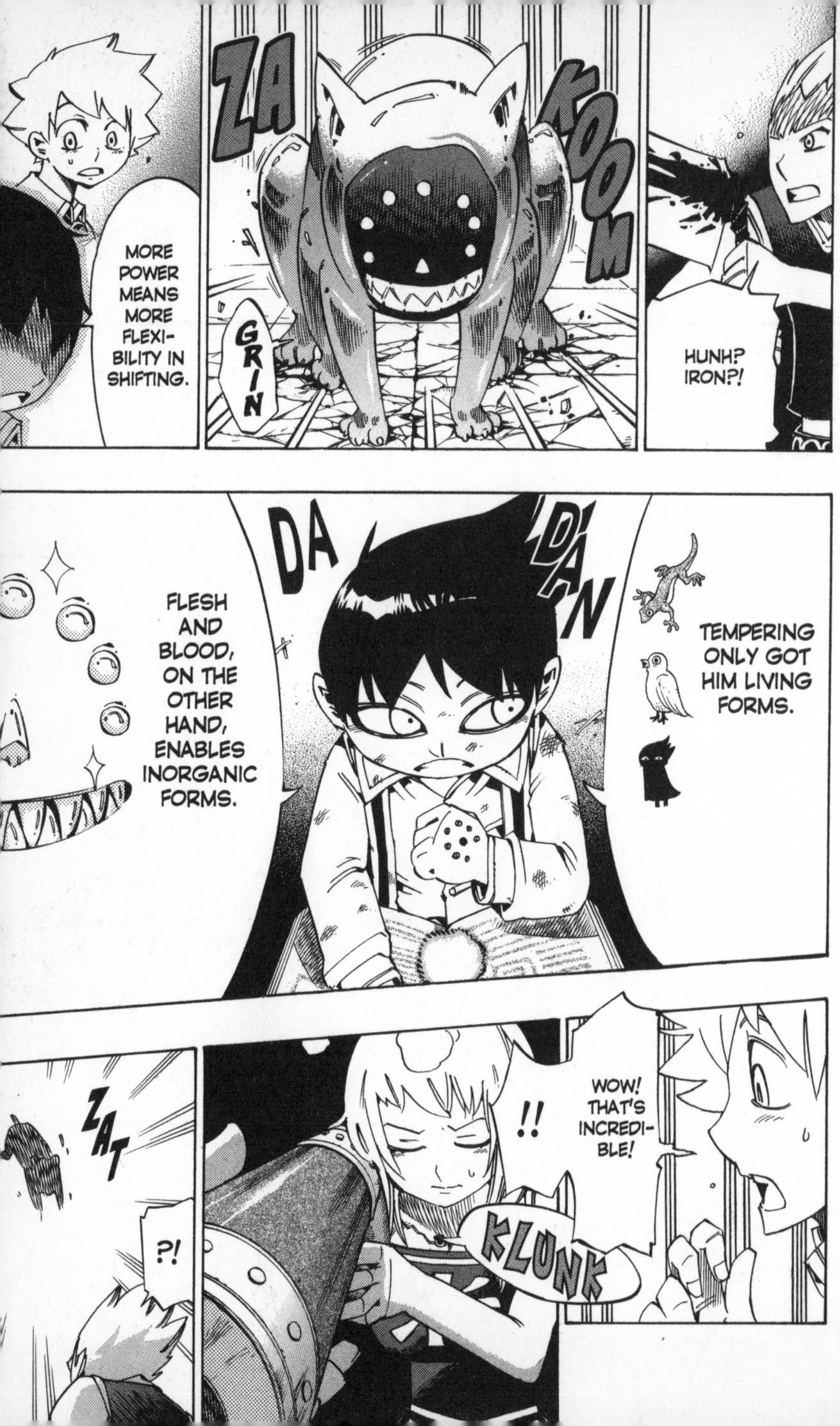
HUNH? IRON?!
ZA
KOOM
GRIN
MORE POWER MEANS MORE FLEXI-BILITY IN SHIFTING.
TEMPERING ONLY GOT HIM LIVING FORMS.
DA
DAN
FLESH AND BLOOD, ON THE OTHER HAND, ENABLES INORGANIC FORMS.
WOW! THAT'S INCREDI-BLE!
!!
KLUNK
ZAT
?!

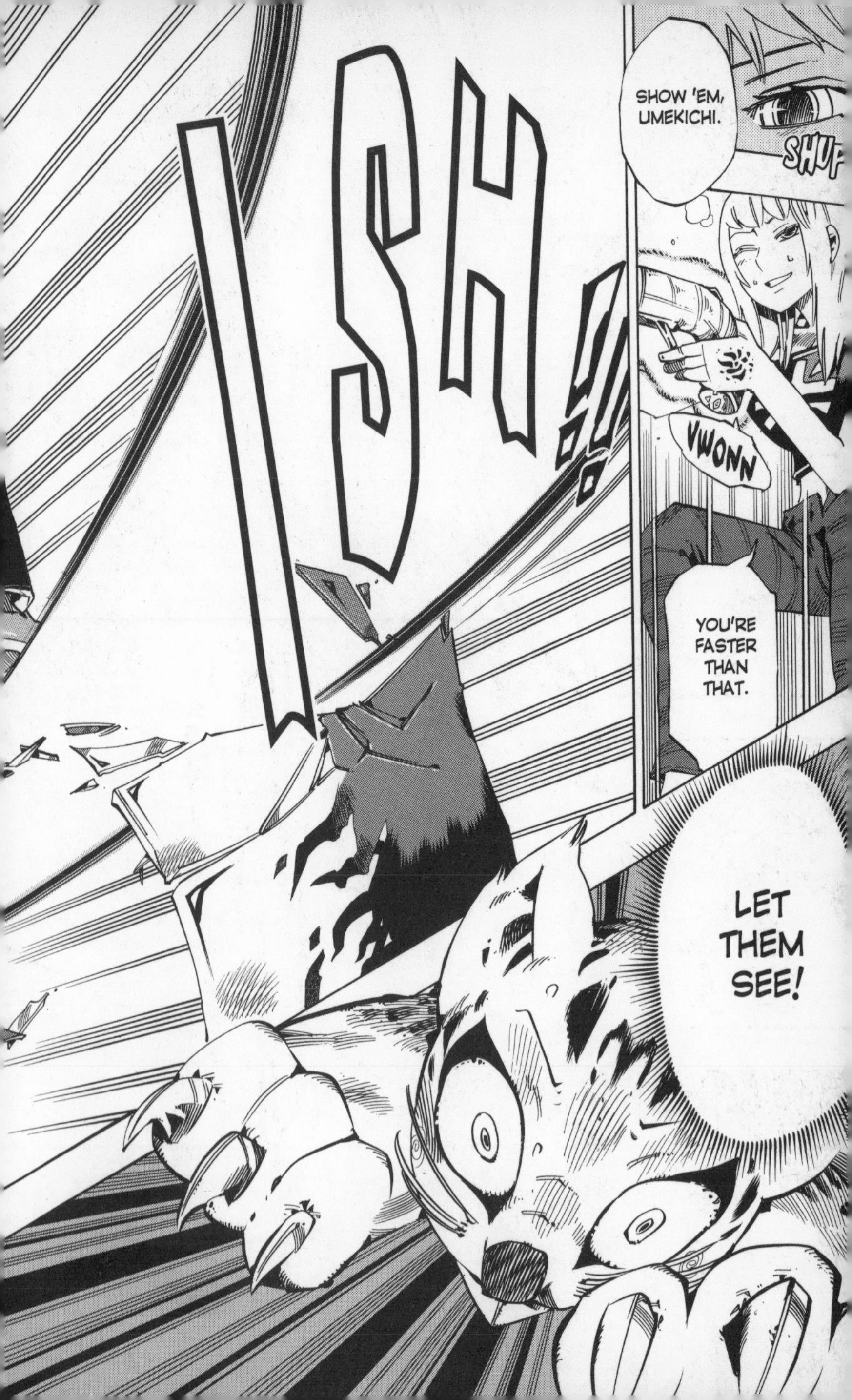
SHOW 'EM, UMEKICHI.
SHUP
VWONN
YOU'RE FASTER THAN THAT.
ISH
LET THEM SEE!

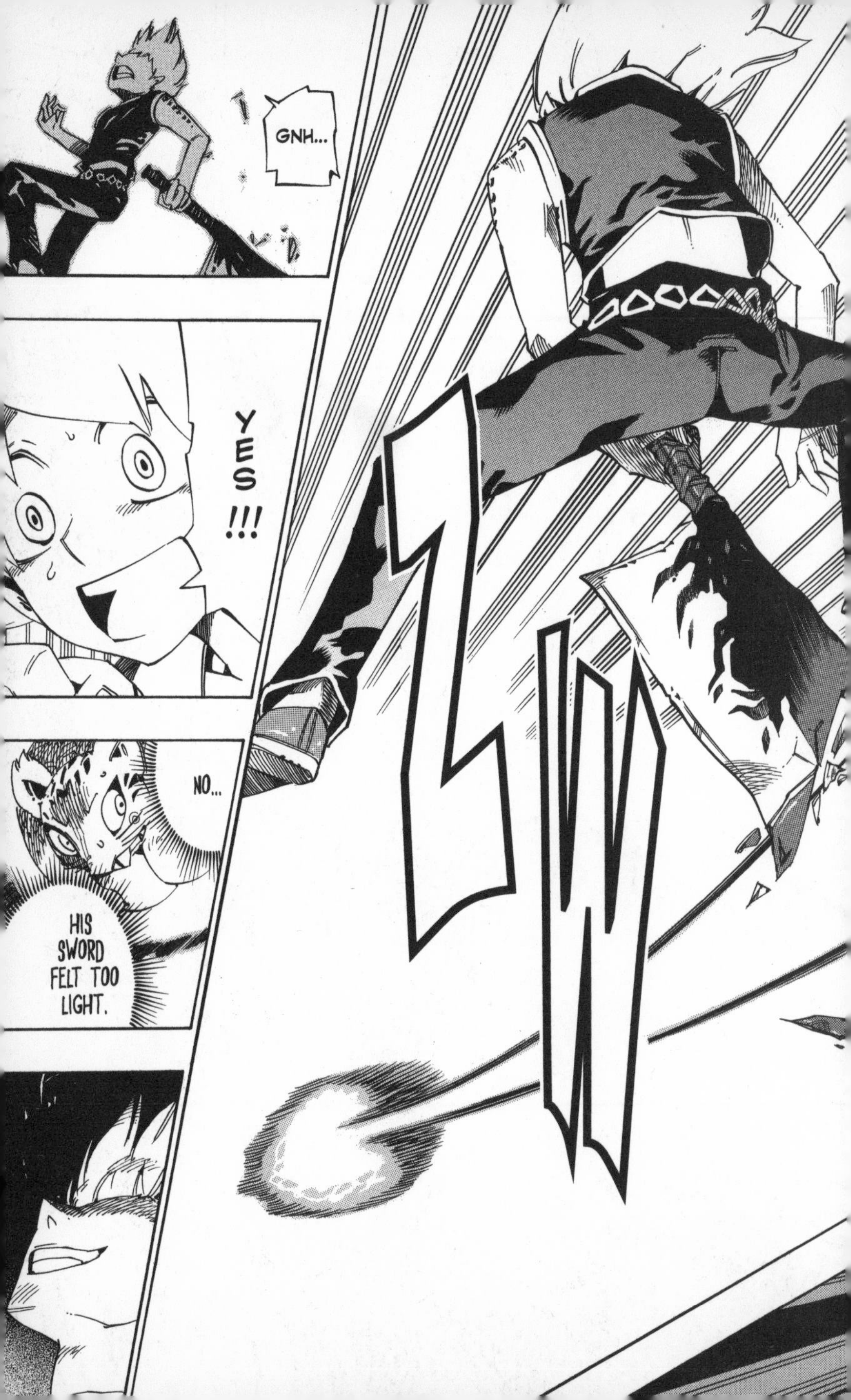
GNH...
YES!!!
NO...
HIS SWORD FELT TOO LIGHT.

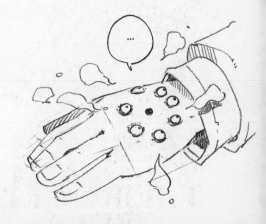

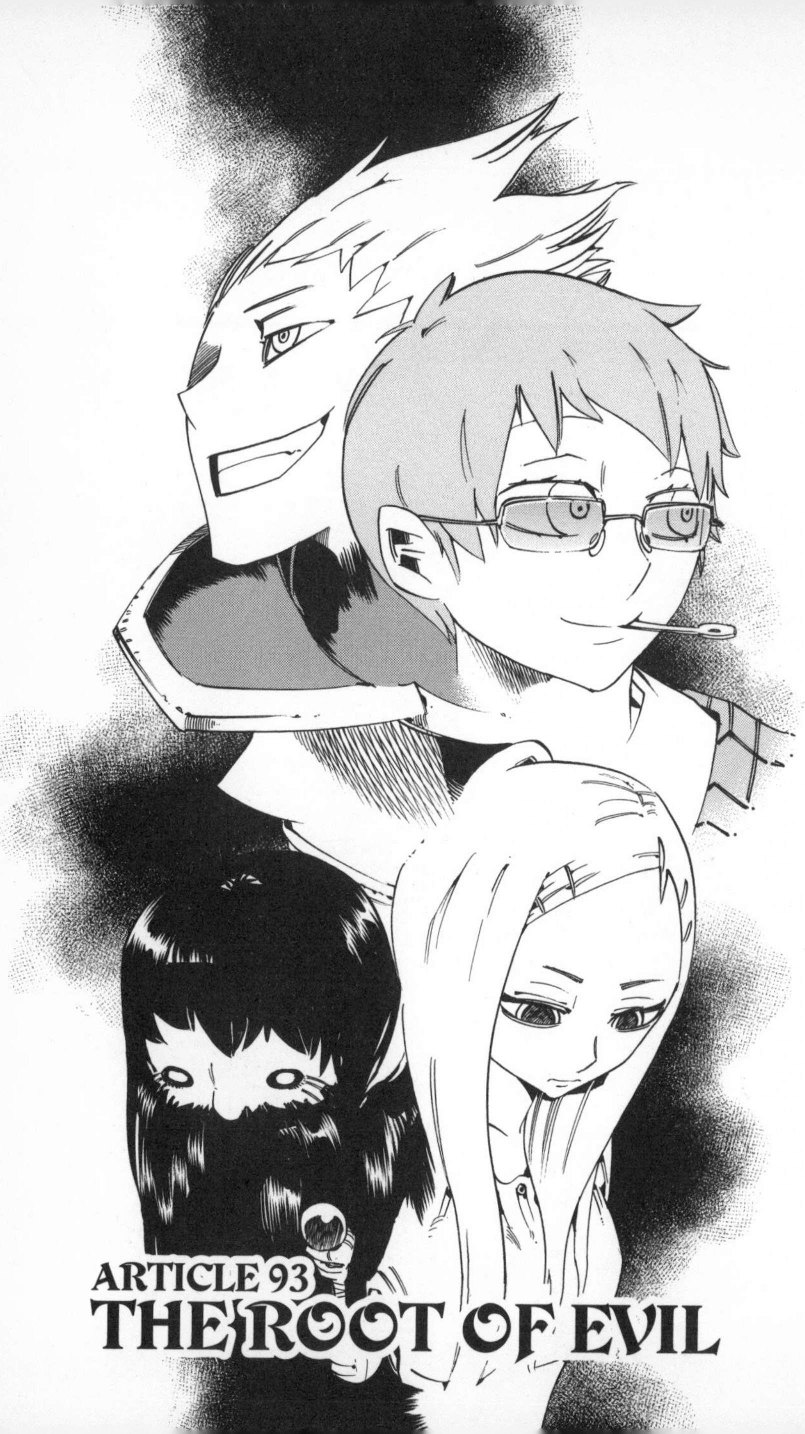

ARTICLE 93
THE ROOT OF EVIL

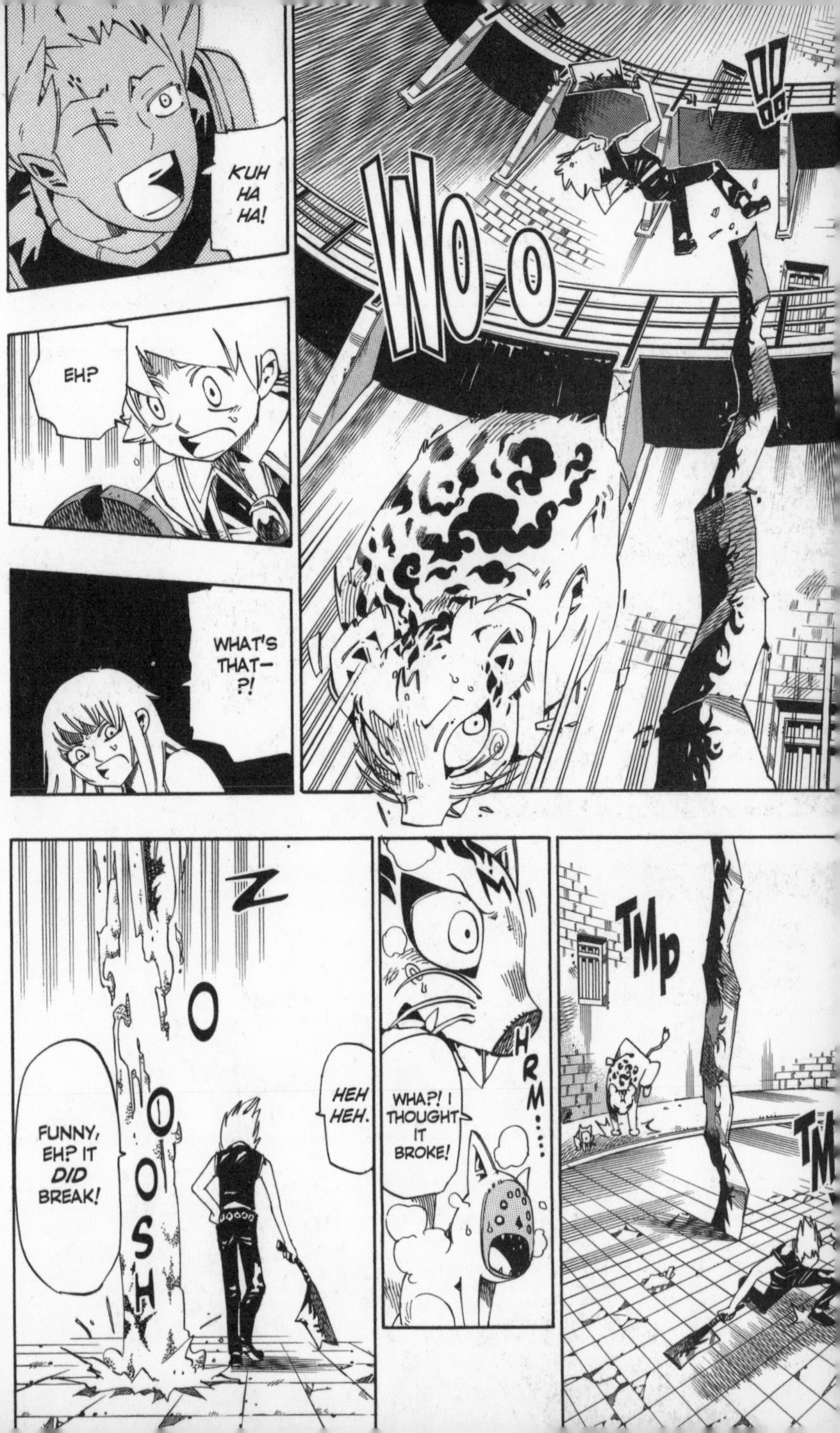
!!
WOO
KUH HA HA!
EH?
WHAT'S THAT—?!
TMP
TMP
HRM.....
WHA?! I THOUGHT IT BROKE!
HEH HEH.
ZOOOSH
FUNNY, EH? IT *DID* BREAK!

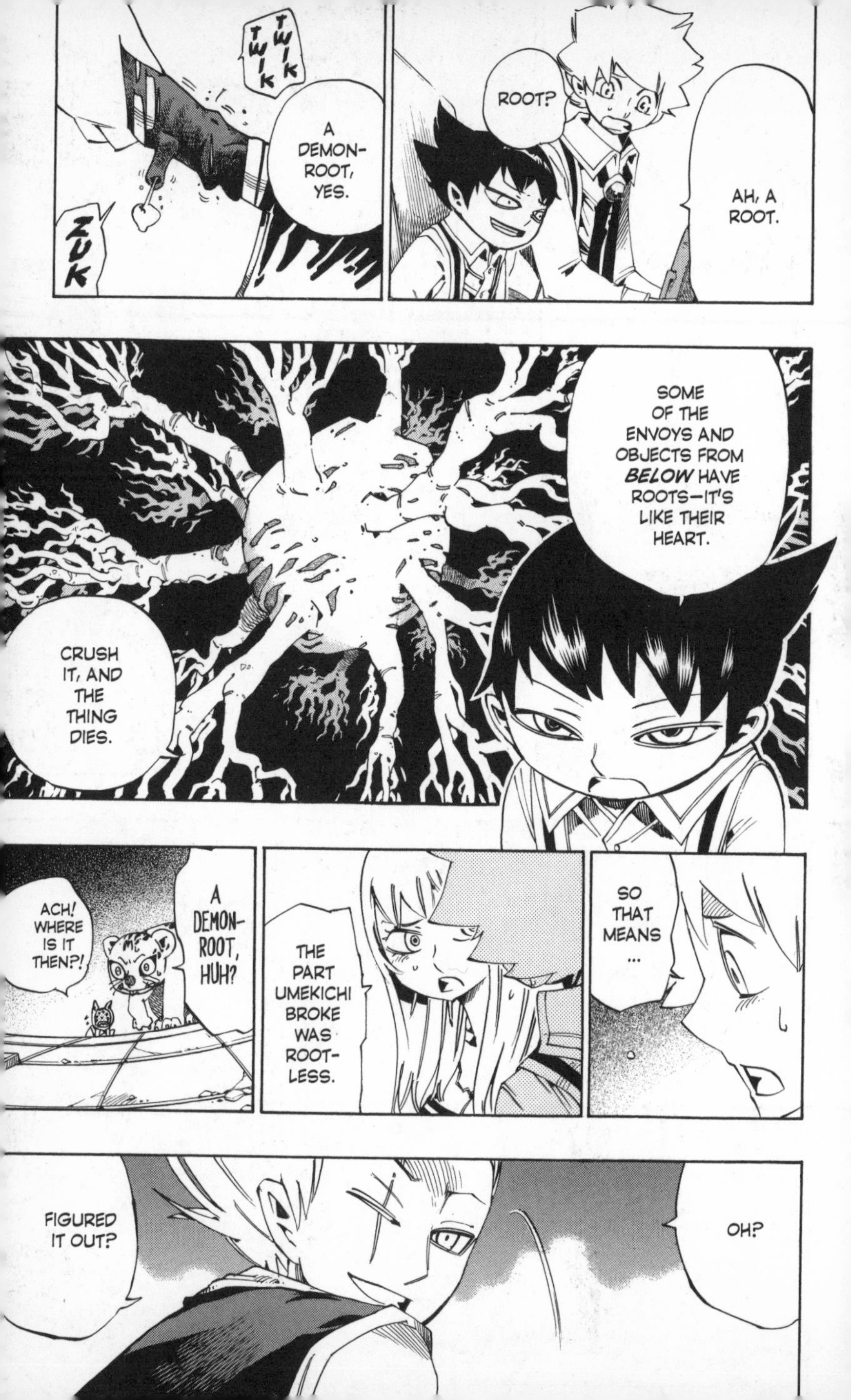
AH, A ROOT.
ROOT?
TWIK TWIK
A DEMON-ROOT, YES.
ZUK
SOME OF THE ENVOYS AND OBJECTS FROM *BELOW* HAVE ROOTS—IT'S LIKE THEIR HEART.
CRUSH IT, AND THE THING DIES.
SO THAT MEANS...
THE PART UMEKICHI BROKE WAS ROOTLESS.
A DEMON-ROOT, HUH?
ACH! WHERE IS IT THEN?!
OH?
FIGURED IT OUT?

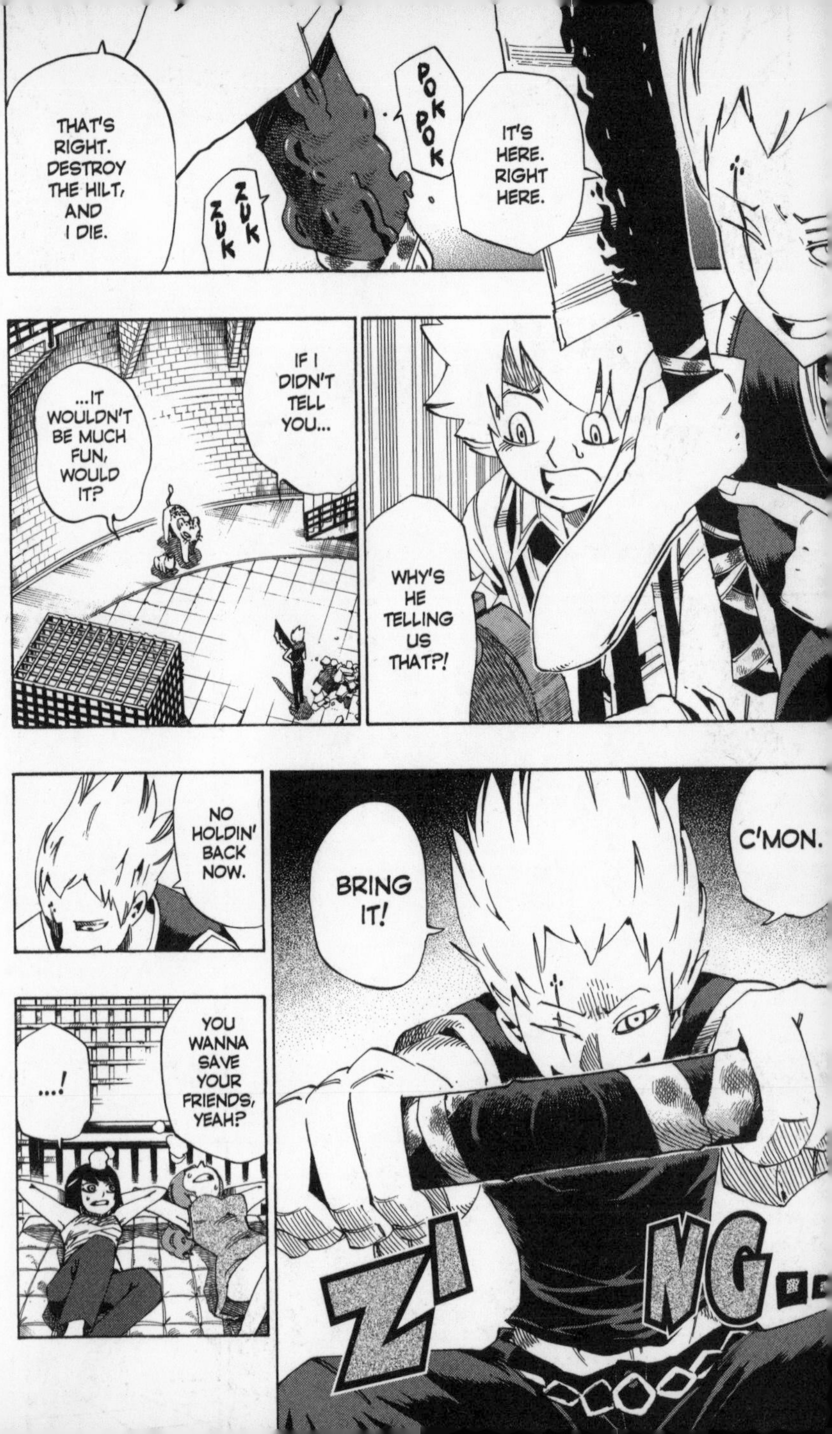
IT'S HERE. RIGHT HERE.
POK POK
ZUK ZUK
THAT'S RIGHT. DESTROY THE HILT, AND I DIE.
WHY'S HE TELLING US THAT?!
IF I DIDN'T TELL YOU...
...IT WOULDN'T BE MUCH FUN, WOULD IT?
C'MON.
BRING IT!
ZING...
NO HOLDIN' BACK NOW.
YOU WANNA SAVE YOUR FRIENDS, YEAH?
...!

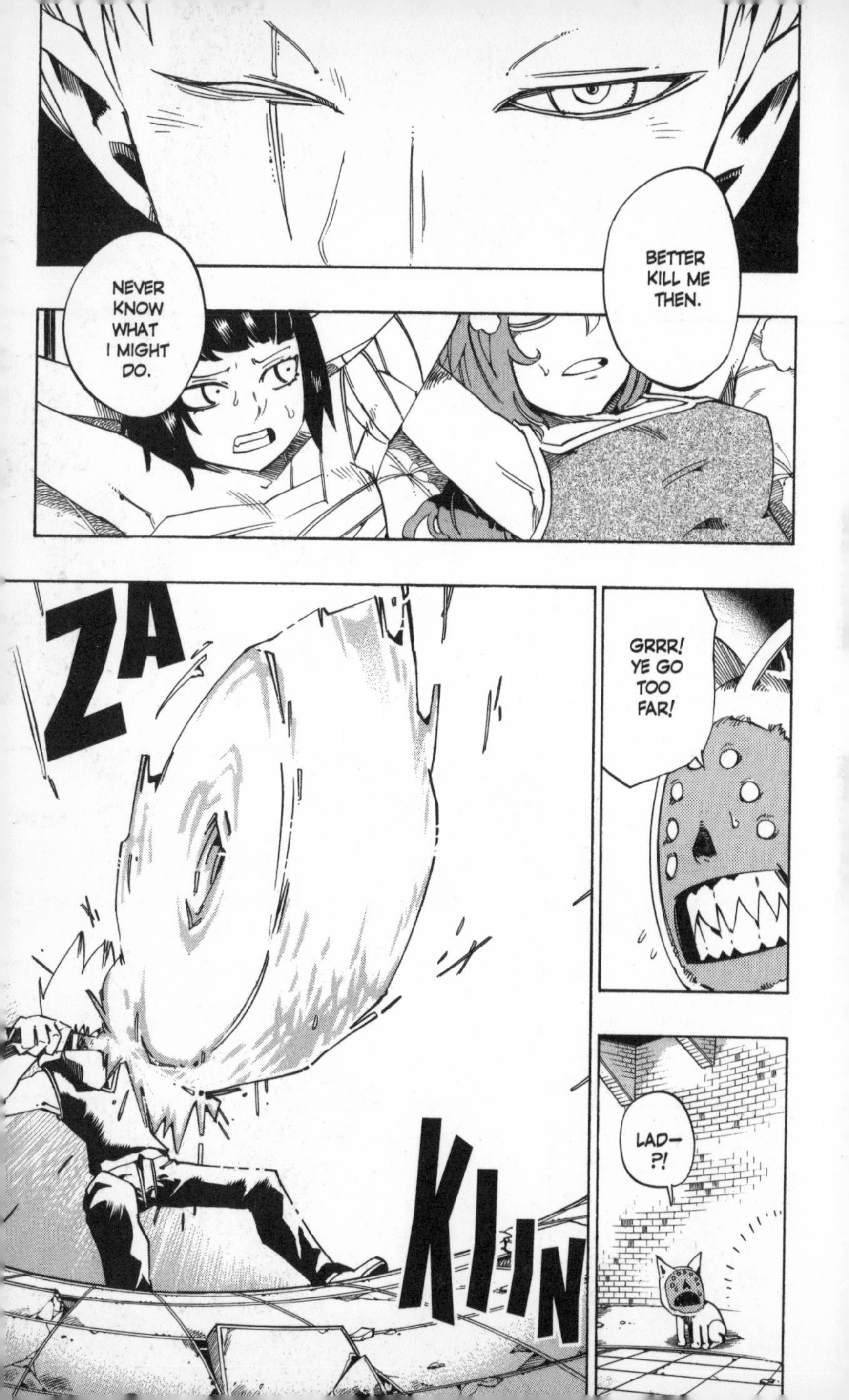
BETTER KILL ME THEN.
NEVER KNOW WHAT I MIGHT DO.
GRRR! YE GO TOO FAR!
LAD—?!
ZA
KLIIN

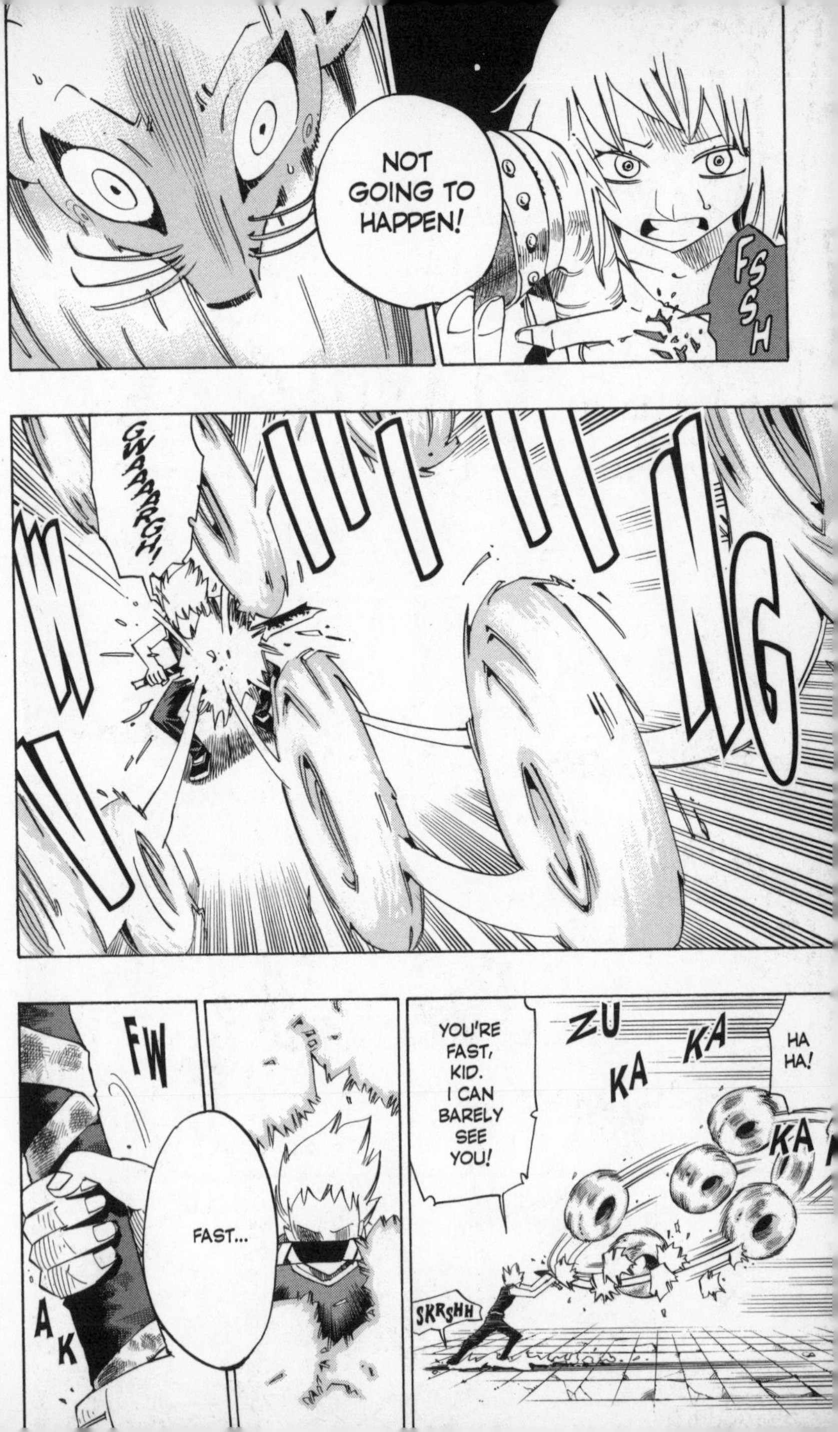
FSSH
NOT GOING TO HAPPEN!
GWAAARGH!
HA HA!
YOU'RE FAST, KID. I CAN BARELY SEE YOU!
ZU KA KA KA
SKRSHH
FW
FAST...
AK

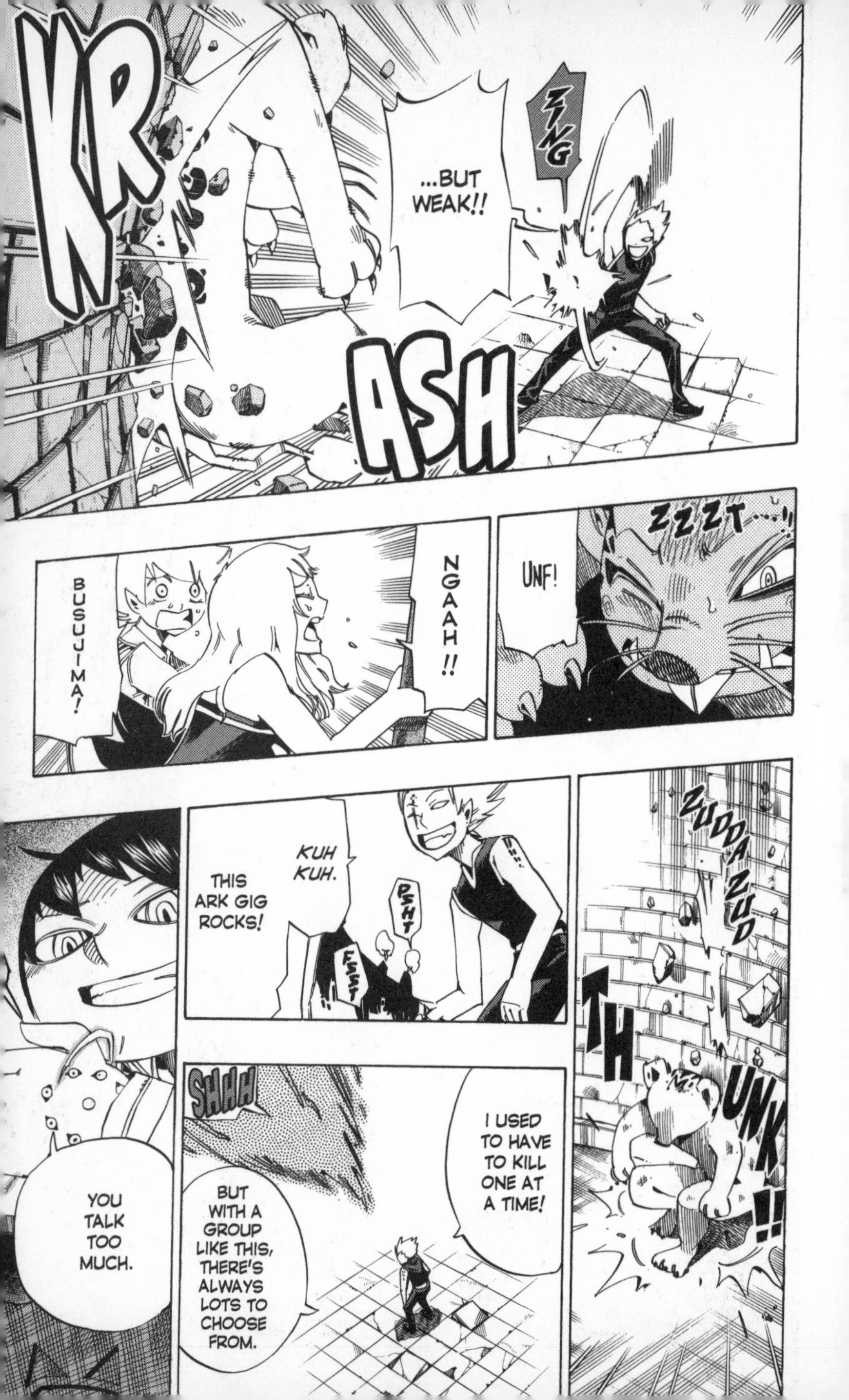
ZING
...BUT WEAK!!
KR
ASH
ZZZT...!!
UNF!
NGAAH!!
BUSUJIMA!
ZUDDAZUD
TH
UNK!!
KUH KUH.
THIS ARK GIG ROCKS!
PSHT
FSST
I USED TO HAVE TO KILL ONE AT A TIME!
BUT WITH A GROUP LIKE THIS, THERE'S ALWAYS LOTS TO CHOOSE FROM.
SHHH
YOU TALK TOO MUCH.

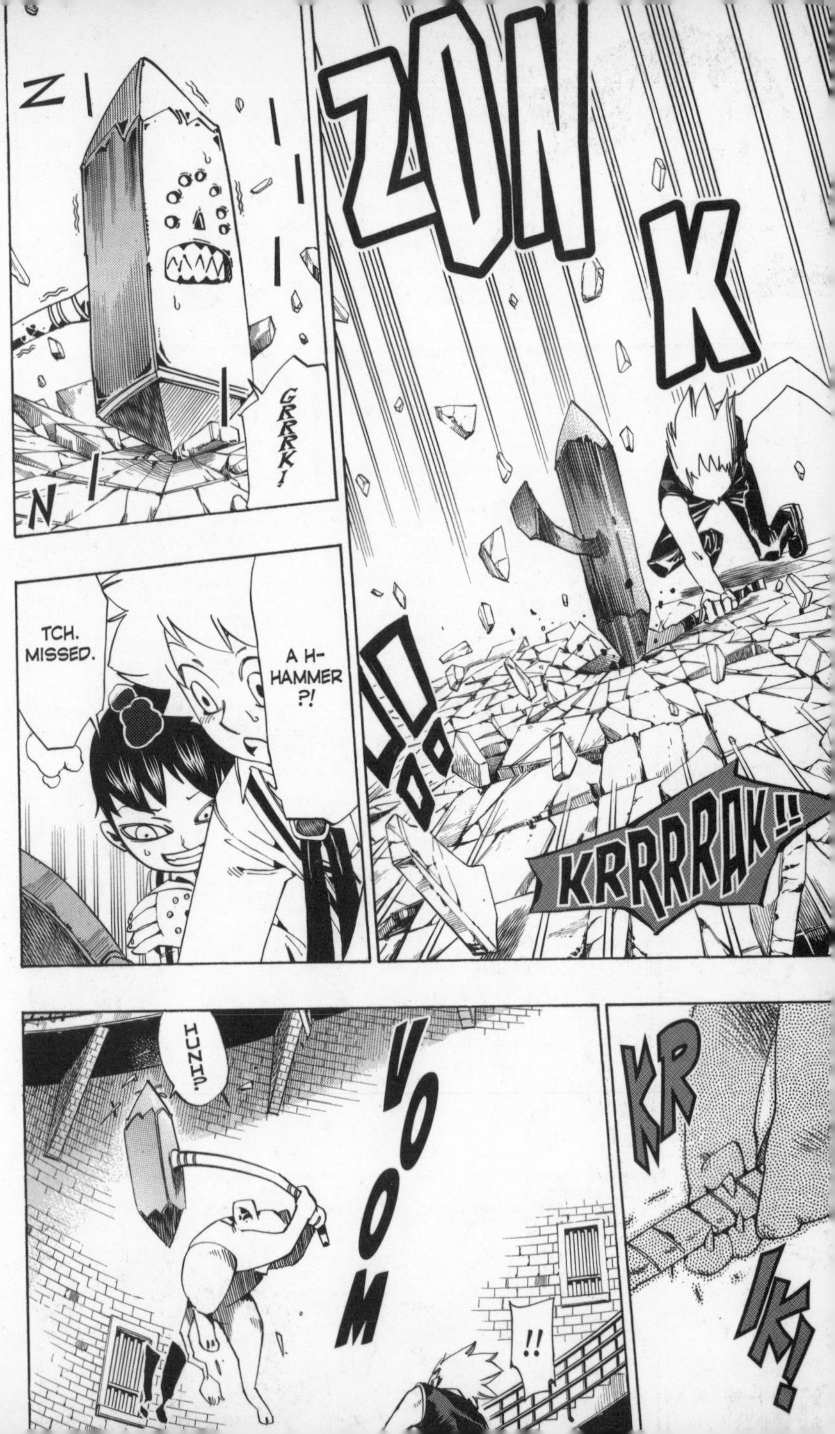
ZONK
!!
KRRRRAK!!
GRRRK!
ZIIIN
A H-HAMMER?!
TCH. MISSED.
KRIK!
VOOOOM
HUNH?
!!

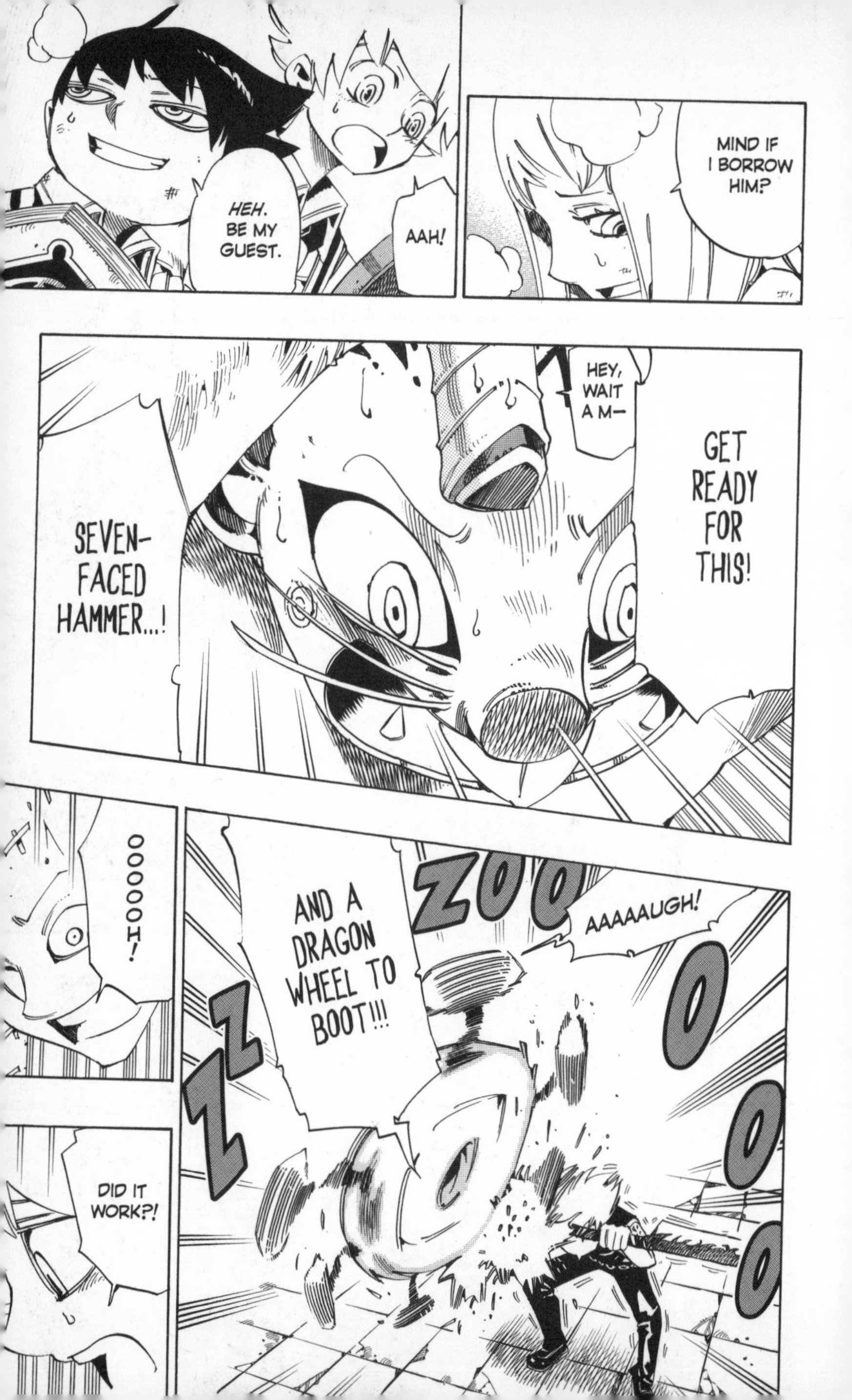
MIND IF I BORROW HIM?
AAH!
HEH. BE MY GUEST.
HEY, WAIT A M—
GET READY FOR THIS!
SEVEN-FACED HAMMER...!
AAAAAUGH!
ZOO
OOO
AND A DRAGON WHEEL TO BOOT!!!
ZZ
OOOOOOH!
DID IT WORK?!

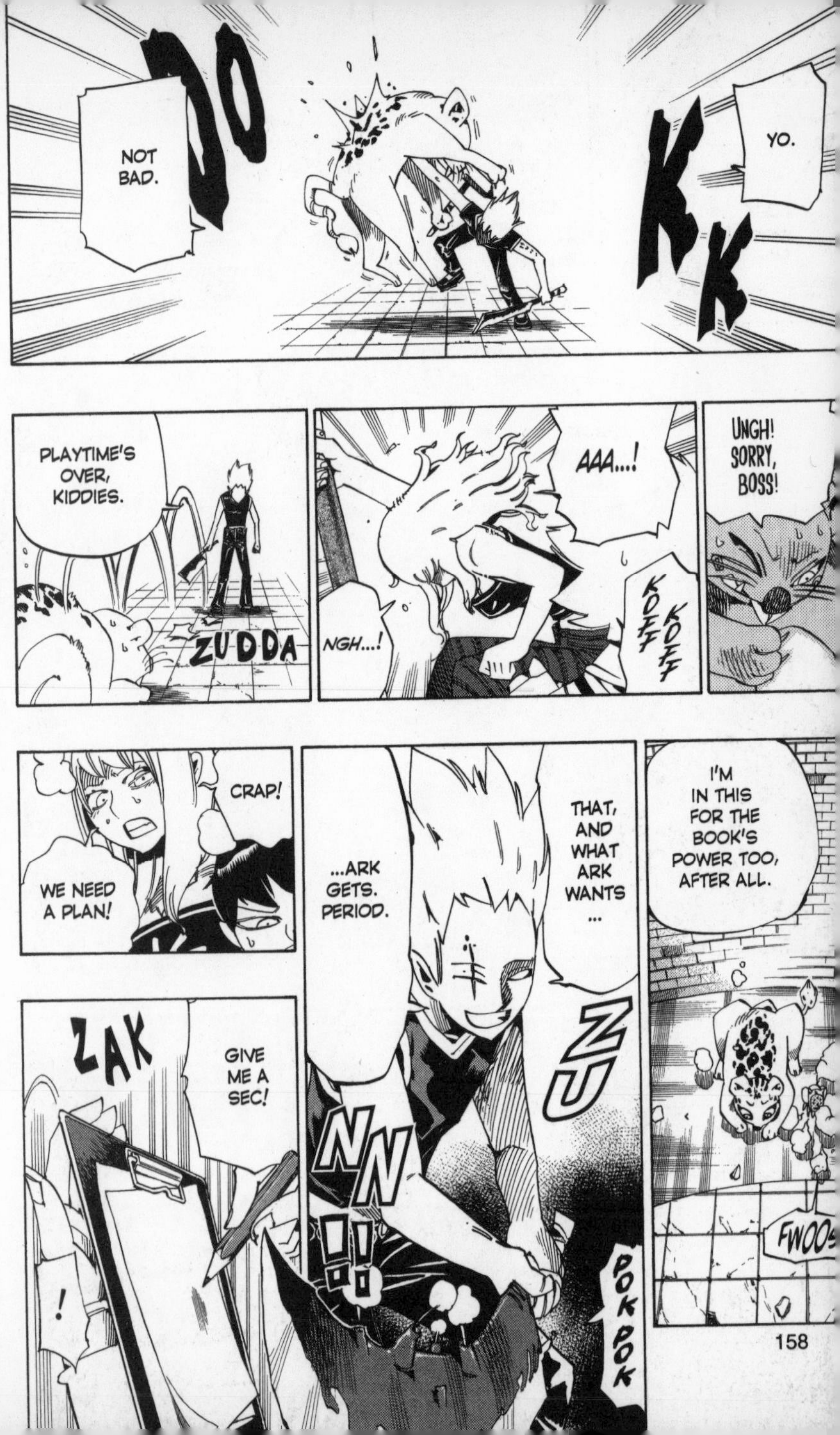
DOKK
YO.
NOT BAD.
UNGH! SORRY, BOSS!
AAA...!
KOFF KOFF
NGH...!
PLAYTIME'S OVER, KIDDIES.
ZUDDA
I'M IN THIS FOR THE BOOK'S POWER TOO, AFTER ALL.
THAT, AND WHAT ARK WANTS ...
...ARK GETS. PERIOD.
ZUNN!!
POK POK
CRAP!
WE NEED A PLAN!
ZAK
GIVE ME A SEC!
!

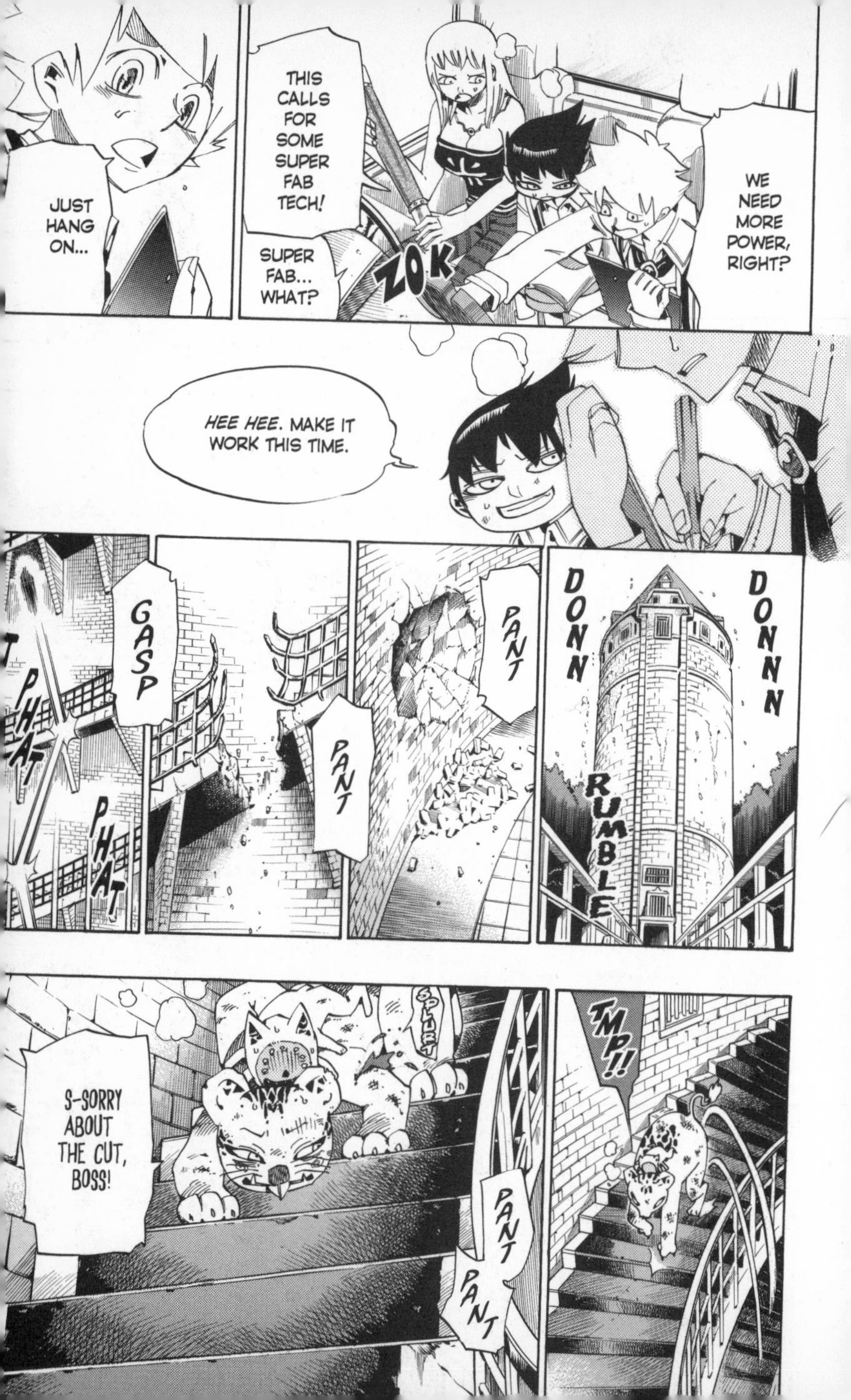

WE NEED MORE POWER, RIGHT?
THIS CALLS FOR SOME SUPER FAB TECH!
ZOK
SUPER FAB... WHAT?
JUST HANG ON...
HEE HEE. MAKE IT WORK THIS TIME.
DONNN
DONN
RUMBLE
PANT
PANT
GASP
PHAT
PHAT
TMP!!
PANT
PANT
SPLURT
S-SORRY ABOUT THE CUT, BOSS!

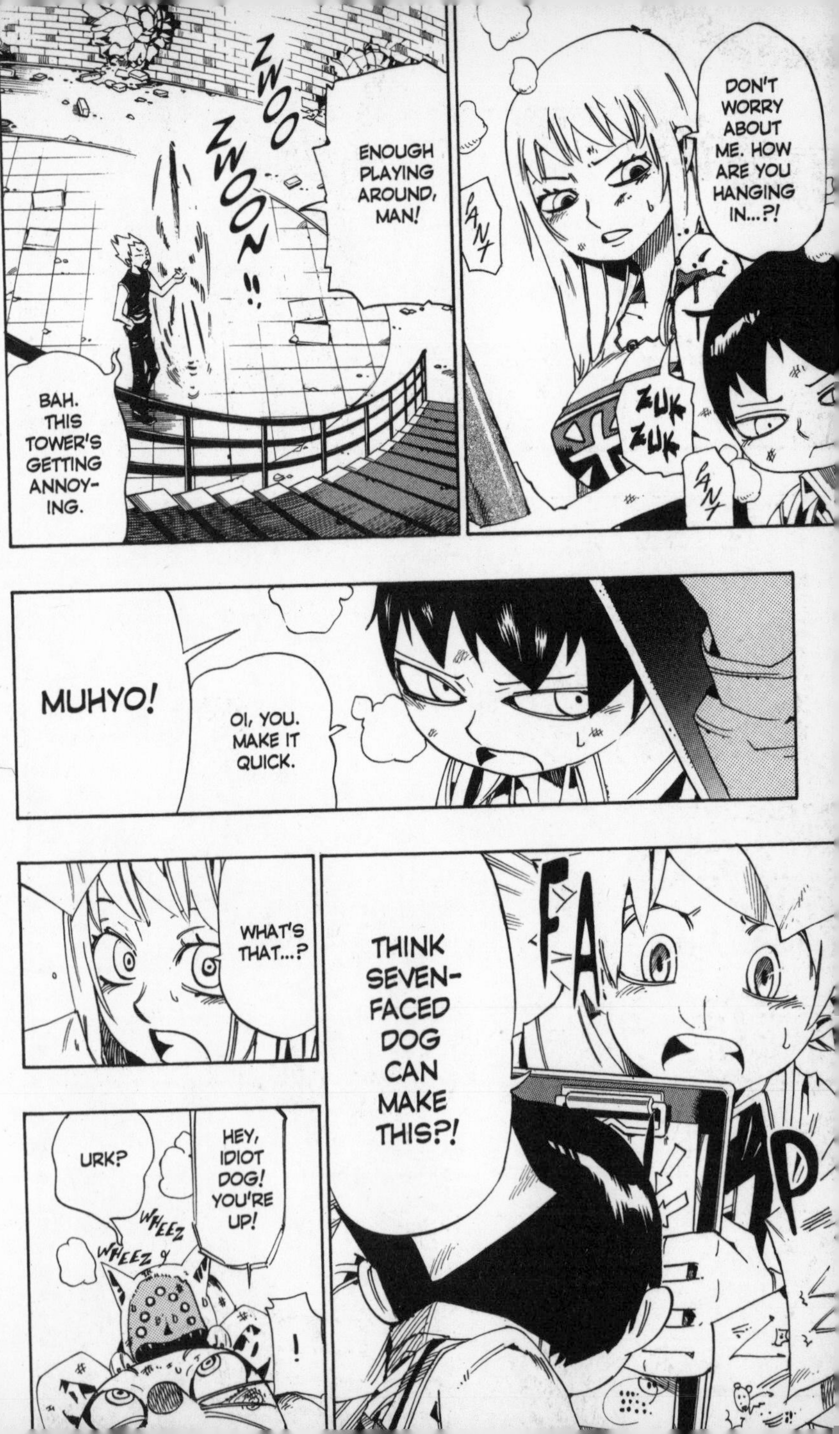
DON'T WORRY ABOUT ME. HOW ARE YOU HANGING IN...?!
PANT
ZUK ZUK
PANT
ENOUGH PLAYING AROUND, MAN!
ZWOO ZWOON!!
BAH. THIS TOWER'S GETTING ANNOY-ING.
OI, YOU. MAKE IT QUICK.
MUHYO!
FA
THINK SEVEN-FACED DOG CAN MAKE THIS?!
TAP
WHAT'S THAT...?
HEY, IDIOT DOG! YOU'RE UP!
URK?
WHEEZ
WHEEZ
!

PLIT PLIT

!

STILL HIGHER...

DOK

TCH.

FLIGHTY LITTLE RUNTS...

STRR

KZZZZZ !!!

ETCH!!

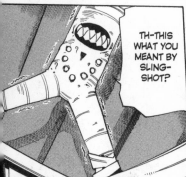

TH-THIS WHAT YOU MEANT BY SLING-SHOT?

VW

...EH?

ZAK

HAH?!

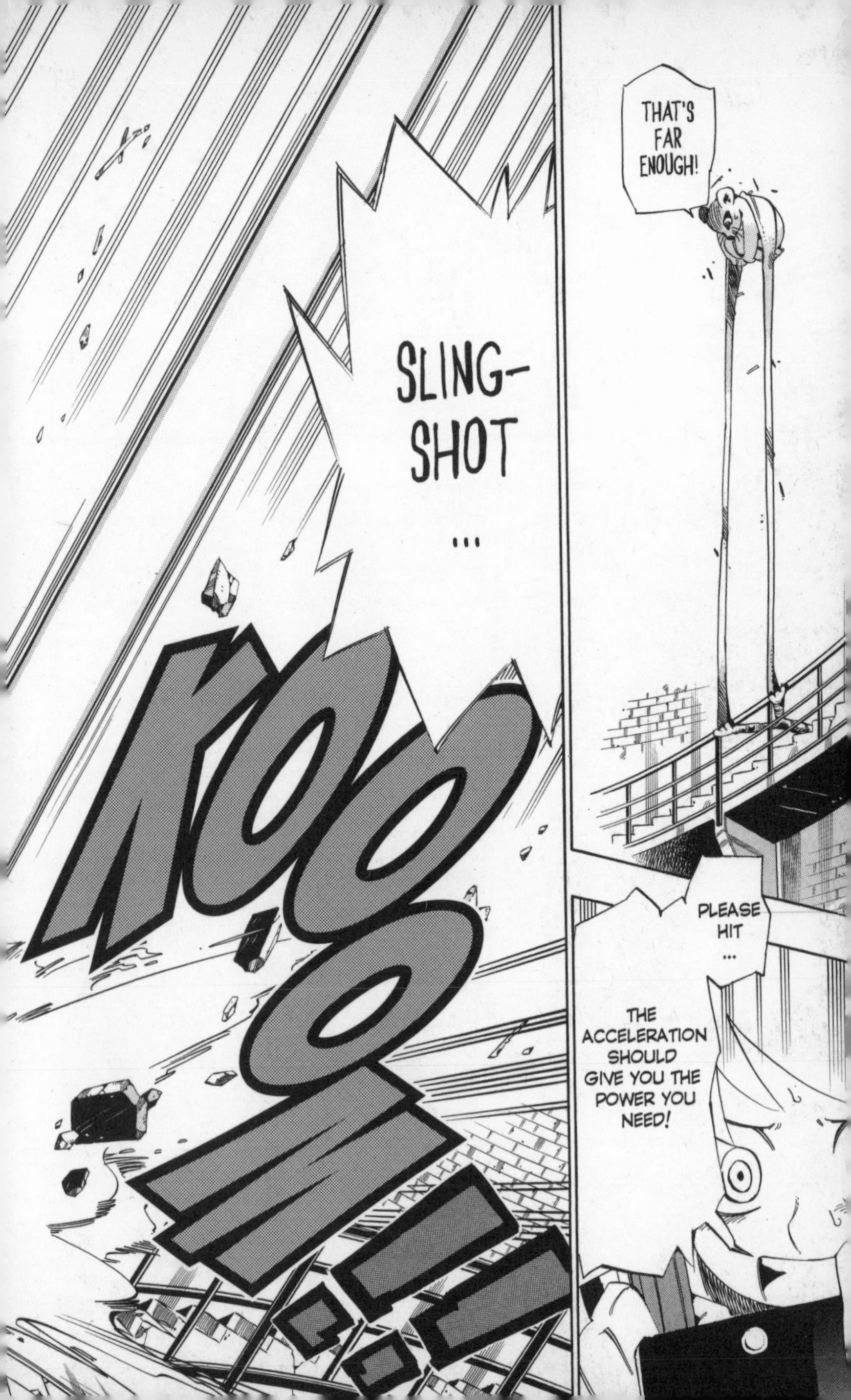
THAT'S FAR ENOUGH!
PLEASE HIT ...
THE ACCELERATION SHOULD GIVE YOU THE POWER YOU NEED!
SLING-SHOT ...

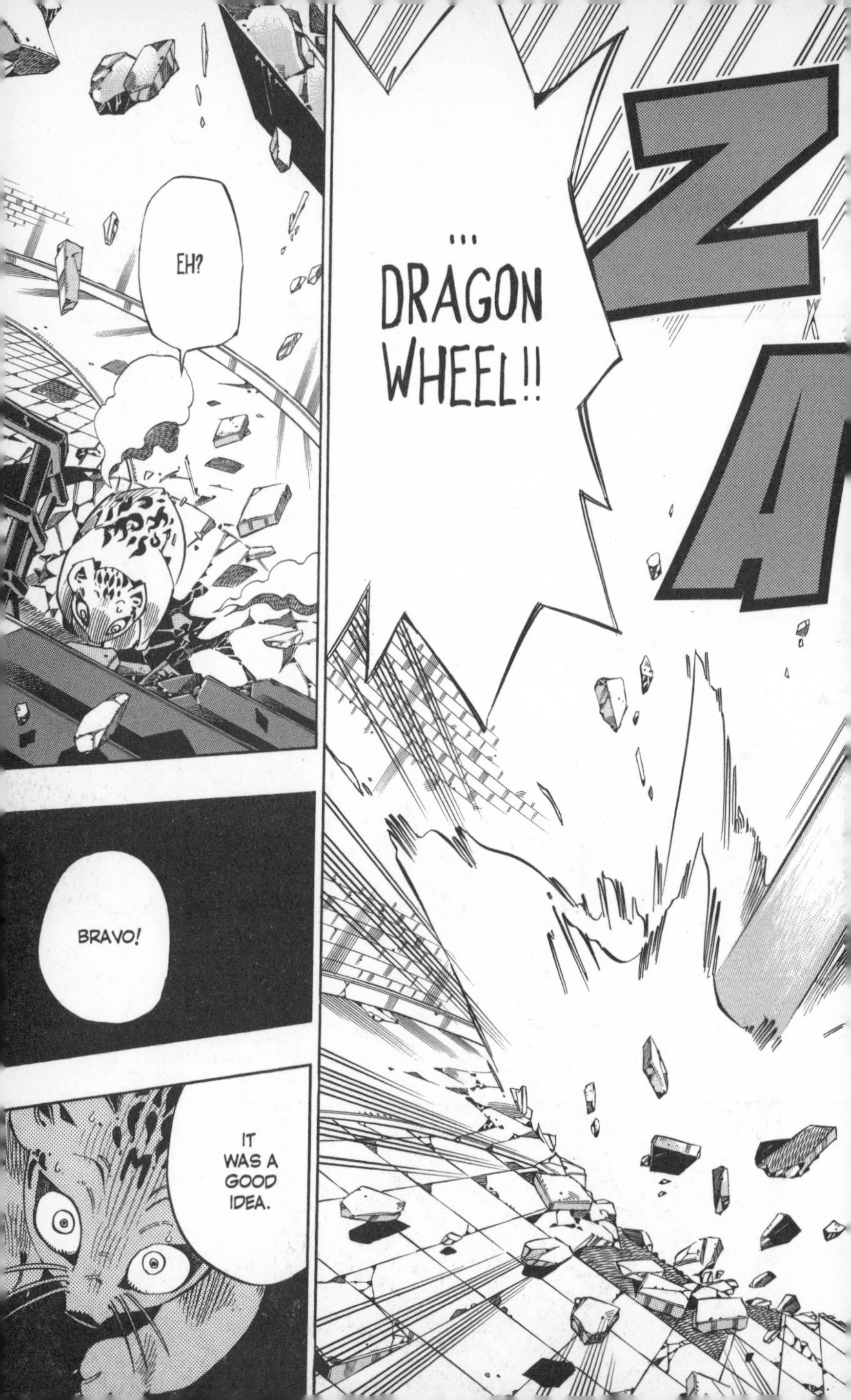
ZA
...DRAGON WHEEL!!
EH?
BRAVO!
IT WAS A GOOD IDEA.

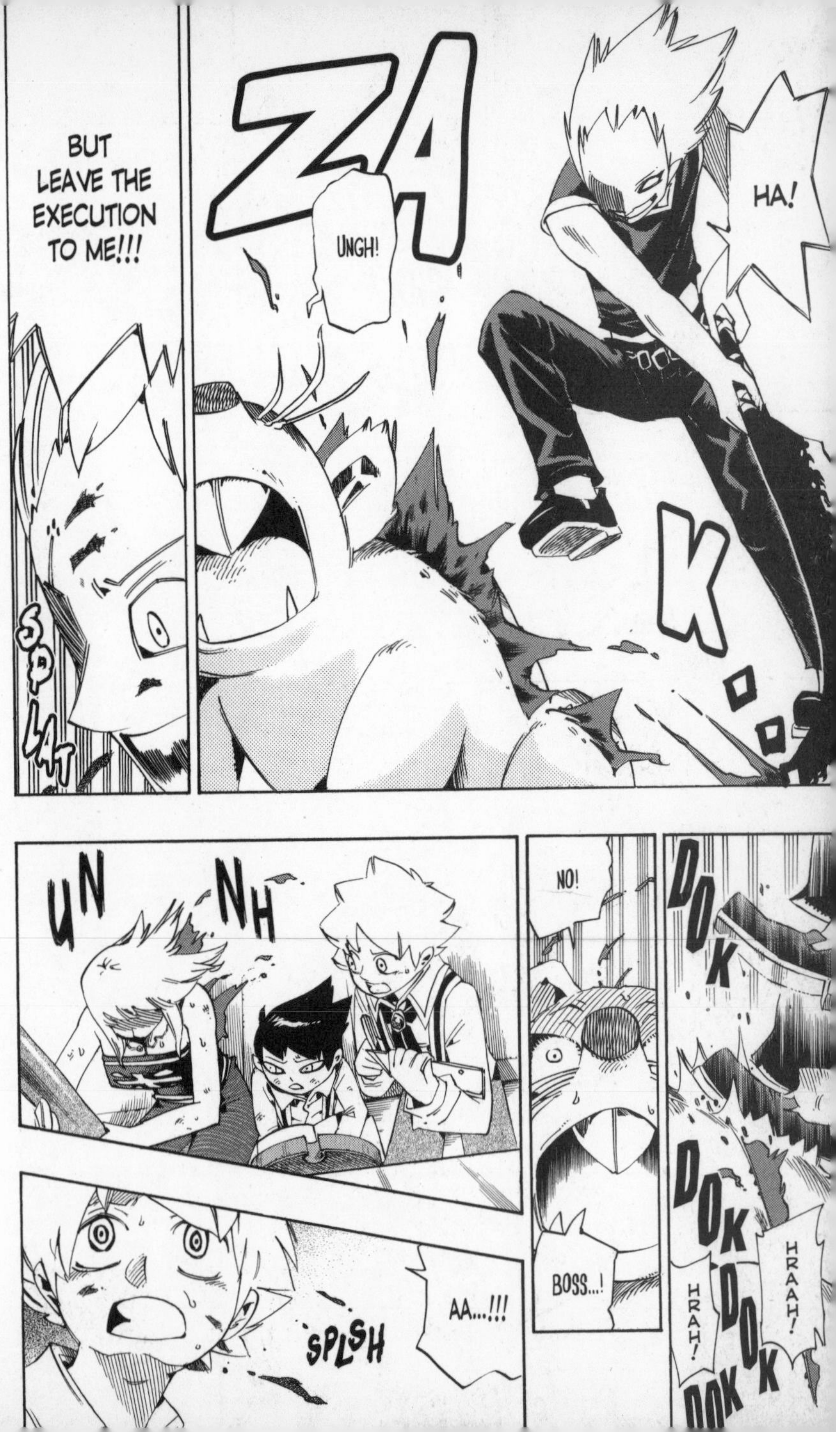

HA!
ZA
UNGH!
K
BUT LEAVE THE EXECUTION TO ME!!!
SPLAT
DOKDOK
DOKDOKDOK
HRAAH!
HRAH!
NO!
BOSS...!
UNNH
AA...!!!
SPLSH

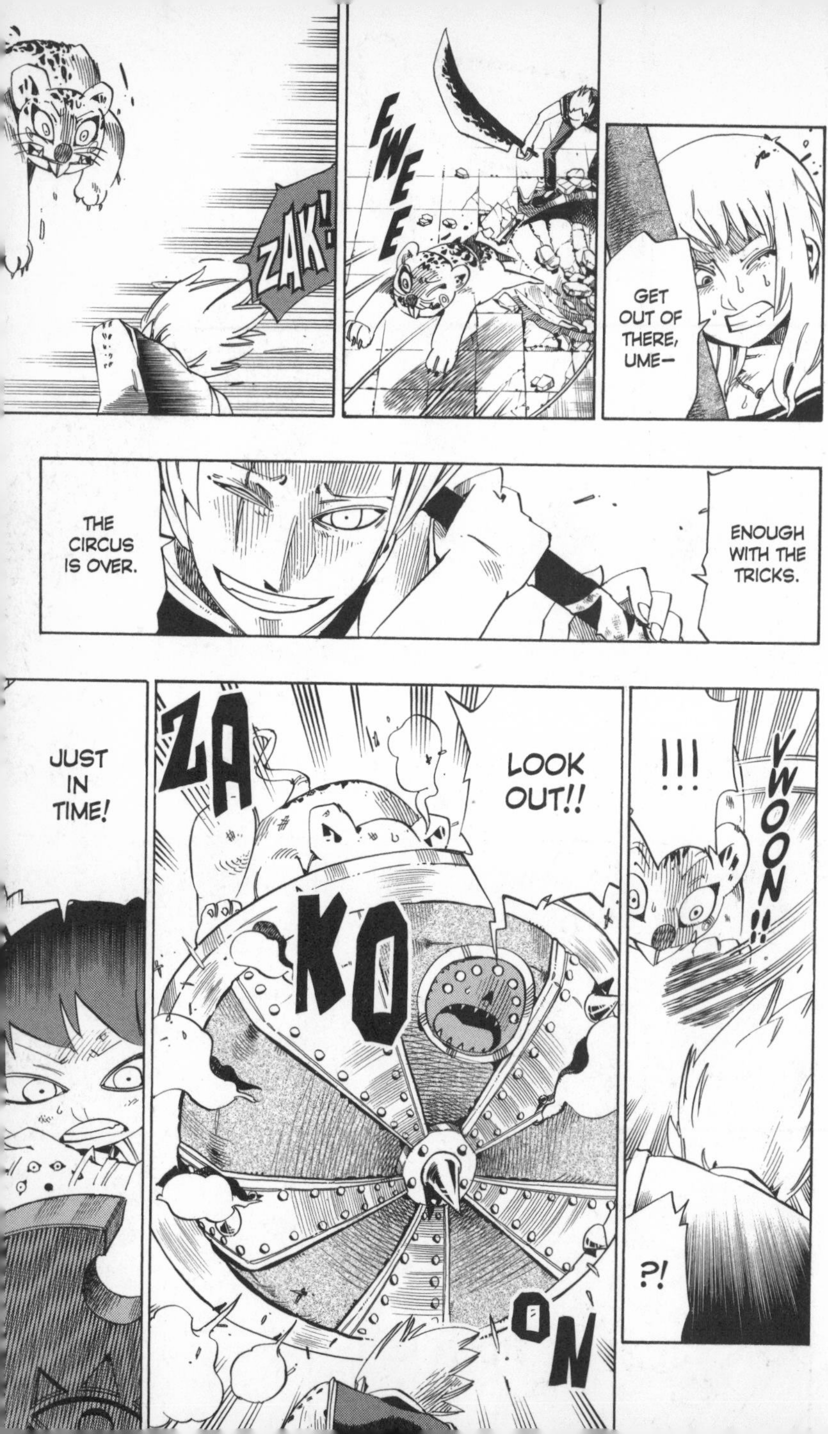
GET OUT OF THERE, UME—
FWEEE
ZAK!
ENOUGH WITH THE TRICKS.
THE CIRCUS IS OVER.
VWOON!!
!!!
?!
LOOK OUT!!
ZA
KO
ON
JUST IN TIME!

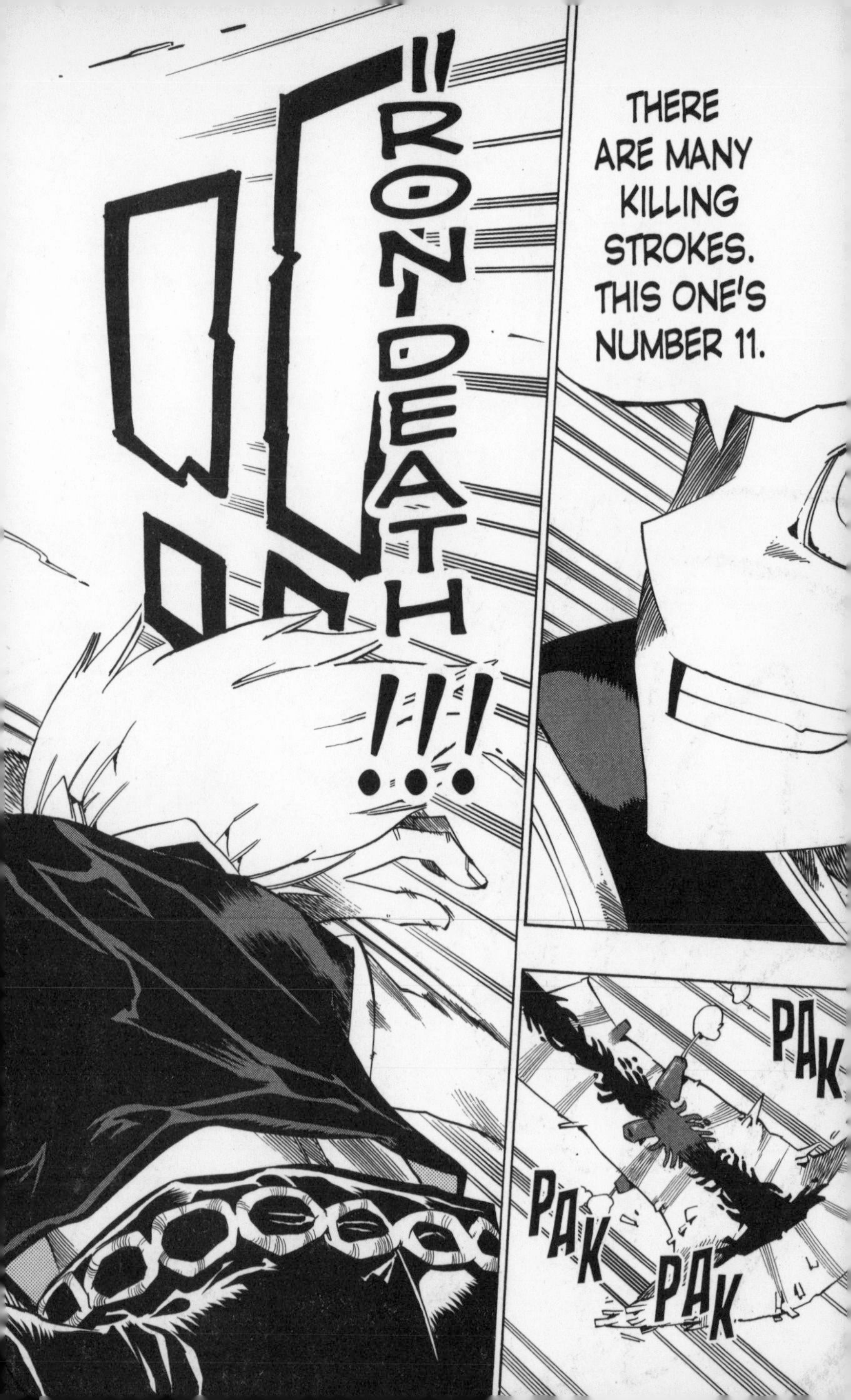
THERE ARE MANY KILLING STROKES. THIS ONE'S NUMBER 11.
PAK
PAK PAK
PAK PAK
IRON DEATH!!!

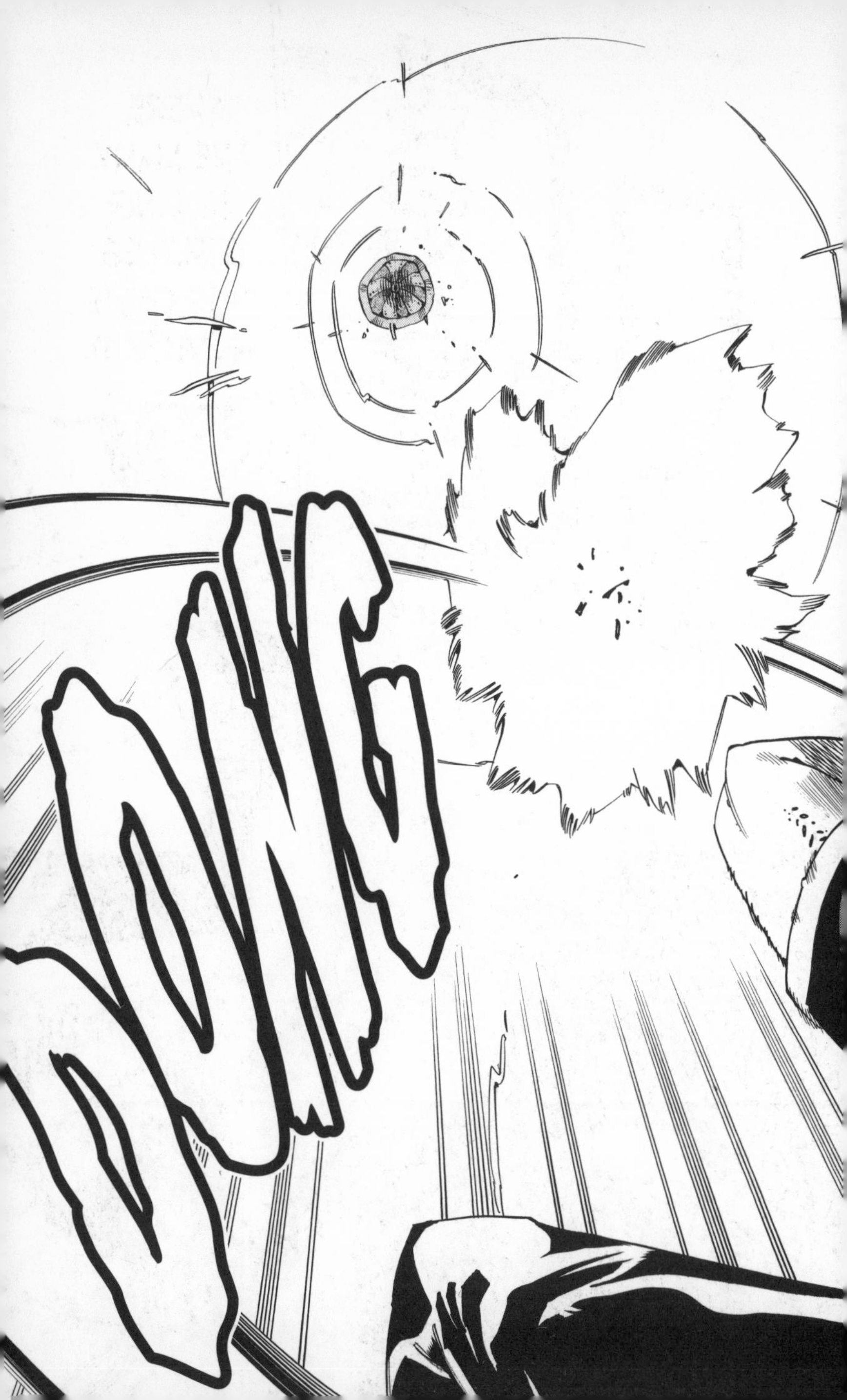

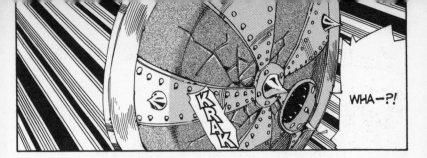

WHA-?!

MUHYO!!!

UNGH!!!

VOO

KRAAK!!

PHUT

ZUUU...

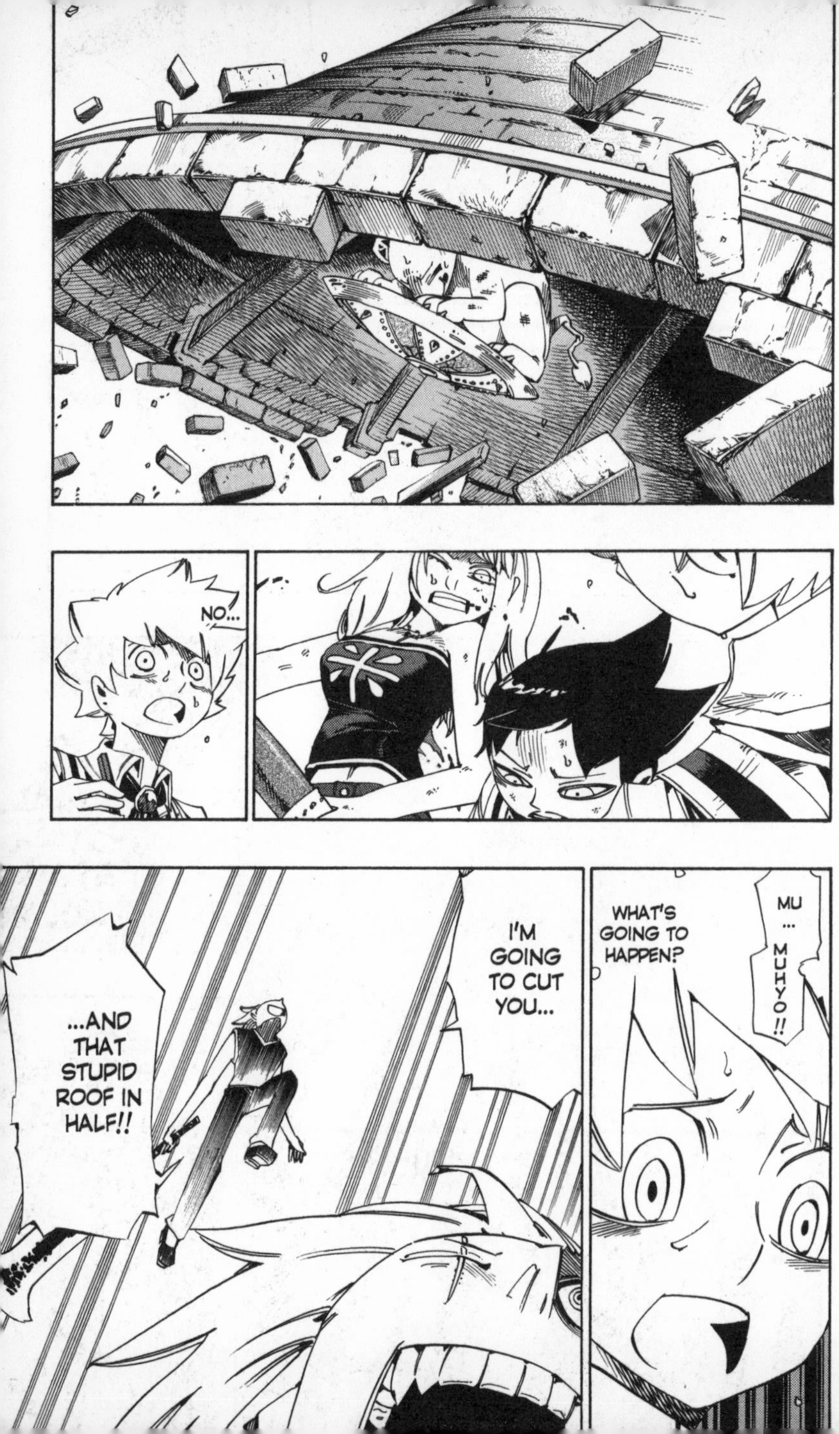
NO...
MU ... MUHYO!!
WHAT'S GOING TO HAPPEN?
I'M GOING TO CUT YOU...
...AND THAT STUPID ROOF IN HALF!!

Muhyo & Roji's
Bureau of Supernatural Investigation
BSI

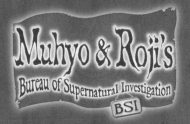

ARTICLE 94
COURAGE

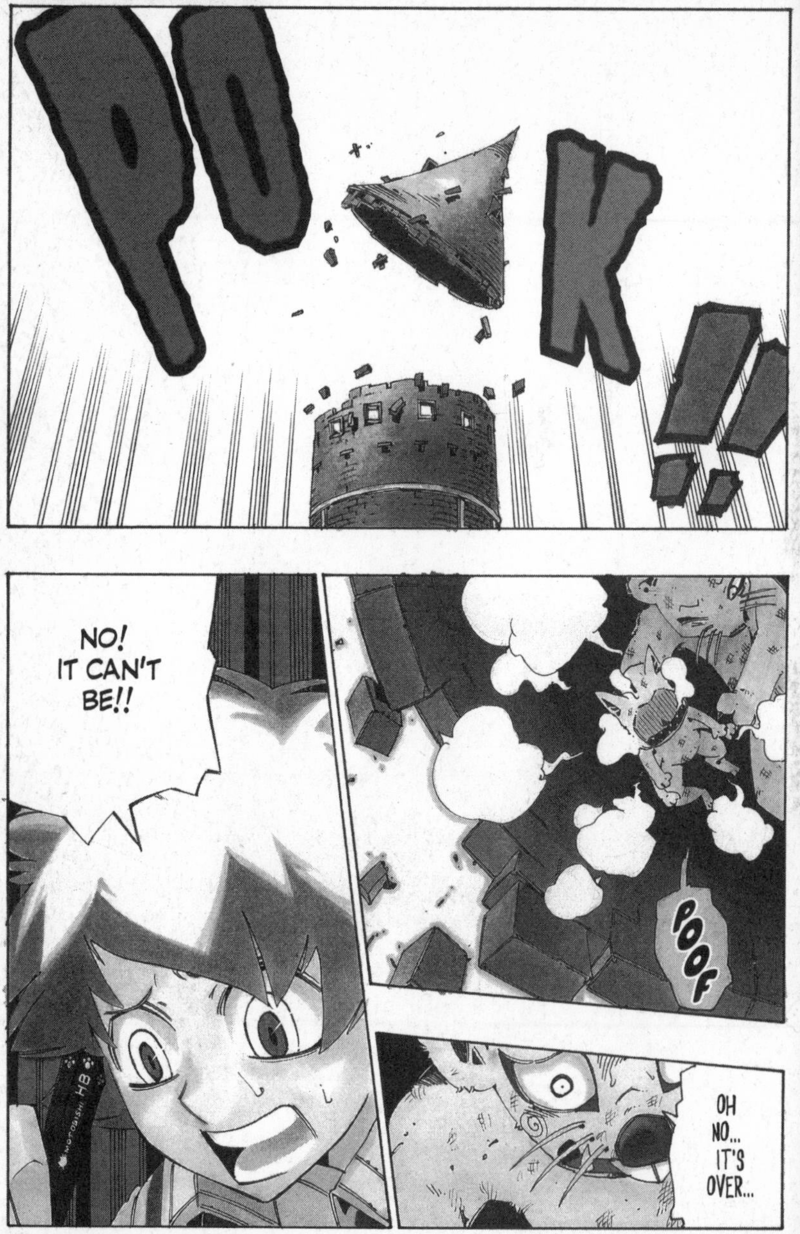
POK!!
POOF
OH NO... IT'S OVER...
NO! IT CAN'T BE!!

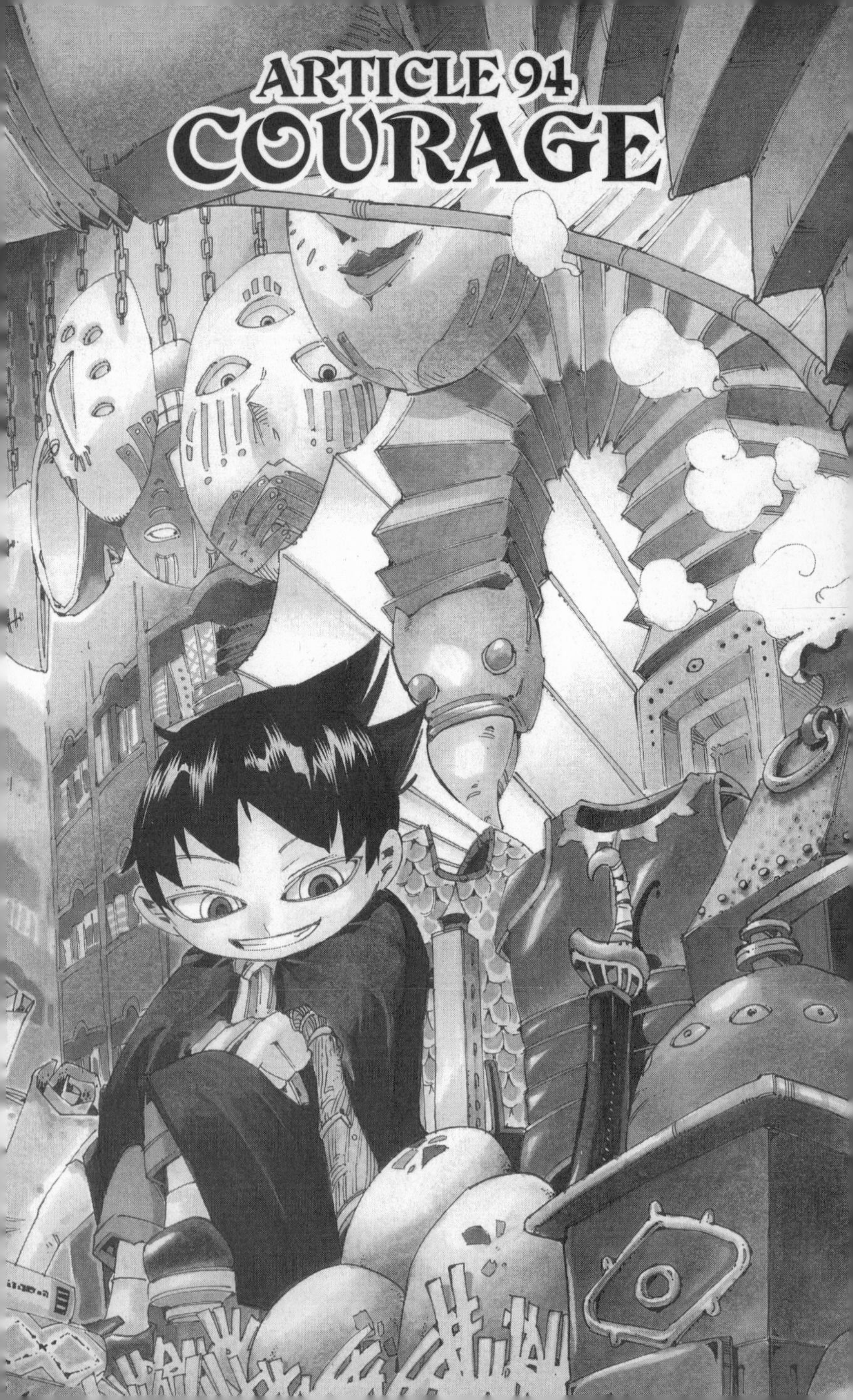
ARTICLE 94
COURAGE

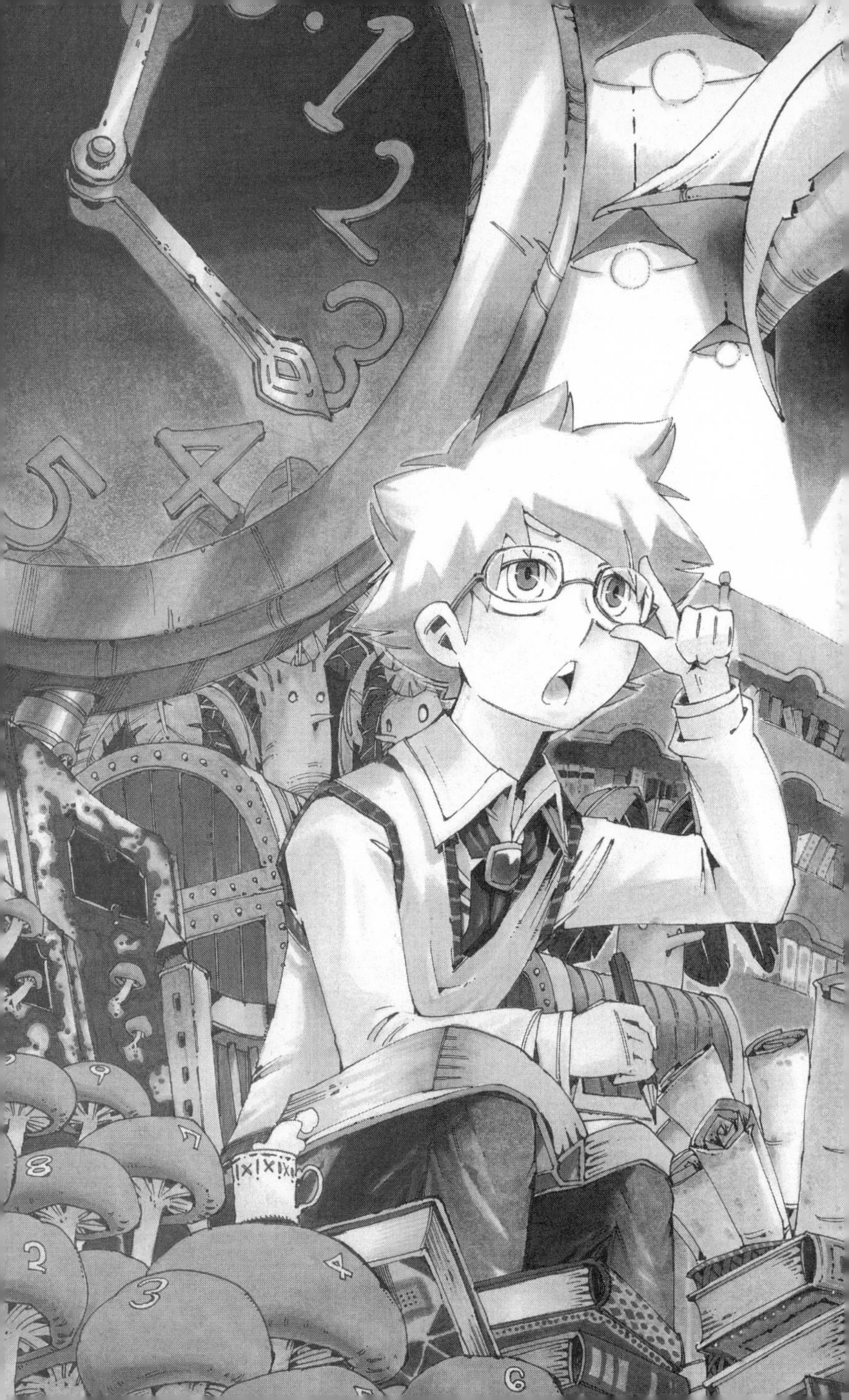

Muhyo & Roji's
Bureau of Supernatural Investigation
BSI

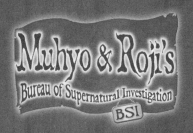

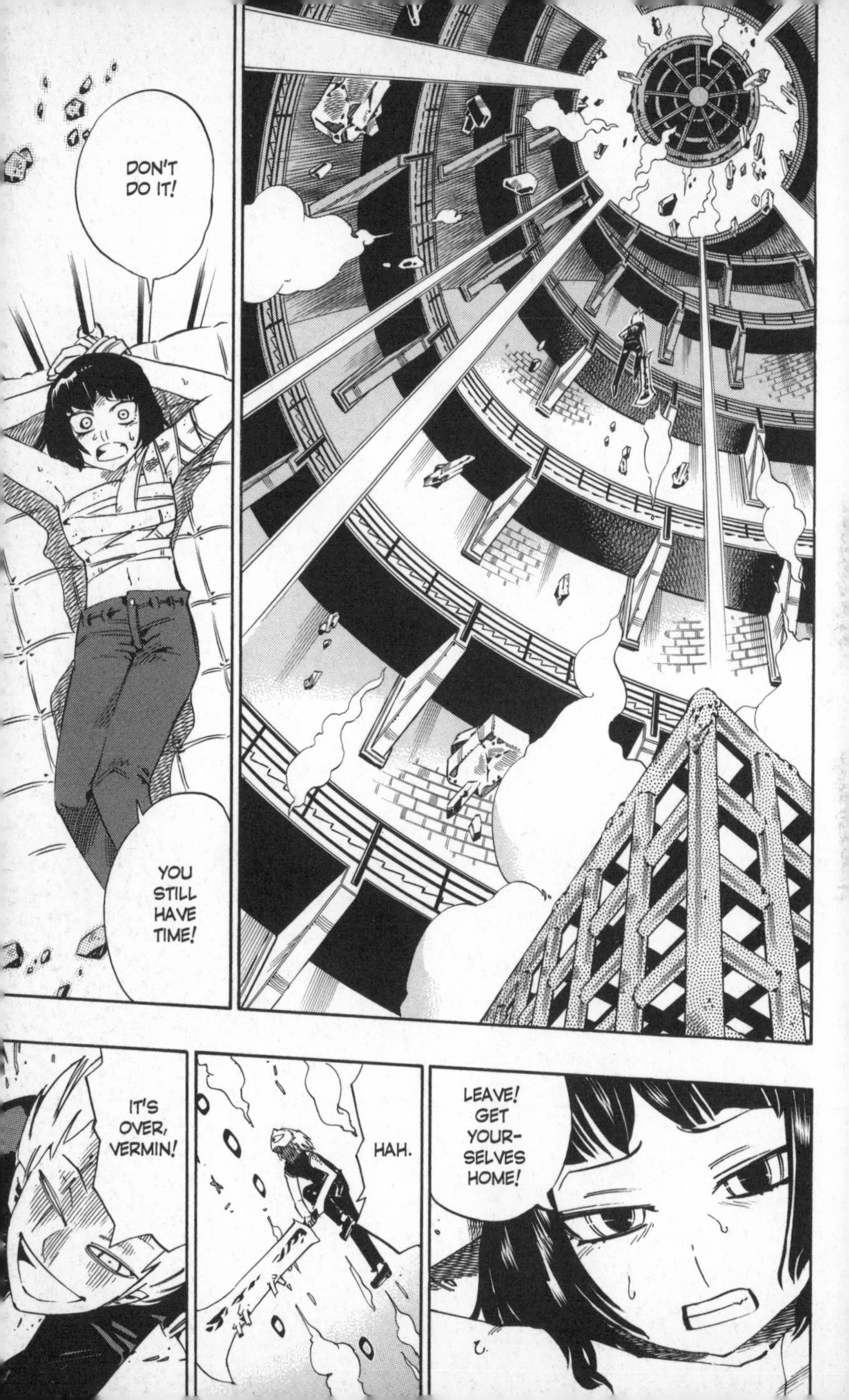
DON'T DO IT!
YOU STILL HAVE TIME!
LEAVE! GET YOUR-SELVES HOME!
HAH.
IT'S OVER, VERMIN!

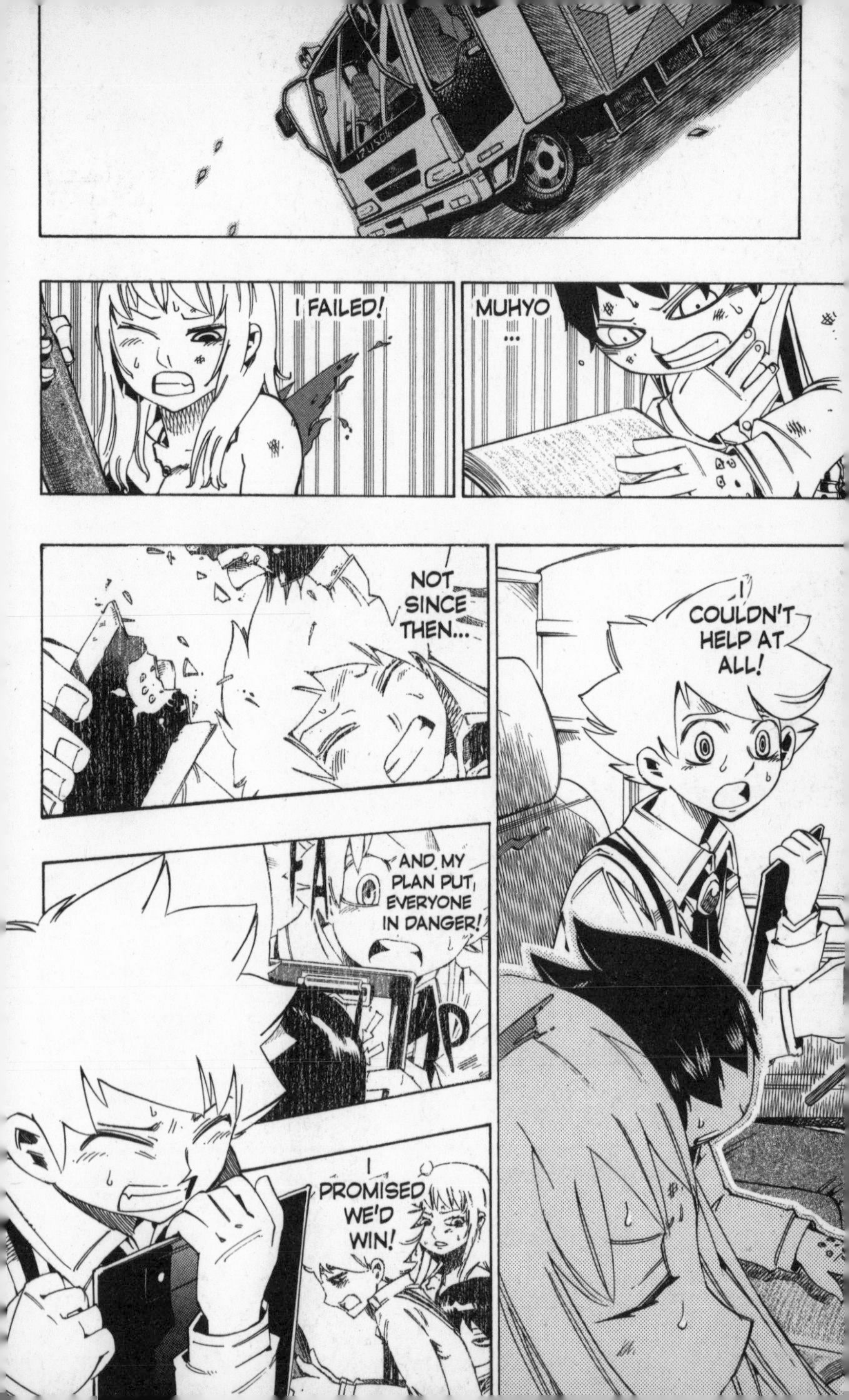
MUHYO ...
I FAILED!
I COULDN'T HELP AT ALL!
NOT SINCE THEN...
AND MY PLAN PUT EVERYONE IN DANGER!
I PROMISED WE'D WIN!

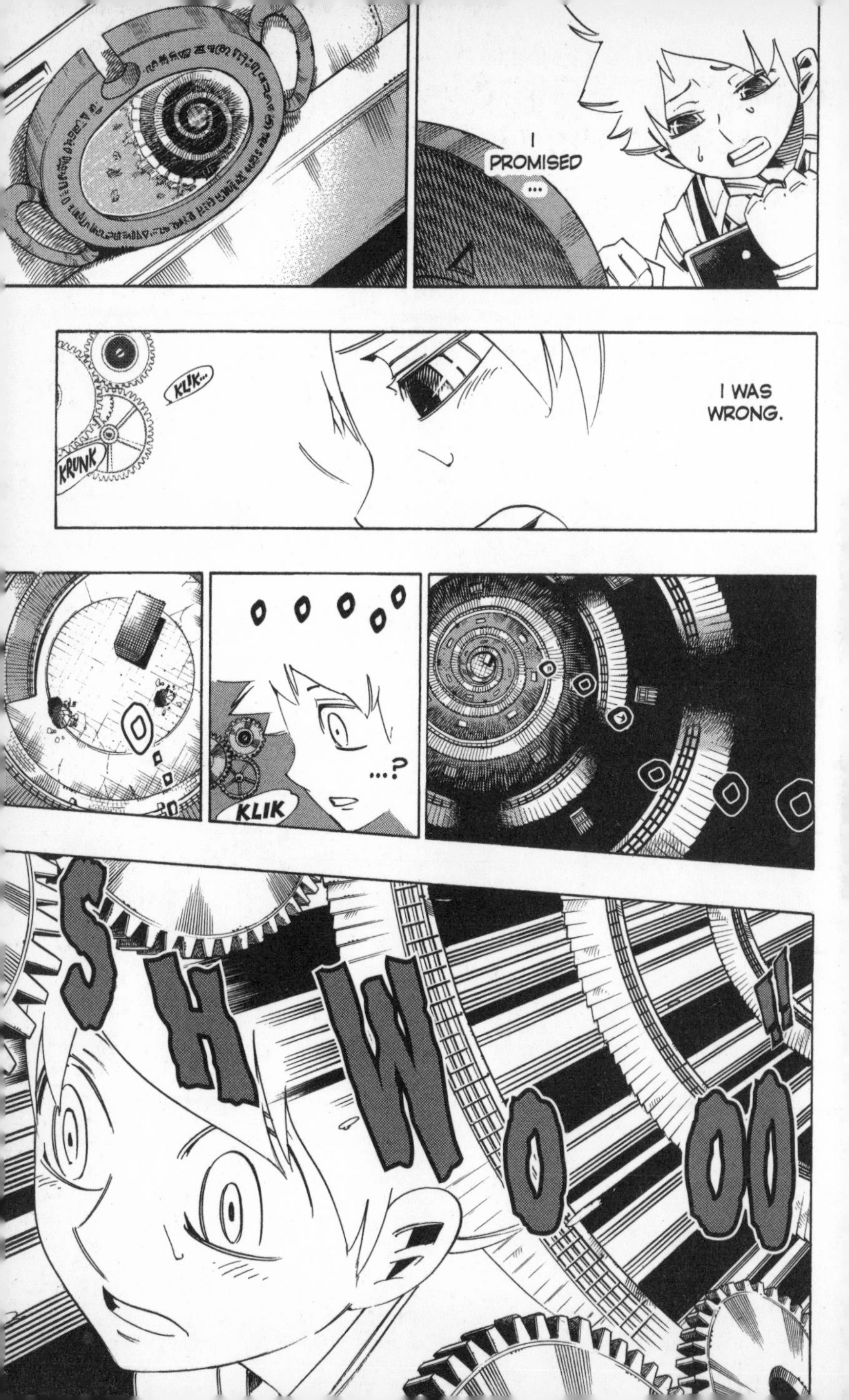
I PROMISED ...
I WAS WRONG.
KLIK...
KRUNK
...?
KLIK
SHWOOO!!

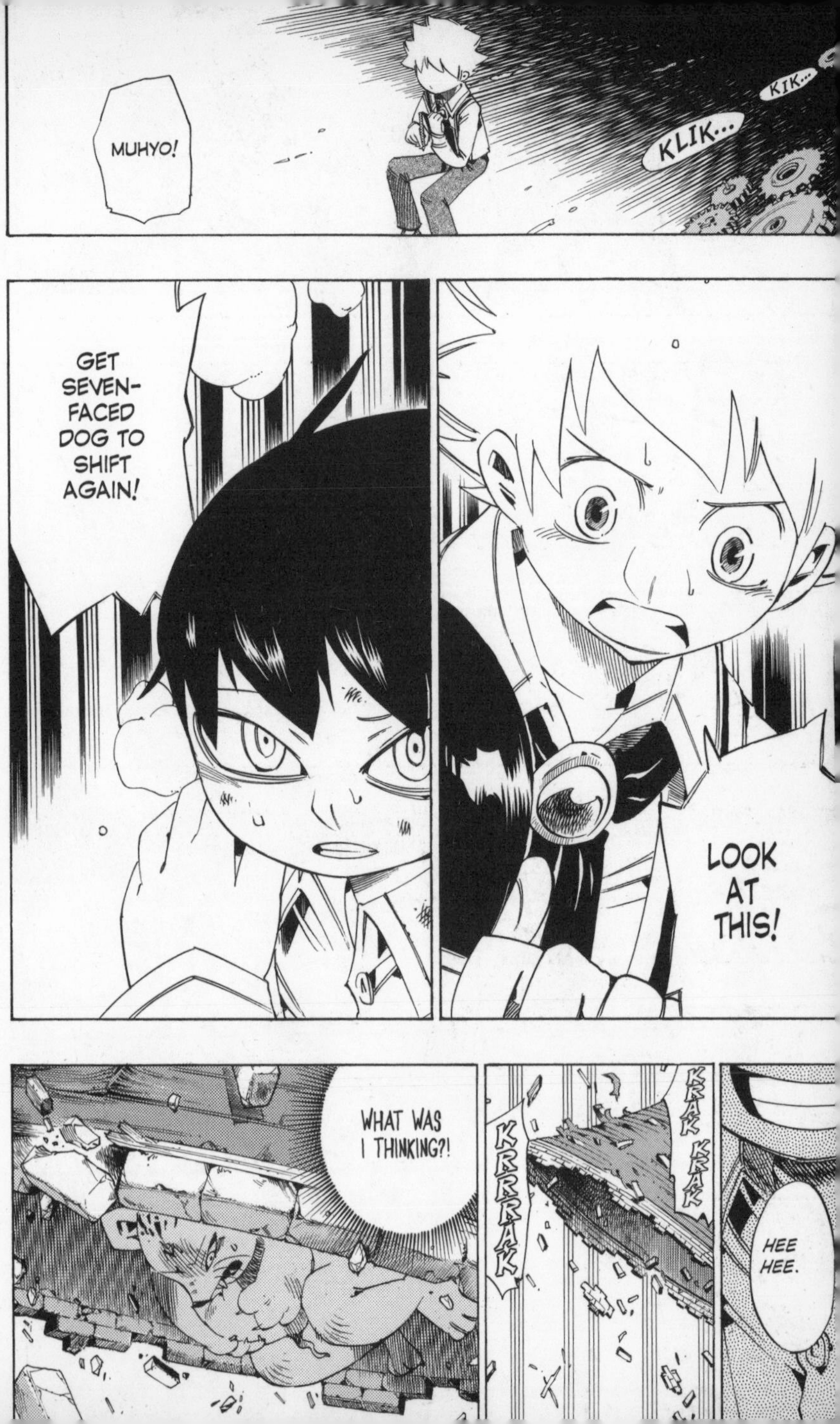
KIK...
KLIK...
MUHYO!
LOOK AT THIS!
GET SEVEN-FACED DOG TO SHIFT AGAIN!
HEE HEE.
KRAK KRAK
KRRRAK
WHAT WAS I THINKING?!

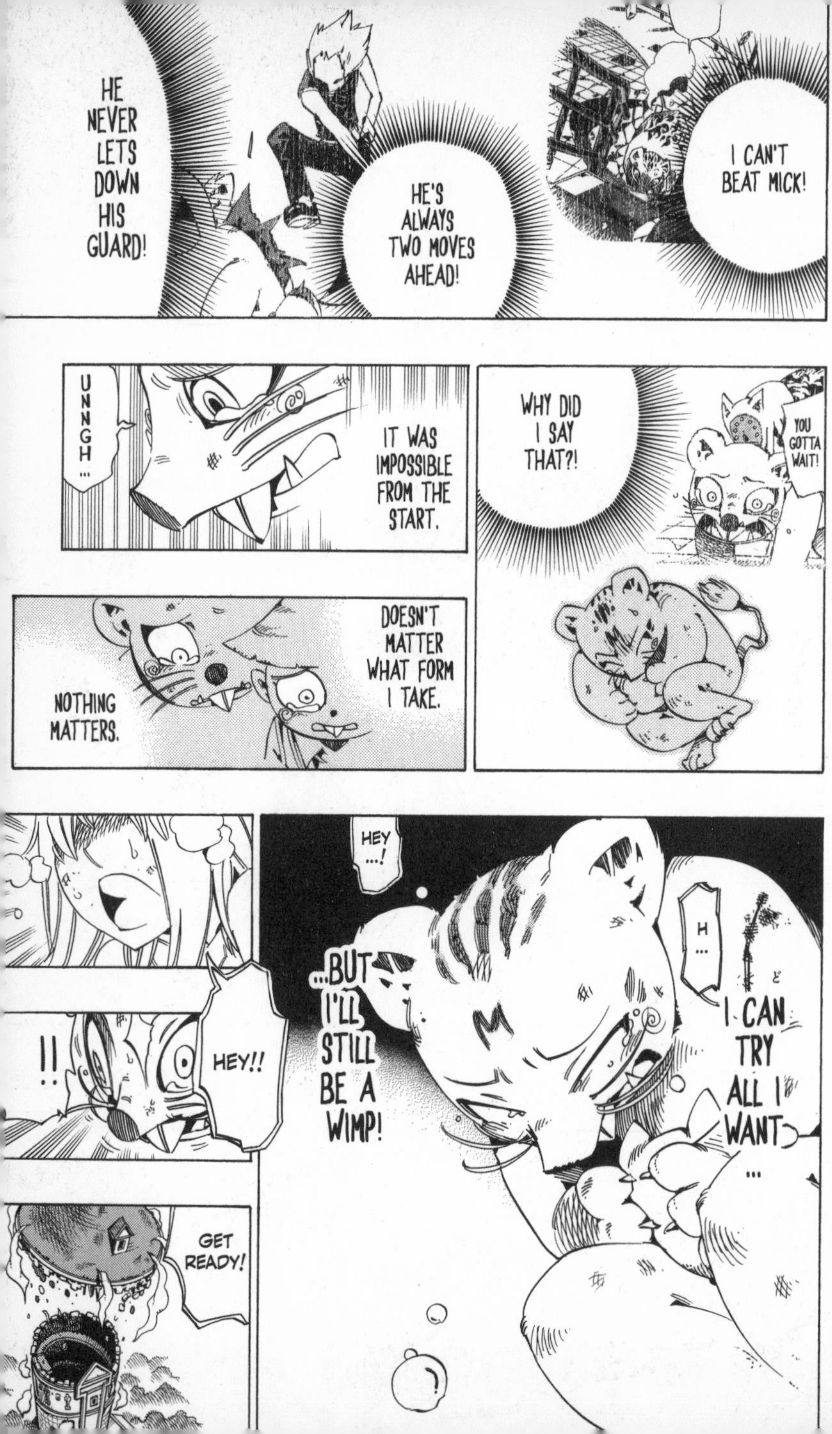

I CAN'T BEAT MICK!
HE'S ALWAYS TWO MOVES AHEAD!
HE NEVER LETS DOWN HIS GUARD!
YOU GOTTA WAIT!
WHY DID I SAY THAT?!
IT WAS IMPOSSIBLE FROM THE START.
UNNGH...
DOESN'T MATTER WHAT FORM I TAKE.
NOTHING MATTERS.
H...
I CAN TRY ALL I WANT...
HEY...!
...BUT I'LL STILL BE A WIMP!
HEY!!
!!
GET READY!

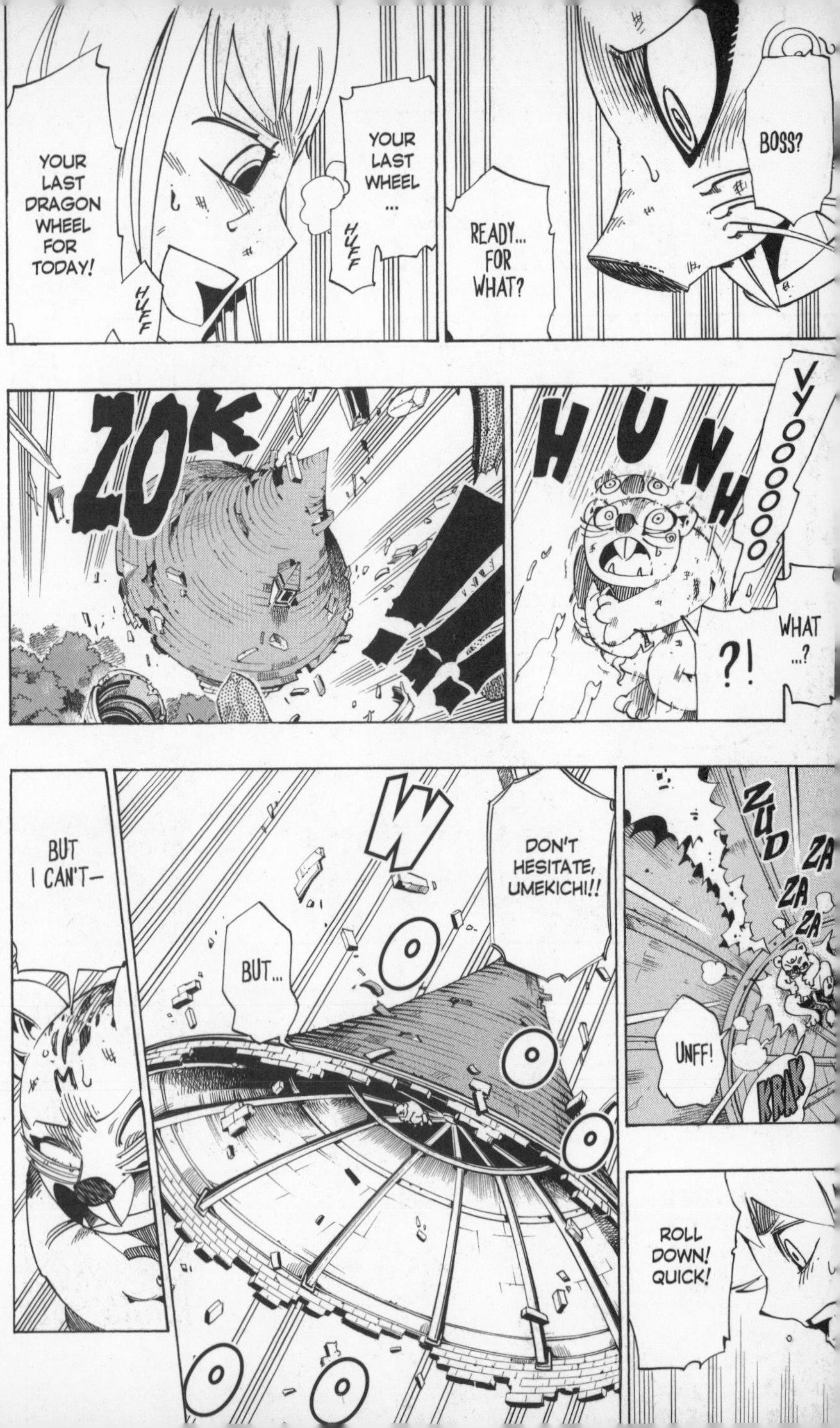
BOSS?
READY... FOR WHAT?
YOUR LAST WHEEL...
HUFF
YOUR LAST DRAGON WHEEL FOR TODAY!
HUFF
VYOOOOOOO
HUNH
WHAT...?
?!
ZOK!!
ZUD
ZA ZA ZA ZA
UNFF!
KRAK
ROLL DOWN! QUICK!
DON'T HESITATE, UMEKICHI!!
W
BUT...
BUT I CAN'T—

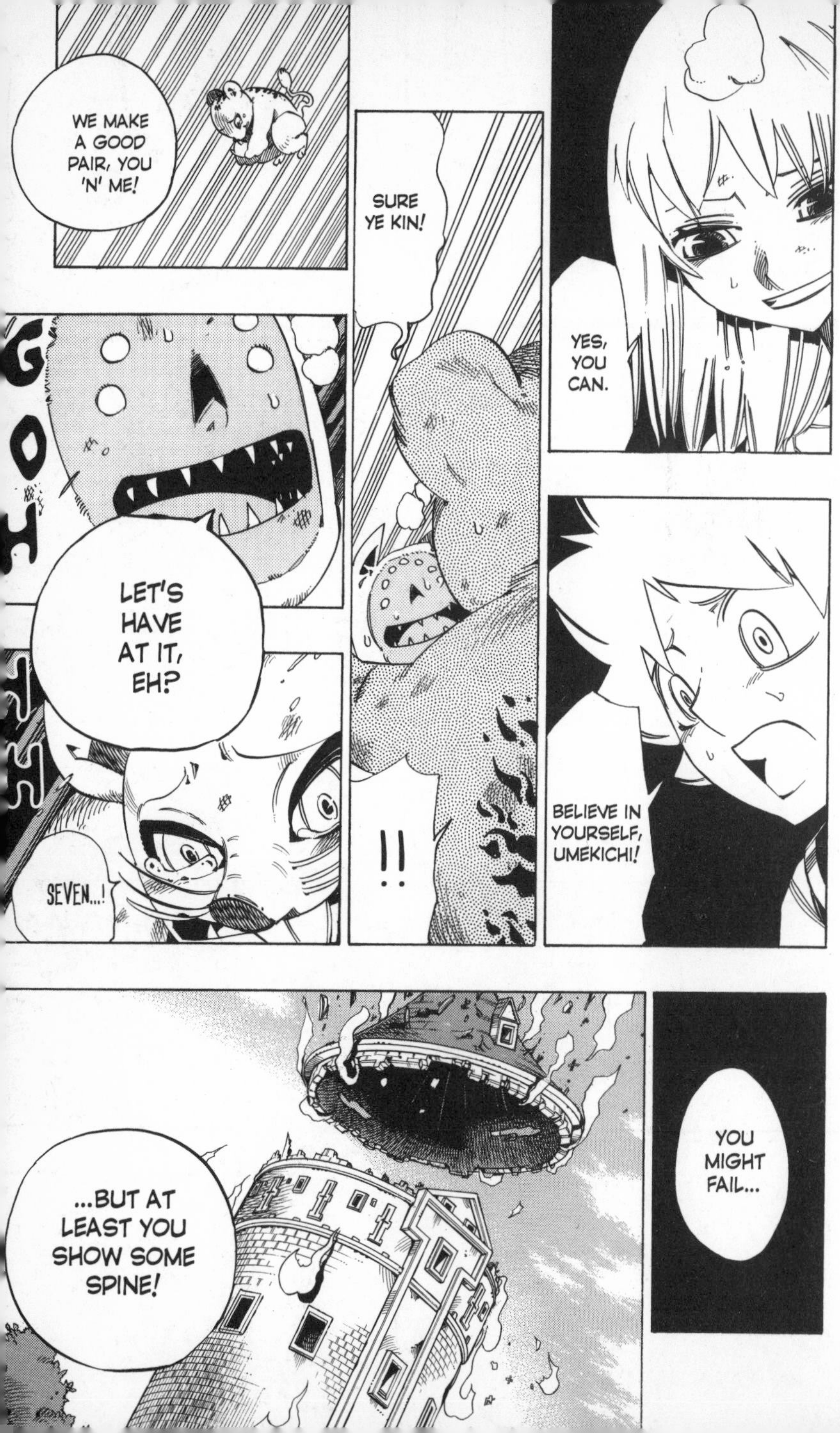
YES, YOU CAN.
BELIEVE IN YOURSELF, UMEKICHI!
SURE YE KIN!
!!
WE MAKE A GOOD PAIR, YOU 'N' ME!
LET'S HAVE AT IT, EH?
SEVEN...!
YOU MIGHT FAIL...
...BUT AT LEAST YOU SHOW SOME SPINE!

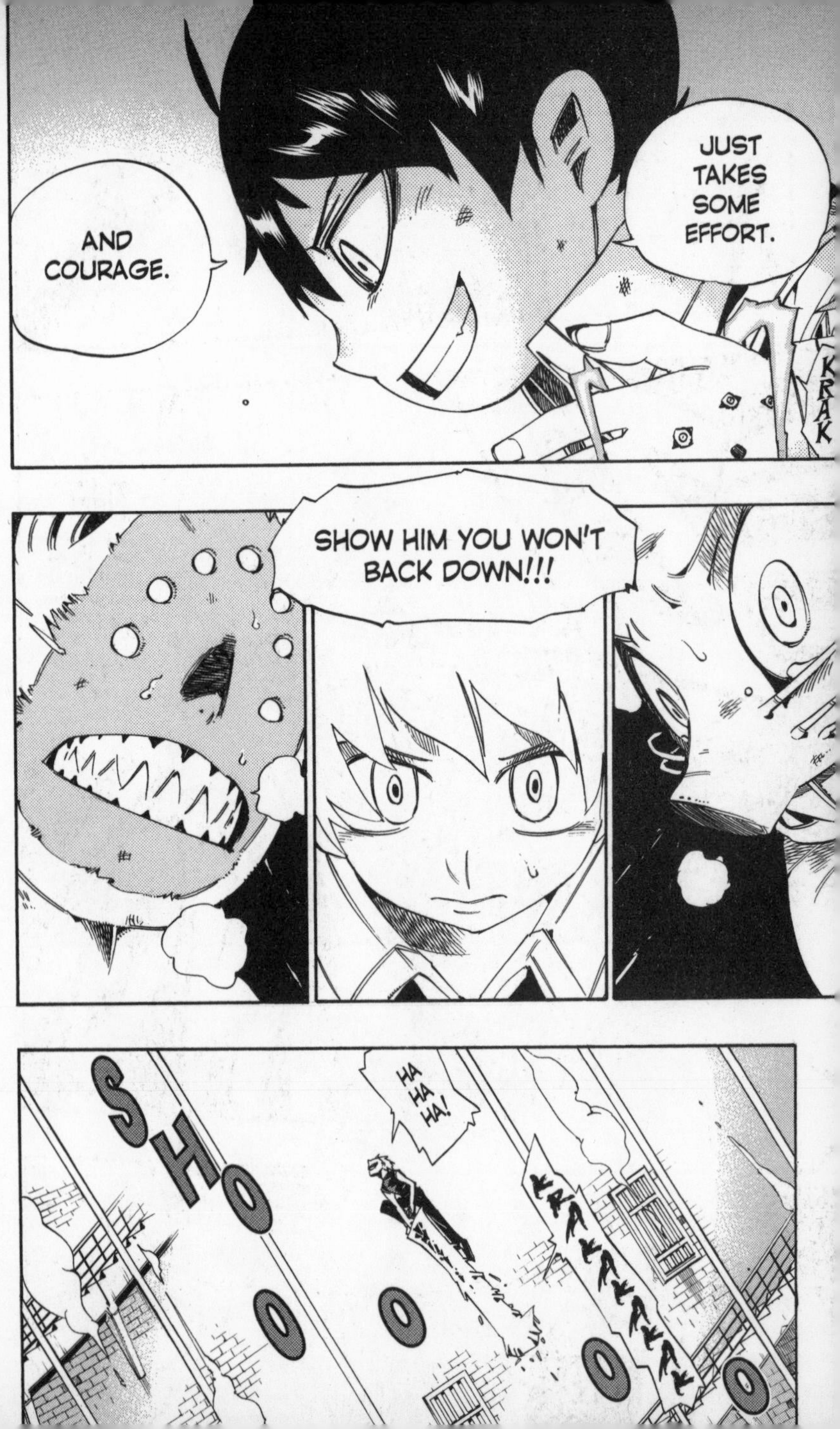
JUST TAKES SOME EFFORT.
KRAK
AND COURAGE.
SHOW HIM YOU WON'T BACK DOWN!!!
KRAKAKAKAK
HA HA HA HA!
SHOOOOOO

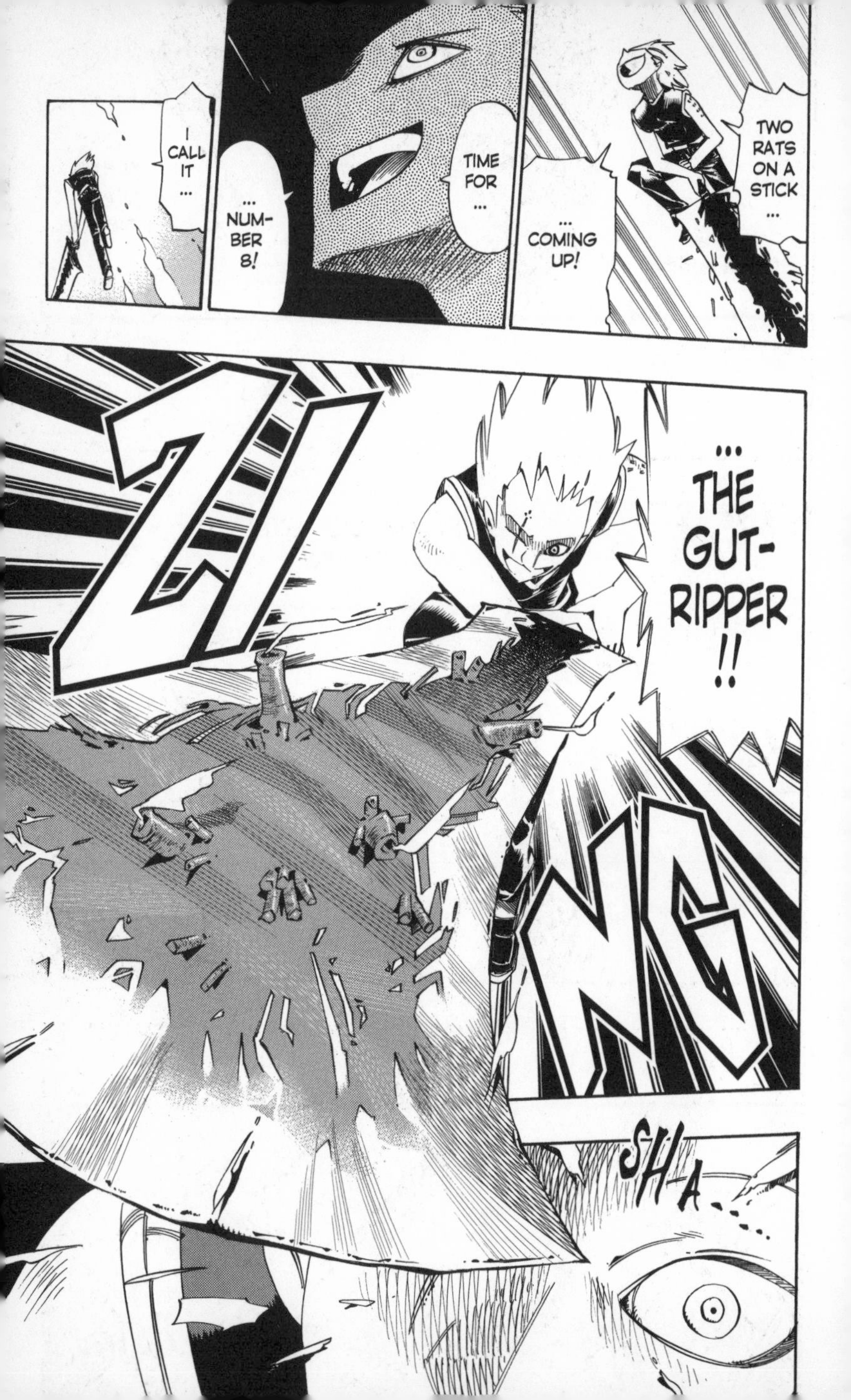
TWO RATS ON A STICK ...
... COMING UP!
TIME FOR ...
... NUMBER 8!
I CALL IT ...
... THE GUT-RIPPER!!
ZI
NG
SHA...

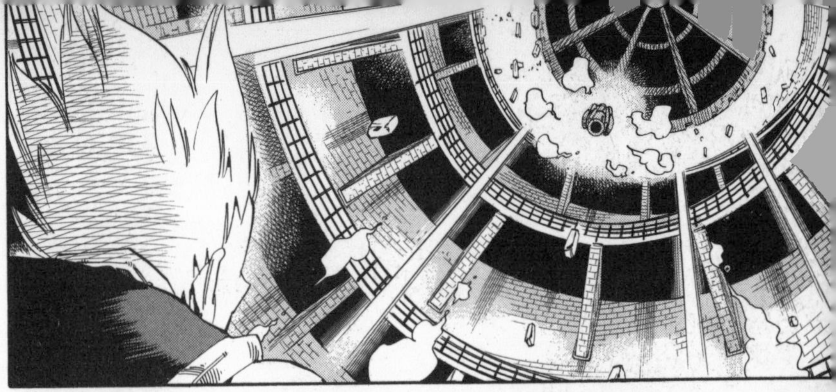

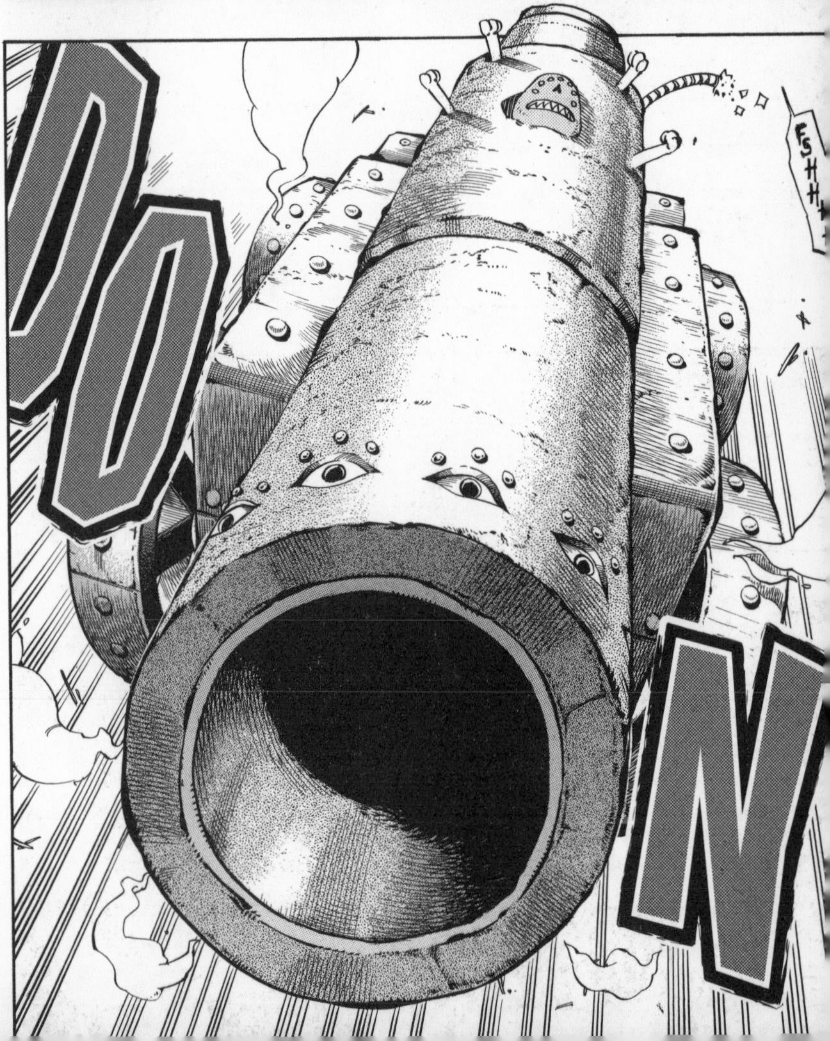
FSHH

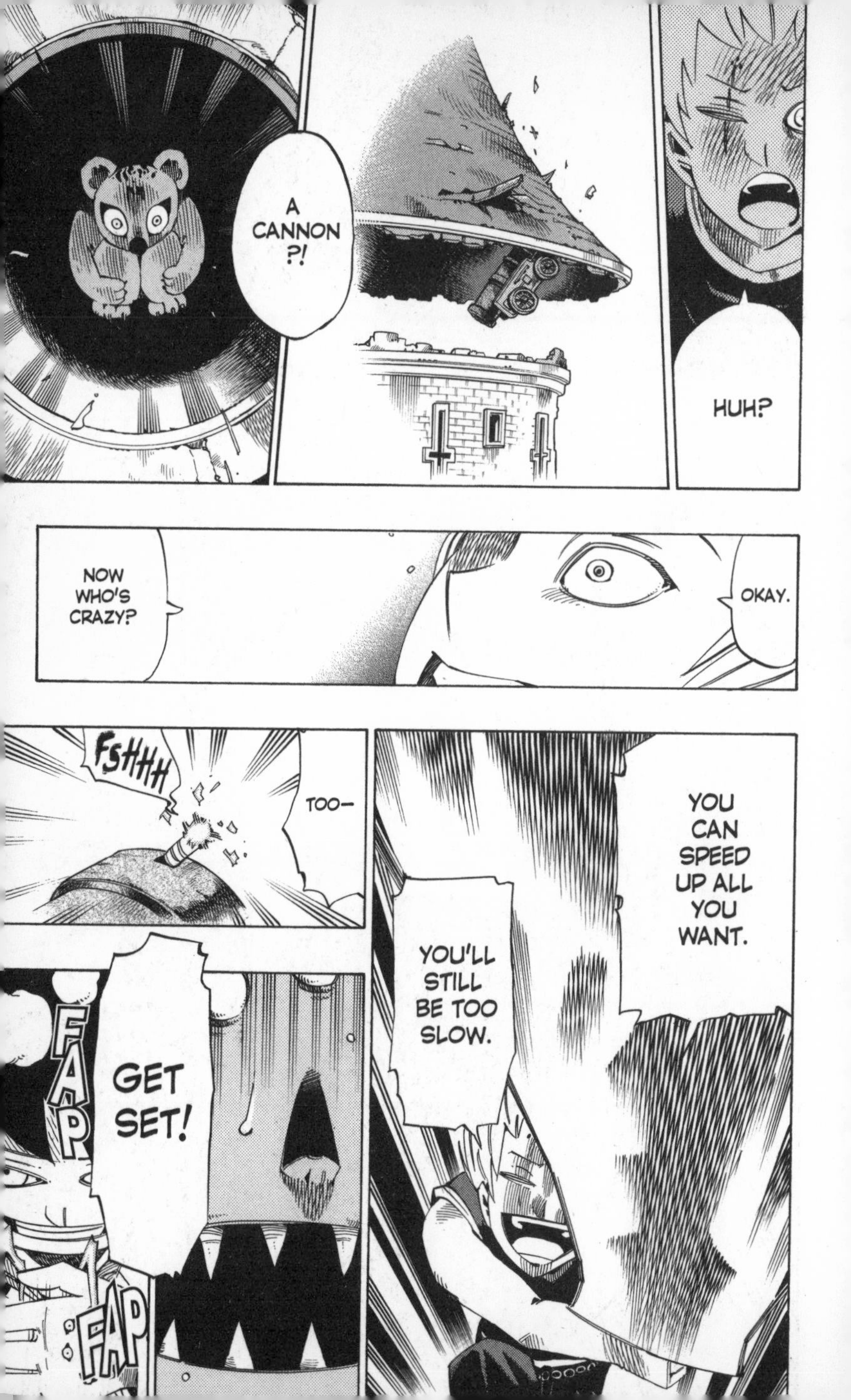
HUH?
A CANNON ?!
OKAY.
NOW WHO'S CRAZY?
YOU CAN SPEED UP ALL YOU WANT.
YOU'LL STILL BE TOO SLOW.
FSHHH
TOO—
GET SET!
FAP
FAP

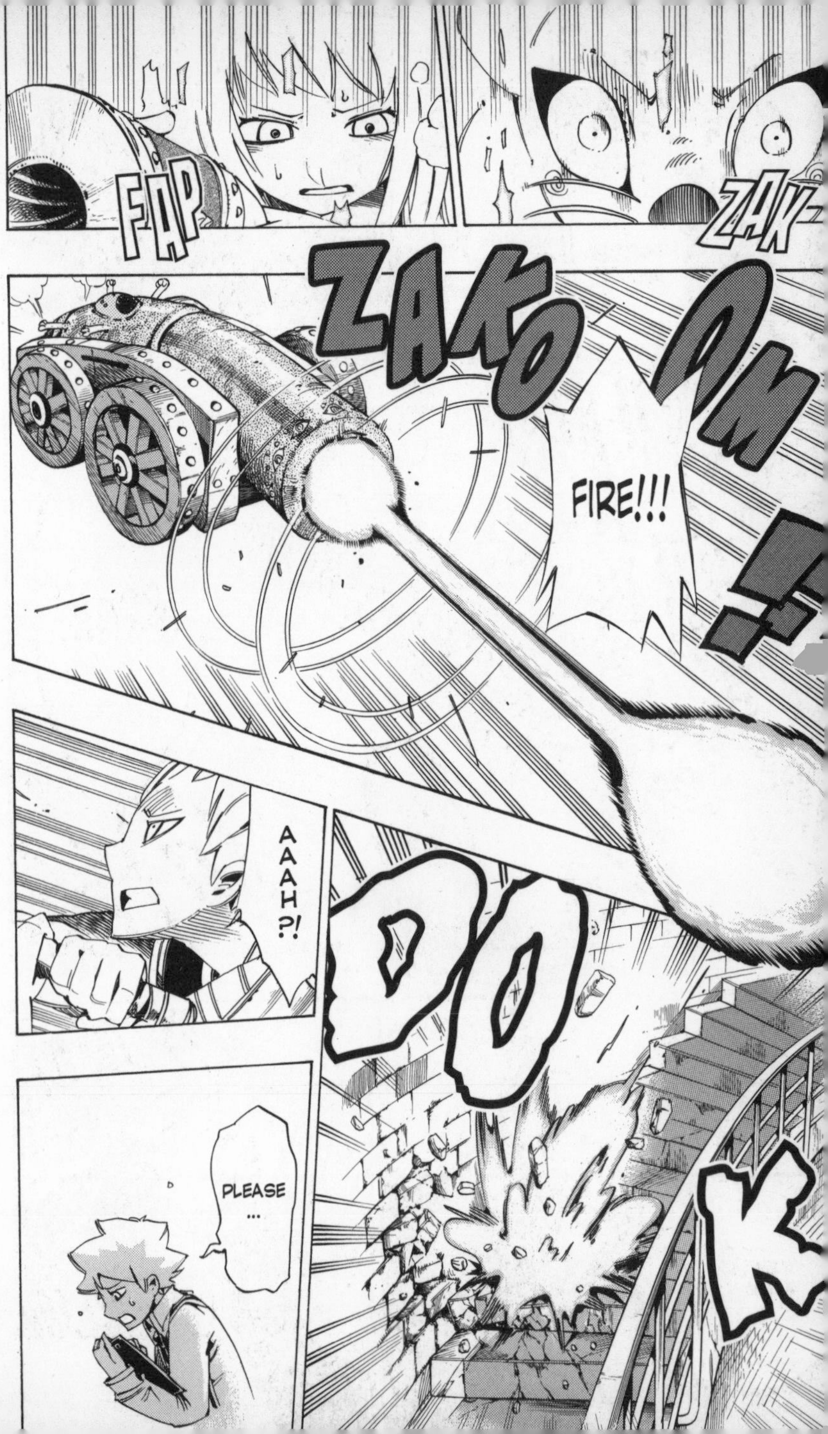
ZAK
FAP
ZAKOOM!!
FIRE!!!
DOK
AAAH?!
PLEASE ...

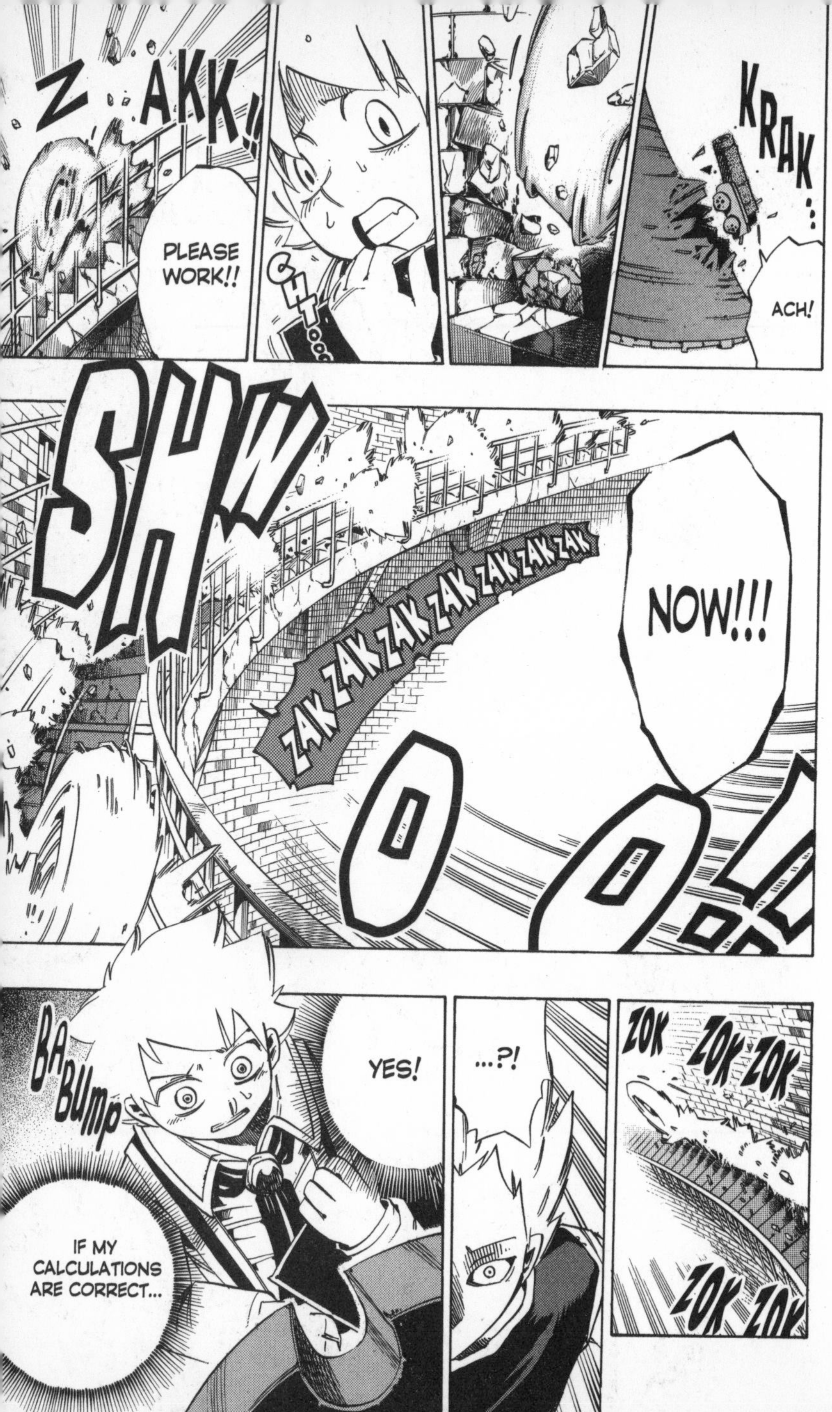
KRAK
ACH!
CHTOOO
ZAKK!!
PLEASE WORK!!
NOW!!!
ZAK ZAK ZAK ZAK ZAK ZAK ZAK
SHW
ZOK ZOK ZOK
ZOK ZOK
...?!
YES!
BABUMP
IF MY CALCULATIONS ARE CORRECT...

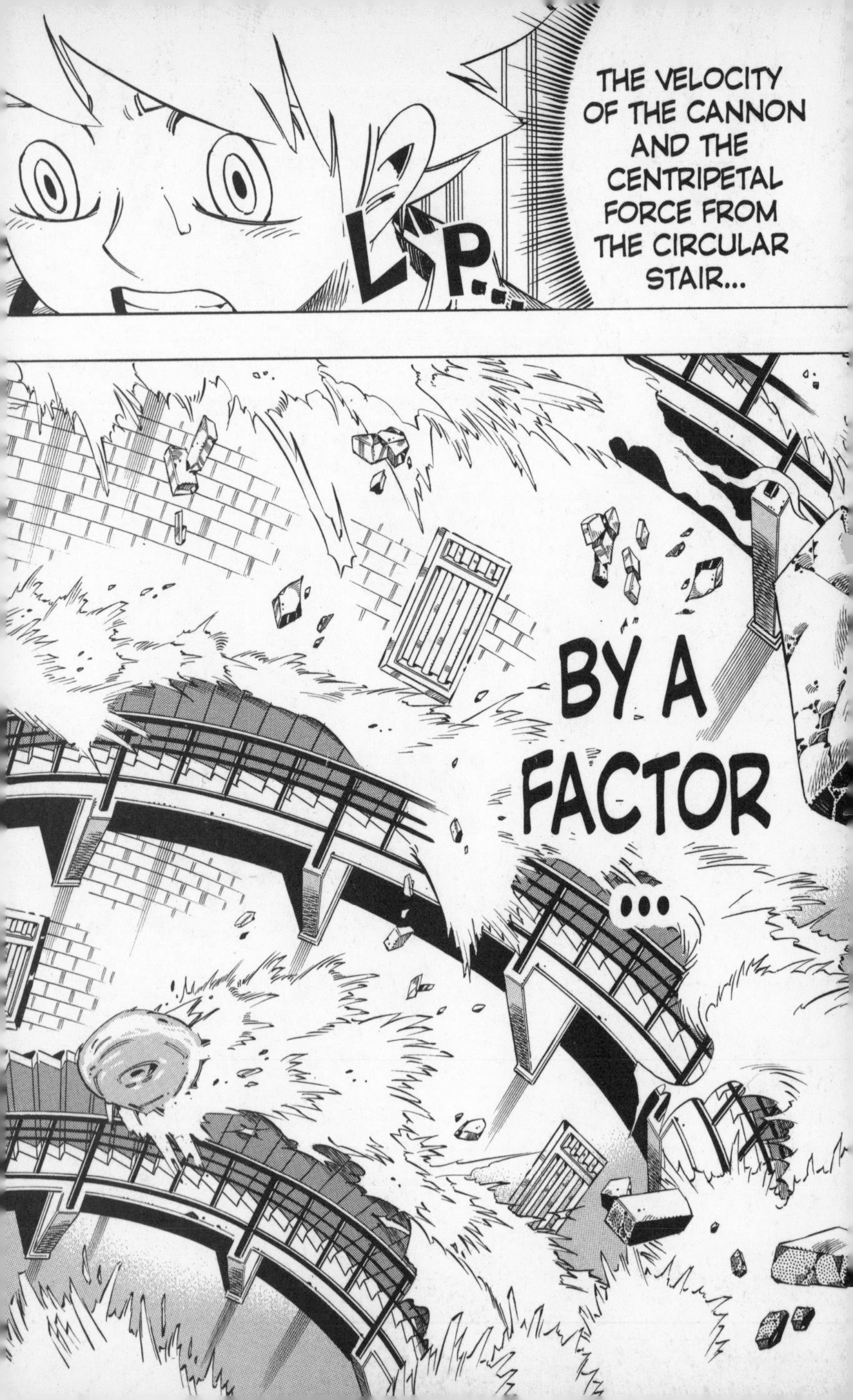
THE VELOCITY OF THE CANNON AND THE CENTRIPETAL FORCE FROM THE CIRCULAR STAIR...
LP...
BY A FACTOR
...

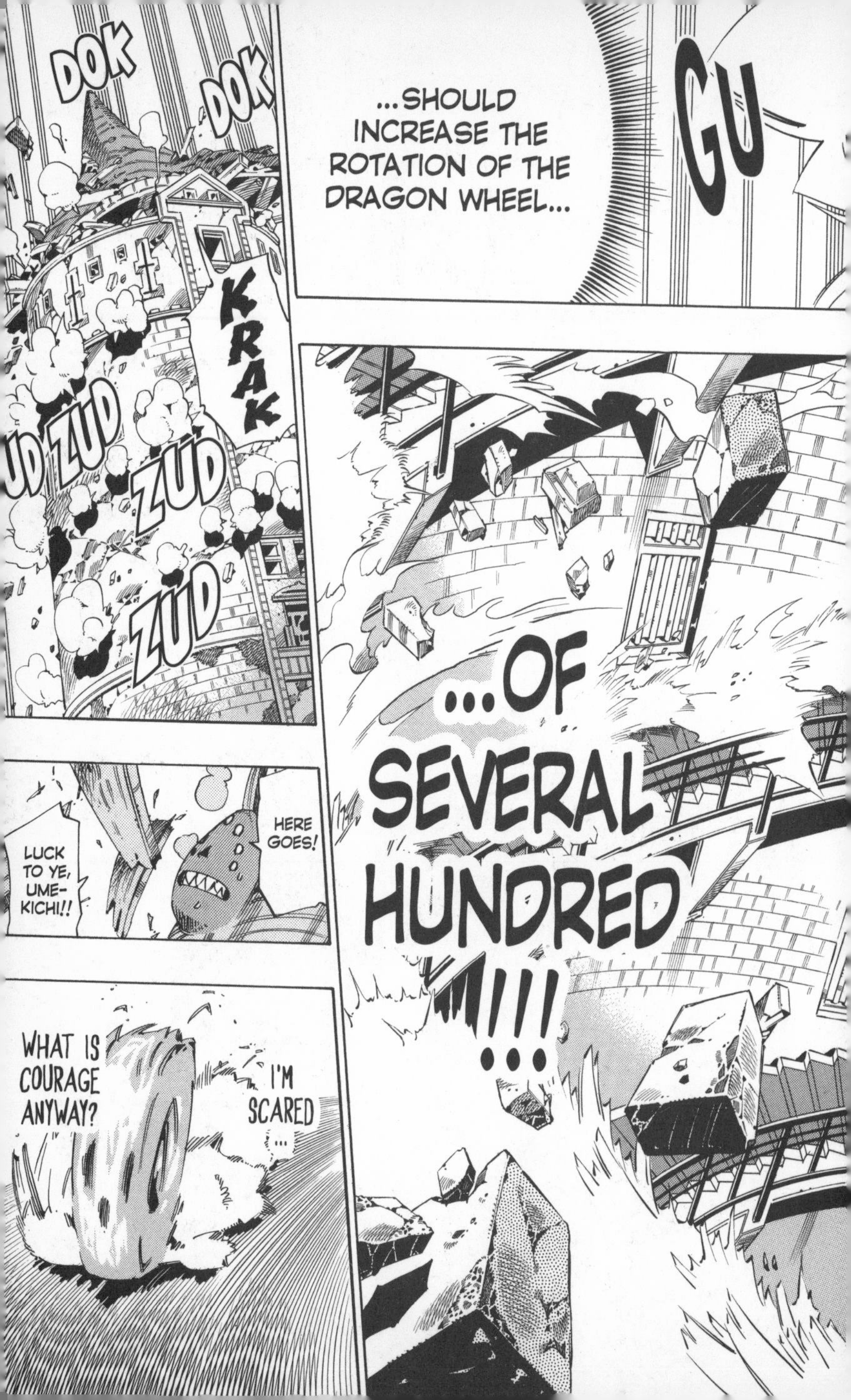
GU
...SHOULD INCREASE THE ROTATION OF THE DRAGON WHEEL...
DOK
DOK
KRAK
ZUD
ZUD
ZUD
ZUD
...OF SEVERAL HUNDRED!!!
HERE GOES!
LUCK TO YE, UME-KICHI!!
I'M SCARED...
WHAT IS COURAGE ANYWAY?

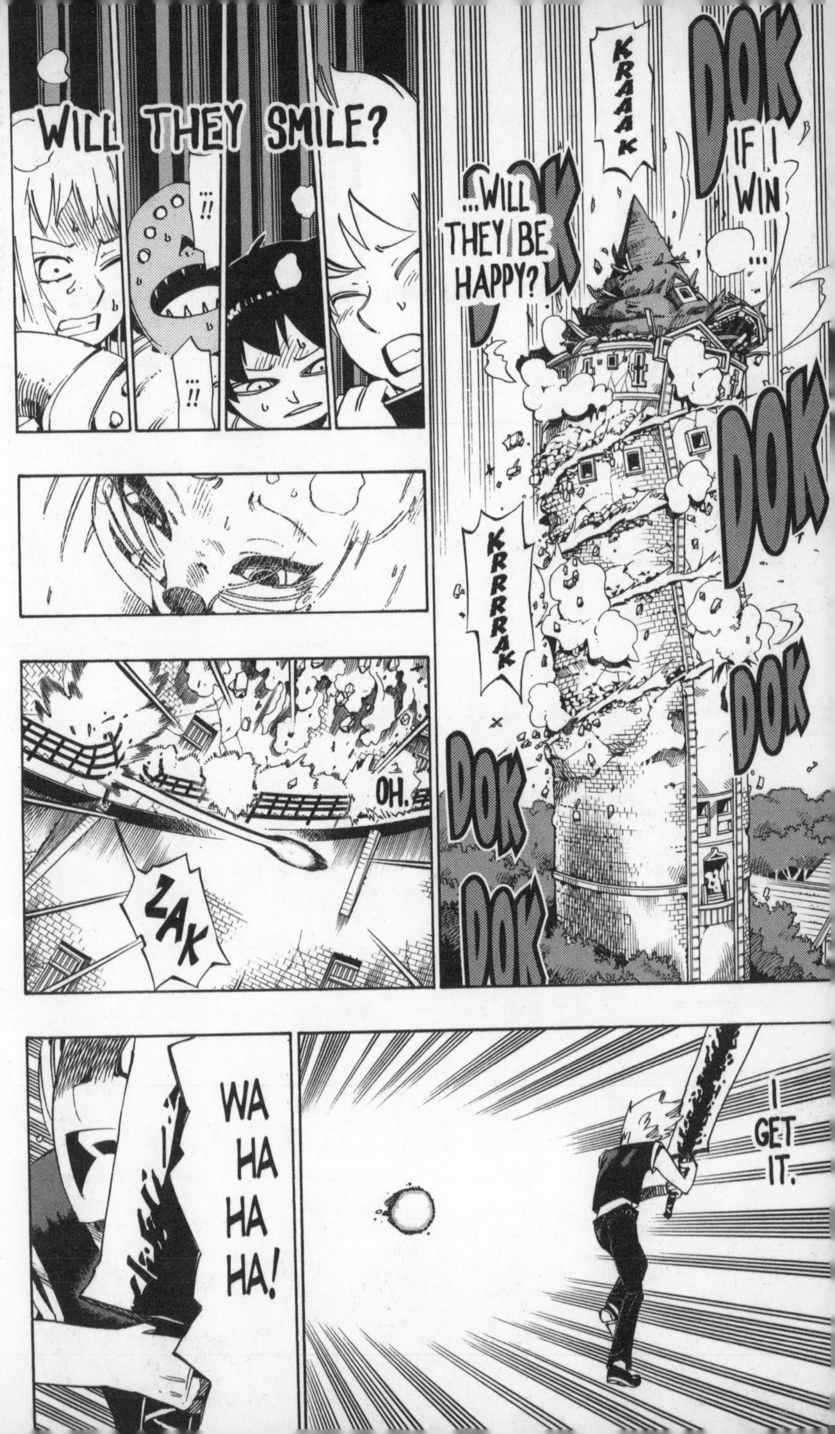
DOK
IF I WIN...
KRAAAAK
...WILL THEY BE HAPPY?
DOK
DOK
KRRRRRAK
DOK
DOK
DOK
WILL THEY SMILE?
...!!
...!!
OH.
ZAK
I GET IT.
WA HA HA HA HA!

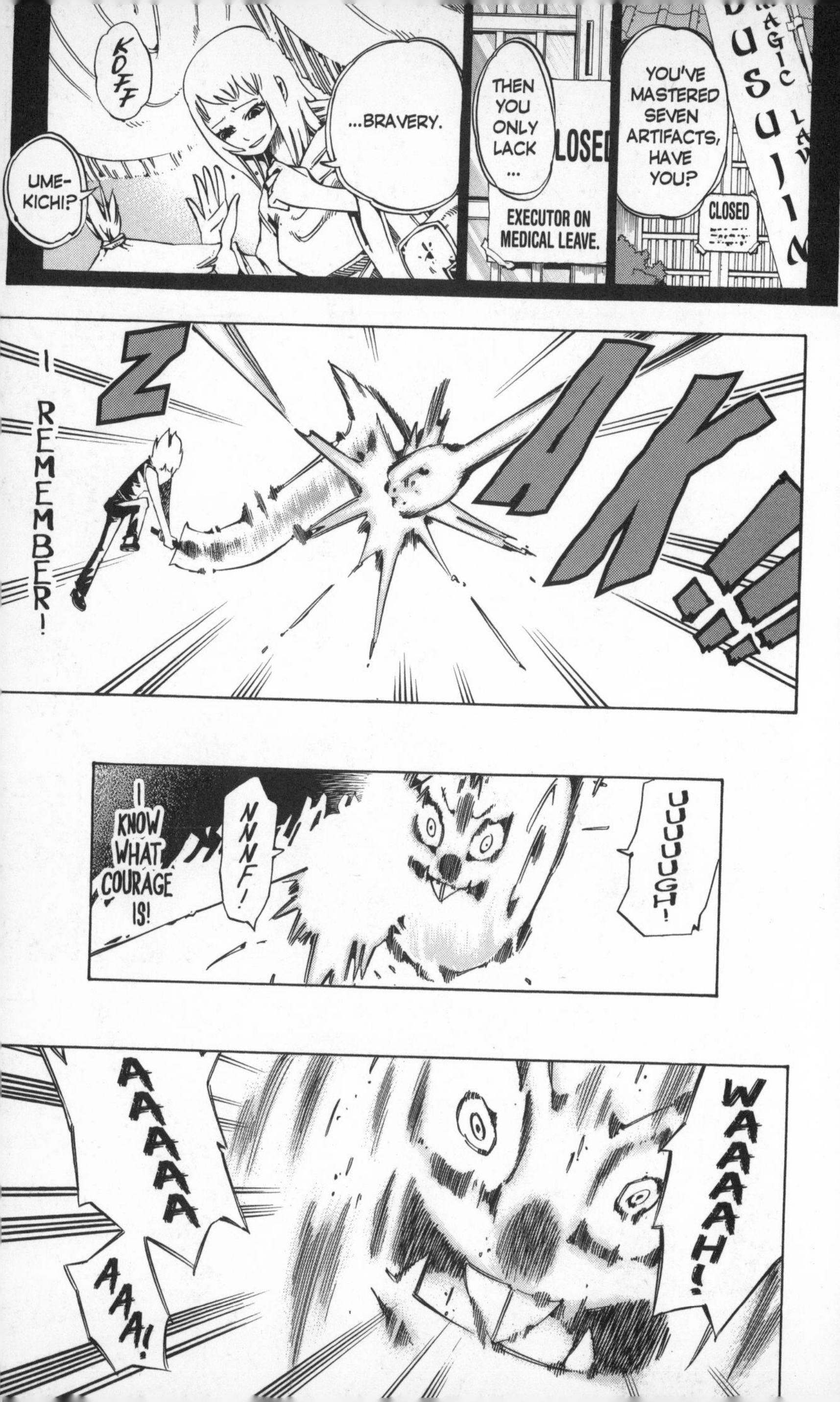
MAGIC LAW
CLOSED
YOU'VE MASTERED SEVEN ARTIFACTS, HAVE YOU?
CLOSED
EXECUTOR ON MEDICAL LEAVE.
THEN YOU ONLY LACK ...
...BRAVERY.
KOFF
UME-KICHI?
ZAK!!
I REMEMBER!
UUUUUGH!
NNNF!
I KNOW WHAT COURAGE IS!
WAAAAAH!
AAAAA
AAA!

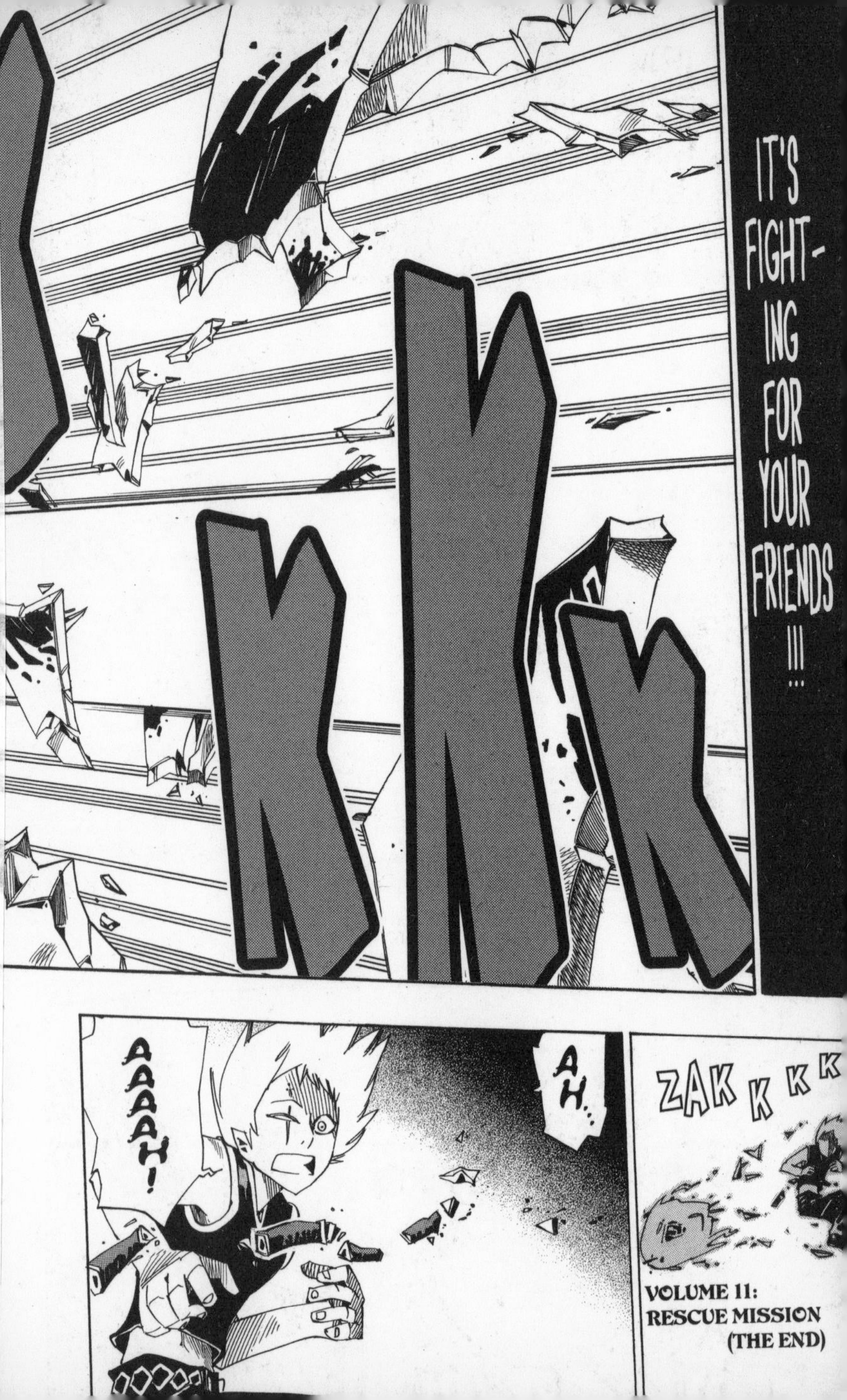
IT'S FIGHT-ING FOR YOUR FRIENDS!!!...
KNK
ZAKKKK
VOLUME 11: RESCUE MISSION (THE END)
AH...
AAAAAH!

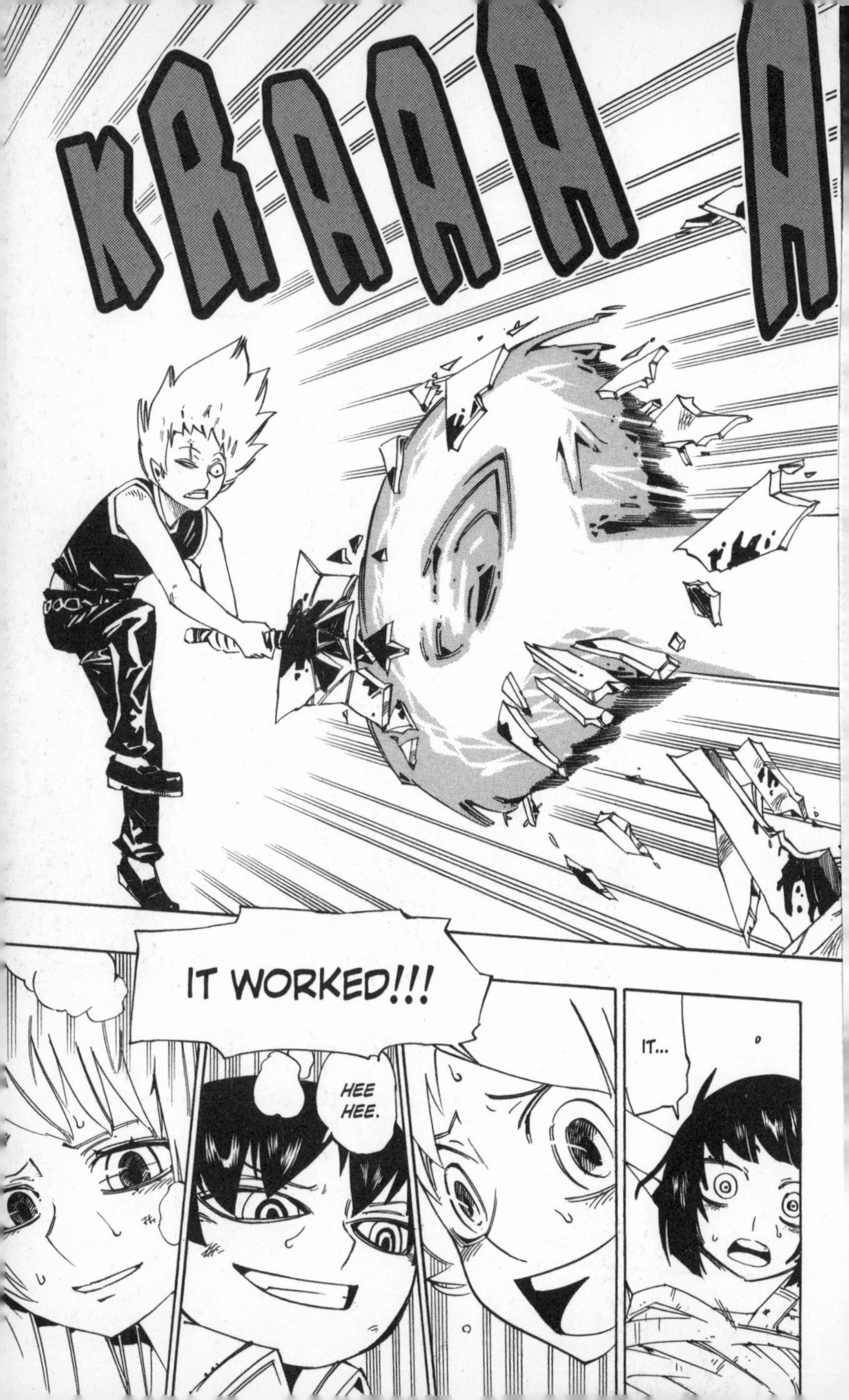
KRAAAA
IT...
IT WORKED!!!
HEE HEE.

THE FOLLOWING APPEARED
IN THE GO!GO! JUMP SPECIAL.
THE POSTER INCLUDED IN
THERE WAS A COLLABORATION
DONE WITH MATSUI-SENSEI,
BUT THE MANGA WAS MINE.
STILL, I GOT A FEELING WE'LL
SEE MORE OF MATSUI-SENSEI
IN THE MANGA SOON! AT
LEAST, I SURE HOPE WE
DO! HOW ABOUT IT,
MATSUI-SENSEI?

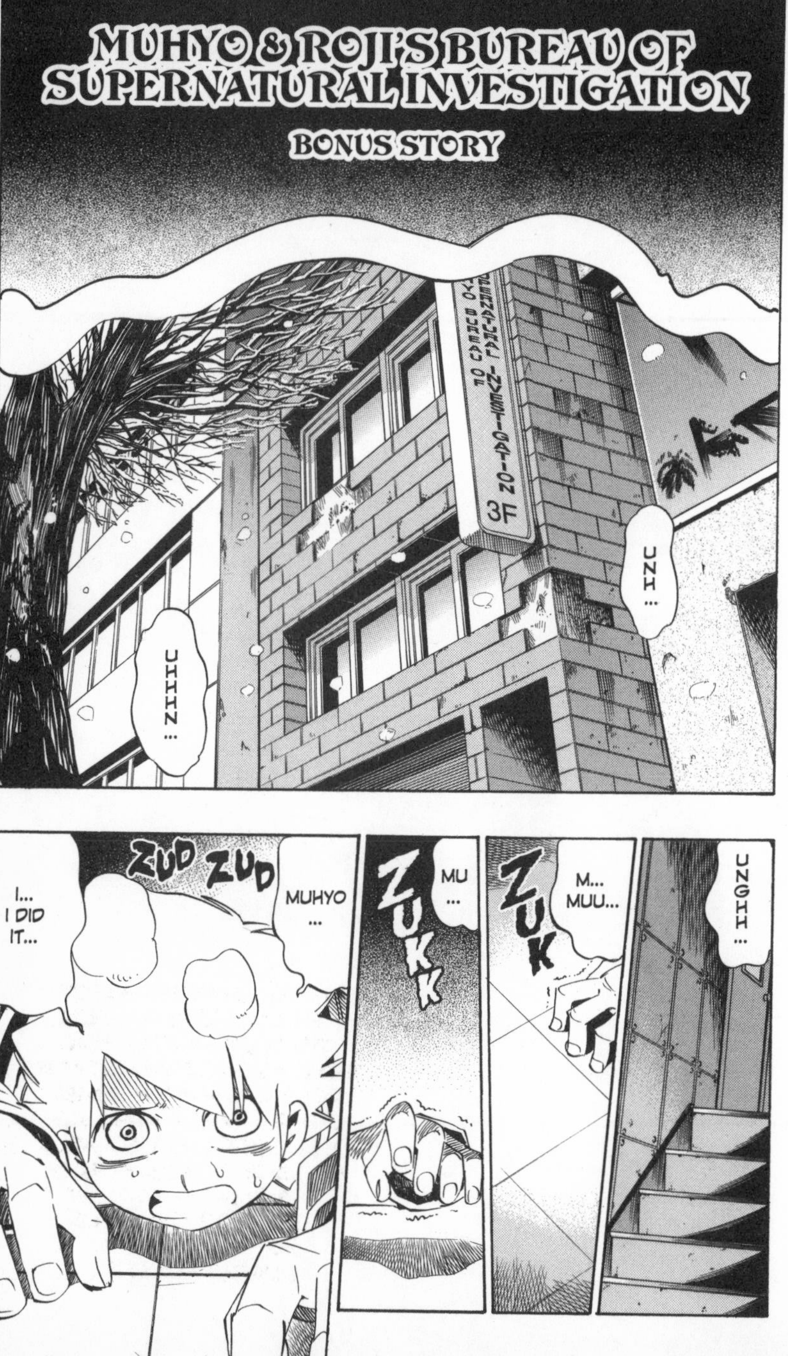
MUHYO & ROJI'S BUREAU OF SUPERNATURAL INVESTIGATION
BONUS STORY
BUREAU OF SUPERNATURAL INVESTIGATION 3F
UNH...
UHHHN...
UNGHH...
M... MUU...
ZUKK
MU...
ZUKK
MUHYO...
ZUD ZUD
I... I DID IT...

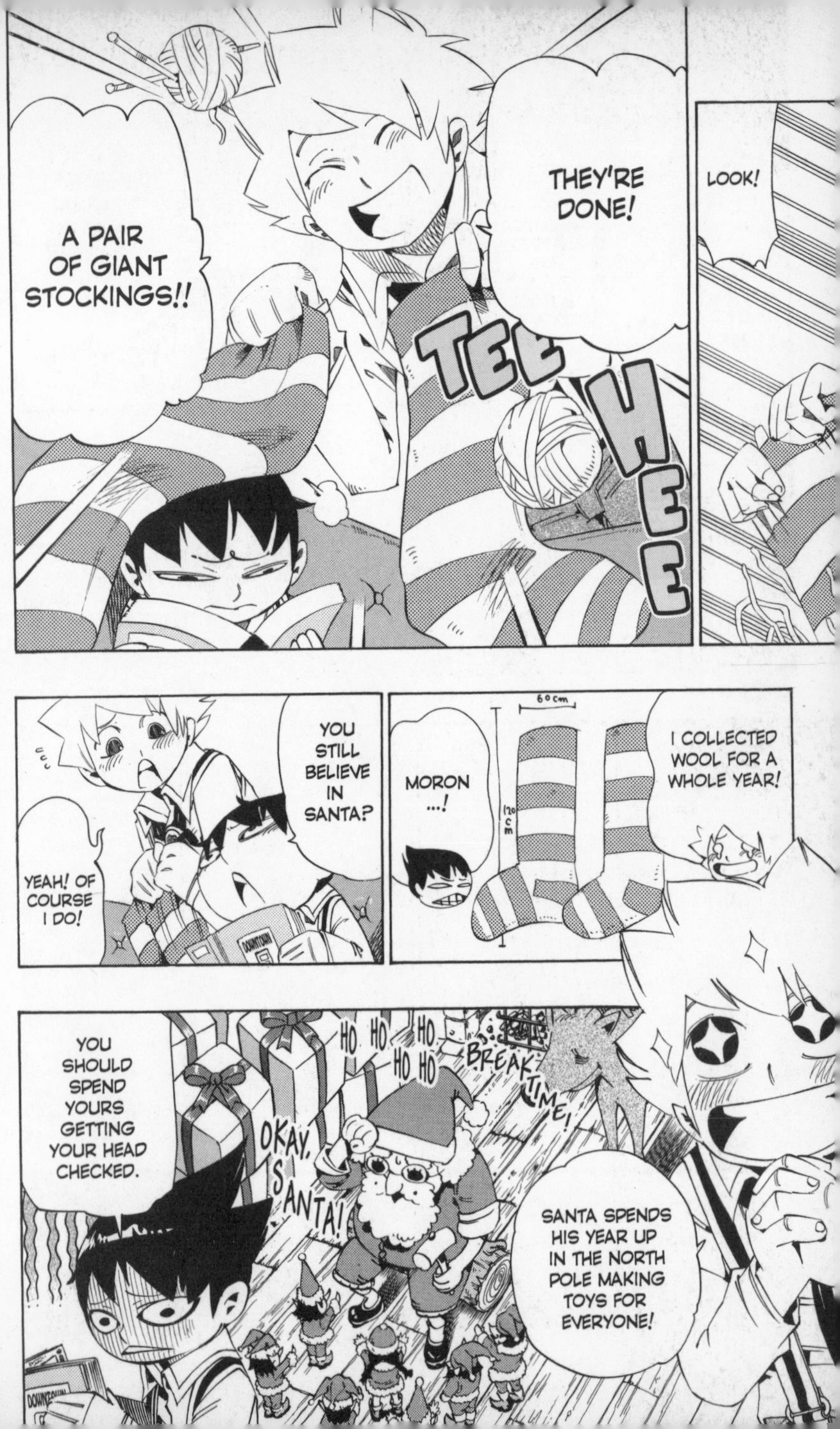
LOOK!
THEY'RE DONE!
TEE HEE
A PAIR OF GIANT STOCKINGS!!
I COLLECTED WOOL FOR A WHOLE YEAR!
60 cm
120 cm
MORON ...!
YOU STILL BELIEVE IN SANTA?
YEAH! OF COURSE I DO!
DOWNTOWN
SANTA SPENDS HIS YEAR UP IN THE NORTH POLE MAKING TOYS FOR EVERYONE!
HO HO HO HO HO
BREAK TIME!
OKAY, SANTA!
YOU SHOULD SPEND YOURS GETTING YOUR HEAD CHECKED.

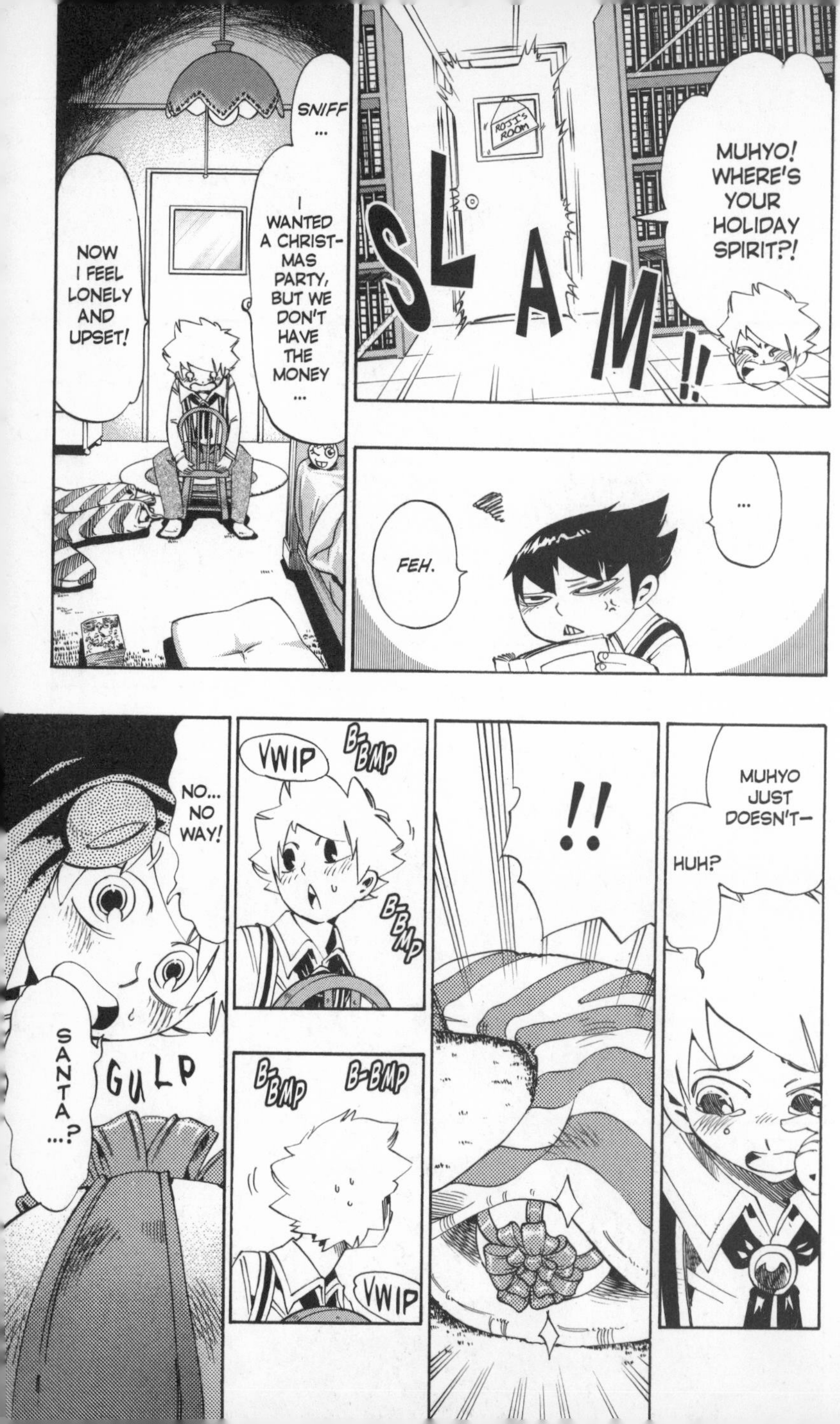
MUHYO! WHERE'S YOUR HOLIDAY SPIRIT?!
ROJI'S ROOM
SLAM!!
...
FEH.
SNIFF ...
I WANTED A CHRISTMAS PARTY, BUT WE DON'T HAVE THE MONEY ...
NOW I FEEL LONELY AND UPSET!
MUHYO JUST DOESN'T—
HUH?
!!
B-BMP
VWIP
B-BMP
B-BMP
B-BMP
VWIP
NO... NO WAY!
GULP
SANTA ...?

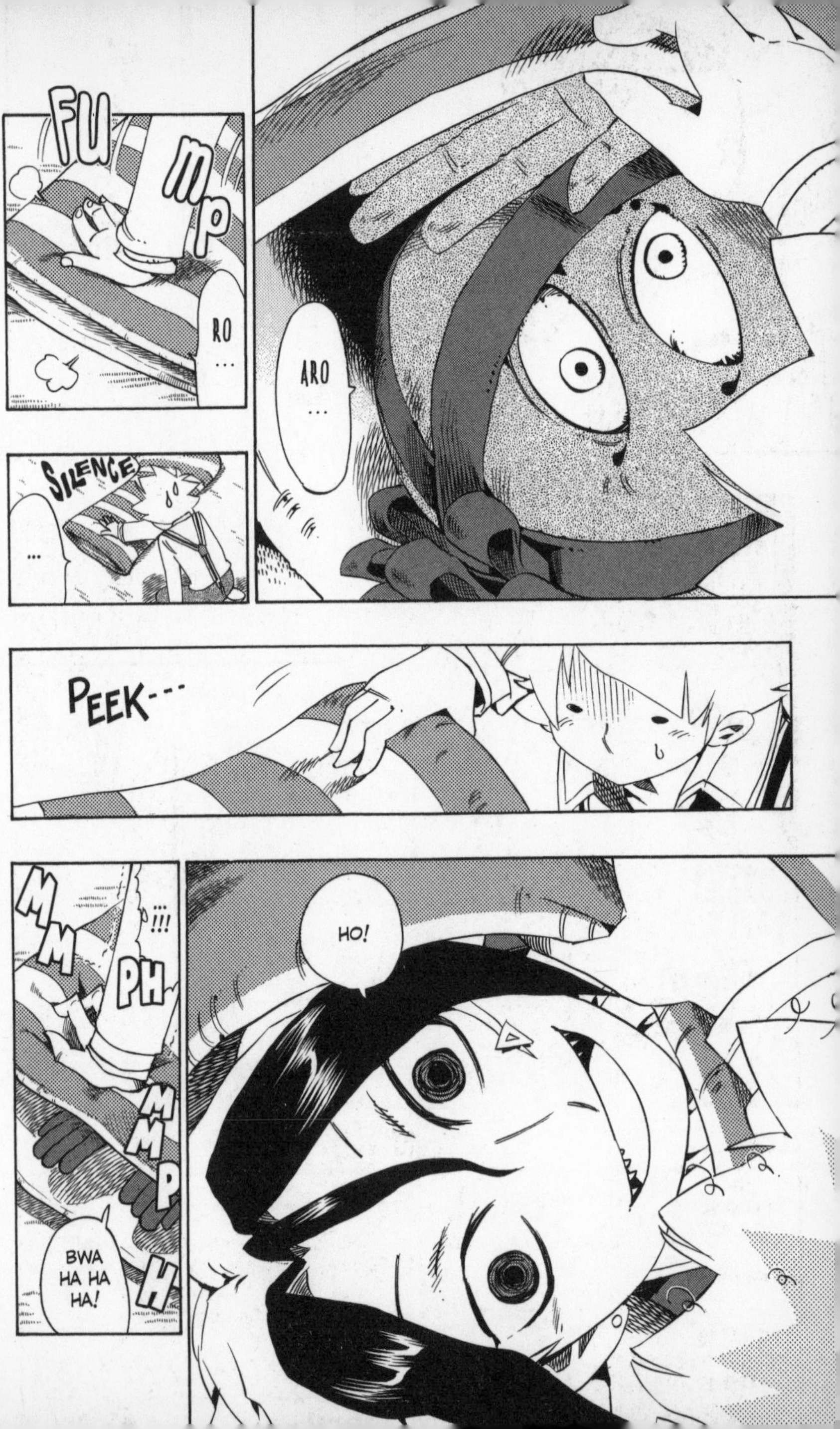
ARO ...
FUmp
RO ...
SILENCE
...
PEEK---
HO!
...!!!
MMPH
MMMPH
BWA HA HA HA!

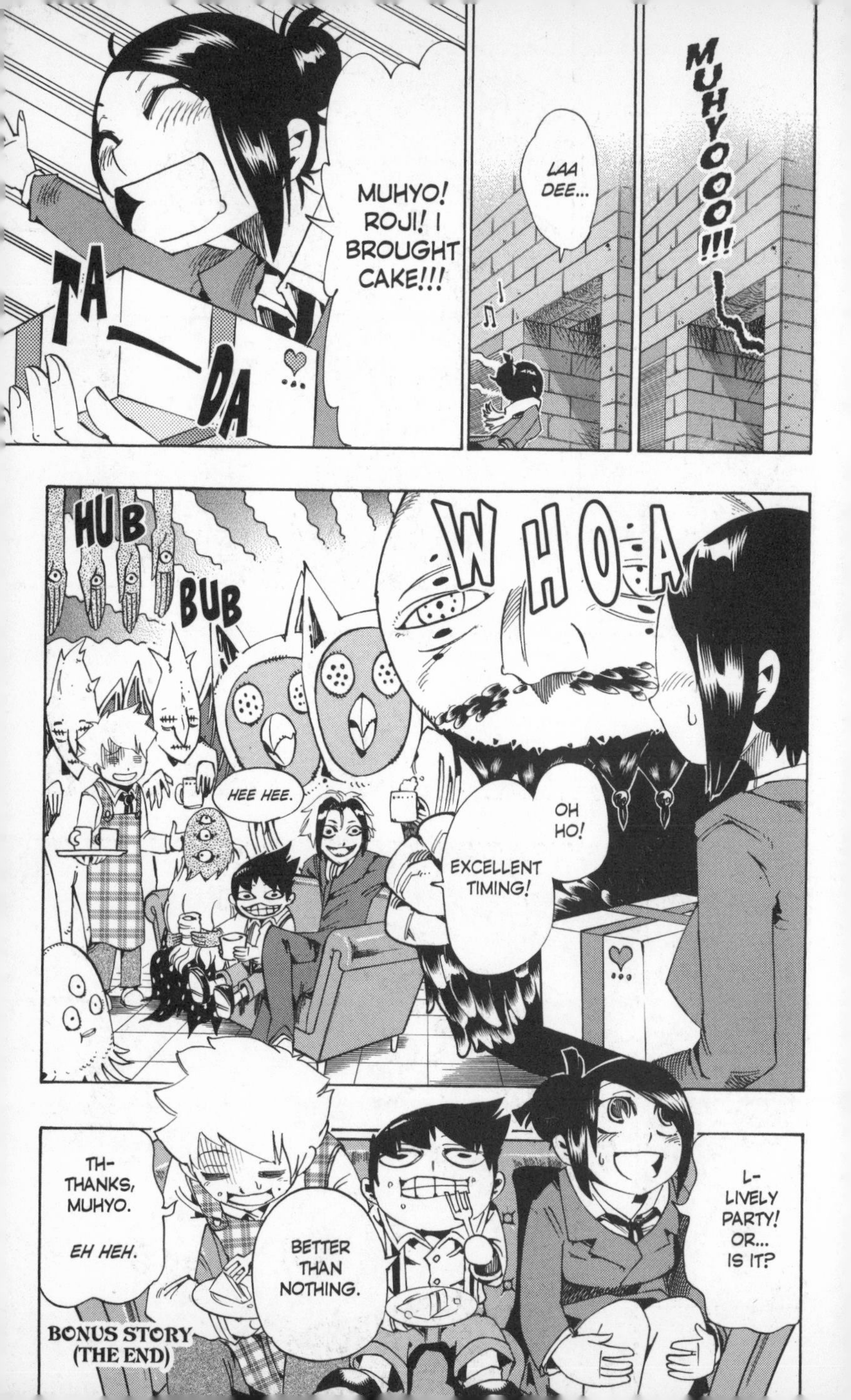
MUHYOOOO!!!
LAA DEE...
TA—DA
MUHYO! ROJI! I BROUGHT CAKE!!!
WHOA
OH HO!
EXCELLENT TIMING!
BUB
HUB
HEE HEE.
L-LIVELY PARTY! OR... IS IT?
BETTER THAN NOTHING.
TH-THANKS, MUHYO.
EH HEH.
BONUS STORY (THE END)

In The Next Volume...

Even as Muhyo and Roji battle against some horrors at M.L.S., another Ark member is cooking up more trouble!

Available August 2009!

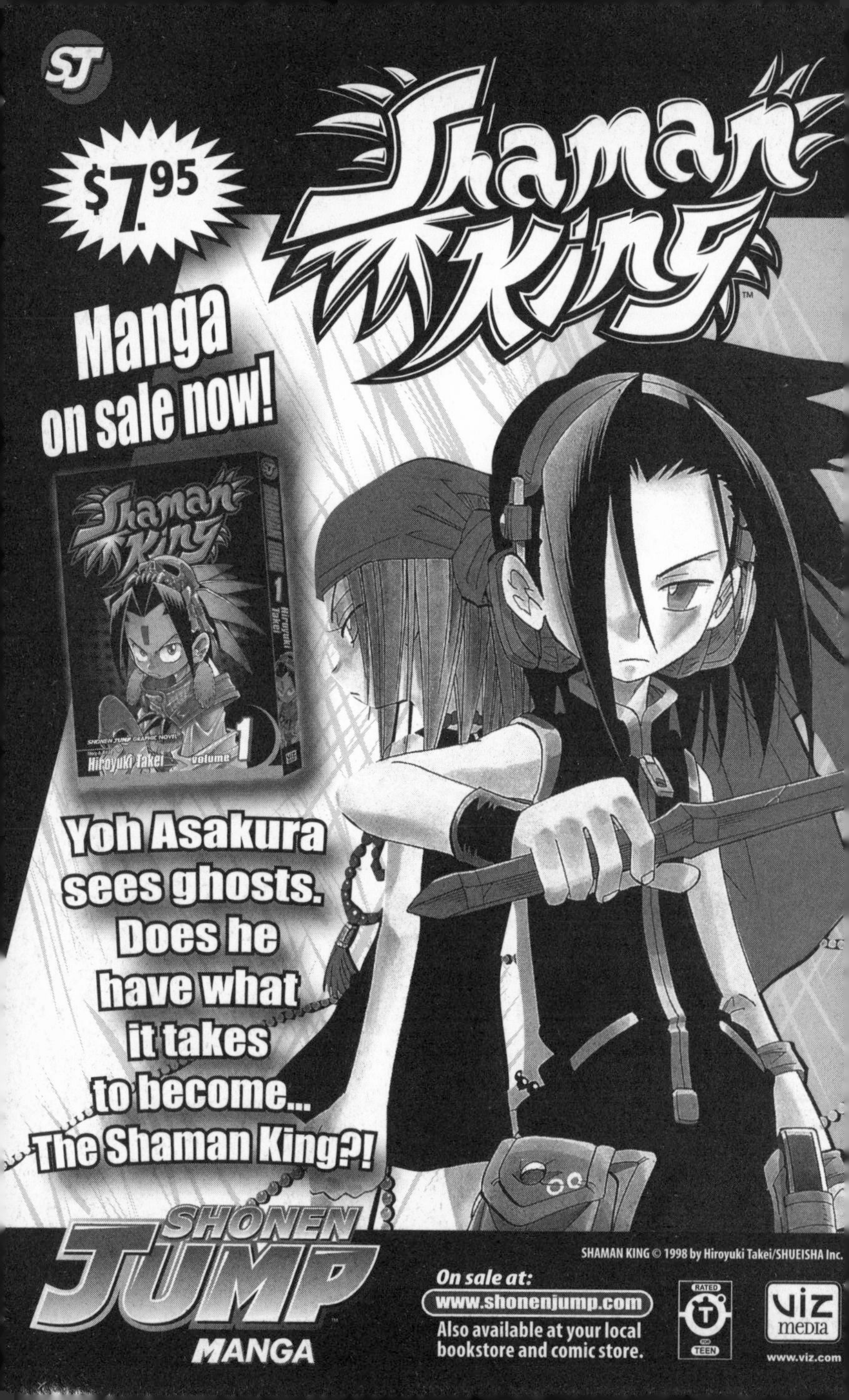
SJ
$7.95
Shaman King™
Manga on sale now!
Shaman King
SHONEN JUMP GRAPHIC NOVEL
Hiroyuki Takei
volume 1
Yoh Asakura sees ghosts. Does he have what it takes to become... The Shaman King?!
SHONEN JUMP
MANGA
SHAMAN KING © 1998 by Hiroyuki Takei/SHUEISHA Inc.
On sale at:
www.shonenjump.com
Also available at your local bookstore and comic store.
RATED T TEEN
viz media
www.viz.com

BOBOBO-BO BO-BOBO

BEWARE THE FIST OF THE NOSE HAIR!

MANGA SERIES ON SALE NOW
by Yoshio Sawai

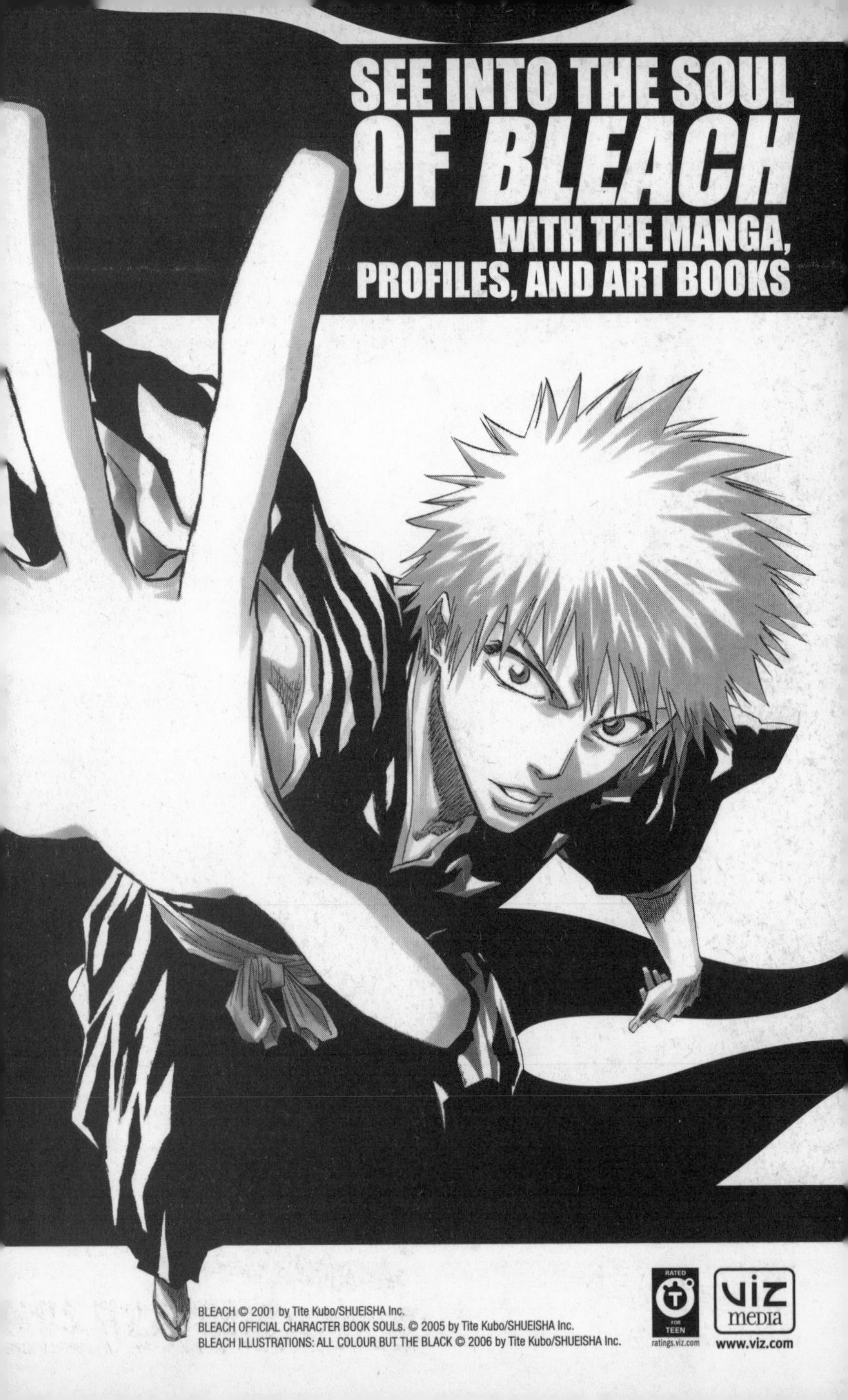
SEE INTO THE SOUL OF *BLEACH*
WITH THE MANGA, PROFILES, AND ART BOOKS
BLEACH © 2001 by Tite Kubo/SHUEISHA Inc.
BLEACH OFFICIAL CHARACTER BOOK SOULs. © 2005 by Tite Kubo/SHUEISHA Inc.
BLEACH ILLUSTRATIONS: ALL COLOUR BUT THE BLACK © 2006 by Tite Kubo/SHUEISHA Inc.
RATED T FOR TEEN
ratings.viz.com
viz media
www.viz.com

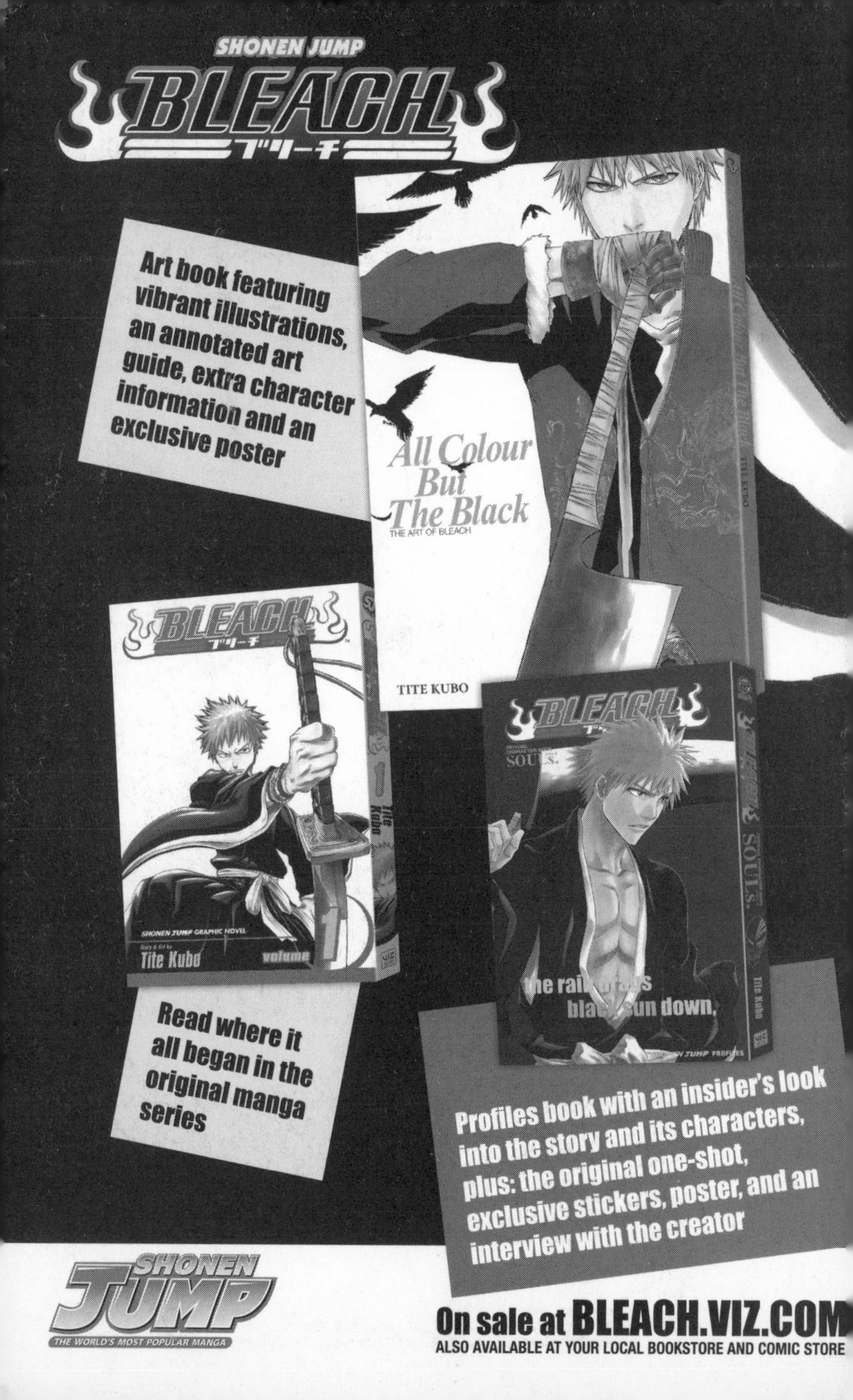
SHONEN JUMP
BLEACH
ブリーチ
Art book featuring vibrant illustrations, an annotated art guide, extra character information and an exclusive poster
All Colour But The Black
THE ART OF BLEACH
TITE KUBO
BLEACH
ブリーチ
SHONEN JUMP GRAPHIC NOVEL
Tite Kubo
volume 1
BLEACH
SOULS.
Tite Kubo
Read where it all began in the original manga series
Profiles book with an insider's look into the story and its characters, plus: the original one-shot, exclusive stickers, poster, and an interview with the creator
SHONEN JUMP
THE WORLD'S MOST POPULAR MANGA
On sale at BLEACH.VIZ.COM
ALSO AVAILABLE AT YOUR LOCAL BOOKSTORE AND COMIC STORE

Tell us what you think about SHONEN JUMP manga!

Our survey is now available online.
Go to: **www.SHONENJUMP.com/mangasurvey**

Help us make our product offering better!